Economic Efficiency in Agricultural and Food Marketing

Economic Efficiency in Agricultural and Food Marketing

EDITED BY

Richard L. Kilmer and Walter J. Armbruster

PUBLISHED FOR

Farm Foundation

AND

*Institute of Food and Agricultural Sciences
of the University of Florida*

BY

Iowa State University Press / Ames

First edition 1987

Library of Congress Cataloging-in-Publication Data

Economic efficiency in agricultural and food marketing.

Includes bibliographies and index.
1. Farm produce—Marketing—Congresses. 2. Food—
Marketing—Congresses. 3. Produce trade—United States—
Congresses. 4. Food industry and trade—United States—
Congresses. 5. Agriculture—Economic aspects—United
States—Congresses. I. Kilmer, Richard L.
II. Armbruster, Walter J. III. Farm Foundation (Chicago,
Ill.) IV. University of Florida. Institute of Food and
Agricultural Sciences.
HD9000.5.E26   1987   381'.41'0973   87-2821
ISBN 0-8138-0533-3

CONTENTS

ACKNOWLEDGMENTS

THE editors wish to express their sincere appreciation to the many people and organizations that made this publication possible. Financial support for this book and the symposium on which it is based was provided by the Agricultural Marketing Service and the Economic Research Service of the United States Department of Agriculture; Farm Foundation; and the Institute of Food and Agricultural Sciences at the University of Florida. Special thanks go to the authors and discussants for the time, thought, and effort devoted to manuscript preparation, presentation, and revision. Emerson Babb, Richard Heifner, Lowell Hill, George Ladd, Terry Roe, and Jim Shaffer made valuable suggestions on early drafts of the symposium outline. Finally, to Teddee Grace, who edited the manuscripts, and to Debbie Barstis, who entered the corrections on the microcomputer, we extend our gratitude for a job well done.

Economic Efficiency
In Agricultural and Food Marketing

Walter J. Armbruster

THE CONCEPT of economic efficiency is a mainstay of agricultural economics criteria for evaluating market performance. While it is only one performance dimension of markets, it is probably the most important tool used by agricultural economists in evaluating agricultural and food markets. However, there is increasing reason to question the credibility of economic efficiency as a concept useful for analysis in today's complex food and agricultural marketing system.

The underlying static concepts of economic efficiency analysis have been developed for a single product firm operating in a competitive spot market environment without regard to time and assuming a certain economic environment. But, the concepts are used to analyze the performance of marketing systems that are made increasingly complex with such vertical market elements as multiple-product firms, conglomerates, and nonspot exchanges as well as increased risk and uncertainty partially related to internationalization of markets. The current interest in free markets, the dynamics of the evolving market structures and realignments, and the changing information environment raise questions about the effects on economic efficiency and other elements of market performance.

To add to the confusion, economic efficiency is not a homogeneous term. Among those concepts frequently incorporated are pricing efficiency, technical efficiency, and overall economic efficiency. A definition of efficiency that is appropriate may well vary depending upon the level of the marketing system in which one is operating or conducting analysis.

WALTER J. ARMBRUSTER is associate managing director, Farm Foundation, Oak Brook, Illinois.

THE RELEVANCE OF ECONOMIC EFFICIENCY

Lang (1980, 772) argues that while economic efficiency is frequently used by economists to evaluate regulation or policy proposals, it is not properly used. He indicates that studies frequently rely on "simply productive efficiency or the private, pecuniary unit cost of production. These measures are quite different from the concept of Pareto optimality, which is the only theoretical definition of economic efficiency. Further, the use of such measures to compare policy alternatives obscures the true nature of the public choice involved."

Despite these criticisms, economists continue to draw upon efficiency analysis to evaluate economic impacts of policy alternatives. It is a widely used tool in the agricultural economist's kit. The question then becomes: How reliable are the results derived from this approach and what is their applicability to the problems addressed?

To be sure, agricultural economists have long been concerned about improving the level of knowledge regarding economic efficiency in food and agricultural marketing. In his 1977 review article, French indicated that serious attempts to improve efficiency of the agricultural marketing system originated in the Agricultural Marketing Act of 1946. As evidence French (1977, 93) cited the allocation of "between $4 million and $8 million per year to projects dealing with efficiency in various parts of the marketing system for agricultural products." He also noted that 700 research reports and journal articles dealing with productive efficiency resulted from these efforts, and that many additional publications focused on related studies of interregional competition and pricing efficiency.

He went on to argue that a good static theoretical framework exists for measuring costs and efficiency of individual firms. Even though he felt that the analyses incorporated realistic specifications on plants and their operating dimensions, French was concerned about the necessity of developing theory for dealing with the more complex marketing systems.

Since that time, research has continued with substantial progress being made. In a 1984 article, Kilmer and Armbruster argued that in recent examinations of agricultural marketing policy, efficiency concepts have become important and there has been pressure to use efficiency criteria in deciding whether economic regulation or federal marketing programs in agriculture are necessary. While arguing (1984, 102) that "efficiency concepts remain relevant in an increasingly integrated production-marketing system," they were concerned that continued diligence is needed to match the current state of knowledge with questions about the production and marketing system. They indicated that improved tools for analyzing productive efficiency and measuring allocative efficiency are becoming available. But there is need for continued development of conceptual models to approximate the complex nature of today's marketing system.

Given the significant structural, organizational, and policy changes in the agricultural and food marketing system in recent years, the chapters that follow explore the usefulness and relevance of efficiency concepts today and advances in their application.

The objectives of this examination include:

• Assessing the implications of economic efficiency for firm decision making and public policy in the agricultural and food marketing system.
• Exploring the conceptual and methodological dimensions to efficiency and their usefulness in the evolving agricultural marketing system.
• Identifying gaps in the conceptual and methodological models and needed directions in marketing efficiency research.

Economic efficiency needs to be closely examined and updated as necessary for today's marketing environment. The chapters in this book provide comprehensive coverage of the subject and identify research directions. The underlying concepts of economic efficiency and the latest methodological developments covering dynamics, uncertainty, and various marketing structures as well as their application to practical management and policy decisions in agricultural and food marketing are included.

As the chapters are developed, it becomes clear that trade-offs among performance dimensions and economic efficiency must be applied within the context of overall market performance.

This book summarizes the current state of knowledge about agricultural and food marketing system efficiency analysis. Reference citations provide a fairly comprehensive review of recent literature to help researchers assess the current state of the art. It should also prove valuable as a supplemental text in graduate level agricultural marketing courses or general economics courses focused on commodity and food marketing. Finally, it should be of interest to all economists interested in a thorough review of the general concepts of efficiency in agricultural and food marketing and the role of welfare economics in analyzing agricultural markets.

While readers could undoubtedly identify specific topics or subsets that they would like to have had included, the present book contains a wide-ranging treatment of the subject by leading researchers in the field. It should be a useful reference for many years to come.

REFERENCES

French, Ben C. "The Analysis of Productive Efficiency in Agricultural Marketing: Models, Methods, and Progress." *A Survey of Agricultural Economics Literature.* Vol. 1, *Traditional Fields in Agricultural Economics, 1940s to 1970s,* ed. L. R. Martin, pp. 93–206. Minneapolis: University of Minnesota Press, 1977.

Kilmer, Richard L., and Walter J. Armbruster. "Methods for Evaluating Economic Efficiency in Agricultural Marketing." *South. J. Agric. Econ.* 16(1984):101–9.

Lang, Malhon George. "Economic Efficiency and Policy Comparisons." *Am. J. Agric. Econ.* 62(1980):772–77.

PART I

Economic Efficiency

CHAPTER 1

The Food Marketing System:
The Relevance of
Economic Efficiency Measures

Gordon C. Rausser, Jeffery M. Perloff, and Pinhas Zusman

IN UNDERTAKING a survey of the relevance of various economic efficiency measures for the analysis of the food marketing system, we encountered in the literature an embarrassing richness of concepts, often poorly defined and unrelated, as is no doubt reflected in the following presentation. However, this state of affairs also provides the opportunity for a meaningful dialogue at this symposium.

The economic evaluation of food marketing systems has had a long history. In general, our profession has followed one of two approaches: (1) focus the analysis on subsystems (processing plants, elevators, transportation systems, etc.) in which the measurement and analytical problems are more tractable or (2) consider the organizational structure of the system and the institutional and policy constraints under which it operates, with the aim of identifying the structural and organizational characteristics likely to generate "inefficiencies." The first approach led to the analysis of productive efficiency of well-defined marketing subsystems.[1] The second approach has motivated market-structure analyses by students of industrial organization. In such analyses, market structure determines market conduct and, consequently, market performance.[2] In the context of the second approach, inefficiencies are ordinarily attributed to monopolistic misallocations.

GORDON C. RAUSSER is Robert Gordon Sproul Chair and Class of 1934 Distinguished Professor, Department of Agricultural and Resource Economics, University of California, Berkeley. JEFFREY M. PERLOFF is associate professor, Department of Agricultural and Resource Economics, University of California, Berkeley. PINHAS ZUSMAN is professor, Hebrew University of Agricultural Economics, Rehovot, Israel.

The methods and criteria employed by both approaches have been instrumental in identifying actual and potential inefficiencies in marketing systems and in developing policy recommendations. For example, market-structure analyses provide the bases for antitrust and other regulatory policies. In any event, as Ladd (1983) has noted, efficiency is only defined by the criteria and constraints imposed. Hence, different criteria and constraints will lead to alternative measurements of inefficiency.

Members of the agricultural economics profession generally fall into one of two schools of thought regarding the measurement of inefficiencies. One school focuses on the deadweight loss efficiency calculations advocated by Harberger (1971). This approach has been widely applied to evaluate various market distortions in a partial equilibrium, static context. People who have used this approach are too numerous to list here, but D. Wallace, A. Schmitz, and B. Gardner come to mind. The second school of thought is, perhaps, most eloquently described by Brandow (1977, 27):

> This reviewer is unwilling to aggregate personal utilities indiscriminately. He is particularly unwilling to accept the assumption that there exist empirical counterparts of either the perfect competition situation or the equivalent situation under the constraints of a program. . . .The neat alignment of resources, output, and prices specified by the perfect competition model is far from duplicated in free markets, and the equally neat alignment assumed under the constraints of a program is not experienced when programs are in effect. In particular, areas under empirically determined supply curves are unlikely to represent opportunity costs.

Basically, this school of thought does not believe that a first-best world is achievable. Measurements from an efficiency frontier that is not singularly attainable can hardly be viewed as socially desirable.

Our purpose is to review and evaluate each of these two schools of thought in the context of the food marketing system. In pursuit of this purpose, we must review a number of basic concepts that should help set the stage for all the presentations to follow. In essence, we will divide the set of potential problems that arise in food marketing systems between those problems that admit an approximate first-best solution and those that do not. In the first instance, conventional welfare analysis will be advanced as providing the relevant criteria and appropriate constraints for the measurement of inefficiencies. In some cases, the standard efficiency calculus can be directly applied, while in other cases it must be modified significantly. For the second subset of problems, nonconventional approaches to efficiency measurement must be advocated. In both instances, of course, a direct empirical analysis of economic efficiency of the food marketing system boils down essentially to a benefit-cost analysis.

REVIEW OF BASIC CONCEPTS

According to the neoclassical paradigm, all exchange is carried out in competitive auction markets. Under full information and in the absence of externalities and nonconvexities, the resulting equilibrium is Pareto efficient. To the extent that this model of the economy is valid, efficiency analysis is, indeed, redundant. Efficiency analysis is of interest only because market imperfections arise and the quantitative implications of such distortions can be used to serve the public interest. At this juncture, it seems appropriate to offer a number of formal definitions that will provide a common ground for the balance of our discussion.

ECONOMIC EFFICIENCY AND PARETO OPTIMALITY

Suppose there are n "goods" in an economy, an economywide endowment of these goods, $\overline{X}$ a production technology that can transform $\overline{X}$ into other aggregate supply vectors, x, and I individuals with preferences defined over the consumption allocation, X, which is an $(n \times I)$ matrix in which the (j, i)th element corresponds to consumption of good j by individual i. Under these conditions, an allocation, X^*, is Pareto efficient if there is no other allocation that makes someone better off and no one less well off. Pareto efficiency is alternatively called *economic efficiency* or *allocative efficiency*. Formally, X^* is Pareto efficient if there does not exist any other feasible X such that each individual i either prefers X to X^* or is indifferent between X and X^* and, for some i, i prefers X to X^*. The $X \cdot e = x$ is a feasible aggregate supply vector given the economy's production technology and endowment, $\bar{x}$, where e is a summation vector over individuals.

COMPENSATION PRINCIPLE AND ECONOMIC SURPLUSES

Formally, the compensation principle tells us that state z' is preferred to state z if, when making the move to z', the gainers can compensate the losers such that everyone is made better off. More formally, if there exists a feasible w', a distribution of incomes among agents, such that $X(z', w')$ is Pareto superior to $X(z, w)$, then the compensation principle states that z' is preferred to z.

The compensation principle is the theoretical underpinning for economic surplus (e.g., consumer-producer surplus, measures of welfare). These measures are based on and answered in the question: How much money (C_i) must each i be given to make him/her just as happy in state (z', w') as in state (z, w)? To derive expressions for this measure, let P denote a vector of equilibrium outcomes (prices) in economy (z, w) and

P', the corresponding vector in economy (z', w'). Further, assume no externalities, and let $V_i(P, w_i)$ denote agent i's indirect utility function. Then, C_i is defined by:

$$V_i(P', w_i' + C_i) = V_i(P, w_i).$$

Agent i's compensating variation (change in surplus), CV_i, for the change from (z, w) to (z', w'), is equal to $-C_i$. An expression for CV_i can also be derived in terms of the agent's expenditure function. Let

$$e_i(P, \bar{u}_i) \equiv \min_{X_{\cdot i}} X_{\cdot i}' P$$

subject to

$$u_i(X_{\cdot i}) = \bar{u}_i.$$

Then,

$$CV_i = e_i(P', u_i^0) - e_i(P, u_i^0) + (w_i - w_i')$$

where $u_i^0 = V(P, w_i)$. If $w_i = w_i'$, then this expression for the compensating variation simplifies to the line integral,

$$\int_P^{P'} \sum h_j(P, u_i^0) dP_j,$$

where $h_j(P, u_i^0)$ represents the compensated demand for good j. Although the vector P is conventionally defined as prices, it can be generalized to include measures of other external arguments in an indirect utility function such as good characteristics. Thus, for example, the compensating variation associated with change in a good characteristic can be measured in exactly the same way as for a price change (Hanemann 1982).

TECHNICAL EFFICIENCY

To describe technical efficiency in production (Farrell 1957), more structure is required. Let production be undertaken by firms that are indexed by k. Each firm's production technology is defined by the set of feasible net-put vectors, $y^k \in R^n$, which will be denoted as Y^k. Positive elements of this vector are outputs and negative elements are inputs.

Given any input bundle, no more output can be produced than is currently being produced. More formally, a production plan, y^k, for firm

k is technically efficient if there does not exist any other feasible plan, y'^k ϵ Y^k such that $y_i'^k \geq y_i^k$ for all i (where y_i denotes the ith element of the y vector) and $y_i'^k > y_i^k$ for some i.

COST EFFICIENCY

Given a net-put vector, y, denote the $(n \times 1)$ vector with all the negative terms in y set equal to zero as y_+ and the $(n \times 1)$ vector with all positive terms set equal to zero as y_-. Let Y^{*k} denote the set of technically efficient y^k and y^{*k} the elements of this set. Define the function $F^k: R^n \rightarrow R$ such that $F^k(y^{*k}) = 0$ for all $y^{*k} \epsilon Y^{*k}$. Finally, let r denote an $(n \times 1)$ price vector for goods.

For a given output, y_+^o, a cost-efficient production plane minimizes input cost. More formally, a production plan, y, is cost efficient relative to w if y_- solves the following cost-minimization problem:

$$\max_{y_-} w'y_-$$

subject to:

$$F^k(y_- + y_+^0) = 0.$$

Note that, assuming a common r faces all firms, the first-order conditions for a solution to this problem imply the standard condition of equality between rates of technical substitution across firms, namely, write as $(r_i/r_j) = (F_i^k/F_j^k) = (F_i^{k'}/F_j^{k'})$ where F_i^k denotes $\partial F^k/\partial y_i^k$ and r_i denotes the ith element of the r vector.

PRODUCTION EFFICIENCY

However, if there are production externalities, cost efficiency within each firm will not generate a social optimum. Hence, economywide production efficiency may be defined as the set of production plans, $\{y^k\}$ that result from solving the following maximization problem for some vector r:

$$\max_{\{y^k\}} r'\left(\sum_k y^k\right)$$

subject to:

$$F^k(y^k|y^{-k}) = 0, \; k = 1,\ldots,K$$
$$\bar{x} + \sum_k y^k \geq 0$$

where y^{-k} is a stacked vector of net puts for all firms except the kth firm, and the vector inequality means that the inequality must hold element by element.

Hence, productive efficiency requires that each firm produces in such a way as to place the economy on its production possibility frontier. Note that when there are no externalities [i.e., $F^k(y^k \mid y^{-k}) = F^k(y^k)$], the first-order conditions for a solution to the above problem also imply equality between rates of technical substitution across firms. In this case, cost efficiency and production efficiency are synonymous.

The above concepts focus on production and neglect the role of consumer preferences. From the standpoint of consumption, similar efficiency notions can be advanced to capture the optimal mix of products and allocation of products among consumers. The relevant conditions for an efficient allocation are that the value placed on produced goods by an individual (marginal rate of substitution) must be equal to the cost of transforming one good into another (marginal rate of transformation); the value of consuming factors of production directly (marginal rate of substitution) must be equal to the cost of transforming the inputs into goods (marginal rate of technical substitution); and the value placed by consumers on consumption of an input and an output (marginal rate of substitution) must be equal to the marginal product.

X-Efficiency and O-Efficiency

Other less formal concepts have also been offered in the literature. In particular, Liebenstein (1966) advances the notion of X-efficiency. Three key determinants of this efficiency are said to be (1) intraplant motivational efficiency, (2) external motivational efficiency (e.g., due to competitive pressures), and (3) nonmarket input efficiency. Liebenstein argues that these forces are significant for four major reasons: (1) contracts for labor are incomplete; (2) not all factors of production (e.g., management knowledge) are marketed; (3) a production function is not completely specified or known; and (4) interdependence and uncertainty lead competing firms to cooperate tacitly with each other in some respects and to imitate each other with respect to technique to some degree. Competitive forces and economic adversities spur cost-reducing measures, which of course imply that the efficiency costs of a monopoly are much greater than the allocative inefficiencies identified by conventional efficiency measures. A formal definition of X-efficiency is not possible in the absence of a model that specifies the processes to which Liebenstein alludes.

Analogously, Helmberger (1968) offered the notion of O-efficiency. Specifically, consider a given set of firms, each engaged in defined economic activities; call this set an O-configuration. Associated with each O-configuration is a set of intrafirm processes ("conscious coordination of economic activities") and market processes ("unconscious coordination") that yield equilibrium. O-configurations that lead to Pareto-efficient equilibria are termed O-efficient.

Efficient Market Hypothesis

Once we relax the assumption of certainty and full information, still other definitions may be advanced. In the context of uncertainty, the efficient market hypothesis has been widely applied in finance and to commodity futures markets. To be sure, uncertainty and limited information are largely responsible for the institutional forms that have emerged in the United States food marketing system.

An asset market is said to be efficient with respect to an information set if revealing that information to all agents would not change equilibrium-asset prices or equilibrium-portfolio holdings.[3] Operationally, this means that a price of an asset will be the discounted expectation of future cash flows, and new information concerning cash flows must be reflected immediately in the price of the asset, where new information is presumed to arrive randomly. In the context of commodity futures markets, this implies that a quoted futures price is nothing more than the expected spot price at some future date based on current information.

Three levels of asset-market efficiency have been distinguished (Fama 1970): (1) *weak form*—the market is efficient with respect to the history of its past prices; (2) *semistrong form*—the market is efficient with respect to all "public information"; and (3) *strong form*—the market is efficient with respect to all information on the economy—public and private.

Recognizing limited information, still other definitions have been advanced. Private information efficiency occurs if an equilibrium allocation is Pareto-optimal and all agents use only their own private or personal information. Price information efficiency occurs if an equilibrium is Pareto-optimal and all agents use any information that can be rationally extracted from observed prices in addition to their private information. Full information efficiency occurs if an equilibrium allocation is Pareto-optimal and every agent has access to all available information. Obviously, private information and price information, when prices are not fully revealing, both imply differential information across individuals.

Some of the above definitions are motivated by the limiting features of the efficient market hypothesis. As Grossman and Stiglitz (1980) have shown, for the property of efficiency to hold, costless information is not only a sufficient but also a necessary condition. In testing the efficiency of futures markets, for example, the implication of these definitions is that, even if a particular model forecast is more accurate than forecasts of futures markets, inefficiency does not necessarily follow. This condition is only necessary; inefficiency implies that a model does exist whose forecasts are more accurate than the futures market forecast (relative accuracy condition). Sufficiency can be obtained by including the condition that the cost of constructing and utilizing the model does not exceed the incremental benefits appropriately adjusted by risk (relative costs/benefits condition). The two conditions—relative accuracy and a favorable cost/benefits relation—are necessary and sufficient for the inefficiency assessment of commodity futures markets to hold.

GLOBAL EFFICIENCY

The above measures of single market efficiency have been extended to a multimarket context by Rausser and Walraven (1985). In their work, the notion of global efficiency is advanced. Formally, a set of multiple interrelated assets markets is efficient if all markets adjust instantaneously and converge to a stable, general equilibrium allocation as a result of the random arrival of any new information. Operationally, global efficiency is a relative concept that measures price dynamics rather than the all-or-nothing characterization of most other concepts. The dynamic properties of the entire set of market prices are employed to assign an accuracy and a speed of convergence measure to each market. As a result, the efficiency of any individual market is considered with a regard not only to its own internal forces but also to its linkages to other markets (i.e., the rest of the system). In a measurement context, price deviations reflecting inaccuracies in the measurement of a conditional expected forward price and its distributed lag adjustments in moving from current prices to a stationary state can be introduced directly into standard welfare loss analysis. To the extent that the speed of convergence is slow or the distributed lag adjustments to shocks and other markets are delayed for a particular asset, the price of that asset will not be the discounted expectation of future cash flows.

MARKET FAILURE VS. GOVERNMENT FAILURE

The above definitions focus on only the private sector economy and neglect the role of government and its influence on the structure, conduct, and performance of a particular economic system. The definitions are couched in standard welfare economics that treats government as a perfect instrument for correcting whatever market failures might be identified by the application of conventional efficiency analysis. This view has been seriously challenged by the accumulation of empirical evidence on the performance of governmental intervention (Rausser 1982). In the rent-seeking literature, the economics of regulation literature, and the theory of state literature, the emphasis is not on market failure but on government failure. In this literature, government policies are not introduced to improve efficiency but rather to redistribute wealth from one group in society to another. In much of this literature, a crude predatory theory of the state is advanced in which government is simply a gigantic transfer mechanism for redistributing wealth and income. In some of these frameworks, the government has no separate autonomy; it is manipulated by powerful interest groups seeking to increase their own welfare to the detriment of society as a whole.

The above perspective quite obviously suggests that the efficiency of government should also be evaluated. This has led Becker (1983) to introduce the notion of "efficient" government redistribution. The Becker framework has been utilized by both Gardner (1983) and de Gorter (1983) to evaluate the efficiency of redistributing economic surplus. Formally, this has led to the following definition: For any particular selection and setting of government policy instruments, there is an equilibrium allocation with a corresponding distribution of utilities among agents. Suppose that there are N instrument mixes and that any one instrument mix is represented by n, and the actual settings or levels of instruments in this mix are represented by the vector X_n. Let $[u_1(n, x_n), \ldots, u_I(n, x_n)]$ denote the utility distribution among the I agents produced by instrument n set at level x_n. Let the set

$$U_n \equiv \{[u_1(n, x_n), \ldots, u_I(n, x_n)] \mid 0 \leq x_n \leq \bar{x}_n\}$$

be the set of utility distributions induced by x_n given n, where $\bar{x}_n$ is the maximal possible level of x_n. Finally, let U^* denote the set of suprema for the union of $U_1, \ldots, U_N$. Now efficient redistribution can be defined: A policymaker's choice of instrument and level of (n^*, x_n^*) achieve efficient redistribution if and only if (n^*, x_n^*) produce a utility distribution that is an element of U^*. In words, a planner has a feasible set of utility distributions that can be obtained by policy means. Redistributive efficiency is achieved when policies are chosen so that the frontier of this feasible set is achieved. Operationally, "utilities" can be measured by economic surplus and agents are aggregated into groups such as producers, consumers, intermediaries, and government. Specifically, redistribution inefficiency has been measured as deadweight loss divided by the amount of economic surplus transferred from consumers (producers) to producers (consumers), (i.e., as the social cost per dollar of economic surplus transferred) (Gardner 1983).

The role of government can be viewed from a number of different perspectives. In each instance, it is important to recognize that political and economic markets are not separable (Rausser 1982). Efficiency in "political/economic markets" can be analyzed from the perspective of political/economic-seeking transfers (PESTs). As noted in the rent-seeking literature, competition in political markets, in contrast to private economic markets, generates social waste rather than social surplus. Interest groups are viewed as competing for political influence by spending time, energy, and money on the production of political pressure to effectuate both the design and tactical implementation of governmental policies. The allocation of these resources is ·directed toward political/economic gain-seeking transfers. In the context of economic efficiency or a first-best world, PESTs activities on the part of interest groups are merely wasteful.

Private agents' PESTs activities were first emphasized by Tullock (1967), who argued that the standard deadweight losses implied by welfare analysis for tariffs, monopolies, and thefts were at best lower bound estimates of the actual cost. This argument was in response to the large number of empirical studies using conventional welfare analysis, which showed that the cost of monopolies and tariffs to society were indeed small.[4] On the basis of his review of these studies, Liebenstein (1966, 392) argues that "microeconomic theory focuses on allocative efficiency to the exclusion of other types of efficiencies that, in fact, are much more significant in many instances."

In Tullock's (1967) analysis, the standard "welfare triangle" is only part of the story. In addition, the transfers from one group in the private sector to another motivate the expenditure of resources in PEST-related activities. Governments do what they do, in part, because they are lobbied or pressured into doing so. Pure transfers cost society nothing; but, for the people engaging in such transfers, they are like any other activity, and this, of course, means that large resources may be invested in attempting to make or prevent transfers. Thus, to achieve accuracy in the measurements of monopoly effects, for example, the standard welfare triangle measures must be extended to include those resources that are invested by potential monopolists who seek the income transfer from their potential customers. As noted by Tullock (1967, 228) "in fact, the investment that could be profitably made in forming a monopoly would be larger than this rectangle since it represents merely the income transfer. The capital value, properly discounted for risk, would be worth much more."

Governments are not only involved in PEST-related activities but, in addition, often generate political/economic resource transactions (PERTs) equivalent to governmental interventions that completely or partially correct market failures by designing a set of rules to reduce transaction costs faced by the private agents (Rausser 1982). The net effect of PERT policies is to increase the size of the pie. Most governmental interventions generate both PERTs and PESTs. The evaluation of these two sets of activities can be performed by the measurement of a "political preference function." Such a function can be used as the criterion for evaluating efficiencies in the private sector as well as in the public sector. As emphasized by Steiner (1969), the choice of weights in such a function is an important dimension of the public interest. Empirically, such a function can also establish an alternative norm for standard efficiency analysis that places weights on both the size and the distribution of the pie.

OTHER COORDINATING MECHANISMS

The given concepts and definitions recognize only three coordinating mechanisms along the vertical marketing chain of the food system, namely, spot markets, futures markets, and the government. There are, of course, numerous other mechanisms or institutions that coordinate the exchange of food products including such things as contracts, cooperatives, vertical integration, horizontal integration, commodity associations, marketing orders and agreements, etc. The neoclassical paradigm, upon which many of the definitions are based, emphasizes competitive spot markets. In the U.S. food marketing system, however, the decline of spot markets has been dramatic. Recent estimates suggest that the spot market accounts for a very small percentage of transactions in a number of commodity systems. For example, only 5 percent of fresh fruits and vegetables, 2 percent of processed fruits and vegetables (Paul et al. 1980), and less than 3 percent of eggs, commercial broilers, and market turkeys (Lasley 1983) are traded through the spot market.

Alternative coordinating mechanisms will influence transaction costs, technology, the quantity and quality of output in a particular commodity system, the size and distribution of profits and losses, and, equally important, the sharing of risk among the various components of the food marketing system. Kilmer and Ward (1982) have advanced a framework for analyzing alternative mechanisms in accordance with their effect on product characteristics, transaction costs, and technology. Unfortunately, uncertainty and risk are not included in their framework.

At the heart of any analytical framework designed to evaluate the performance of alternative coordinating mechanisms is the notion of a contract. In fact, the organization or configuration of coordinating mechanisms can be viewed as a system of interrelated contracts. Such a perspective can be traced to the concept of a firm adopted long ago by Coase (1937). More recently, the Coasean perspective has been accepted and employed by students of economic organizations (e.g., Fama and Jensen 1983).

Unfortunately, the choice of contractual arrangements and the evolution of stable contractual systems have been generally ignored by the market structure literature. Since it is analytically necessary to view any organizational form, including hierarchy (internal organization) as a nexus of contracts, traditional market structure analysis is insufficient for evaluating economic efficiency of marketing systems. As Williamson (1971) has shown, the phenomenon of vertical integration, so central in many markets, can hardly be explained without considering the alternative underlying contractual arrangements and the transaction costs they entail.

The importance of contracts in the development of a theory of market organization can be seen by distinguishing the four general types of exchange systems that arise. The first type consists of the competitive auction markets that are assumed by the neoclassical paradigm. Although several kinds of complex contracts (e.g., securities) are often traded in auction markets, such markets can be clearly distinguished from contractual markets. The second type consists of imperfect noncontractual markets. These are comprised of various forms of imperfectly competitive trade in goods and services. The noncontractual nature of the transactions is characterized by the virtual absence of trade over states of nature even when uncertainty prevails. Therefore, no risk bearing is allocated in these transactions. An example of this type is a monopolistically competitive retail market for food products in which no long-term, state-contingent commitments are undertaken. The third type consists of contractual markets in which transactions involve complex contractual arrangements among independent transactors. Contracts struck in these markets ordinarily include trade over states of nature under conditions of uncertainty and under conditions of imperfect and asymmetric information structures. Thus, risk bearing is traded as part of the transaction of goods and services. An example of this type is the grower-processor contractual arrangement in which prices depend on delivery dates, the quality characteristic of the product, etc. The fourth type of exchange mechanism consists of trade among different components of a single hierarchical economic entity (e.g., a wine producer who also grows the grapes used as raw material). Here the terms of exchange are often, though not always, determined by fiat. Note, however, that since an internal organization may also be viewed as a network of contracts there is no sharp distinction between contractual exchange and hierarchies. Furthermore, noncontractual exchange, too, may be regarded as a special extreme case of contractual exchange. Contracts, in their variety of shapes and forms, thus become the common building blocks and the unifying concept in any theory of market organization.

ACHIEVABILITY OF FIRST-BEST SOLUTION

When the cost of resources consumed in the marketing process and the various benefits that are created can be summarized in some net value measure and compared to a feasible net value-maximizing norm, the efficiency problem is adequately treated. Unfortunately, this is virtually impossible under many circumstances for two reasons: (1) the cost and benefits are not easily identified and are often difficult to measure; and (2) a feasible net value-maximizing norm may not be achievable. To be sure, it is not too difficult, at least in principle, to measure the net social surpluses associated with certain price-quantity combinations due to the instability of these variables. But how should such benefits as availability of food products near buyers' homes, product quality and variety, in-store conveniences, low probability of stock outs, unrestricted choice of quantity (nonrationing), and short queues be valued?[5] Similarly, how should the availability of information on transaction opportunities, the lowering of uncertainty and risk to the various market participants (farmers, processors, market-clearing intermediaries, and final consumers), and the saving of precious time and efforts of farmers seeking out potential buyers in implementing exchange be valued?

Where information is incomplete and asymmetrically distributed among transactors, states of nature uncertain, and nonconvexities exist, a first-best solution or a feasible net value-maximizing norm cannot be obtained. Uncertainty itself is not the culprit responsible for the inability to obtain a first-best solution. As Debreu (1959) has shown, competitive markets in state-contingent claims could still constitute a perfectly efficient system of exchange. However, as information is imperfect and asymmetrically distributed, many markets in contingent claims will fail to emerge (Radner 1982). Complex contracts, which allow trade over states of nature while taking into account the information compatibility constraints, may then provide more efficient solutions, although these solutions are only second-best results. Under these arrangements, risk bearing is traded in conjunction with the transaction of goods and services. The determination of the contractual terms ordinarily depends on the market structure in which the exchange is carried out. The typology of market structures traditionally adopted in the industrial organization literature applies here as well. It should be emphasized, however, that the diversity of buyers and sellers is often conducive to differentiated customized contracts and, hence, to multiple thin markets ruled by bargaining relations.

For circumstances where a first-best solution is not achievable or cannot be approximated, conventional efficiency comparisons must be discarded. In this situation, analysts are left with one of two alternatives. The first alternative would be to define a new norm. For example, a political preference function based on the notion of political efficiency could be advanced (Rausser 1982; Zusman 1976). In fact, such a political preference function could admit nonmaterial well-being. The "trade-off weights" appearing in the political preference function can be utilized parametrically in the derivation of political efficiency measures. For analysts who are not prepared to operate with such norms and who prefer to continue with conventional economic efficiency norms, we have no recourse but to turn to the theory of second-best. In this case, the actual efficiency is compared to the "second-best" solution rather than to an infeasible first-best solution. Moreover, with this approach, analysts must be concerned with the constrained Pareto efficiency and the theorem of second-best.

Constrained Pareto efficiency follows if markets are incomplete so that allocations are constrained by the feasible trading space. Specifically, an allocation X is constrained Pareto efficient relative to available markets if, without the implicit or explicit addition of markets, no feasible Pareto-superior allocation exists (Newberry and Stiglitz 1981). The theorem of the second-best sheds further light on this concept. Lipsey and Lancaster (1956) state the theorem as follows: Let there be some function $F(x_1, \ldots, x_n)$ of the n variables $x_1, \ldots, x_n$, which is to be maximized (minimized) subject to a constraint on the variables $\phi(x_1, \ldots, x_n) = 0$. This is a formalization of the typical choice situation in economic analysis. Let the solution of this problem (the Paretian optimum) be the $n - 1$ conditions $\theta^i(x_1, \ldots, x_n) = 0$, $i = 1, \ldots, n - 1$. Then the following theorem, the theorem of the second-best is:

> If there is an additional constraint that makes the satisfaction of the jth condition impossible, i.e., $\theta^j \neq 0$, then the maximum (minimum) of F subject to both the constraint ϕ and the additional constraint 0 will, in general, be such that none of the still attainable Paretian conditions $\theta^i = 0$, $i \neq j$, will be satisfied.

In a world of second-best, initial conditions are crucial and intransitivities, along with paradoxes, can arise. Under limited and asymmetric information, conventional efficiency norms force comparisons of second-best solutions. As a result, we cannot be assured that unambiguous evaluations can be performed.

For circumstances in which a first-best solution is achievable or can be approximated, conventional efficiency methods can and should be used. There are, however, many problems in food marketing in which these circumstances do not arise. In what follows, we examine a number of cases in which the conventional efficiency analysis is misleading and should be avoided. These cases are grouped into one of two categories: (1) dynamic measures of efficiency, which are examined in the next section and (2) second-best outcomes, which are examined in the section on Second-Best Solutions.

DYNAMIC MEASURES OF EFFICIENCY

Traditional static measures of efficiency, market power, and welfare are inappropriate for use in markets in which prices and output levels are intertemporally determined. In the case of the food marketing system, most prices and output levels are generated from dynamic markets. The inappropriateness of such measures is particularly obvious in the case of renewable and nonrenewable resource industries, markets with learning curve effects or dynamic demand functions, and agricultural markets in which supply adjustments take years to complete. The latter type of adjustment is particularly common in perennial crops and in the livestock sector. Indeed, dynamic adjustments may take years in many, if not most, agricultural markets; thus, traditional static measures may be highly misleading. Also, under technological progress and growth, a noncompetitive structure may be more efficient in the long run whereas, in the short run, conventional measures would imply inefficiencies.

In a general equilibrium context, it is important to recognize that the effect of economic forces from "outside markets" on the various components of the food industry can be quite different. In the context of storable commodities, asset arbitrage opportunities have a much more pronounced effect on tradeables relative to nontradeables. In the formation of the price of food at the retail level, both tradeable and nontradeable goods play important roles. Nontradeables for most food products represent a greater proportion of the retail value than the tradeable component (e.g., the raw agricultural commodity value). The static measures of efficiency, market power, and welfare will be misleading to the degree that long waves appear in the dynamic paths of these two general types of goods.

DYNAMIC PARTIAL EQUILIBRIUM MEASURES OF EFFICIENCY

The biases from using static measures are often substantial. For example, La France and de Gorter (1985) found that it takes more than ten years for the dairy industry to adjust so that the average annual dynamic welfare change is three times the static estimate in evaluating dairy support programs.[6] Baumann and Kalt (1983) have used dynamic models to calculate consumer surplus over time from freezing natural gas prices. They conclude that the appropriate static analysis overestimates the present value of such a program by 15 percent ($12 billion).

Thus, traditional types of studies, such as the efficiency and welfare effects of marketing orders, should take these adjustments into account. To illustrate this point, consider an agricultural market subject to a marketing order that allows for market allocations and the elimination of some of the crop.[7] If entry takes time, which seems the case in all these types of marketing orders, early entrants make large short-run gains while, in the long run, marginal firms break even. Consumers, correspondingly, suffer larger welfare losses at first than in the long run when supply increases. Due to the supply allocation rule between two markets, however, price falls more substantially over time in the secondary market than in the primary market.

Because these types of adjustments can take years or decades, the present value of the efficiency or welfare losses and gains depends crucially on the interest rate, both for discounting reasons and because it affects the rate of entry. As the interest rate increases, the present value of profits for each new entrant decreases. Thus, during the adjustment period, supply is lower, price is higher, and consumer surplus is lower.

Similarly, anything that affects the rate of entry will affect the adjustment path and the present discounted value of efficiency or welfare. As the rate of entry increases, the supply increases, the price falls, consumers are better off, and producers' profits may rise or fall. Most static analysts, because they have only looked at the long-run steady state, neglect the gains of early entrants. Similarly, such studies typically ignore the larger losses that consumers face in the short run than in the steady state.

Pindyck (1985) has shown that Lerner's approach to measuring monopoly power in a static model can be generalized for use in a dynamic model. Lerner's index of monopoly power is $L = (P - MC)/P$ (where P = price and MC = marginal cost) which, in the static case, depends only on the elasticity of demand. In a dynamic market, however, such a measure will depend on more than just the elasticity of demand so that the Lerner measure is inappropriate even as an instantaneous measure of monopoly power. For example, the price and production trajectories of an exhaustible natural resource monopolist, who faces an isoelastic demand curve and has zero extraction costs, are identical to those of a competitive market (Stiglitz 1976). Thus, the monopolist has no monopoly power; yet, the Lerner measure would equal one at every point in time.

Similarly, if a monopolist is using a new technology in which the learning curve is important, current prices will be below current marginal cost. As a result, even though output is less than in a competitive market, the Lerner index is negative.

Pindyck (1985) argues that, even if the Lerner index sufficed as an instantaneous measure, averaging such short-run measures would not be informative for two reasons: (1) the short-run monopoly price depends on more than the firm's short-run demand curve so that using the short-run elasticity would be misleading; and (2) the firm's gain and consumer's loss from monopoly power depend on the rate at which demand adjusts, which in turn depends on the firm's price trajectory. Thus, Pindyck recommends a measure that reflects the trajectory of monopoly power over time weighted by the firm's revenues (consumer's expenditures).[8]

FLEXIBLE/INFLEXIBLE MARKETS AND OVERSHOOTING

In both macroeconomics and general equilibrium theory, analysts have begun to recognize the incentive for long-term contracting in a number of important markets. For example, labor contracts generally fix the wage rate over long periods of time. Over the period of the contract, wages are pegged to some general indices such as the consumer price index. The incentives for long-term contracting have been found to be particularly important for nontradeables, heterogeneous goods, markets in which information is limited, and markets in which price adjustments are costly. These characteristics arise in many of the input markets to the assembly, processing, and distribution components of the food marketing system. In contrast, the more homogeneous, storable, and tradeable raw commodities produced at the farm level offer fewer incentives for long-term contracting. This simple dichotomy of markets in the general economy, fixed and flex, leads to the nonneutrality of money and overshooting in the more flexible price markets.

With short-run nonneutrality of money, relative prices will become distorted, even though all expectations are formed rationally. It means that the dynamic path of food commodity markets depends critically upon the linkages between these markets, exchange rates, and domestic as well as international money markets. Exchange rates or storable food commodity prices will overshoot their long-run equilibrium because other markets in the general economy respond only with very long lags to any permanent change in money supply (Rausser et al. 1985).[9]

Empirical evidence has been advanced to support the hypothesis of a mixture of fixed- and flex-price markets in the general economy and the overshooting of farm-level prices (Rausser et al. 1985). In the context of efficiency analysis, these phenomena preclude the application of conventional static measures of efficiency. In effect, due to the fixed-price markets, permanent changes in money supply will impose externalities on raw commodity prices. Static measures will not recognize these externalities or the resulting overshooting and, thus, will incorrectly evaluate the inherent instabilities in a particular market. Hence, the use of observed data to perform welfare analysis of various stabilization policies will prove misleading.

The overshooting phenomenon and the composition of fixed- and flex-price markets strongly suggest that, as we move from the farm gate to the food store, much "industrial contamination" occurs that increases the degree of "stickiness" of food prices as we move up the vertical marketing chain.[10] Widening margins or abnormally large profits in the short run do not necessarily imply that oligolopolistic or monopolistic competition is on the rise. Similarly, narrowing margins or decreasing rates of profit do not necessarily mean that competitive behavior has somehow been reasserted. These movements may, in fact, reflect nothing more than the differential response of one market versus another to a perceived permanent change in money supply. This suggests, of course, that dynamic welfare analysis in food marketing must concern itself with the linkage effects of money markets, interest rates, and exchange rates before arriving at any unambiguous conclusion.

SECOND-BEST SOLUTIONS

Great care must be exercised in using efficiency and welfare measures in markets with limited information and/or where contracting is pervasive. The traditional partial equilibrium measures, which implicitly assume full information or spot-market exchange, are almost certainly misleading. A few approaches have been developed, however, that can be used in some, but not all, of these situations. In the following two subsections, a thumbnail sketch of these approaches is outlined.

LIMITED INFORMATION AND EFFICIENCY COMPARISONS

Unfortunately, in the presence of limited information, moving from one second-best to another second-best equilibrium can raise or lower welfare or various efficiency measures. Eliminating a "distortion" that would raise efficiency in a world of full information can lower efficiency or welfare in a world of limited information. Such effects may be missed by traditional partial equilibrium measures either because they ignore the general equilibrium effects or because they implicitly assume full information.

Were this point only an unlikely theoretical possibility, we could continue to use traditional methods. In many final agricultural and re-source goods markets (e.g., grocery stores, breakfast cereals, and fast foods), however, there are reasons to believe that informational problems exist. Chief among these is the presence of market power derived from limited information about the price or the quality of products.

Many papers have shown that, in markets for even homogeneous commodities, limited price information endows firms with informationally based market power that may result in price dispersion.[11] In a model advanced by Perloff and Rausser (1983), market power in one sector of an industry can provide a firm with information that it can use to gain market power in another sector. In this limited and asymmetric information model, an increase in public information known to the competitive fringe can increase or decrease the distortions in various agricultural markets. This ambiguous result simply reflects the general principle that, in moving from one second-best to another, there is no assurance that society's welfare is enhanced.

In markets with heterogeneous goods, consumers are concerned with the quality and variety of goods as well as their prices (Salop 1977).[12] Thus, since differences in product attributes across brands affect the value per dollar of the products, even if prices of products are known, limited information about attributes can also convey market power to firms. The surprising result of most of these articles on limited information is that an increase in information may not increase efficiency or welfare (properly measured). Unless consumers obtain full information, the increase in information will cause the economy to shift from one second-best equilibrium to another. As the literature on limited price information shows, such an increase in information may leave efficiency and welfare unchanged. The literature on limited information about product attributes indicates that welfare can even be lowered.[13]

However, an even more striking result is that where other market imperfections exist, providing full information can actually reduce welfare. In a competitive market, the elimination of limits to information must increase efficiency and welfare. However, it is easy to imagine counter examples in monopolistically competitive markets. Suppose that an industry is monopolistically competitive (as is the case of many processed foods, drugs, and other markets), and consumers have limited information about the health attributes of these products. The government informs consumers with high blood pressure that they should not eat certain of these products because of their inherently high levels of sodium or cholesterol.

If consumers heed these warnings, demand for various products will change. The result may be to drive up the price for products with low sodium or cholesterol levels, which harms some consumers who are not on a restricted diet. It is possible that the damage to this latter group could exceed the benefit to the group with high blood pressure. Indeed, it is possible that the shifts in demand could drive up the prices for so many related goods that all consumers (including those rationally responding to the warnings) are worse off.

Such health warnings are becoming increasingly common. The U.S. Department of Agriculture, the Food and Drug Administration, and the Federal Trade Commission have held joint public hearings on the issue of food labeling. These agencies have issued health warnings concerning aflatoxin, cholesterol, sodium, potassium, saccharin, cyclamates, calories, protein levels, and other components and attributes of foods and drugs. Obviously, when the government actually removes certain products (e.g., those with cyclamates) from the market, the impact of their actions is even greater.

Warnings on cholesterol appear to have had a substantial impact on U.S. consumption of meat and eggs; warnings on saccharin, cyclamates, and other sugar substitutes have affected a number of markets, especially the soft drink industry; and cigarette warnings have greatly affected the tobacco industry. For example, since 1965, milk and cream consumption have declined 21 percent, butter consumption has declined 28 percent, and consumption of eggs has fallen from 334 per capita in 1960 to 283 in 1979 (Commodity Research Bureau, Inc.; Consumer Reports 1981).

In the cases discussed above, standard partial equilibrium efficiency and welfare measures may be misleading because they ignore the general equilibrium effects. A much more important theoretical issue is that efficiency and welfare comparisons are not well defined in those situations in which consumers' welfare levels change. Obviously, calculations will depend upon the information levels assumed in the analysis.

Some attempts have been made to come to grips with this problem.[14] Using a clever analysis, Dixit and Norman (1978) argue that in certain cases efficiency and welfare statements can be made even when these measures are ambiguous due to information problems because both measures move in the same direction.

There have also been a number of empirical and theoretical studies that have attempted to make efficiency and welfare calculations in situations in which government regulations or warnings impact a market (Sexton 1979; Colantoni et al. 1965). Where the primary impact of limited information is on price and the minimal impact is on quality and variety, the efficiency effects of providing more information may be measured in the traditional way (Devine and Marion 1979; Perloff and Salop 1985a, 1985b; Boynton and Perloff 1982).

SECOND-BEST WORLD: CONTRACTS

Contracts may involve only two parties (dyadic contracts) as most contracts do, or the number of parties to a contract may exceed two (multiadic contracts).[15] They may be prespecified (e.g., futures contracts) or they may be reached through individual, independent contracting or through collective bargaining. Contractual forms also abound; they vary with respect to the rights and obligations of the parties, the payoff schedules, the risk-sharing arrangements, the extent to which state-contingent actions and payoffs are specified, the procedures established to deal with situations on which the contract is not explicit, the agreed duration of the agreement, termination clauses, the scope for individual discretionary actions, the monitoring and enforcement arrangements, etc. Underlying the wide diversity of contracts is a general unified structure, while the observed contractual forms are manifestations of its adaptation in specific circumstances.

TRANSACTION COSTS AND ECONOMIC EFFICIENCY

In a second-best world, transactions involve various costs—*transaction costs*. The term refers to welfare losses entailed by the actual second-best contractual arrangements relative to a first-best solution in which technology and resource availability are the only constraints. First-best solutions are reached in competitive markets with perfect information. It will prove analytically useful to identify the main categories of transaction costs, their sources, and the determinants.

Information Cost. In the absence of nonpersonal competitive auction markets, individual transactors have to seek potential partners to exchange and determine their respective offers. The search, obviously, is not costless. Also, having concluded an agreement, each party must monitor certain variables related to the states of nature and the parties' actions to select optimally its own discretionary actions and to detect deviations of the other parties from their agreed contractual obligations. Information cost, therefore, depends on the ease of search, on the parties' access to information, on the informational requirements determined by the contract, on the value of information in optimizing decisions, and on the technology of information processing and communication.

Bargaining Cost. When contractual terms are determined through negotiation rather than unilateral dictation by "contract makers" or the announcement of auctioneers, bargaining costs are incurred by the parties concerned. Bargaining situations also arise during the contract implementation phase when circumstances occur that are unaccounted for in the original contract. The level of the bargaining cost depends on the extent of the bargaining space as reflected in the range of potential payoffs to the parties; the number of parties involved and their attitude toward compromise; the complexity and completeness of the original contract (the more complete the contract, the greater the bargaining cost at the formulation phase and the smaller at the implementation phase); and the rules adopted for dealing with disagreement in the implementation phase.

Enforcement Cost. This refers to the actual and subjective costs incurred by the parties in enforcing the contract. It includes the cost of standby enforcement mechanisms (e.g., entering a legally binding contract in order to permit enforcement by the state) and the costs of actual enforcement (e.g., litigation costs and the cost of remedial actions).

Externality Cost. In the present context, the externality cost arises whenever a party or parties select actions that, while being within their contractual rights, affect the well-being of other parties. Presumably, the deciding party maximizes its own gains while ignoring the effects on the others. All "moral hazard" phenomena in agency contracts (agency cost) fall into this category. In authority contracts (e.g., employment contracts), the principal is contractually entitled to decide the agent's actions, which also creates externalities if the effects of the action on the agent's utility are ignored by the principal. In incomplete multiadic contracts, contractually prescribed group decision rules for circumstances unaccounted for in the original contract do not always espouse unanimity. When the deciding subgroup (i.e., a simple majority) ignores the effects of its decision on the utilities of the other parties, externality costs may again be created. These will be referred to as externality costs in group decisions.[16] Welfare loss due to "free riding" may also be included in the present category. Externality costs, in general, may be interpreted as misguided incentives.

The Cost of Nonoptimal Risk Sharing. In a first-best world in which every individual has perfect information (i.e., monitoring, communications, and search are costless), risk bearing can be optimally allocated among individuals. In a second-best world in which information is scarce, optimal allocation of risk bearing is, in general, attainable only at the expense of an increase in the other types of transaction costs. The parties may then opt for suboptimal risk sharing to save on total transaction costs. The welfare loss due to suboptimal risk sharing is, therefore, regarded as a transaction cost. This cost depends on the degree of environmental uncertainty and the parties' aversion to risk.

Other Types of Transaction Costs. There are, in fact, many more types of transaction costs, all of which may be found in marketing systems. Among these, one may list *complexity costs* reflecting the limited capacity of humans to deal with complex relationships; *exclusion costs,* which are the cost of resources that individuals or groups may have to invest to protect their property rights (e.g., protection of patent rights); etc.

The various transaction costs are interrelated through various substitution relations. Thus, agency costs may be lowered by accepting nonoptimal risk-sharing arrangements, and both agency and nonoptimal risk-sharing costs may be lowered by increasing the monitoring and enforcement costs. In internal organizations, consisting of a hierarchy of authority contracts, high monitoring and enforcement costs yield pronounced agency relations throughout the hierarchical structure, leading to "organizational slack" or X-inefficiency, to use Liebenstein's term.

In negotiating a contract, each party seeks to further its own objective, which implies that the resulting contract will be constrained Pareto-optimal, namely, a second-best solution in which the various transaction costs are traded off to minimize the overall cost.[17] But individual contracts are not concluded in a vacuum; they clearly depend on the environment, but also on the other contracts, thus giving rise to the concept of an equilibrium set of contracts. As Zusman and Etgar (1981) have shown, it is descriptively correct and analytically useful to regard a marketing channel as an equilibrium set of contracts.

The following normative question then arises: Given that individual contracts are Pareto-efficient, is the equilibrium set of contracts also efficient? Note that systemic inefficiencies may arise in several ways. First, the pattern of contractual exchange, namely, the matching of buyers and sellers, may be inefficient. Second, productive resources employed by the various parties may be misallocated across contracts, and goods and services may be inefficiently distributed. Finally, the number of parties to a contract may be nonoptimal. The last problem has not yet been adequately researched and will, therefore, not be discussed. The first three sources of inefficiency in systems of dyadic contracts were studied by Zusman and Etgar (1981) as well as Zusman and Bell (1982). It was found that, in the absence of intercontractual externalities and when lump-sum transfers are allowed, the equilibrium set of dyadic contracts is indeed efficient. Unfortunately, in a second-best world, intercontractual externalities are pervasive; and despite the second-best efficiency of individual contracts, the entire system need not be efficient. However, it can be shown that with better informed traders, more effective enforcement measures, and lower overall uncertainty, the systemic inefficiencies are diminished. It should be emphasized that the equilibrium set of contracts, among others, is characterized by the condition that no subset of transactors can improve its members' positions by entering new contracts or by altering existing ones. Hence, inefficiencies often derive from institutional restrictions on free contracting.

POLICY IMPLICATIONS

What are the policy implications of the contractual theory of economic organization discussed? Perhaps the most important implication is a negative one: Minimize institutional barriers to free contracting. There are, however, several important qualifications to this imperative. First, free contracting may benefit the group of actors entering the contracts, but this may be attained at the expense of other participants in the economic process. To the extent that overall social welfare is thereby impaired (e.g., the formation of cartels), a regulatory policy is needed. Second, when public goods may be profitably produced through collective action, but due to free riding the needed voluntary contracts (organizations) fail to emerge, deliberate public action may prove desirable (e.g., setting national grades and standards). Third, public gathering and dissemination of information and legally established mandatory reporting systems are likely to improve market performance. Fourth, strengthening legal support to contract formulation and enforcement will lead to improvements in contractual exchange. Finally, besides other beneficial effects, market stabilization programs are likely to lower transaction costs by lowering the uncertainty due to instability.

The implications for research seem clear. More studies of contractual arrangements and organizational structures are needed in food marketing systems.[18] Future research should focus on the relationship between contractual organizational forms and policy programs and social institutions (e.g., marketing orders and bargaining cooperatives).

CONCLUDING REMARKS

Aside from the political preference function and the notion of political efficiency, the vast majority of definitions and corresponding efficiency measures are all consistent with the first school of thought, which operates with the conventional norm of a first-best solution. The major value of this perspective is simplicity. It results in simple measurements of consumer and producer surpluses and deadweight losses. For circumstances in which a first-best solution can be approximated or is almost achievable, conventional efficiency measures can and should be used. As we have emphasized, however, for many problems in food marketing these circumstances do not arise. As a result, we must turn to the theory of second-best, assuming, of course, that we are not prepared to operate with some other new norm (e.g., political efficiency).

Our survey of economic efficiency measures clearly signals an urgent need to clarify and focus our view of economic efficiency and the implied operational measures. What seems to be missing is a general approach to the problem in which the various concepts and measures outlined are special cases induced by the particular simplifying assumptions and the analysts' interest. As our survey would suggest, the general framework should be dynamic and fully allow for uncertainty, limited and asymmetric information structures, and a host of other transactional problems and costs. The "constrained Pareto" criteria may then be employed in efficiency comparisons and in constructing appropriate efficiency measures. Moreover, in any efficiency analysis, the constraints imposed by the political system, existing institutions, and equity considerations should be clearly delineated. Initially, it would seem most appropriate for us to treat these particular constraints as exogenously given. However, for those of us who are very ambitious, an endogenous treatment of such constraints can be entertained.

NOTES

1. These attempts have been surveyed by French (1977). Industrywide productivity studies (Heien 1983) also belong to this category.
2. For example, see Blake and Helmberger (1971); Manchester (1974); Helmberger et al. (1977); and Connor (1981).
3. See Latham (1984) for an extensive discussion of the merits of this definition, vis-à-vis definitions proposed by Fama (1976), Jensen (1978), and Beaver (1981).
4. These studies led Mundell (1962) to comment that "unless there is a thorough theoretical reexamination of the validity of the tools upon which these studies are founded . . . some one (sic) will inevitably draw the conclusion that economics has ceased to be important!"
5. Indirect methods may be employed in the evaluation of certain costs and benefits produced in the marketing systems. For example, Zusman (1969) attempted an indirect approach to the evaluation of buyers' travel efforts and nonprice offer variations in a network of food retail stores. We are not aware of any attempt at estimating the subjective cost of rationing and time spent in queues. In market economies these costs are obviously negligible. However, in nonmarket economies, in which rationing and queues serve as principal market clearing mechanisms, these costs can be enormous.
6. Taking the present discounted value of the short-run measures of welfare has problems, however. See Schmalensee (1982) and discussion below.
7. The following discussion is based on Berck and Perloff (1985). The results discussed below are conditional on the specific assumptions of that model.

8. Pindyck's (1985) approach is to incorporate any relevant "user costs" (the sum of discounted future costs or benefits that result from current production decisions where the user costs are calculated assuming that the firm is a pricetaker) in the measure of marginal cost: $L^*(t) = P_t - FMC_t)/P_t$ (where FMC_t is the full marginal social cost at time t, evaluated at the monopoly output level). $L^*(t)$ lies between 0 (perfect competition) and 1 for all t. His measure is of potential monopoly power rather than actual monopoly power (which depends on how oligopolistic firms interact with each other). To aggregate this measure over time, Pindyck recommends multiplying $L^*(t)$ by expenditure at time t and summing. Alternative weighting variables include quantity and price. The bias of the standard Lerner measure in the case of natural resources is pronounced. For example, in his simulations using values appropriate for oil, copper, or nickel and assuming the elasticity of demand is elastic (say, equal to 5), L is in the range of 0.23 to 0.44, but L^* is in the range of only 0.15 to 0.06. Similarly, in the learning-by-doing case, the standard Lerner index underestimates the true degree of monopoly power, and by a significant amount, where demand is elastic.

9. As the share of flex-price markets rises, the extent of overshooting falls. In the case of the United States food system, the introduction of flexible exchange rates in 1973 and, more recently, the introduction of flexible interest rates in late 1979, imply less overshooting for a given shock. Of course, the amount of observed overshooting may be greater, even though more markets become flex-price, if the shocks in money markets are larger.

10. For empirical evidence supporting this observation, see Rausser et al. (1985).

11. Probably the first paper to clearly make this point was Scitovsky (1950). The first paper to present a formal mathematical analysis that illustrates this issue is in Diamond (1981). Stiglitz (1979) presents an excellent survey of this literature.

12. Salop (1977) distinguishes between quality, identified as characteristics about whose value all consumers agree, and variety, those variations across brands for which there is no consensus or for which consumers' preferences differ.

13. *Ibid.* See, also, Perloff (1981).

14. See, for example, the recent literature on advertising and welfare.

15. A marketing cooperative is a good example of a highly complex, long-term multiadic contract.

16. Externality costs due to group decisions were recognized and analyzed by Buchanan and Tullock (1962).

17. Lang (1980) cites several interesting examples of Pareto improvements in contractual arrangements in vegetable marketing achieved through collective bargaining. It is worth noting that all the cited improvements were achieved through the internalization of externalities accomplished by shifting the consequences of decisions to those who actually make them (because they possess the relevant information or, otherwise, control the operation). Externality costs due to moral hazard behavior (agency costs) were, thus, minimized. Lang also found that collective bargaining was more effective than independent contracting in bringing about the improvement. Though explainable on the basis of cognitive misperceptions, this finding seems to contradict a priori theorizing.

18. Lang (1980) is an interesting first step in this direction.

REFERENCES

Bauman, Michael G., and Joseph P. Kalt. "Intertemporal Consumer Surplus in Lagged-Adjustment Demand Models." Harvard Institute of Economic Research Discussion Paper No. 956, Harvard University, Jan. 1983.

Beaver, W. H. "Market Efficiency." *Account. Rev.* 56(1981):23–27.

Becker, G. S. "A Theory of Competition Among Pressure Groups for Political Influence." *Q. J. Econ.* 98(1983):371–400.

Berck, Peter, and Jeffrey M. Perloff. "A Dynamic Analysis of Marketing Orders, Voting, and Welfare." *Am. J. Agric. Econ.* 67(1985):487–96.

Blake, I., and P. Helmberger. "Estimation of Structure-Profit Relationships with Application to the Food Processing Sector." *Am. Econ. Rev.* 61(1971):614–27.

Boynton, Robert D., and Jeffrey M. Perloff. *The Short- and Long-run Effects of the Vector Grocery Store Consumer Price Information Program.* Report prepared for the Federal Trade Commission, Bureau of Economics, March 1982.

Brandow, George E. "Policy for Commercial Agriculture for 1945–71." *A Survey of Agricultural Economics Literature,* Vol. 1, ed. Lee R. Martin, pp. 209–92. Minneapolis: University of Minnesota Press, 1977.

Buchanan, J. M., and G. Tullock. *The Calculus of Consent.* Ann Arbor: University of Michigan Press, 1962.

Coase, R. L. "The Nature of the Firm." *Economica* 4(1937):386–405.

Colantoni, C. S., O. A. Davis, and M. Swaminuthan. "Imperfect Consumers and Welfare Comparisons of Policies Concerning Information and Regulation." *Bell J. Econ.* 7(1965):602–15.

Commodity Research Bureau, Inc. *Commodity Yearbook.* New York: various issues.

Connor, J. M. "Food Product Proliferation: A Market Structure Analysis." *Am. J. Agric. Econ.* 63(1981):605–17.

Debreu, G. *Theory of Value.* New York: John Wiley & Sons, 1959.

de Gorter, Harry. "Agricultural Policies: A Study in Political Economy." Ph.D. diss., University of California-Berkeley, 1983.

Devine, D. Grant, and Bruce W. Marion. "The Influence of Consumer Price Information on Retail Pricing and Consumer Behavior." *Am. J. Agric. Econ.* 61(1979):228–37.

Diamond, P. "A Model of Price Adjustment." *J. Econ. Theory* 3(1981):156–68.

"Diet and Heart Disease." *Consumer Reports,* (May 1981): 256–60.

Dixit, A., and V. Norman. "Advertising and Welfare." *Bell J. Econ.* 9(1978):1–17.

Fama, E. "Efficient Capital Markets: A Review of Theory and Empirical Work." *J. Fin.* 25(1970):335–58.

———. "Efficient Capital Markets: A Reply." *J. Fin.* 30(1976):143–45.

Fama, E. F., and C. M. Jensen. "Separation of Ownership and Control." *J. Law and Econ.* 26(1983):301–26.

Farrell, M. "The Measurement of Productive Efficiency." *J. Royal Stat. Soc.* 120 Series A (1957):253–81.

French, B. C. "The Analysis of Productive Efficiency in Agricultural Marketing: Models, Methods, and Progress." *A Survey of Agricultural Economics Literature,* Vol. 1, ed. L. R. Martin, pp. 93–206. Minneapolis: University of Minnesota Press, 1977.

Gardner, Bruce. "Efficient Redistribution through Commodity Markets." *Am. J. Agric. Econ.* 65(1983):225–34.

Grossman, S. T., and J. E. Stiglitz. "The Impossibility of Informationally Efficient Markets." *Am. J. Agric. Econ.* 70(1980):393–408.

Hanemann, M. "Quality and Demand Analysis." *New Directions in Econometric Modeling and Forecasting in U.S. Agriculture,* ed. G. C. Rausser, pp. 55–98. New York: North-Holland Publishing Co., 1982.

Harberger, A. C. "Three Basic Postulates for Applied Welfare Economics: An Interpretive Essay." *J. Econ. Lit.* 9(1971):785–97.

Heien, D. M. "Productivity in U.S. Food Processing and Distribution." *Am. J. Agric. Econ.* 65(1983):297–302.

Helmberger, P. "O-Efficiency and the Economic Organization of Agriculture." *Agricultural Organization in the Modern Industrial Economy,* pp. 18–28. Columbus: Ohio State University, April 1968.

Helmberger, P. G., G. R. Campbell, and W. D. Dobson. "Organization and Performance of Agricultural Markets." *A Survey of Agricultural Economics Literature,* Vol. 3, ed. L. R. Martin, pp. 503–653. Minneapolis: University of Minnesota Press, 1977.

Jensen, M. "Some Anomalous Evidence Regarding Market Efficiency." *J. Fin. Econ.* 6(1978):95–101.

Kilmer, Richard L., and Ronald W. Ward. "Simulating the Performance of a Multiple Exchange Mechanism Market." *South. J. Agric. Econ.* 14(1982):17–21.

Ladd, George W. "Value Judgments and Efficiency in Publicly Supported Research." *South. J. Agric. Econ.* 15(1983):1–7.

La France, Jeffrey T., and Harry de Gorter. "Regulation in a Dynamic Market: The U.S. Dairy Industry." *Am. J. Agric. Econ.* 67(1985):821–32.

Lang, M. G. "Marketing Alternatives and Resource Allocation: Case Studies of Collective Bargaining." *Am. J. Agric. Econ.* 62(1980):760–65.

Lasley, Floyd L. *The U.S. Poultry Industry: Changing Economics and Structure.* Washington, D.C.: USDA ERS Rep. 502, July 1983.

Latham, M. "Defining Capital-Market Efficiency." Ph.D. diss., Massachusetts Institute of Technology, 1984.

Liebenstein, H. "Allocative Efficiency vs. X-Efficiency." *Am. Econ. Rev.* 56(1966):392–415.

Lipsey, R., and R. K. Lancaster. "The General Theory of the Second Best." *Rev. Econ. Studies* 24(1956):11–32.

Manchester, A. C. *Market Structure, Institutions and Performance in the Fluid Milk Industry.* Washington, D.C.: USDA ERS Rep. No. 248, Jan. 1974.

Mundell, R. A. "Review of L. H. Janssen, 'Free Trade, Protection, and Custom Unions.' " *Am. Econ. Rev.* 52(1962):621–22.

Newberry, D., and J. Stiglitz. *The Theory of Commodity Price Stabilization.* Oxford: Clarendon Press, 1981.

Paul, Allen P., Robert W. Bohall, and Gerald E. Plato. *Farmers Access to Markets.* Washington, D.C.: USDA ESCS, NED, Sept. 1980.

Perloff, Jeffrey M. "Can Health Warnings and Nutritional Information Lower Welfare?" Dept. Agric. Econ. Working Paper 181, University of California-Berkeley, June 1981.

Perloff, Jeffrey, M., and Gordon C. Rausser. "The Effect of Asymmetrically Held Information and Market Power in Agricultural Markets." *Am. J. Agric. Econ.* 65(1983):366–72.

Perloff, Jeffrey M., and Steven C. Salop. "Equilibrium with Product Differentiation." *Rev. Econ. Studies* 52(1985a):107–20.

———. "Imperfect Information, Product Differentiation, and Entry." Dept. Agric. Econ. Working Paper 154, University of California-Berkeley, 1985b.

Pindyck, Robert S. "The Measurement of Monopoly Power in Dynamic Markets." *J. Law and Econ.* 28(1985):193–222.

Radner, R. "Equilibrium Under Uncertainty." *Handbook of Mathematical Economics,* Vol. 2, ed. K. J. Arrow and M. D. Intriligator, pp. 923–1006. Amsterdam: North-Holland Publishing Co., 1982.

Rausser, Gordon C. "Political Economic Markets: PERTs and PESTs in Food and Agriculture." *Am. J. Agric. Econ.* 64(1982):821–33.

Rausser, Gordon C., James A. Chalfant, and Kostis G. Stamoulis. "Instability in Agricultural Markets: The U.S. Experience." Dept. Agric. Econ. Working Paper 359, University of California-Berkeley, March 1985.

Rausser, Gordon C., and Nicholas Walraven. "Futures Markets Efficiency: A Global Perspective." University of California-Berkeley, Aug. 1985.

Salop, Steven C. "Second-Best Policies in Imperfect Competition: How Improved Information May Lower Welfare." Center for the Study of Organization Innovation Discussion Paper No. 11, Georgetown University, Aug. 1977.

Schmalensee, Richard. "Another Look at Market Power." *Harvard Law Rev.* 95(1982): 1789–1816.

Scitovsky, T. "Ignorance as a Source of Oligopoly Power." *Am. Econ. Rev.* 40(1950):48–53.

Sexton, Richard J. "A Theory on Information and Its Application to the Effect of Labeling on Food Products." Dept. Agric. and Appl. Econ. Staff Paper P79-35, University of Minnesota, Oct. 1979.

Steiner, P. O. *The Public Sector in the Public Interest, the Analysis and Evaluation of Public Expenditures: The PPB System.* Washington, D.C.: Compendium of papers submitted to the U.S. Congress, Joint Economic Committee, Subcommittee on Economy and Government, 1969.

Stiglitz, Joseph E. "Monopoly and the Rate of Extraction of Exhaustible Resources." *Am. Econ. Rev.* 66(1976):655–61.

———. "Equilibrium in Product Markets with Imperfect Information." *Am. Econ. Rev.* 69(1979):339–45.

Tullock, Gordon. "Welfare Costs of Tariffs, Monopolies, and Theft." *West. Econ. J.* 5 (1967):224–32.

Williamson, O. E. "The Vertical Integration of Production: The Market Failure Considerations." *Am. Econ. Rev.* 61(1971):112–23.

Zusman, P. "Welfare Implications and Evaluation of Buyers Travel Inputs and Non-Price Offer Variations in Networks of Retail Food Stores." *Econometrica* 37(1969):439–55.

———. "The Incorporation and Measurement of Social Power and Economic Models." *Int. Econ. Rev.* 17(1976):447–62.

Zusman, P., and C. Bell. "The Equilibrium Set of Dyadic Contracts," Reprint Series 8201. Rehvot, Israel: The Center for Agricultural Economic Research, Jan. 1982.

Zusman, P., and M. Etgar. "The Marketing Channel as an Equilibrium Set of Contracts." *Manage. Sci.* 27(1981):284–302.

The Food Marketing System:
The Relevance of
Economic Efficiency Measures

A DISCUSSION

George W. Ladd

I COMMEND the authors for a useful survey and evaluation that gets this conference off to an excellent start. They found "an embarrassing richness of concepts"; it disturbs me to realize that people can be inefficient in so many different ways.

The thrust of my review will be that they are too generous in their evaluation. They state that equilibrium is Pareto-efficient if all markets are competitive, if people have full information, and if externalities and convexities do not exist. They treat limitations that arise from dynamics, limited information, contracting, and general equilibrium considerations.

In my view, our efficiency measures are of severely limited usefulness even under static conditions of perfect information. To summarize my position: (1) "Efficient" means no more than "efficient according to the criterion used and under the constraints imposed"; (2) we cannot judge the efficiency of an actor's behavior unless we know the actor's goals; and (3) we do not know society's goals. Therefore, we cannot judge the efficiency of public policies nor the effect of private behavior upon these goals.

The constraints need not be formal restrictions, but may affect input prices or input-output ratios. Farrell (1957) presents measures of efficiency of a multi-input, single product, profit-maximizer. If a firm values means as well as ends and successfully maximizes a utility function of profit and amount of one input used, the Farrell measures tell us it is inefficient. I once wrote (Ladd 1983, 2),

> Public policy issues involve identifying desirable and undesirable results and means. Until these are identified, it is impossible to develop a yardstick for measuring the efficiency of a policy. When economists presume to tell society, or its elected or appointed officials in government, what is efficient, they over-value their contribution, being at most qualified to say "I have chosen to measure results in this way

GEORGE W. LADD is professor, Department of Economics, Iowa State University.

and costs in that way and have imposed these constraints. Under these limiting specifications, this outcome is superior and I use 'efficient' to describe this superior outcome. Society may be interested in other results and costs or may want to impose more or fewer restrictions. I do not know the best outcome under these alternative public choices."

My position leads me to favor Rausser's idea of using a "political preference function." But I prefer "public" over "political," "goals" over "preferences," and "values" over "goals." Values are standards that determine selection of goals and means; and goals influence preferences. I also prefer "functions" over "function."

My position leads me to reject the author's stand that conventional welfare analysis provides relevant criteria and appropriate constraints for measurement of inefficiencies in problems that admit a first-best solution, and to respond to their statement, "It is not too difficult, at least in principle, to measure the net social surpluses associated with certain price-quantity combinations . . . " by replying, "but surpluses need not have any relation to welfare."

To demonstrate the importance of knowing the publics' goals and to illustrate the errors we make when we do not know them, I argue that Pareto efficiency is impossible in our society without government intervention; there exist five conditions in U.S. society that require public intervention in order to maximize a social welfare function (SWF).

1. Merit goods (Pazner 1973). They may be a means of providing consumer information or allowing for externalities or voluntary giving or they may represent imposed choices; as laws requiring public school attendance.

2. Universal hedonists. A universal hedonist's utility is affected by other persons' utilities or levels of consumption.

3. Pollution and environmental degradation. These are inescapable results of production and consumption activities.

4. Sacred (in a sociological sense) or existence values. Economics applies instrumental values: Things and employees are valued as means to ends. Things and people have sacred value when they are valued for themselves. For some of us, wildlife and wilderness areas are sacred objects. They are valuable even though we will never see them; their existence is valued.

5. Concern for distributive justice, fairness, equity.

To show the necessity for public intervention in the case of merit goods, I follow Pazner (1973). Let x_{ih} be the quantity of item i consumed, or supplied, by person h; X_h be the vector whose typical element is x_{ih};

$$x_i = \sum_{h=1}^{H} x_{ih}$$

The SWF is

$$W[U_1(X_1), U_2(X_2), \ldots, U_H(X_H); x_1, x_2, \ldots, x_J].$$

Here x_j is the quantity for merit good j. From the first-order conditions for maximizing W subject to $F(X) = 0$, if item i is not a merit good we obtain (consumer's marginal rate of substitution = MRS).

$$MRS_{ij} = MRT_{ij} - (\partial W/\partial x_j)/(\lambda \partial F/\partial x_i) \qquad (1)$$

The right hand side of (1) can be interpreted as a price ratio or exchange ratio. Discrepancy "from the marginal rate of transformation indicates that unfettered reliance on the competitive price mechanism cannot lead to an optimal outcome. It suggests . . . that consumers and producers should be made somehow to face different prices . . . " (Pazner 1973, 468). If item j is a merit bad, $\partial W/\partial x_j < 0$, item j should be taxed. Pazner suggests that society taxes cigarettes and liquor because they are merit bads.

If item j is a merit good, item j should be subsidized. The Employment Act of 1946 specifies it to be public policy to "promote maximum employment, production, and purchasing power." I interpret the act to mean that society has declared employment to be a merit good. We traditionally distinguish between efficiency effects and employment effects of policies. This argument tells me that we are wrong to do so. Subsidizing employment can be efficient public policy. Maximizing economic surplus at the expense of lower employment may be inefficient. Likewise, because individuals and society care about equity, we cannot be sure that a policy is efficient unless we have considered its effect on equity.

Notice that (1) requires measures of marginal social utility of each merit good and merit bad. This takes us back to the importance of knowing publics' goal functions or publics' value systems. Expression (1) is typical of outcomes in conditions 1 through 5. Maximization of a SWF under each of these conditions requires that consumer's MRS differs systematically from society's MRT, and that consumers and producers face different prices—conditions not satisfied by competitive markets.

The fact that these prevalent conditions cause competitive outcomes to be less than optimal has important implications.

1. Competitive prices can measure private benefits and private costs, but not social benefits nor social costs.

2. In the presence of 1, 2, 3—and 4 if pollution affects sacred values—an individual's family of indifference curves is fixed only if everyone else's levels of consumption remain constant.

3. Under 3, the area under the compensated demand function is not a measure of welfare.

4. Under 3 or 4, consumer surplus does not measure welfare. A price reduction or a general increase in consumer income can reduce consumer welfare.

5. Each condition makes it impossible to infer welfare changes from changes in behavior. Observed market behavior tells us little about preference for nonmarketed items.

I propose that we can contribute more to sound choice of public policies if we turn our work in the direction of social indicators. In 1982, the Organization for Economic Cooperation and Development (OECD) published a list of social indicators. It includes 33 specific indicators grouped under eight major "social concerns": health, education and learning, employment and quality of working life, time and leisure, physical environment, social environment, personal safety, and command over goods and services. The indicators included under the last named are the only ones that require prices for measurement. Under physical environment, for example, the indicators are indoor dwelling space, access to outdoor space, basic amenities, proximity of selected services, exposure to air pollutants, and exposure to noise.

We can view the social indicators as arguments of publics' preference functions. (Without additional work we cannot know whether the OECD list is adequate for work in the United States.) Fox (1983, 898) observes that, "Each of its 33 indicators is treated as a distinct entity. Even within a group . . . , the various indicators involve different units of measure and there is no obvious way to assign 'relative importance' weights to these units. Similarly there is no obvious way to weight the relative importance of the eight major groups or social concerns."

In the spirit of this quotation, and in keeping with my biases, we would report effects of alternative policies upon each social indicator. Each person could then apply his own set of subjective weights to select his preferred policy.

Rausser, Perloff, and Zusman show a number of problems encountered in applying efficiency concepts in a second-best world. Social indicators provide a way of circumventing some of these problems.

REFERENCES

Farrell, M. J. "The Measurement of Productive Efficiency." *J. Royal Stat. Soc.* Series A, Part 3, 120(1957):253–81.

Fox, Karl A. "The Eco-Behavioral View of Human Societies and Its Implications for Social Science." *Int. J. Systems Sci.* 14(1983):895–914.

Ladd, George W. "Value Judgments and Efficiency Criteria in Publicly Supported Research." *South. J. Agric. Econ.* 15(1983):1–7.

Organization for Economic Cooperation and Development. *The OECD List of Social Indicators.* Paris: OECD, 1982.

Pazner, Elisha A. "Merit Wants and the Theory of Taxation." *Public Finance* 28 (1973): 460–72.

CHAPTER 2

Economic Efficiency and Welfare Measurement in a Dynamic, Uncertain, Multimarket World

Richard E. Just

ECONOMIC EFFICIENCY is almost as illusive in the conceptual world of economic theory as it is in reality. As economic thought progresses, more arguments are advanced explaining why the traditional concept of economic efficiency may not or cannot be attained. Initially these arguments centered around simple distortions related, for example, to market structure. In the classical, single market framework, most such distortions could be easily corrected by some form of government intervention to attain a Pareto-efficient competitive equilibrium.

As the *multimarket* nature of the economy began to be considered, however, the problem of second-best showed that these considerations are not so simple if distortions exist elsewhere in the economy (Lipsey and Lancaster 1956). Further consideration of externality problems showed that even economywide competitive equilibrium may not be Pareto-efficient. Some of this literature focused on the need to create additional markets (e.g., Coase 1960) while other literature emphasized the need to compile public information to guide policymaking (e.g., in the provision of public goods such as market infrastructure or in the tax/subsidy approach to controlling externalities).

Consideration of the *dynamic* nature of the economy further complicated these problems. For example, policy issues surrounding public expenditures on research and development, or markets affected by learning and long periods of supply adjustment, present cases in which externality

RICHARD E. JUST is professor, Department of Agricultural and Resource Economics, University of Maryland, College Park.

markets cannot be created and needed information is not accessible because future market participants cannot represent themselves. Thus, consideration of their welfare as well as the rate by which their welfare should be discounted over time necessarily becomes subjective. As a result, even considerations of Pareto efficiency become unclear (see Just et al. 1982, Chap. 13, for a more detailed discussion).

More recently, problems of uncertainty and information have further exacerbated consideration of economic efficiency (Stiglitz 1985). Some have argued that efficient levels of price stabilization can be attained by allowing private storage markets to work, but this would not be true if the public sector is less risk averse than the private sector. Others have argued that creating more markets in which risk and information can be traded (such as insurance, futures, and options markets) can lead to more efficiency. However, Hart (1975) has demonstrated that the second-best problem extends to risk markets (i.e., adding one risk market may reduce welfare if another does not exist). Furthermore, it may be impossible to add some risk markets because of various kinds of transactions costs related to moral hazard and adverse selection. Borch (1962), Hart (1975), and Stiglitz (1982), among others, have shown that competitive equilibrium is not Pareto-efficient when risk markets are incomplete or information is imperfect. These various issues arising in the context of a dynamic, uncertain, multimarket world have led to the need to rethink some of the fundamental issues and concepts of welfare economics. A few issues suggest that even the criteria by which efficiency is measured require modification or, as Stiglitz (1985, 31) concludes in the context of imperfect information and incomplete risk markets, that "the separation between equity and efficiency considerations is no longer generally valid." For example, with imperfect information, the gainers and losers from a change may not be identifiable so lump sum redistribution is impossible (Runge 1985). Even if they can be identified, but have differing levels of risk aversion or differing labor-leisure preferences, redistribution has distinct efficiency effects (Stiglitz 1985; Layard and Walters 1978).

Against the backdrop of these considerations this paper turns first to a discussion of the criteria by which economic efficiency is measured. Because of the issues involved, the discussion necessarily takes on distinct policy connotations and begins at a fairly basic level in the welfare economics literature. Following this discussion, the paper considers problems of measuring efficiency in dynamic, uncertain, and multimarket worlds. In each case, the major difficulties with conventional efficiency analysis are discussed and appropriate practices are demonstrated under conventional assumptions. Finally, further considerations under more general and realistic assumptions are discussed. Throughout the paper, however, the primary focus is restricted to empirical welfare measurement of efficiency in market level analysis.

WELFARE MEASUREMENT AND ECONOMIC EFFICIENCY

The emphasis on conceptualizing economic efficiency stems from an inability to make objective interpersonal comparisons (de Graaf 1957; Scitovsky 1951), which follows from an inability to determine the social welfare function. Without a social welfare function, economists have a limited basis for choosing among alternative states of the economy. Pareto argued that the only objective basis under which one can say society is better off is when at least one person is better off and no one is worse off. Since, according to the Adam Smith result, competitive equilibrium is a state from which no such changes can be made, competitive equilibrium has been intimately linked with the concepts of economic efficiency and Pareto efficiency (Arrow 1970). However, many Pareto-efficient states (many competitive equilibria) exist and many pairs of states are not Pareto-comparable so the Pareto concept has proven to be of limited usefulness in reality.

Kaldor (1939) and Hicks (1939) proposed the compensation principle in an attempt to expand the set of comparable alternatives. In this approach, a new state of the economy is pronounced potentially Pareto-efficient relative to a current one if the sum of willingness to pay for the change (possibly negative) over all individuals is positive (gainers can compensate losers so that no one is worse off). However, application of this principle without actually paying compensation involves a strong value judgment implying equal weighting of individuals in the social welfare function (Chipman and Moore 1978) while application of the principle with compensation is often impractical because nondistorting lump sum transfer payments are not realistically possible (Layard and Walters 1978). Furthermore, the compensation principle suffers from problems of reversals and intransitivities (Scitovsky 1941; Gorman 1955). These problems with the Pareto concept and the compensation principle have led some economists and politicians to conclude that welfare economics has little to say about choosing among realistic economic alternatives (Cochrane 1980; van den Doel 1979). Nevertheless, the willingness-to-pay approach has continued to serve as the basis for conventional applied economic welfare analysis (Just et al. 1982).

Along a much different line, Arrow (1963) examined the possibility of ranking alternative social states based solely on individuals' preference orderings. His famous Impossibility Theorem suggests that quantitative (cardinal) information about the intensity of preferences is necessary to rank social alternatives; rankings by individuals are not sufficient (Kemp and Ng 1977). Arrow's work has spawned a voluminous literature on "possibility theorems" by relaxing his axioms (for surveys see Sen 1970, 1982; Fishburn 1973).[1] However, this line of research has also neglected some important practical considerations that render the work of limited usefulness for choosing among realistic social alternatives. First, the transactions costs of compiling votes or rankings from all individuals on each issue may be impractical. Buchanan and Tullock (1962), for example, show that the decision-making costs of reaching a Pareto optimum may be prohibitive and a true optimum may be attainable only when the criterion of Pareto efficiency is discarded.

Second, possibilities of impartiality and moral consideration are not given adequate attention (Mueller 1979; Rawls 1971). Without these possibilities, intensities do not matter and the welfare of some individuals or generations may not matter. Suppose, for example, that society consists of three individuals and a change is considered that takes $1000 from one individual to give $100 to each of the other two. If the three individuals were to vote selfishly on the change, knowing who the benefactors are, the majority would likely favor the change. On the other hand, if the voting were done with impartiality (not knowing which of the three they would be), then the majority would be against the change. Finally, adding moral consideration of others, the change could be favored even with impartiality if the $1000 were taken from a rich person to give $100 to each of two poor people.

Third, the concept of rights implicit in such notions as liberty and exploitation has peculiar implications involving the impossibility of a Paretian liberal (Sen 1982). For example, simple individual freedoms such as choosing reading material, sleeping positions, or practicing religion are not consistent with the Pareto principle. While the examples of this issue in the literature on the Paretian liberal may appear of little relevance to agricultural economists on the surface, the issue itself is at the heart of some environmental problems involving the right to pollute versus the right to a clean environment, etc.

These considerations have led to a two- (or more-) stage view of social decision making in the literature on justice and public choice whereby impartial moral and social considerations guide formulation of rules at the first stage. Harsanyi (1955) gave the first formal treatment of the role of moral consideration by distinguishing between an individual's personal preferences and his moral or social preferences. He considers the latter set of preferences as the basis for the interpersonal comparisons that are ultimately required in public choice. Using three relatively weak assumptions (that both sets of preferences satisfy the von Neumann-Morgenstern axioms of choice and that two states are indifferent socially if they are indifferent for every individual), he proves that the social welfare function is a weighted sum of individual personal von Neumann-Morgenstern utility indexes,

$$W = \sum_i a_i U_i,$$

wherein each individual's utility possibly depends on externality-related factors like consumption of other individuals. This welfare function (or a simplification of it associated with impartiality) has been called the Just Social Welfare Function.[2] The difficulties associated with the Harsanyi approach relate to (1) the possibility and cost of all individuals obtaining sufficient information about others (subjective probabilities, risk attitudes, etc.) to engage in interpersonal comparisons; and (2) whether individuals can be impartial in choosing weights.[3]

The same concerns led Buchanan and Tullock (1962) to develop a theory of constitutional government in a setting resembling that depicted by Harsanyi (1955) (see Mueller 1979 for a comparative discussion). They view democratic government as a two-stage process in which the constitution is written in the first stage, where moral concerns and impartiality guide formulation of constitutional rules because individuals are uncertain of their future positions. The conflict of individual liberties with the Pareto principle can be resolved by establishing a protected sphere for individual choice or by putting in place a mechanism that can override the Pareto principle when ethical issues such as personal liberties are involved. As suggested by Sen (1982, Chap. 14), these are the most appealing approaches to resolving the conflict of individual rights with the Pareto principle. Thus, individuals can be free to pursue their own self-interest in the later parliamentary stage subject to constitutional rules and institutions. A constitution formulated in this context has been called the Just Political Constitution and is viewed as forming the basis for the social welfare function (Mueller 1979). For example, if Harsanyi's assumptions apply, then the constitutional rules can be regarded as setting a framework in place that will choose weights and maximize a Harsanyi-type of social welfare function (subject to certain other constitutional rules that may apply to issues such as ethics and personal liberties).

Without digressing too far into the area of political science, some discussion of the relevance of this framework to the United States and Western economies in general is worthwhile. A number of studies have found reasons why a representative form of democracy may be an optimal outcome of the constitutional stage. For example, representative democracy is preferred to direct democracy because meeting assemblies become impossible and lead to endless debate with large numbers of voters (Dahl

1970) and participation by the masses in all decisions results in high costs of decision making for each participating individual (Buchanan and Tullock 1962) (i.e., because of *transactions costs* and *limited information*). On the other hand, representative democracy is preferred to dictatorship because of the *external costs* and *moral hazard* associated with dictatorships, because dictatorship may impinge on certain personal liberties, and because some debate facilitates better decisions (van den Doel 1979). Shubik (1970) further argues that the time lags involved in representative debate prevent unpremeditated decisions. Finally, Downs (1957), Shubik (1968), and van den Doel (1979) show that two-party democracy attains the same optimum welfare as an omniscient, benevolent philosopher-king.[4]

These considerations suggest that major provisions of the United States Constitution specify rules for decision making at the parliamentary stage consistent with maximization of welfare given transactions costs, limited and costly information, externalities, moral hazard, etc. In other words, the constitutional rules are directed to the realistic possibilities under which competitive equilibrium is not Pareto-efficient and under which, following Stiglitz (1985), issues of efficiency and distribution cannot be separated. This raises a fundamental question about which criteria should be used to measure economic efficiency.

Traditionally, economic efficiency in agricultural marketing and agricultural policy has been measured according to the standard of competitive equilibrium. Under traditional assumptions wherein competitive equilibrium is Pareto-efficient and nondistorting lump sum transfers are possible, the case for this approach is strong and there is little reason to expect it to be inconsistent with public choice under a Just Political Constitution. That is, if efficiency and distribution are separable issues, then the Pareto criterion is appropriate for addressing efficiency issues as long as any individual's weighting in the social welfare function is positive. Thus, if competitive equilibrium is Pareto-efficient, competitive equilibrium can serve as an ultimate efficiency norm. Even when competition fails, Pareto efficiency can still provide a useful, although empirically less tractable, standard of comparison (Arrow 1970). However, when competition fails because of more realistic possibilities (e.g., transactions costs, limited information, externalities, moral hazard, etc.) and the impossibility of nondistorting lump sum transfers leads to an inability to separate efficiency considerations from distributional considerations, then it seems that the criteria governing public choice in the context of a Just Political Constitution may provide a better norm for measuring economic efficiency. That is, the assumptions required for this approach may be a more accurate abstraction of reality than those of the conventional approach.

According to the literature on public choice, the process for determining society's values are set once the constitutional stage is completed (Mueller 1979). Thus, it seems reasonable to interpret the social welfare function as arising from the constitution (Arrow 1963). In this context, evidence about the social welfare function can be obtained from behavior of the political system (Tinbergen 1956; Theil 1964; Friedlaender 1973). Then, under assumptions where competitive equilibrium does not provide Pareto efficiency and lump sum transfers are not possible, efficiency can be measured according to the social values of true relevance. This approach is more consistent with the political science literature that studies how society's values are determined. For example, Easton (1965a, 1965b, 21), in harmony with his definition of political science, defines a political system as "those interactions through which values are authoritatively allocated for a society."

How can economists ignore the authoritative values of society in cases in which the basis for their own concept of social value fails? It is difficult to see how the traditional measure of efficiency in economics (departure from competitive equilibrium) can carry much weight when more realistic aspects of the economy are of realized importance. This problem has long led to sharp criticism of economic analyses by economists and politicians alike. For example, even in the context of agriculture, which some argue is more competitive than others, Brandow (1977, 271) argues that "the perfect competition model is far from duplicated in free markets" and its assumptions are "breathtakingly heroic." Cochrane (1980) argues that the welfare measures derived from it are simply irrelevant to actual issues of agricultural policy analysis. These conclusions follow from the impracticality of nondistorting lump sum transfers and the insensitivity of welfare measures to distributional issues and noneconomic considerations, such as ethical concerns that become important under more realistic conditions.

On the surface, these considerations may seem of greater concern in the areas of agricultural policy than in marketing research. However, suppose some marketing institution is established or abolished by Congress based on considerations of distribution, limited information, the distorting nature of any transfers, etc. Then it is entirely inappropriate to evaluate the performance of the marketing institution in a framework that ignores those considerations. And yet, following the discussion of the introduction, these are the kinds of considerations that are often relevant in a dynamic, uncertain, multimarket world. Thus, the traditional approach to evaluating economic efficiency may not be appropriate for many dynamic, uncertain, multimarket problems.

The analysis of marketing orders provides a good example. The language of the enabling legislation and the circumstances that led to it suggest an objective of orderly marketing and stabilization for agricultural commodities in which risk and dynamic problems are important. For some agricultural products, particularly perennial crops and dairy, free markets can get into boom-bust cycles. During periods of shortage, high prices can induce overinvestment because of imperfect information. Then in ensuing periods of surplus, low prices can cause disinvestment beyond the rate of depreciation. As a result, the response of industry stabilization associated with a quota or controlled price, due both to reasons of risk aversion and the dynamics of investment, can cause benefits that exceed the usual deadweight loss triangle. For example, in recent hearings on the federal marketing order for hops, the results of an econometric study were used to show that the effects of a quota regulation were potentially if not actually Pareto-superior to a free market for these reasons.

In most cases, questions of economic efficiency must be addressed in the context of an economic model. Economic models are necessarily abstractions from reality. As such, they are based on assumptions. The extent to which the conclusions are relevant to the real world depends largely on how realistic the assumptions are. If a model follows the traditional assumptions, wherein competition leads to Pareto efficiency and nondistorting lump sum transfers are possible, then efficiency and distribution are separable considerations and the traditional criteria of economic efficiency are appropriate within the confines of the model. However, loosely speaking, the results apply in reality only to the extent that the assumptions apply in reality.

Suppose, on the other hand, a model admits more general assumptions. If competition does not lead to Pareto efficiency, then economic efficiency cannot be measured by the departure from competitive equilibrium. If nondistorting lump sum transfers are not possible, then efficiency cannot be separated from distribution and Pareto efficiency is also not a useful standard of comparison. Alternatively, efficiency—in this case, social efficiency—must be measured according to society's values (i.e., the departure of the current value of the social welfare function from its optimum). In this context, a workable approach following Buchanan and Tullock (1962) is to use the constitution as a starting point in establishing society's values. Then, following Tinbergen (1956) and Theil (1964), the collective preferences of elected politicians at the parliamentary stage can be regarded as a manifestation of the social welfare function, which thus makes it observable given the constitutional rules. In this context, the concept of social efficiency becomes synonymous with Zusman's (1976) concept of political efficiency, so empirical measurement is possible. Alternatively, if no assumptions are made so that the social welfare function is observable and if efficiency and distribution are not separable because of other generalities, then empirical welfare measurement of economic

efficiency is not possible. Many Pareto optima may be distinctly suboptimal socially.

Several studies have attempted to estimate the collective preferences of elected politicians by observing enacted policies (e.g., Rausser
and Freebairn 1974). However, the approach suggested here differs distinctly although subtly. Most previous attempts to estimate policymaker
preferences have been regarded as positive studies, whereas estimates of
policy preferences in the context of this paper take on normative significance. Indeed, the two-stage theory of public choice proposed by Buchanan and Tullock (1962) is both positive and normative. Furthermore,
in this framework, estimation of the social welfare function given the
constitution can involve estimating how preferences of elected officials
change through political regimes as the economic and political environment changes.

If one adopts this approach to observation of the social welfare
function, a fundamental question is raised about the potential role for
economic welfare measurement. That is, if observed policies are regarded
as maximizing the social welfare function, then they are tautologically
efficient. So what is the need for economic welfare measurement? The
answer rests squarely on the same considerations that cause a departure
of competitive equilibrium from Pareto efficiency. Policymakers also face
uncertainties, transactions costs, limited information, etc. (Theil 1964).
Thus, the policies that are optimal in one set of circumstances may become decidedly inefficient in another. The contribution of welfare measurement in this context is to point out where improvements are possible
or where social inefficiencies exist with changes in available information,
the set of possible decisions, the economic and political environment, etc.
Or if policy preferences are assumed to be reflected with random disturbances in the policy process, economic analysis can serve to point out
policies that differ substantially from the usual social welfare norm and,
thus, may require revision.

The arguments of this section do not discredit the conventional
approach of economic welfare analysis under appropriate assumptions.
Rather, this section focuses on the restrictions under which it is applicable
and, since the restrictions apparently do not apply in some dynamic,
uncertain, multimarket problems, a workable alternative is suggested.
While the alternative constitutional approach requires an alternative assumption (that the constitution is a Just Political Constitution or in some
way institutes a political process that manifests the social welfare function), it also enables analysis of the thorny distributional issues on which
the conventional approach is silent much along the lines investigated
formally by Sen (1982, Chap. 18).[5]

The choice of which approach to use must be based on a subjective evaluation of which set of assumptions better approximates reality and on which kinds of issues the welfare analysis is to serve. For example, the provision of a certain shopping convenience may have relatively small distributional implications at the margin and, thus, the distorting effects of any transfers required to return to a similar distribution may be insignificant. In such a case, conventional analysis may be quite justified if efficiency issues dominate distributional issues. On the other hand, in questions of providing crop yield insurance, some of the major issues relate to limited information, moral hazard, adverse selection, risk aversion, and thus the distorting effect that any transfers may have on risk behavior. For such problems, the conventional approach may provide such a poor approximation of reality that it becomes misleading. Thus, the constitutional approach may be preferable.[6]

Because each of these approaches may provide a better approximation of reality for different problems, both will be considered. For each of the major considerations of this paper, use of the conventional approach is discussed first and then modifications for use with a Harsanyi-type social welfare function are considered. Estimation of the weights for such a function based on observed policy choices is not considered explicitly but is assumed to be accomplished using procedures similar to previous positive studies of political preferences with further parameterization to reflect changing political and economic climates.

WELFARE MEASUREMENT IN AN UNCERTAIN WORLD

Measurement of the welfare effects of uncertainty was a very misunderstood subject through the 1960s and 1970s. Based on the work of Oi (1961) and Massell (1969), the welfare associated with price variability came to be measured by the expected producer or consumer surplus associated with a given supply or demand curve. While their theoretical derivations are internally correct, the assumptions offer a poor approximation of reality for agriculture. The difficulty with this approach is that it represents only the case of instability with certainty; both producers and consumers are assumed to know the price in time to adjust to it along their supply and demand curves. In agriculture, however, producers cannot predict their output prices well at the time production decisions are made; they can respond only to the parameters of a subjective price distribution rather than to the price itself. Furthermore, with risk aversion, the supply curve may change simply in response to the variance of price. Finally, in most agricultural problems, production is also risky so one must distinguish between expected (*ex ante*) supply and actual (*ex post*) supply (see Just et al. 1982, Chap. 11, for a detailed discussion of these problems).

Modifications in conventional welfare measurement for the case of uncertainty have been developed by Just et al. (1982) and by Pope et al. (1983).[7] The results are derived in the context of willingness-to-pay (compensating or equivalent variation) in one case and certainty equivalent in the other. The willingness-to-pay approach makes the criteria of Kaldor (1939), Hicks (1939), and Scitovsky (1941) directly applicable and is thus better suited to the conventional approach, while the certainty equivalent approach is better suited to the constitutional approach of this paper. Nevertheless, results of the two approaches coincide under constant absolute risk aversion.

To demonstrate these results, consider Fig. 2.1 in which the supply of a good depends on both the mean, μ, and variance, σ^2, of the probability distribution of price. The supply curve $S_\alpha(0)$ is the supply curve corresponding to no risk (the mean price is the actual price) and α represents the level of risk aversion. Of course, changes in the area above this supply curve and below price associated with changes in price, technology, etc., have the usual willingness-to-pay connotations of conventional welfare analysis; thus, the associated producer surplus "triangle" serves as a meaningful conventional welfare measure. Note further that the supply curve with risk neutrality ($\alpha = 0$) and variance σ^2, represented by $S_0(\sigma^2)$ in Fig. 2.1, coincides with the no risk supply curve $S_\alpha(0)$, so the related producer surplus triangle has a similar welfare interpretation.

Now suppose risk is introduced at level σ^2 with risk aversion. The supply curve as a function of mean price then becomes $S_\alpha(\sigma^2)$. With constant absolute risk aversion, the vertical difference in the two supply curves is $2\alpha q \sigma^2$ at a quantity q which reflects the marginal risk premium. At a given quantity q', the area under the marginal risk premium curve thus measures the total risk premium. By construction, this is the same as area *b*. Thus, the certainty equivalent of profit with mean price μ' and variance of price σ^2 is area *a* and is equal to expected profit, area *a* + *b*, less the risk premium, area *b*. From this result, one finds that the area below expected price and above the supply curve taken as a function of mean price and conditioned on variance of price can serve as an appropriate welfare measure. It measures the certainty equivalent of profit while changes in it (associated with changes in the price distribution, technology, input prices, etc.) measure compensating and equivalent variation.

These results extend under constant absolute risk aversion only to the case of measuring welfare effects in any market where quantities are determined with certainty by the decision maker at the time of decision making (for which the good is essential in the related production or consumption process). This implies that measurement of the consumer

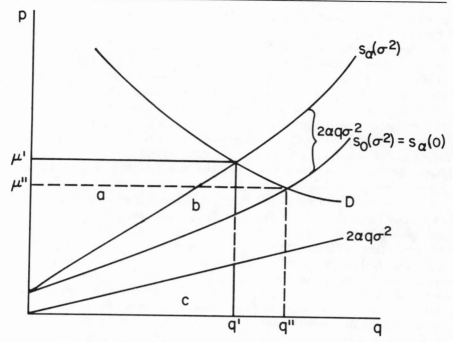

FIG. 2.1.   Welfare measurement under uncertainty.

surplus triangle in input markets (e.g., associated with wheat producers'
acreage demand rather then their wheat supply) is necessary in the case
of stochastic production; the producer surplus triangle in an output market associated with stochastic production is not appropriate for welfare
measurement without a correction factor (see Pope et al. 1983).

   With these results, many of the practices of conventional welfare
measurement can be extended to market level welfare measurement with
risk at least under constant absolute risk aversion. That is, since the area
under an aggregate supply (demand) curve and above expected price is
the sum of such areas under individual supply (demand) curves, the producer (consumer) surplus triangles associated with aggregate supply (demand) measure the sum of willingness to pay over all producers (consumers) and can be added to obtain overall willingness to pay for various
groups of producers and consumers. In this framework several restrictive
assumptions of conventional welfare measurement can be relaxed. First,
not only can risk be introduced into market level welfare measurement,
but willingness-to-pay measurements can be facilitated in cases in which
competitive equilibrium is not Pareto-efficient. For example, willingness-
to-pay measurement can be possible in the context of Fig. 2.1 when

another risk market is missing; indeed, risk averse behavior may only be significant when certain risk markets such as crop insurance are missing. Suppose expected consumer demand is represented by D. Then competitive equilibrium occurs at expected price μ' and output q'. If, however, consumers are risk neutral, they may be better off to provide a stable profit for producers purchasing quantity q'' at price p'' regardless of actual demand. This is, in fact, the Pareto optimum with risk neutral consumers assuming vertically parallel random shifts in demand and zero interest rates.

More generally, there is no inherent reason why the role of externalities (transactions costs, moral hazard, adverse selection, etc.) that can be incorporated into market level relationships cannot be incorporated into models of aggregate supply and demand behavior under risk (assuming supply and demand continue to exist). These are merely additional factors conditioning supply and demand (see Chap. 9). Thus, conventional welfare measurement under constant absolute risk aversion may be feasible methodologically, based on market concepts of supply and demand, even though competitive equilibrium is not Pareto-efficient. The major difficulty thus becomes the ability to represent the role of these various factors in determining supply and demand. For example, empirical studies have been able to estimate the effect of changes in risk on aggregate supply assuming producers face the same price for every state of nature and that all producers have constant absolute risk aversion (Just 1975). More realistic empirical models are often impossible to estimate because of insufficient data.

More fundamental difficulties in welfare measurement under uncertainty arise when absolute risk aversion is not constant. In this case, supply or demand relationships must be conditioned on the level of risk aversion, on the utility level, or on the level of wealth. Of course, only the latter is empirically practical in which case calculation of compensating or equivalent variation requires solution of a differential equation problem (see Just et al. 1982, Sec. A.6). Using this approach, one can also calculate the certainty equivalent of wealth as the equivalent variation of removing risk, plus wealth at expected prices (and quantities).[8] Thus, calculation of common welfare measures for individuals is still a methodologically tractable problem.

There are two fundamental difficulties associated with welfare measurement under nonconstant risk aversion. First, aggregate supply or demand curves depend on how each individual's risk preferences change with changes in wealth. Except under special circumstances (e.g., identical utility functions), this is tantamount to knowing every individual's supply or demand. Second and more importantly, since risk preferences and thus risk behavior depend on wealth, nondistorting lump sum transfers are inherently impossible. Thus, conventional efficiency considerations cannot be separated from distributional concerns.

The case of nonconstant risk aversion thus calls for an alternative to the conventional approach. The constitutional approach offers such an alternative. Although supply or demand must be measured, in effect, at the individual level for the reasons given, the associated individual certainty equivalents can be used in approximating a Harsanyi-type social welfare function empirically. That is, each von Neumann-Morgenstern utility index, U_i, is a monotonically increasing function of the certainty equivalent. Thus, introducing a first order Taylor-series representation of this function allows the Harsanyi-type social welfare function to be written as a weighted sum of certainty equivalents with weights possibly depending on the respective certainty equivalents. Such a function can then be estimated from observed policy decisions (with weights also possible depending on the current political and economic environment) following the previous discussion. The welfare analysis of alternative policies, marketing institutions, etc., can then be performed by calculating effects on the social welfare function. Thus, as for many of the other assumptions of conventional analysis, relaxing the assumption of constant risk aversion leads to extremely demanding data requirements even though the analysis is methodologically tractable.

Nevertheless, consideration of these difficulties may be of increasing importance. With the increasing role of monetary phenomena, the internationalization of U.S. grain markets and accompanying price volatility, and the rapid devaluation of assets in U.S. agriculture, the behavior of agricultural markets today may be markedly different today than several years ago. Perceived uncertainty may be much greater while the reduction in wealth may have sharply increased absolute risk aversion. These changes could thus have significant implications for welfare measurement of economic efficiency in agriculture.

WELFARE MEASUREMENT IN A DYNAMIC WORLD[9]

Welfare measurement in dynamic situations has also presented many difficult and misunderstood problems. The most difficult issue, which for the most part has avoided resolution, relates to the social discount rate. That is, how should one dollar of benefits today be compared with one dollar of benefits tomorrow, next year, or in the next century? Some have argued that the market interest rate can serve as a social discount rate. However, this is appropriate only if the capital market is perfect and the same set of individuals are involved in each of the time periods considered. These are the only assumptions under which social discounting can be considered in a reasonably objective (value-free) context similar to that proposed by Pareto (1896), Kaldor (1939), Hicks (1939), and Scitovsky (1941). Nevertheless, these assumptions are usually regarded to fail on both counts. Capital markets carry significant transactions costs and credit limits based on collateral. Also many important dynamic problems extend beyond the life of a significant portion of producers and consumers so that part of some future generations cannot register their preferences in current markets.

While many studies have used the market interest rate approach with an opportunity cost justification despite these problems, another approach is to choose a discount rate consistent with the revealed preferences of policymakers (see Just et al. 1982 for a critical discussion of the opportunity cost approach). Although economists have been somewhat reluctant to view outcomes of the policy process as maximizing the applicable social welfare function in static problems (such as in the previous section), it is interesting to note that this approach has become a major accepted means of choosing a social discount rate. Dynamic problems of social discounting involving considerations that cause clear departure of competitive equilibrium from Pareto efficiency and nondistorting lump sum transfers are obviously impossible. Furthermore, choosing a discount rate is often tantamount to choosing income distribution over time. These are exactly the conditions under which the "objectivity" of the conventional approach is unattainable. Thus, the accepted practice of choosing social discount rates consistent with rejection of policies that have been rejected and acceptance of policies that have been accepted is fully in line with the constitutional approach suggested for such circumstances.

Another crucial consideration in dynamic welfare measurement relates to investment. The implicit role of investment in shifting supplies and demands over time and the resulting implications for welfare measurement is probably the most misunderstood problem in dynamic welfare measurement. Countless studies have evaluated the effects of some change on producers by measuring the producer surplus triangle associated with short-run supply over several successive time periods. This is appropriate if all fixed factors remain fixed. However, some fixed factors are usually variable beyond the short run. Changes in short-run supply from period to period thus involve investments or disinvestments in these factors that are also affected by changes in a firm's economic environment. Many empirical supply models used in such calculations involve lag specifications that are explicitly designed to accommodate such effects, yet the role of investment is not reflected in welfare calculations.

To illustrate the problem, consider the firm with short-run marginal cost curve S_1 operating at initial price p_0 in Fig. 2.2. Now suppose the price increases from p_0 to p_1 over two production periods. In the short run

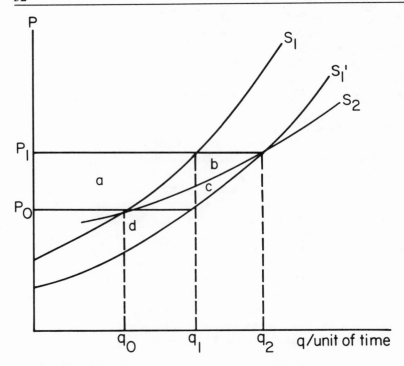

FIG. 2.2. Dynamic welfare measurement.

(during the first period), production increases from q_0 to q_1 along the short-run marginal cost curve. Thus, the increase in producer surplus or quasi-rent in the first period is area a. By the second period, however, the firm will have had time to adjust some of its fixed factors in response to the price increase. Suppose these investments shift the short-run supply curve to S'_1 so that production is q_2 in period 2. If the price increase were evaluated in period 2 simply according to the short-run supply curve in period 2 as it stands after the higher period 1 price, the change in short-run producer surplus is area $a + b + c$. Alternatively, if the price increase were evaluated in period 2 by the change in short-run producer surplus with p_0 prevailing in both periods versus p_1 prevailing in both periods, then the change is area $a + b + c + d$. Neither of these approaches, however, reflects the period 2 difference in producer welfare associated with a two-period price change, because the investment cost (area $c + d$) required to shift the short-run marginal cost curve from S_1 to S'_1 is ignored. The correct measure of producer welfare change in period 2, considering the investment undertaken, is a gain of area $a + b$ so that total gain over two periods is area $2a + b$. Alternatively, the producer

welfare change in period 2 can be measured by the change in short-run
producer surplus in period 2 (area $a + b + c + d$) less the cost of
investment (area $c + d$) incurred to get it (see Just et al. 1982, Sec. 4.5).

These results readily generalize to multiple periods with discounting
to obtain the following results. The welfare effect (compensating or
equivalent variation) of any change on a firm is given by the discounted
sum of producer (consumer) surplus changes associated with respective
supply (demand) curves of all relevant lengths of run (as viewed from the
initial point in time), i.e.,

$$\Delta \pi_t^T = \sum_{k=t}^{T} \delta^{k-t} \Delta P_t^k = \sum_{k=t}^{T} \delta^{k-t} \Delta C_t^k$$

where δ is the firm's private discount rate, $\Delta \pi_t^T$ represents the total welfare effect on the firm of a change in the sequence of prices over periods
$t, \ldots, T$, and ΔP_t^k (ΔC_t^k) is the corresponding change in producer (consumer) surplus associated with a one-period supply (demand) curve with
$k - t + 1$ period foresight. Alternatively, the welfare effect of any change
affecting a firm over time can be measured by the discounted sum of
changes in short-run producer (consumer) surplus minus the discounted
sum of changes in investments, i.e.,

$$\Delta \pi_t^T = \sum_{k=t}^{T} \delta^{k-t} \Delta P_k^k - \sum_{K=t}^{T} \sum_{n=l}^{k-t} \delta^{k-t-n} \Delta I_{k-n}^k$$

$$= \sum_{k=t}^{T} \delta^{k-t} \Delta C_k^k - \sum_{k=t}^{T} \sum_{n=l}^{k-t} \delta^{k-t-n} \Delta I_{k-n}^k$$

where I_{k-n}^k is the change in investment undertaken at time $k - n$ in
planning for production in period k. From these results one finds the
solution to calculating changes in investment implicit in supply or demand
curves that are shifting over time in response to own-price changes,

$$\Delta I_k^k = \delta^{k-t} (\Delta P_{t+1}^k - \Delta P_t^k) = \delta^{k-t} (\Delta C_{t+1}^k - \Delta C_t^k)$$

Similar results too numerous to review here have been developed
for cases including risk and final consumption. In each case, the results
are similar except that supply and demand curves become conditioned on
(expected) utility levels or wealth. Thus, for producers, the compensating
and equivalent variations and the certainty equivalent generally coincide
if and only if absolute risk aversion is constant for the same reasons
discussed previously. In the final consumer case, the compensating and
equivalent variations generally coincide if and only if income elasticities

are zero for all goods with changing prices just as in the conventional static case. Conditions have been developed under which the related producer and consumer surplus triangles generally approximate these welfare quantities in the static case (Willig 1976; Pope and Chavas 1982). Similar results carry through for the dynamic case as well, but the validity of approximating properties after temporal aggregation is open to question. Alternatively, exact measures of these welfare quantities can be obtained by solving differential equation problems based on supply and demand functions.

Turning to the possibilities of market measurement of welfare and efficiency, however, the latter generalities create serious problems. Again, as in the static uncertainty case, if producer and consumer surplus triangles provide meaningful measures of willingness to pay for individuals in individual time periods, then producer and consumer surplus triangles associated with aggregate supply and demand provide a meaningful measure of aggregate willingness to pay in the corresponding time periods. Thus, conventional market-based welfare measurement (free of value judgments beyond willingness-to-pay criteria) is strictly applicable if and only if (1) all producers face no risk or have constant absolute risk aversion; (2) all consumers have zero income elasticities for goods with changing prices; (3) a perfect capital market exists; and (4) the set of market participants and their preferences is fixed over the relevant time horizon.

If the latter two conditions fail, then an alternative means of social discounting (e.g., the constitutional approach) must be used, although aggregate willingness-to-pay measures within time periods are still appropriate since intratemporal nondistorting lump sum transfers are possible (under other usual assumptions of the conventional approach).[10] Thus, either Willig-type results must be applied to use surplus measures associated with aggregate supply and demand as approximations, or a disaggregated constitutional approach is necessary. However, the approximating properties of surplus triangles developed by Willig (1976) do not carry through in comparing groups of individuals or calculating the conventional concept of deadweight loss (Hausman 1981). Thus, the constitutional approach may be preferable if departures from the first two assumptions are serious.

Again, following the constitutional approach, as in the previous section, a Harsanyi social welfare function can be approximated using certainty equivalents for producers and money measures of utility change for consumers. Following the arguments of Chipman and Moore (1980), the appropriate money measure of utility for consumers in this case is the money metric defined by initial income plus the equivalent variation of any change (willingness-to-pay criteria are not of direct relevance). These welfare measures can be estimated on the basis of individual behavior or group behavior (if groups are internally identical) and then used in the estimation of welfare weights based on revealed policy preferences. Again, however, the associated data requirements are very demanding even though the analysis is methodologically tractable.

Consideration of dynamic processes of adjustment is apparently a crucial aspect of welfare measurement in agriculture. For example, in evaluating dairy price-support programs, LaFrance and de Gorter (1985) found that the average annual dynamic welfare change is three times the static change. The difference is primarily due to a lengthy process of adjusting herd size and other investments. Many agricultural production activities, particularly in livestock and perennial crops, involve similarly long adjustment cycles. Furthermore, some have postulated dynamic adjustments in consumer preferences (e.g., beef consumption) due to habit formation. Given such phenomena, welfare measurement of the effects of agricultural market policies and institutions must give careful attention to the dynamic aspects of welfare measurement.

WELFARE MEASUREMENT IN A MULTIMARKET WORLD

Aside from the difficulty with interpersonal comparisons, the lack of multimarket considerations has been the reason for perhaps the bulk of the criticism of welfare economics over the past 50 years. When applied in measuring producer and consumer surplus changes in a single market, critics claim the results are partial and, thus, do not reflect true welfare effects of various alternatives.

Consider, for example, a two-market economy as in Fig. 2.3 in which a competitive final goods industry produces good q using good x as a single factor of production. Initially, the final goods industry faces input price w_0 and output price p_0 and thus produces output quantity q_0 according to the associated supply curve $S(w_0)$ using input quantity x_0 consistent with the derived demand curve $D(p_0)$. Now suppose output price is reduced to p_1. Initially, the final goods industry will attempt to adjust along its supply curve $S(w_0)$ to produce quantity q_2. According to a partial welfare analysis, this would cause a loss in producer welfare of area u. However, if good x is available in imperfectly elastic supply, S', the lower output price and associated lower derived demand, $D(p_1)$, cause a decline in the input price to w_1. As a result, output supply increases to $S(w_1)$ so that quantity q_1 is produced at the new price p_1. Thus, producer welfare actually declines from area $u + y$ to area $y + z$ for a net loss of area $u - z$. Equivalently, this effect is measured by a loss in consumer surplus in the input market from area $a + b$ to area $b + c$ for a net loss of area $a - c$ (i.e., area $u - z$ = area $a - c$).

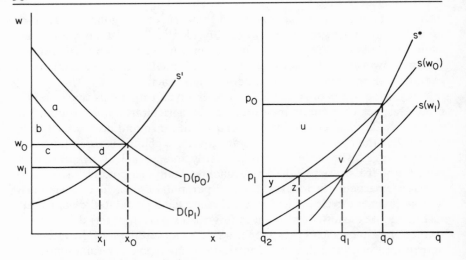

FIG. 2.3.   Multimarket welfare measurement.

The latter accounting, however, is also partial because it does not reflect the loss that suppliers of the input suffer with a decline in input price. Their loss in producer surplus is area $c + d$. Thus, under conditions in which these surpluses measure willingness to pay, the net willingness to pay to keep the original price, considering all producers and input suppliers, is area $a + d$. Equivalently, this effect can be measured as area $u + v$ in the final goods market where S^* is an equilibrium supply curve that takes account of the input price adjustment that takes place with changes in output price. Thus, the partial criticism of classical welfare economics is avoided in this simple two-market economy by measuring welfare change according to equilibrium supply in the output market.

Many generalizations of this result are demonstrated by Just et al. (1982, Chap. 9 and Append. D) on the demand side as well as the supply side. To the extent that producer and consumer surplus triangles reflect willingness to pay (e.g., to the extent that final consumer income elasticities are zero for all goods with changing prices or to the extent that Willig-type approximations are appropriate), these generalizations show that the effect of introducing a single distortion in an otherwise competitive economy can be measured completely in the market in which the distortion is introduced. That is, the net willingness to pay by society can be found by using surplus triangle concepts in a single market in a rather standard way even though many prices and many markets are affected. However, to do so one must use general equilibrium supply and demand curves that take account of all price adjustments caused elsewhere in the economy as the distortion is altered. This makes the appropriate general equilibrium supply and demand dependent on the particular type of distortion.

While this result greatly extends some theoretical results developed in partial frameworks, several problems hinder its empirical applicability. First, when altering a distortion is considered, it is not in an economy otherwise free of distortions. Second, consumer income elasticities are clearly nonzero for many goods. Third, estimation of general equilibrium supply and demand requires information about all of the conditioning factors of the economy, which together with information about all prices is sufficient to estimate all supplies and demands. Thus, the data requirements are demanding. Finally, the equilibrium approach described produces no distributional information about who gains and who loses with a change in the distortion. In many welfare analyses, the limited distributional results that show which groups gain or lose are of great interest.

When the possibility of distortions in other markets is introduced, a generalization of these results implies that equilibrium relationships must also be estimated to determine the change in net government revenues and the change in noncompetitive benefits (demand price minus supply price multiplied by quantity) accruing to producers or consumers in all markets directly involving price controls or noncompetitive behavior. To accommodate the problem of nonzero income elasticities, either Willig-type results (that have not been investigated in the context of general equilibrium measurement) must be invoked or behavior of final consumers must be estimated in all final goods (and labor) markets to measure the departure of willingness to pay from standard surplus measures. As with dynamic considerations, however, nondistorting lump sum transfers are not possible in the latter case so a disaggregated constitutional approach is necessary.

Given these considerations, the data requirements of both the conventional and constitutional approaches are very great if many realistic assumptions are incorporated. Nevertheless, these considerations appear to be important in agricultural marketing problems. Many sectors of the agricultural economy have important vertical market relationships. For example, a change in a retail milk pricing program can have important effects on milk consumers, milk producers, milk processors, grocery stores, and even producers of feed grains. Many farms are diverse producers of many commodities, so changes that affect one crop may be passed through to varying degrees to other crop markets both domestically and internationally. Important effects can also be transmitted to input markets as in some of the Russian grain deals. Or input market developments can be passed through to final goods markets as in the case of oil price increases in the 1970s. These considerations suggest that welfare measurement of efficiency in agriculture can benefit substantially by improving empirical abilities to identify intermarket relationships.

EMPIRICAL CONSIDERATIONS AND CONCLUSIONS

The methodological means for welfare measurement have been extended in many ways to the case of a dynamic, uncertain, multimarket world. However, welfare measurement based on market-level concepts of supply and demand and the associated producer and consumer surplus triangles is strictly appropriate only under restrictive conditions. Adding many realistic assumptions associated with risk, externalities, transactions costs, imperfect information, etc., causes competitive equilibrium to lose its identity with Pareto optimality. For such cases, welfare practitioners must be careful not to apply the standard results that show Pareto inferiority of quotas, price supports, etc., simply because they depart from competitive equilibrium. These considerations become crucial in evaluating many provisions included, for example, in marketing orders.

Furthermore, unless consumers have zero income elasticities for all goods with changing prices and producers have constant absolute risk aversion, the usual surplus triangles measure neither willingness to pay nor other useful money metrics such as certainty equivalent. While correction factors and differential equation approaches are available for calculating useful welfare quantities from market supplies and demands in these cases (e.g., assuming identical individuals if at the market level), lump sum redistribution is no longer nondistorting. For such cases, the conventional approach to welfare measurement that focuses only on efficiency may not be appropriate; thus, one must carefully weigh the applicability of its assumptions relative to those of an alternative (constitutional) approach. Such considerations may be crucial in evaluating policies related, for example, to crop insurance (where risk as well as moral hazard and adverse selection are major problems) and futures markets (where risk as well as imperfect information and transactions costs are major problems).

In conclusion, the methodologies to handle welfare measurement with these various problems are fairly well developed. Development of the methodology for welfare measurement has progressed almost hand in hand with the development of new models that demonstrate the role of alternative behavioral criteria under various assumptions. From a practical point of view, the major constraint to their use is at the empirical stage. Many of the generalizations discussed in this paper greatly increase the data requirements of empirical modeling. Empirical models have considered an ever expanding set of markets, intermarket relationships, and dynamic investment relationships, as data and computer power have increased. But this movement has met increasing difficulty of identification or, conversely, has come only at the expense of including more assumptions and arbitrary specifications. Relatively few empirical models have included risk-related behavior. Fewer have considered limited information, transactions costs, moral hazard, etc. As the assumptions in empirical models are broadened and more realistic behavior is incorporated, econometricians find that the results become less clear and the apparent statistical clarity in a model based on many specific assumptions can be entirely misleading (see McAleer et al. 1985; Leamer 1985). These same reservations also apply to the welfare calculations based on such models and paint a somewhat bleak picture of our abilities to generate accurate welfare measurements for the difficult issues of a complex, dynamic, uncertain, multimarket world. Rather than hope for a simple paradigm that can converge on reality and eventually encompass all seemingly relevant phenomena, market and welfare analysts are apparently doomed to continue to view economic phenomena from various alternative perspectives (alternative sets of assumptions) that generate different levels of clarity versus conflict in each new problem.

NOTES

1. Arrow's axioms involve unrestricted domain, the weak Pareto principle, non-dictatorship, and independence of irrelevant alternatives.
2. Imposing impartiality implies $W = \Sigma_i U_i$. Note that any social welfare functional with unrestricted domain and satisfying independence of irrelevant alternatives, the strong Pareto principle, anonymity, separability of unconcerned individuals, and cardinality with interpersonal comparability must be of this form (Maskin 1978; Sen 1982). Note further, however, that simply replacing cardinality with ordinality and adding a minimal equity assumption (the best-off individual's preferences can never be served when they conflict with all worse-off individuals' preferences) results in the Rawlsian social welfare functional where the worst-off individual becomes dictator (Sen 1982). Although Rawls's (1971) theory of justice is closely related to much of the literature considered here, it is not considered to be of practical relevance because of the overriding importance it places on the preferences of one individual.
3. Diamond (1967) has also criticized Harsanyi's (1955) social aggregation based on its implicit use of the "sure thing" principle. This is not a strong criticism in the context of most economic research that makes use of von Neumann-Morgenstern utility, however, since it involves treating the prospect of a given level of utility differently than an uncertain prospect with the same level of expected utility in the social welfare function. See Sen (1982, Chap. 9) for a recent discussion.
4. Some have argued that vote trading in Congress and the economic influence of the rich in political markets has undermined these desirable properties of

representative democracy. However, Buchanan and Tullock (1962, 154) have shown that "if some vote trading is not introduced, no allowance can be made for possible variations in individual intensities of preferences." Furthermore, the work of Becker (1983, 1984) suggests that a political interest group's activities depend on its willingness to pay for various alternatives; thus, political interest group activities can possibly be a useful guide to policy formulation. Zusman (1976), however, derives conflicting results in a different model in which social power is not based on willingness to pay.

5. The term "constitutional approach" is more appropriate here than a term such as "political approach" because welfare significance and measurement of economic efficiency is attainable only when the constitution plays a particular role. Otherwise, the approach simply measures political efficiency (how well political preferences are satisfied).

6. In examining the literature, one finds some cases where the assumptions of the conventional approach to welfare measurement are apparently assumed to hold (as evidenced by the use of the deadweight social loss concept) but yet distributional issues are a competing concern. For example, Becker (1984) uses deadweight social loss as a measure of social costs incurred to attain a given distributional outcome. In this paper, however, such an approach is viewed as inappropriate. If distributional concerns are systematically at odds with the deadweight loss criterion of the conventional approach, then some of the associated simplifying assumptions that lead to separability of efficiency and distribution are not applicable.

7. This section considers welfare measurement under risk only for producers although in both input and output markets. The risk problem is not important for typical consumer decisions since choices are made based on actual prices. One important exception arises in the case of consumer durables wherein the durable must be chosen before prices of related goods are known. For example, a car purchaser may not know what the price of gasoline will be during the life of the car. Such cases, however, can be handled in the household production framework by integrating the usual approach to consumer welfare measurement for end goods with the approach to producer welfare measurement in this and the following section. See Just et al. (1982, Sect. C.3).

8. That is, the equivalent variation, e, of removing risk is defined by

$$V(\bar{p},\alpha,W_0) = V(\bar{p},0,W_0 + e)$$

where p is a vector of expected *ex ante* prices of both inputs and outputs, α is a vector of parameters determining risk with $\alpha = 0$ for no risk, W_0 is initial wealth, and V is the indirect expected utility function. The result follows upon noting that

$$E[U(W)] = V(\bar{p},\alpha, W_0) \text{ and } U(W) = V(\bar{p},0, W_0 + e)$$

where $W = W_0 + pq$ is actual *ex post* wealth, $\overline{W} = W_0 + e + \bar{p}\bar{q}$ is the certainty equivalent of wealth, p and q are actual *ex post* price and quantity vectors, q is a vector of expected *ex ante* quantities, and U is the direct utility function defined on wealth.

9. The discussion of conventional welfare measurement in this section follows

Just et al. (1982, Chap. 13 and Append. C); supporting details and references can be found there.
10. That is, even though use of compensated supply and demand curves can be used to determine potential Pareto improvements based on compensating and equivalent variations, one cannot then move to any redistribution from the resulting Pareto-superior outcome without possibly reducing the amount available for distribution. A Pareto-superior outcome would necessarily be obtained when the first two conditions fail only if any redistribution is substantially restricted.

REFERENCES

Arrow, K. J. *Social Choice and Individual Values.* New York: John Wiley & Sons, 1963.
———. "The Organization of Economic Activity: Issues Pertinent to the Choice of Market Versus Nonmarket Allocation." *Public Expenditures and Policy Analysis,* eds. J. Margolis and Robert H. Haveman, pp. 59–73. Chicago: Markham Publishing Company, 1970.
Becker, G. S. "A Theory of Competition Among Pressure Groups for Political Influence." *Q. J. Econ.* 98(1983):371–400.
———. "Public Policies, Pressure Groups, and Dead Weight Costs." Paper presented to the Nobel Symposium on the Growth of Government, Stockholm, 15–17 Aug. 1984.
Borch, K. "Equilibrium in a Reinsurance Market." *Econometrica* 30(1962):424–44.
Brandow, G. E. "Policy for Commercial Agriculture, 1945–71." *A Summary of Agricultural Economics Literature,* Vol. 1, ed. L. R. Martin, pp. 209–92. Minneapolis: University of Minnesota Press, 1977.
Buchanan, J. M., and G. Tullock. *The Calculus of Consent.* Ann Arbor: University of Michigan Press, 1962.
Chipman, J. S., and J. C. Moore. "The New Welfare Economics 1939–1974." *Int. Econ. Rev.* 19(1978):547–81.
———. "Compensating Variation, Consumer's Surplus, and Welfare." *Am. Econ. Rev.* 70(1980):933–49.
Coase, R. H. "The Problem of Social Cost." *J. Law and Econ.* 3(1960):1–44.
Cochrane, W. W. "Some Nonconformist Thoughts on Welfare Economics and Commodity Stabilization Policy." *Am. J. Agric. Econ.* 62(1980):508–11.
Dahl, R. A. *After the Revolution?* New Haven: Yale University Press, 1970.
de Graaf, J. *Theoretical Welfare Economics.* London: Cambridge University Press, 1957.
Diamond, P. "Cardinal Welfare, Individualistic Ethics and Interpersonal Comparisons of Utility." *J. Polit. Econ.* 75(1967):765.
Downs, A. *An Economic Theory of Democracy.* New York: Harper and Row, 1957.
Easton, D. *A Framework for Political Analysis.* Englewood Cliffs, N.J.: Prentice-Hall, 1965a.
———. *A Systems Analysis of Political Life.* New York: John Wiley & Sons, 1965b.
Fishburn, P. C. *The Theory of Social Choice.* Princeton: Princeton University Press, 1973.
Friedlaender, A. F. "Macro Policy Goals in the Postwar Period: A Study in Revealed Preference." *Q. J. Econ.* 87(1973):25–43.
Gorman, W. M. "The Intransitivity of Certain Criteria Used in Welfare Economics." *Oxford Econ. Papers,* New Series 7(1955):25–35.
Harsanyi, J. C. "Cardinal Welfare, Individualistic Ethics, and Interpersonal Comparisons of Utility." *J. Polit. Econ.* 63(1955):309–21.
Hart, O. "On the Optimality of Equilibrium When the Market Structure is Incomplete." *J. Econ. Theory* 11(1975):418–43.
Hausman, J. A. "Exact Consumer's Surplus and Deadweight Loss." *Am. Econ. Rev.* 71(1981):662–76.
Hicks, J. R. "The Foundations of Welfare Economics." *Econ. J.* 49(1939):696–712.
Just, R. E. *Econometric Analysis of Production Decisions: The Case of the California Field*

Crops. Giannini Foundation Monograph No. 33, University of California-Berkeley, 1975.

Just, R. E., D. L. Hueth, and A. Schmitz. *Applied Welfare Economics and Public Policy.* New York: Prentice-Hall, 1982.

Kaldor, Nicholas. "Welfare Propositions of Economics and Interpersonal Comparisons of Utility." *Econ. J.* 49(1939):549–52.

Kemp, M. C., and Y. K. Ng. "More on Social Welfare Functions: The Incompatability of Individualism and Ordinalism." *Economica* 44(1977):89–90.

LaFrance, J. T., and H. de Gorter. "Regulation in a Dynamic Market: The U.S. Dairy Industry." *Am. J. Agric. Econ.* 67(1985):821–32.

Layard, P. R. G., and A. A. Walters. *Microeconomic Theory.* New York: McGraw-Hill, 1978.

Leamer, E. E. "Sensitivity Analysis Would Help." *Am. Econ. Rev.* 75(1985):308–13.

Lipsey, R. G., and R. K. Lancaster. "The General Theory of the Second Best." *Rev. Econ. Studies* 24(1956):11–32.

McAleer, M., A. R. Pagan, and P. A. Volker. "What Will Take the Con Out of Econometrics?" *Am. Econ. Rev.* 75(1985):293–307.

Maskin, E. "A Theorem on Utilitarianism." *Rev. Econ. Studies* 45(1978):93–96.

Massell, B. F. "Price Stabilization and Welfare." *Q. J. Econ.* 83(1969):285–97.

Mueller, Dennis C. *Public Choice.* London: Cambridge University Press, 1979.

Oi, W. Y. "The Desirability of Price Instability under Perfect Competition." *Econometrica* 27(1961):58–64.

Pareto, Vilfredo. *Cours d'Economie Politique.* Vol. 2. Lausanne, Switzerland: F. Rouge, 1896.

Pope, R. D., and J. P. Chavas. "Producer's Surplus and Risk." Dept. Agric. Econ. Working Paper, Texas A & M University, 1982.

Pope, R. D., J. P. Chavas, and R. E. Just. "Economic Welfare Evaluations for Producers under Uncertainty." *Am. J. Agric. Econ.* 65(1983):98–107.

Rausser, G. C., and J. W. Freebairn. "Estimation of Policy Preference Functions: An Application to U.S. Beef Import Quotas." *Rev. Econ. and Stat.* 56(1974):437–49.

Rawls, J. *A Theory of Justice.* New York: Oxford University Press, 1971.

Runge, C. F., and R. J. Myers. "Shifting Foundations of Agricultural Policy Analysis: Welfare Economics When Risk Markets Are Incomplete." *Am. J. Agric. Econ.* 67(1985):1010–16.

Scitovsky, T. "A Note on Welfare Propositions in Economics." *Rev. Econ. Studies* 9(1941):77–88.

———. "The State of Welfare Economics." *Am. Econ. Rev.* 41(1951):303–15.

Sen, A. K. *Collective Choice and Social Welfare.* San Francisco: Holden-Day, 1970.

———. *Choice, Welfare and Measurement.* Cambridge, Mass.: MIT Press, 1982.

Shubik, M. "A Two Party System, General Equilibrium and the Voters' Paradox." *Z. Nationalo.* (1968):341–54.

———. "On Homo Politicus and the Instant Referendum." *Public Choice* 9(1970):79–84.

Stiglitz, J. E. "The Inefficiency of the Stock Market Equilibrium." *Rev. Econ. Studies* 49(1982):241–61.

———. "Information and Economic Analysis: A Perspective." *Econ. J.* 95(Conference Papers Supplement 1985):21–41.

Theil, H. *Optimal Decision Rules for Government and Industry.* Amsterdam: North-Holland Publishing Co., 1964.

Tinbergen, J. *Economic Policy: Principles and Design.* Amsterdam: North-Holland Publishing Co., 1956.

van den Doel, Hans. *Democracy and Welfare Economics.* London: Cambridge University Press, 1979.

Willig, Robert D. "Consumer's Surplus Without Apology." *Am. Econ. Rev.* 66(1976):589–97.

Zusman, P. "The Incorporation and Measurement of Social Power in Economic Models." *Int. Econ. Rev.* 17(1976):447–62.

Economic Efficiency and Welfare Measurement in a Dynamic, Uncertain, Multimarket World

A DISCUSSION

Rulon Pope

PROFESSOR JUST has provided a useful review of the measurement of welfare under conditions especially suited to agriculture. These methods are difficult, but not impossible, to apply due to data and modeling problems. In addition to rather conventional Chicago-style welfare methods, Just seems to be arguing that the profession be about characterizing the social welfare function of society by examining political or bureaucratic behavior.

Given the immense impact that welfare economics has on economic analysis, it does seem fruitful to examine extensions of common practice and possibly other approaches involving welfare functions that do not weight equally gainers and losers.

EX ANTE OR EX POST

I want to briefly comment on the techniques that Professor Just has ably exposited in the paper. These techniques readily translate into the exhaustion of gains from trade. With competitive type markets, which include those with imperfect information, these gains can be measured using private behavior and are generally approximated by consumer and producer surplus. When markets fail due to externalities, whether conventionally defined or expanded to include public goods, adverse selection, moral hazard, or other phenomena where markets cannot exhaust these gains, then one must rely on other than solely market means to obtain welfare measures.

When markets exist, then the techniques described by Just are especially useful and rather readily implemented. It seems to me that constant absolute risk aversion is sufficiently reasonable at this stage of risk analysis. Such behaviors have the property in which real and nominal wealth-

RULON POPE is professor, Department of Economics, Brigham Young University, Provo, Utah.

based decisions differ but in which likely errors are small. Secondly, in all of the analysis, I am persuaded that changes in the distribution of risks and information across agents could be vitally important (e.g., Pope and Chambers 1985). Even without risk aversion of any kind, risk type measures seem to be crucial for measuring aggregate responses using aggregate data. Thirdly, one must be careful to incorporate institutions and markets that affect risk. For example, when there is hedging, as in Feder et al. (1980), then welfare under constant absolute risk aversion is the area above supply minus the quantity hedged and below expected price. The former quantity is independent of expected cash price but still must be used in the calculation (Pope and Chavas 1985a, Suppl. C). If mean cash price and futures price are functionally related, then welfare methods must recognize this in the calculations. Further, forward prices can be easily included in the measures as well. If expected cash price can be independently varied, then the welfare measure involves output minus (forward plus futures) contracted output. Thus, markets for risk are vital to the analysis. These comments aside, Just has used the expected utility maximization of individual agents as an important component of the social norm.

Probably the most confusing word in economics is efficiency. Its meaning is specific to an underlying model and even when the model is understood, it is often unclear what efficiency means. Under static certainty, the firm or consumer is said to be technically efficient if it is on the boundary of a production or utility possibility set. The firm or consumer is said to be efficient in allocation if the economic agent sets the marginal rate of substitution equal to the price ratio. Usually for a firm, there is an additional output effect where one must also examine efficiency. Hence, even within this simple static paradigm, there are at least three meanings of efficiency.

When uncertainty is introduced, *ex post* notions of efficiency correspond to the above for each random draw of the state of nature. In nearly all studies of economic efficiency, *ex post* choices are used to infer efficiency. Thus, if C_i is the ith firm's cost of producing output y, the efficiency index is C_i/C where C is the *ex post* cost function calculated by the researcher. This is the common Farrell technique used frequently in agricultural economics or its econometric analogue (Schmidt and Lovell 1979). In virtually no cases are such analyses calculated using the *ex ante* costs and accounting for the possibility of risk averse behavior. It is easy to show that most inferences in the literature on firm efficiency are full of conceptual and measurement errors when production uncertainty is admitted for a competitive firm (Pope 1980).

Since the cost function is used ubiquitously for efficiency and other measurements because it is fairly robust to model specification, it seems useful to ask what cost minimization means in a world where outputs are not known for certain as input choices are applied. One of the first jobs of the researcher is to decide which inputs are to be included in the cost calculation. One's immediate reaction might be all of them—except perhaps management. Yet routinely, all informational inputs are ignored in consumer and producer efficiency considerations except apologetically in one's qualifications about the significance or accuracy of conclusions. This omission is crucial. It is the sole microlink to the debate over whether markets (or a particular market) are efficient. One cannot discuss the value of grades or standards in marketing orders without explicitly facing up to this issue in the consumer case (Pope, forthcoming). Finding that a futures or options trading strategy is systematically preferred when transactions or computing and research costs are ignored says virtually nothing about whether markets or individual agents are inefficient. Therefore, if one is to use a concept like cost minimization, it seems that a coherent *ex ante* efficiency norm should be developed. The incorporation of information gathering activities will rule out the usual static cost minimization notions. It may greatly alter the form of the problem as well. For example, let information be omitted, and assume a competitive firm that has a production function $y = f(x) + h(x)e$ where y is output and x is a vector of inputs, and e is a random disturbance. *Ex ante* cost minimization must hold fixed mean and variance of production or f and h. This is in marked contrast to minimizing costs holding f fixed or minimizing cost subject to *ex post y*. This could change some conclusions of agricultural studies based upon the cost function (e.g., the classic study by Binswanger 1974). The dynamic analogue of the above problem when information is included is found in Pope and Chavas (1985b).

As Stiglitz (1985) and others correctly argue, imperfect information and more particularly asymmetrically held information, does cause one to ask interesting questions. The pooling (adverse selection) and moral hazard problems associated with agricultural insurance, capital markets, and labor markets are real, and it would be wise to study these problems seriously to see when inefficiencies might be mitigated by government policy. It is particularly interesting that monitoring and taxing or subsidizing complementary activities might be an optimal policy. Though Stiglitz argues that the fundamental theorem of welfare economics will not hold in these cases, it is still unclear to me what specific institutions he has in mind to remedy these market failures. These issues of public finance seem especially important and have received scant attention for agricultural issues.

THE IMPOSSIBILITY OF INFERRING SOCIAL UTILITY

I am afraid that I must be less sanguine about the Harsanyi-based approach proposed by Just. I agree that the usual welfare triangles, whether including risk, dynamics, or market dependence, are incomplete but useful. However, their frequent use in policy analysis attests to their usefulness until something better comes along. Is the Harsanyi approach this better approach? I think not.

Again incomplete information is the key. There is by now a large literature in public choice on rent-seeking and agency problems. This literature seems to say that the agency problem is real and will not be resolved by a proper contractual instrument. If the agent were fully informed, this may not be the case. Secondly, key features of our economic system are the large transactions costs of representation, the free-rider problem, and the inability of the public to "punish" the agent when behavior is not Pareto-efficient. Thirdly, the fact that the program parameters change so often will make economic analysis very difficult. Presumably, the populace has rather stable tastes if analysis is to be effective. Hence, some constraint on opportunities or perceptions must be driving the change in political behavior. These are not identified in Just's paper but are surely important.

Finally, it seems to me that the public choice literature is routinely not given the attention it deserves. Rent-seeking behavior has not been sufficiently examined. The extent to which real resources are used to obtain rents should be measured and assessed. This may mean that a bribe is more efficient than lobbying to obtain these rents. Yet lobbying may merely be an expensive means for the public to convey intensity of preferences and information to elected officials.

REFERENCES

Binswanger, H. "The Measurement of Technical Change Biases with Many Factors of Production." *Am. Econ. Rev.* 65(1974):964–76.
Feder, G., R. E. Just, and A. Schmitz. "Futures Markets and the Theory of the Firm under Price Uncertainty." *Q. J. Econ.* 44(1980):317–28.
Pope, R. "The Effects of Production Uncertainty." *Operations Research in Agriculture and Water Resources,* ed. D. Yaron and C. S. Tapiero, pp. 123–36. Amsterdam: North-Holland Publishing Co., 1980.
———. "The Value of Information about Food-Concepts and Their Implications for Measurement." Washington, D.C.: USDA ERS Tech. Bull. Forthcoming.
Pope, R., and R. Chambers. "Consistent Aggregation When Competitive Firms' Output Prices Vary." Dept. of Econ. Working Paper, Brigham Young University, 1985.
Pope, R., and J. P. Chavas. "Producer Surplus and Risk." *Q. J. Econ.* Supplement C, Dec. 1985a.
———. "Risk, Dynamics and Cost Minimization." Dept. of Agric. Econ. Working Paper, University of Wisconsin, 1985b.
Schmidt, P., and A. Lovell. "Estimating Technical and Allocative Inefficiency Relative to Stochastic Production and Cost Frontiers." *J. of Econometrics* 9(1979):343–66.
Stiglitz, J. E. "Information and Economic Analysis: A Perspective." *Econ. J.* 95(Conference Papers Supplement 1985):21–41.

CHAPTER 3

The Science and Art
of Efficiency Analysis:
The Role of Other
Performance Criteria

J. Walter Milon

EFFICIENCY ANALYSIS is a growth industry. In fact, efficiency analysis may be the premier growth industry among economists. During the past decade the profession has brought to market a dazzling array of new efficiency models and precepts for traditional subjects such as market structure and firm rivalry, and has moved boldly into new territories once considered outside the realm of the discipline—sports and traffic rules, marriage, criminal justice, litigation, politics, government administration, etc.[1] In the process a new lexicon of efficiency terms has developed. In addition to the familiar technical, allocative, and economic efficiencies, we now have purely technical efficiency, overall technical efficiency, relative efficiency, scale efficiency, congestion efficiency, overall efficiency, absolute price efficiency, wealth efficiency, social efficiency, Pareto efficiency, and last, but certainly not least, the mysterious X-efficiency.

Like Alice observing the splendor of Wonderland, we might question what this activity is all about. Certainly we might be tempted to observe through the rose-colored glasses of some who argue that, "in a world where each and every individual is asserted to behave consistently with the postulate of constrained maximization, economic inefficiency presents a contradiction in terms. . . . The world is efficient, if the model

J. WALTER MILON is associate professor, Department of Food and Resource Economics, University of Florida, Gainesville and formerly a visiting senior economist, Office of Policy, Planning and Evaluation, U.S. Environmental Protection Agency, Washington, D.C.

describing it sufficiently specifies the gains and costs to make it so . . ." (Cheung 1974, 71). In this idyllic world, efficiency analysis is little more than proper specification and clever integration. But, alas, there are agnostics. Recent articles by Bromley (1982), Cochrane (1980), Ladd (1983), Lang (1980), and others reveal lingering doubts and concerns about the scope and meaning of efficiency analysis. Indeed, the fact that this book includes the topic of "Other Performance Criteria" suggests that efficiency analysis alone may not provide sufficient guidance for individual and public decisions about the agricultural and food marketing system.[2]

What are these other criteria? The traditional structure, conduct, and performance framework emphasizes that market structure (number of firms, concentration, etc.) and conduct (collusive behavior, discrimination, etc.) determine economic performance (primarily market price). Within this framework, inefficiencies result principally from noncompetitive behavior that restricts the free flow of resources and unduly enhances price. Properly designed economic regulation can be used to correct these market failures.

We also observe numerous examples of government intervention to satisfy other performance criteria for the food system: transfer programs to redistribute income; regulatory programs to assure quality, safety, and environmental protection; and research to enhance productivity. If we combine federal regulatory efforts through the United States Department of Agriculture (USDA), Food and Drug Administration (FDA), Environmental Protection Agency (EPA), Consumer Product Safety Commission (CPSC) and Occupational Safety and Health Administration (OSHA) with state and local regulatory programs to assure abundant, nutritious, safe food products, the United States food distribution system may well be the most heavily regulated sector of the economy. The objectives of these diverse forms of social regulation raise some perplexing questions. Can the food system be efficient and still fail to satisfy other performance criteria? What other criteria might be deemed more important so that inefficiencies are acceptable? While both questions are interesting, they imply the commonly held perspective that efficiency must be traded off against other criteria (e.g., the familiar efficiency-equity trade-off). A more useful question would be, "Why doesn't efficiency analysis include these other performance criteria?"

I believe the answer to this question can be found in a careful investigation of the philosophical and methodological origins of efficiency analysis. This inquiry compels us to recognize that efficiency analysis is simply welfare economics and that our interpretation of welfare inevitably requires value judgments.[3] In this regard, John Neville Keynes's (1917) trichotomy of economic methods is especially illuminating. Keynes distinguished three branches: (1) the identification of economic uniformities, which was the subject of positive economic science; (2) the comparison of observed and ideal economic behavior, which was normative economic science; and (3) the prescription of specific rules to attain economic ends, which was termed an art. To be clear, Keynes did not use the term *art* in a pejorative way but rather in the spirit of Aristotle's pragmatism: "Every art and every inquiry, and similarly every action and pursuit, is thought to aim at some good" (Thomson 1976, 63). Thus, what the profession now calls normative or welfare economics can be seen as both a science and an art.[4] The scope of efficiency analysis is determined by value judgments about the means and ends of economic activity.

Despite the growing number of efficiency analysts, surprisingly few practitioners would describe themselves as welfare economists. Indeed, misunderstanding about the nature of welfare economics has encouraged economists to treat it like a captured spy—simply torture it until it confesses the answer you want to hear. Stigler (1981, 73) describes welfare economics as ". . . that branch of economic theory in which one economist achieves fame by demonstrating a flaw in the price system and a second economist achieves equal fame by discovering the flaw in this demonstration."

This poor regard for formal welfare economics while numerous practitioners are developing "efficient" solutions for economic and social problems is unfortunate. This situation subsumes several important conflicts over the scope and practice of efficiency analysis. It is appropriate that a book on efficiency analysis gives serious consideration to the theoretical underpinnings of the practice. Theoretical explorations into economic methods, however, have not played a large role in agricultural economics. The discipline developed in an environment of scientific positivism that narrowly defined economists' methods (Barkley 1984). But circumstances and academic fashion change. A growing number of economists are questioning the discipline's methodological premises (Caldwell and Coats 1984). This is all for the good of the profession at large and agricultural economists in particular because, as McCloskey (1983, 482) persuasively argues, economists ". . . will then better know why they agree or disagree, and will find it less easy to dismiss contrary arguments on merely methodological grounds."

COMMODITY AND NON-COMMODITY VALUES: SCHISM AND SYNTHESIS

The *locus classicus* for modern welfare theory is Pareto's *Manual of Political Economy* (1935). Pareto's results are well known so an explanation is not necessary. For my purposes it suffices to note that Pareto constructed a theory of allocation based on free exchange and ordinal preferences. In this framework, perfectly competitive markets would achieve the norm of efficient allocation. For positive economic science (Keynes's definition), this formulation had no significance. As Blaug (1978, 372–74) points out, virtually all economic uniformities (e.g., downward sloping demands, positively sloped supply curves) can be deduced and tested without appealing to optimality conditions. For normative economic science, however, the implications were extensive. Pareto had begun the transformation of what was primarily a moral theory of social good based on intrinsic values (utilitarian welfare theory) into a behavioral study of individual actions and instrumental values. Pareto's framework made it possible to (theoretically) compare the relative efficiency of an idealized competitive model with actual market structures without appealing to additional normative assumptions (e.g., interpersonal comparability of preferences). The implications for the art of economic analysis, however, were quite limited. The problem of interpersonal comparability that restricted the earlier welfare analyses of Bentham, Jevons, and Marshall would turn up as a major obstacle to actual application of the Pareto model.

Before addressing the interpersonal comparability issue, it is important to discuss a critical element of Pareto's analysis that has been neglected and is the source of much confusion in the efficiency literature. Pareto's social theory was a synthesis of separate, specialized social sciences (Tarascio 1969). In his theoretical framework, a social equilibrium results from the interplay of diverse motives, conditions, and objectives. While Pareto described this equilibrium as a maximum of social utility, he carefully explained that social utility did not depend only on individual preferences or the quantity and distribution of economic goods and services. Tarascio (1969, 7) urges economists to recognize that, "it is important to keep in mind that [Pareto's utility] has nothing to do with economic utility as we use the term today—it is a social concept, deriving from ethical, moral, religious, political, etc. as well as economic causes."

Pareto used the term *ophelimity* to describe the preferences for and satisfactions from economic goods and services. Ophelimity was unique to the individual but determined in part by social interaction (Tarascio 1969, 9–10). Given this limited definition and scope, Pareto argued that a welfare economics built on *commodity values* could only provide a partial understanding of individual satisfaction and overall social welfare. To evaluate individual utility and the overall level of utility for society, Pareto believed it was necessary to understand the role of noncommodity values in individual and social welfare and to integrate these values into policy analysis.

Despite Pareto's explicit distinction between ophelimity and utility as the proper basis of welfare economics, modern welfare economics equates individual utility with individual welfare and defines social welfare as the aggregation of individual utility. All sources of individual or social satisfactions, whether or not derived from goods and services, are taken as the subject matter of welfare economics. This widely held perspective on the scope of welfare analysis is reflected in Just et al. (1982, 3), "Welfare economics is concerned with the total welfare of the individual, not simply with the welfare level resulting from market goods and services."

The difficulty with this broad definition of welfare economics occurs in the transition from individual to collective welfare. While Pareto explicitly ruled out interpersonal comparisons as the basis for a normative economic science (Tarascio 1969, 6), modern welfare economics critically depends on a *comparability convention* (Cooter and Rappoport 1984, 509) to measure and aggregate individual welfare. The commonly accepted modern convention is the Barone-Kaldor-Hicks compensation test based on money-metric measures of *individual* marginal utility (marginal rate of substitution) changes (compensating and equivalent variations).

Professional acceptance of the compensation test convention can be traced in part to the dominance of logical positivism as the method of modern economics. During the methodological controversy of the 1930s, the term *value judgment* acquired a negative, nonscientific connotation due largely to Robbins's (1935) attacks on the policy prescriptions of the classical economists. Robbins argued that the classical economists' premise of a declining marginal utility of income could not be tested scientifically and was thus a value judgment. Amidst this controversy, Kaldor's (1939) assertion that hypothetical transfers of equally weighted monetary units are an objective basis for economic science was generally accepted by the profession with little discussion of the fact that Kaldor had simply substituted one value convention for that adopted by economists from Smith to Pigou. As Cooter and Rappoport (1984, 526) point out, the result was ". . . that a generation of economists was trained to believe that science treats a dollar as equally valuable to everyone, whereas a nonscientific approach treats a dollar as more valuable to the poor than to the rich."

Also contributing to the acceptance of the compensation test convention as the cornerstone of the New Welfare Economics was the growing perception that economics should emphasize the behavioral aspects of economic exchange for the purpose of predicting economic activity. Friedman's (1935) article on positivist methodology helped to turn the concepts of *utility* and *value* into instrumental variables that served the purpose of abstract theorizing, but distorted whatever connection remained with the intrinsic meaning of utility in the welfare economics of Bentham, Edgeworth, and Pareto.

The efficiency paradigm that resulted from this methodological framework is straightforward: homogeneous or "representative" consumers and firms engage in exchange of homogeneous products through discrete contracts; changes in the basic exchange structure that lead to a net surplus (comparing consumers' and producers' surplus) are (allocatively) efficient. In terms of the compensation test criteria, an efficient change is deemed an improvement in community welfare.[5] It is explicitly assumed that all relevant performance criteria are embodied in the valuation process and exchange contract: the income distribution is optimal, consumers have homothetic preferences and perfect information about product characteristics, producers have identical production functions and maximize profits, no externalities result from the exchange, and no noncommodity values are relevant to the exchange. Quite simply, all the interesting "other criteria" I might consider are assumed away.

The problem with the use of abstract assumptions for normative science objectives is that it has shaped the profession's view of the world to see social objectives defined exclusively in terms of commodity values and a particular judgment on interpersonal comparability. Certainly abstract assumptions are important for a qualitative calculus,[6] but their merit is questionable in efficiency analysis wherein quantitative measurement, not prediction, is the objective. In addition, while we freely use the term *Pareto efficiency* to describe the desirability of particular exchange relationships, it should be clear that the term is only loosely related to the full set of social interactions that characterized the "real" Pareto optimum. Is the problem of other performance criteria merely one of assumptions and value judgments? My pessimistic answer is yes, but I believe some basic changes in the scope and practice of efficiency analysis can remedy these problems and put the art of efficiency analysis on a sounder methodological, less value-dependent footing. Before I address these changes, consider a few examples of how the conventional approach to productive, allocative, and economic efficiency has inherent limitations that reduce its effectiveness in evaluating social welfare.[7]

"SCIENTIFIC BIASES" IN NEOCLASSICAL EFFICIENCY ANALYSIS

PRODUCTION EFFICIENCY

The standard approach to modeling production efficiency establishes a neoclassical frontier production function based on either a homogeneous (Farrell 1957) or nonhomogeneous (Kopp 1981) technology for a group of firms (farms or plants) based on known factor prices. The purpose is to establish a ranking basis for comparing a firm's performance relative to the frontier. Inherent in the basic approach is the notion that firms off the frontier are inefficient.

The value premises for this efficiency analysis deserve careful consideration. Contractual relations in the agricultural sector are characterized by considerable diversity; no single theory provides a complete explanation for the simultaneous presence of family, fixed wage, rental, sharecrop, and cooperative contracts between the factors of production.[8] In fact, most recent theories emphasize the importance of unmarketed factor inputs in the choice of contractual arrangements (Eswaran and Kotwal 1985; Murrell 1983; and Pollak 1985). Regardless of which theory is correct, all imply that firms pursue different means and ends that are subjective to the individual decision maker. Individuals' utility objectives and their preference intensities are not completely revealed in factor prices or output results; thus, the so-called frontier is efficient only for the production technology of the firms that lie on the frontier. Firms off the frontier cannot be labeled inefficient since the observer cannot objectively know which combination of factor inputs yields the most utility to factor owners. Personal satisfactions that may result from particular forms of business organization or in the pursuit of certain noncommodity values associated with production activities are not measured. Ladd (1983, 3) has observed that such comparisons of individual firms in the name of productive efficiency require "an interpersonal comparison in the form of an assertion that people who value only ends should get what they want but people who value means and ends should not get what they want."

A second shortcoming of the standard production efficiency analysis is that it implicitly assumes no technological externalities. Firms' production activities generate no harmful effects on recreational waterways, wildlife habitat, or people in surrounding communities. Laborers' wages include a risk premium to compensate for employment-related health and safety risks such as exposure to toxic substances and dangerous work conditions. In other words, all firms have internalized externalities in the neoclassical input prices and production technology.

The reality of course is quite different. Agriculture is a major source of nonpoint surface water pollution (Clark et al. 1985) and groundwater contamination; food processing plants are point source water polluters; and poorly informed laborers are exposed to toxic substances and dangerous work conditions. While environmental and safety regulations attempt to control these harmful effects, certainly all firms do not comply fully.

The standard production efficiency model simply does not consider these external effects and the problem of noncompliance. A firm on the frontier may be the least cost producer but still be responsible for significant external costs. A firm off the frontier that has internalized these negative effects would be labeled an inefficient producer. In this setting, the economic advice, whether to private or public interests, that firms should move toward greater production efficiency is a value judgment that commodity output is more desirable than foregone noncommodity values. Perhaps we should follow Mishan's (1984) suggestion and honestly describe production efficiency as productive "virtue" in our policy prescriptions.

ALLOCATIVE EFFICIENCY

Analyses of allocative efficiency focus on the market for a (homogeneous or heterogeneous) good and are concerned with changes in consumers' and producers' welfare due to market structure, regulations, or other exogenous influences. The theoretical normative results and ambiguities for imperfect competition and market interventions such as grades, marketing orders, and stabilization policies are documented elsewhere (Just et al. 1982). It is sufficient to note in passing that, in general, definitive efficiency results are obtained only in the context of the neoclassical consumer and firm in markets for homogeneous goods with perfect information. Empirical applications to determine changes in allocative efficiency in even the most restricted models, however, have encountered serious problems (French 1982). This point has an important bearing on the art of efficiency analysis, which I will return to later.

Consider instead the problem of assessing the allocative efficiency of quality controls and health risks in food production and consumption. The traditional approach is to introduce quality as either a continuous or discrete spectrum of product characteristics in consumer and producer decision sets. Assuming both consumers and producers perceive all dimensions of product quality prior to contracting, any restrictions on quality choice are allocatively inefficient (Bockstael 1984). Ambiguity arises though when uncertainty about quality enters the analysis.

Uncertainty about food quality can be considered as two distinct but related problems. First, food sanitation is a short-run concern in that consumers cannot fully know sanitation levels prior to purchase, but the health effects are typically known shortly after consumption. The results may be manifested as temporary illness or, in the extreme, immediate death. Food additives are a second problem that also are not fully known to the consumer at purchase. Their results are not revealed until after a considerable time lag and only then in generic health effects such as cancers or birth defects. The critical issue bearing on allocative efficiency in both settings is who chooses the health risk levels for food safety.

From an economic perspective, this issue can be viewed as a quality search problem in which consumers incur costs to obtain information about product quality. Following Akerlof's (1970) "lemon principle" for nonbranded goods, consumer choice with uncertain product safety leads to a "low quality only" equilibrium that is allocatively efficient but inferior to a perfect (first-best) information equilibrium (Stuart 1981). This high risk outcome is due in part to asymmetric information and can be improved through information dissemination in the form of brands, labels, or other product specific devices. Food producers will invest in product safety and information dissemination until incremental costs exceed revenue gains and a desired level of product safety is determined by the market. Note that this allocatively efficient solution requires transactions costs for both buyers and sellers: for buyers in the form of search costs and higher product prices, and for sellers in the form of increased production costs. Note also that unless all consumers can utilize this product safety information and there is a sufficiently wide range of price and health risk trade-offs, some consumers may be exposed to health risks they would otherwise be unwilling to take. A final consideration is the type of liability binding the exchange contract. Strict liability for product safety will generally tend to encourage greater safety (Goldberg 1974).

Applied to the food sanitation problem, this consumer choice with brand information solution has both desirable and undesirable implications. Consumers are free to select an efficient level of health risk but the actual distribution of risks may not be well known. Consumers may understate the probability of fatal risk leading to *ex post* results that are inconsistent with *ex ante* expectations. In addition, liability claims may force producers out of the market and cause uncertainty about future supply.

The food additive problem is even more difficult due to the time lag between consumption and resultant health effect. Consumer perceptions of health-related risks are widely distributed and many consumers understate the long-term health risks even for such well-known health risks as tobacco (Ippolito and Ippolito 1984). Consumers may not be able to evaluate technical information and liability claims may not be feasible due to producer dissolution and/or weak cause-effect relationships.

Thus, while the freedom of choice models of health risk selection in food markets may lead to allocatively efficient solutions, these solutions may impose high transactions costs and unexpected, disproportionate health costs on some consumers. The alternative, of course, is direct regulation through minimum quality standards that restrict consumer choice. Whether this solution is more or less desirable cannot be readily determined on efficiency criteria.

Consider the problems of comparing the costs and benefits of choice versus regulatory alternatives. The easy part is determining the direct costs of regulatory controls to determine, enforce, and implement food safety standards and the direct costs to consumers and producers in the form of search costs, transactions costs, and labeling costs in the free choice setting. The difficulty comes in determining the relative benefits of health risk regulation. Ideally we should know each consumer's Hicksian willingness to pay (compensating variation) for all types of health risk reductions and the relative differences in the distribution of health risks for the two alternatives. While the latter is primarily a medical issue, the valuation of health risks, both morbidity and mortality, is solely an economic issue.

The technical and ethical dilemmas in health risk valuation, however, are numerous. Direct medical costs from illness cannot measure psychic disutility and are a poor proxy for true willingness to pay. Labor market studies may provide some insight into worker valuation of risk/income trade-offs, but these studies suffer from selectivity biases, risk interdependencies, and other interdependent influences characteristic of labor markets. In those few instances in which direct expressions of willingness to pay for health risk reductions have been elicited through personal interviews, individuals could not readily evaluate the risk/income trade-offs and many expressed ethical objections to the choice setting.[9]

In light of the technical and ethical problems of determining the allocative efficiency of choice versus regulatory alternatives, it is not surprising that food safety laws in the United States are based primarily on health considerations. Enabling statutes for food safety regulation by USDA, FDA, EPA, and OSHA explicitly rule out the use of benefit-cost criteria in regulatory decisions.[10] Like child labor and maximum hour legislation, these regulations are not justified by allocative efficiency considerations but instead by the democratically expressed desire for government to protect public safety and health. This certainly does not rule out inconsistencies in regulatory policy, such as the concurrent approval of cigarette sales and enforcement of the Delaney clause prohibiting carcinogenic substances in food products. But, the notion that food safety might be traded off with economic cost is ethically wrong if legislative action is a statement of publicly held values.

Another aspect of food safety regulation not easily addressed in the allocative efficiency framework relates to long-run expectations and consumer confidence in food system quality. Von Weizsacker's (1984, 1086) principle of extrapolation suggests that markets benefit from readily accessible quality information that "serves as a surrogate for unavailable information or costly information about the present and the future."

While food brands clearly serve this purpose, there are many instances in which branding or other types of quality signals are unenforceable. State and federal regulations to prevent adulteration, misbranding, or other abuses create a type of goodwill or a public good that defines the conditions for allocative efficiency but itself is not easily defined in efficiency terms. This subjective element of food system performance may explain why United States food safety laws are a collective choice anomaly. Despite the opposition of well-organized industry groups and the well-known difficulties of organizing widely dispersed consumer interests, the food safety laws enacted during the past 50 years have retained their basic consumer protection character. It is difficult to believe that this commitment reflects nothing more in the public mind than a desire for market efficiency.

ECONOMIC EFFICIENCY

Consider next the use of efficiency analysis for counseling public officials on policy decisions regarding direct government intervention in agricultural commodity markets. Economic efficiency in this context is defined by the Barone-Kaldor-Hicks compensation test. It is a recognition that any policy action is likely to leave at least one person worse off.

There is an uneasy alliance between the compensation test principle for commodity price analysis in normative economic science and its application in policy decisions in which both price and other market performance measures are concerned. Economists generally see the compensation test as an objective, neutral measure of potential changes in social welfare. However, most recognize that the compensation test is a dominant indicator of welfare improvements only when dollar gains and losses are weighted equally across recipients. In comparative statics this restriction is inconsequential given homogeneous consumers and producers. But, in policy analysis, equal weighting implies cardinal comparability and utilitarian values. In lieu of the mythical social welfare function, we defer to the political process to determine the appropriate "weights" for other performance objectives such as distributional concerns, employment stability, and the character of competition.

Economists since Adam Smith have been uncomfortable with the notion that political choice is necessary to determine the socially preferred allocation of resources. In recent years the merits of government intervention have been increasingly questioned in the development of a "new political economy." The nature of this controversy has an important bearing on the use of efficiency analysis in policy decisions and the importance of other performance criteria in determining public policy.

This new political economy can be characterized by what Rausser

(1982, 832) describes as a perspective that ". . . recognizes the nonsepa-rability of political and economic markets, the nonexistence of pure trans-fers, and the second-best world in which we live." This analysis can be briefly described using game theoretic concepts. The key elements are welfare improving activities or positive sum games, pure distributional activities or zero sum games, and rent-seeking activities or negative sum games.[11]

At the simplest level, political action can be explained as a collective solution to prisoner-dilemma type games in which cooperation yields a positive sum payoff. Agriculture and food programs such as biological research, price stabilization, or quality regulations can be described as minimizing the transactions costs of social coordination and thereby im-proving resource allocation.

Political action also serves to create income redistribution institu-tions or other forms of entitlements (property rights, legal exemptions, etc.) to achieve general social objectives. These institutions serve not just as instruments of transfer and production, they also define social relations and noncommodity values that are democratically selected. To propo-nents of participatory democracy, the norms or institutional relations that result from this political super game are themselves a source of social utility (Elkin 1985).

Several agricultural institutions can be viewed in this context. Founding of the Farm Bureau by the United States Agricultural Exten-sion Service was an effort to provide rural farmers with a collective voice in national legislation. Capper-Volstead served not only to protect small producers from oligopsonistic middlemen but also to cultivate participa-tion in employee controlled organizations (Johnson and Jesse 1981). The income transfer systems in the various agriculture acts served to foster asset ownership, resource conservation, individual independence, and ru-ral stability. While all these objectives were not fully realized (Penn 1984), contrast the results for the farm sector with the results of the income assistance programs in urban communities as described by Gilder (1979).

Proponents of the rent-seeking view of political action argue that political action by interest groups inevitably leads to coercion, resource waste, and inequality-preserving institutions. Taken to the limit as Man-cur Olson does in *The Rise and Decline of Nations* (1982), the result is rigid distributional coalitions and special-interest organizations that re-duce total social product and cause eventual economic stagnation. The modern Leviathan (Buchanan 1975) turns out instead to be a multiheaded Hydra. Several examples of rent-seeking behavior in agriculture have been discussed recently (Rausser 1982; Gardner 1985).

Recognition that political and economic analysis are not mutually exclusive and that positive, zero, or negative sum outcomes are possible raises some important issues about the science and art of efficiency analysis. First, from the perspective of a normative science, the political-economic market linkage creates a rich set of behavioral propositions about consumer, producer, voter, and legislator interactions. A positivist research agenda to identify the significance of interest groups, constituents, bureaucrats, and ideology on committee and chamber voting can provide useful insights about the importance of redistribution in democratic policy choice. It emphasizes that socially desirable policies are selected for both the magnitude and distribution of benefits and costs and suggests that the normative efficiency results of neoclassical market models have more limited usefulness than many of us would like to believe. There is a serious danger, however, that the political choice function will become just another economic black box into which dollars go in and policies come out. The narrow positivist research program should not become the only economic interpretation of political choice processes and dictate the agenda for the art of efficiency analysis.

One implication for the art of efficiency analysis is the need to explicitly consider both income and geographic differences in the benefits and costs of policies. Nationally aggregated demand and supply curves based on homogeneous producers and consumers may provide useful qualitative information, but the aggregate quantitative results may be quite misleading. Since few policies will have uniform results on randomly distributed representative consumers, the need for disaggregated analysis is evident. For example, regional dairy markets are characterized by different degrees of competition and varying income distributions across consumers and producers. Given that a uniform policy change is likely to cause quite different welfare impacts across regions, disagreement about the efficiency of alternative policies is hardly surprising.[12]

In addition, traditional efficiency analysis all too often frames a policy issue around a limited economic interpretation that substitutes for wider discussion of the noncommodity values that underlie the issue. The root question of redistribution, namely how the welfare of an individual relates to others, is about defining basic civil rights. Simply converting these issues of basic rights into monetary equivalents for the sake of maximizing exercises will not reveal much about real policy choices. For example, individuals who qualify for food stamps or other in-kind transfers are granted an entitlement that has a specific ethical foundation. To argue that cash transfers are equivalent from a "neutral" efficiency perspective obscures the basic ethical consideration involved in public choice[13] (Kelman 1983).

Finally, the perverse dynamics of the rent-seeking/negative sum public choice perspective raises some perplexing concerns about the scope of efficiency analysis. The policy conclusion of the Olson (1982) analysis is that only by neutralizing special interest activities is it possible to achieve efficient, long-term economic growth. This view is reflected in recent proposals for independent boards and legislative reform for agricultural programs (Gardner 1985). An alternative perspective on rent-seeking behavior is offered in a recent book by Kuttner (1985) who argues that a corporatist structure of competing interest groups is necessary to determine long-term investment objectives and to maintain a stable, adaptable social structure. While interest groups may have some narrow objectives, on balance their concerns encompass a broad spectrum of social objectives. He cites the experience of several modern industrial states in which concern for special interest issues has contributed to positive, not negative, economic growth.

With regard to the agricultural sector, an important question to consider is whether public support for long-term efficiency enhancing activities such as research and education would be forthcoming if agricultural interest groups were stripped of their lobbying incentives. The well-known problem of underinvestment in long-term research in competitive industries could readily limit future growth in domestic agriculture.[14] Deregulated markets and neutral regulatory agencies may limit rent-seeking activities and yield short-term efficiency gains but at the expense of a viable, countervailing voice in an increasingly urban, industrial society. These considerations do not fit easily in standard compensation test calculations nor do I offer any simple solution. But they are an important concern, especially if we give serious attention to other performance objectives in the art of efficiency analysis.

EFFICIENCY CRITERIA, EMPIRICISM, AND FOOD POLICY

Efficiency criteria have been accorded a regal status in our profession although some have dissented, insisting that "the emperor has no clothes." The traditional defense asserts the need for an objective standard to appraise hypothetical or actual states of the world. Yet, the objectivity of efficiency criteria as pedagogic tools in normative economic science need not blind our vision of real world ideals and concerns. As economists we have an uncommon Platonic urge to manipulate exact images of imprecise economic reality and to disparage those who see other images as lacking in scientific rigor (Pokorny 1978). This "cult of objectivity," as Lerner (1972) described it, may serve a useful purpose in advocating a specific a priori concept of economic welfare as an initial working hypothesis. But, this perspective cannot lead to fruitful policy analysis if efficiency becomes the first and only principle of economic policy that we consider.

What other objectives then can we as economists use as guides for the art of policy analysis? Perhaps it may be useful to consider Philbrook's (1953, 858) contention that, "Only one type of serious defense of a policy is open to an economist or anyone else: he must maintain that the policy is good." Certainly defining the notion of good is a task relished only by philosophers, preachers, and bartenders, but I submit that a consensus would agree that any theory of the good involves both distributional implications and the noncommodity values engendered by policy choices. This latter aspect is a function of broad social norms and institutions that are not easily addressed in a typical efficiency analysis framework. On the other hand, distributional implications are tractable and can be readily integrated with only a few modifications of our analytical procedures.

A COMPARABILITY CONVENTION FOR
EFFICIENCY AND DISTRIBUTION

For policy analysis of economic efficiency, consider Ng's (1984) comparability convention alternative to the standard compensation test. Ng's quasi-Pareto criterion requires a comparison of gains and losses *within* income groups affected by a policy. If compensation would be possible within each income group after a policy change, the policy is socially desirable.[15]

The advantage of the quasi-Pareto criterion is that it requires explicit consideration of a policy's distributional consequences. Individuals are assumed to have the same marginal rate of income substitution (Bergson 1980) within income groups, but differences in the marginal rate across groups necessitate group-specific comparisons. Two special cases of the test are also of interest. On one extreme, if all individuals have homothetic preferences and the marginal rate of income substitution is constant across income groups, the test collapses to the standard Barone-Kaldor-Hicks test. On the other hand, if individuals are unique and noncomparable, the test is the same as the Pareto criterion requiring no one to be worse off as the result of a policy change (i.e., unanimity).

The quasi-Pareto criterion also provides a more objective basis for evaluating the distributional value judgments that enter a policy analysis. In contrast to the standard compensation test practice of assuming constant marginal income effects for surplus calculations and ignoring distributional effects, proper implementation of the quasi-Pareto criterion would require a direct assessment of group-specific income effects and explicit reporting of distributional consequences. In addition, more encompassing welfare criteria such as Willig's (1981) social welfare dominance criterion (which might have been renamed "Welfare Economics Without Apology") can be evaluated using the same information output from the analysis. Alternatively, this information could be used in conjunction with different distributional weights (Little 1957) to determine the policy implications of preferential rates of income substitution across groups. These additional analytical exercises would heed the spirit of Ladd's (1983) call for "efficient reporting" about value judgments in economic research.

It is remarkable that a profession caught in controversy over "data mining" (Lovell 1983) and "trying to take the con out of econometrics" (Leamer 1983) has given so little attention to the value judgments inherent in efficiency analysis. How often have you seen an analysis of a proposed policy change in which the surplus measures are calculated using a single approximating formula based on the "best fit" demand and supply curves? Have we really reduced value judgments to simple arithmetic formulas? Can we really claim that this type of analysis is consistent with the spirit of the scientific method?

OTHER PERFORMANCE OBJECTIVES AND FOOD POLICY

The strong empiricist flavor of these suggestions and criticisms applies with equal validity to considerations of noncommodity values and objectives in agricultural and food policy. The preceding discussion highlights some of the difficulties in evaluating these other objectives within the traditional normative science framework. Yet it is surprising how vigorously the profession holds up the efficiency norm as the criterion for the good of public policy. It is a bit like the old joke about the man searching under a streetlight who answers a passerby's question that he is looking for the watch he knows he lost one block away. When asked why he continues to look for it here, he replies, "Because the light is better." Indeed, Pareto (1935, 1413) himself, the namesake for most contemporary efficiency jargon, chided the economists of his own day for

> . . . obstinately (trying) to get from their science alone the materials they know are needed for a closer approximation to fact; whereas they should resort to other sciences and go into them thoroughly—not just incidentally—for their bearing on the given economic problem. Many economists are paying no attention to such interrelations, for mastery of them is a long and fatiguing task requiring an extensive knowledge of facts; whereas anyone with a little

imagination, a pen, and a few reams of paper can relieve himself of a chat on "principles."

The history of food policy in the United States reveals a deep concern for noncommodity objectives. The policy decisions that shaped the current food distribution and regulatory system clearly reflect a commitment to solve basic economic and social problems that were quite distinct from other sectors of the economy. Certainly there are no other regulatory agencies like USDA in Washington, D.C.!

It is a legitimate task for agricultural economists to question whether the policy concerns and objectives of a prior period are relevant for the contemporary economy. It is an equally legitimate task—no, it is a responsibility—that economists also consider how the policy concerns and objectives of today are addressed in their policy prescriptions. Agricultural and food policy is inextricably linked to general social policy in the modern welfare state. Narrow economic concepts and considerations, even those employed along with a broader concept of the range of economic transactions, are not likely to be decisive on matters of policy. Quite simply, an artistic economist must also be a good social philosopher.

An earlier generation of economists spent a great deal of time and effort trying to work out a framework of workable competition that reconciled the abstract world of perfect competition with the real world of industrial policy (Sosnick 1958). Considering the numerous other performance objectives that limit the policy effectiveness of traditional efficiency analysis, perhaps we should direct our attention to a theory of workable regulation for agriculture and the food system.

NOTES

1. The literature on these subjects is so voluminous that one can do no more than cite key works. On sports and traffic rules, see Wittman (1982); on marriage, see Becker (1973); on criminal justice, see Becker (1968); on litigation, see Posner (1973); on politics, see Mueller (1979); and on government administration, see Atkinson and Stiglitz (1980).
2. These "other" criteria are quite encompassing. My original charge from Dick Kilmer suggested I address: equity, quality, legality, administrative feasibility, growth, and technological progress.
3. The term "value judgment" causes great difficulty in the profession so to avoid ambiguity I adopt Nagel's (1967, 76) description: "Value judgments as commonly understood in moral philosophy are statements expressing a reasoned approval (or disapproval) of something by someone in the light of deliberation concerning what is desirable."
4. The distinction is sometimes labeled "pure" and "applied" welfare economics but this implies that the latter is simply an application of the former. The next

section will argue that this commonly held view is incorrect since the underlying assumptions are different.

5. It is important to note that the form of the compensation test differs from that developed by Hicks (1939). Conceptually the test is the sum of *individual* compensating and equivalent variations, not consumers' and producers' surpluses. The net surplus definition is technically correct only when consumers have homothetic preference functions with constant marginal utility of income and producers are homogeneous.

6. Blaug (1978, 702) also questions some of the qualitative value of abstract assumptions that obscure reality: "A moment's reflection, therefore, will show that a great many neoclassical theories are empty from the viewpoint of the 'qualitative calculus'; unless they are fed with more facts to further restrict the relevant functions, they tell us only that equilibrium is what equilibrium must be."

7. The terms productive and allocative efficiency represent firm and market level analyses, respectively, as defined by Kilmer and Armbruster (1984). Economic efficiency refers to applications of the compensation test criterion in public policy. This differs from use of the term in Lang (1980) who equates economic efficiency with Pareto efficiency. I believe the two terms should be distinct since the latter correctly denotes unanimity.

8. An overview of theoretical approaches to agricultural contracts is provided in Eswaran and Kotwal (1985).

9. Several recent publications summarize the conceptual and practical issues in morbidity and mortality valuation. A review and evaluation of labor market studies is provided in Viscusi (1983). Violette and Chesnut (1983) summarize the literature on mortality valuation, and Chesnut and Violette (1984) evaluate the state of the art in morbidity valuation. Smith et al. (1985) report the results of recent research on valuation of health risk reductions.

10. Some agencies do use a risk-benefit analysis for regulatory decisions but this approach is very different from cost-benefit analysis.

11. Rausser (1982, 822) describes rent-seeking activities as,

> . . . ways of generating income by undertaking activities which are directly unproductive, i.e., they yield pecuniary returns but do not produce *goods or services* that enter a utility function directly or indirectly via increased production or availability to the economy of goods that enter a utility function. Insofar as such activities use real resources, they result in a contraction of the availability set open to the economy. (Emphasis added.)

12. See the symposium on dairy policy reform in the *American Journal of Agricultural Economics,* December 1984.

13. Senauer (1985) argues that food stamps and income transfers also do not have the same economic impact on consumer food purchases. Davis (1982) makes a similar point with regard to nutrition.

14. Inadequate investment in basic research and weak political power by agricultural interests are frequently cited as primary problems in countries with poor agricultural performance.

15. Formally the test can be described as: For all individuals i defined as members of income group $j = 1, \ldots, J$, a policy is a social welfare improvement if and only if $(CV_j > - CV_j)$ for all j and CV is the compensating variation measure of gains and losses. The test is a sufficient, not a necessary, condition for a welfare improvement.

REFERENCES

Akerlof, G. "The Market for 'Lemons': Quality Uncertainty and the Market Mechanism." *Q. J. Econ.* 84(1970):487–500.
Atkinson, Anthony B., and Joseph E. Stiglitz. *Lectures on Public Economics.* New York: McGraw-Hill, 1980.
Barkley, Paul W. "Rethinking the Mainstream: Discussion." *Am. J. Agric. Econ.* 66 (1984):798–801.
Becker, Gary. "Crime and Punishment: An Economic Approach." *J. Polit. Econ.* 76 (1968):169–90.
———. "A Theory of Marriage: Part I." *J. Polit. Econ.* 81(1973):813–35.
Bergson, Abram. "Consumer's Surplus and Income Redistribution." *J. Public Econ.* 14(1980):31–47.
Blaug, Mark. *Economic Theory in Retrospect,* 3d ed. Cambridge, England: Cambridge University Press, 1978.
Bockstael, Nancy E. "The Welfare Implications of Minimum Quality Standards." *Am. J. Agric. Econ.* 66(1984):466–71.
Bromley, Daniel W. "Land and Water Problems: An Institutional Perspective." *Am. J. Agric. Econ.* 64(1982):834–44.
Buchanan, James M. *The Limits of Liberty: Between Anarchy and Leviathan.* Chicago: University of Chicago Press, 1975.
Caldwell, Bruce J., and A. W. Coats. "The Rhetoric of Economists: A Comment on McCloskey." *J. Econ. Lit.* 22(1984):575–78.
Chesnut, L. G., and D. M. Violette. *Estimates of Willingness to Pay for Pollution-Induced Changes in Morbidity: A Critique for Benefit-Cost Analysis of Pollution Regulation.* Washington, D.C.: Report to the Office of Policy Analysis, U.S. Environmental Protection Agency, Sept. 1984.
Cheung, Steven N. G. "A Theory of Price Control." *J. Law Econ.* 17(1974):53–71.
Clark, Edwin H., II, Jennifer A. Haverkamp, and William Chapman. *Eroding Soils: The Off-Farm Impacts.* Washington, D.C.: The Conservation Foundation, 1985.
Cochrane, Willard W. "Some Nonconformist Thoughts on Welfare Economics and Commodity Stabilization Policy." *Am. J. Agric. Econ.* 62(1980):508–11.
Cooter, Robert, and Peter Rappoport. "Were the Ordinalists Wrong About Welfare Economics?" *J. Econ. Lit.* 22(1984):507–30.
Davis, Carlton G. "Linkages Between Socioeconomic Characteristics, Food Expenditure Patterns, and Nutritional Status of Low Income Households: A Critical Review." *Am. J. Agric. Econ.* 64(1982):1017–25.
Elkin, Stephen L. "Regulation as a Political Question." *Policy Sciences* 18(1985):95–108.
Eswaran, Mukesh, and Ashok Kotwal. "A Theory of Contractual Structure in Agriculture." *Am. Econ. Rev.* 75(1985):352–67.
Farrell, Maurice J. "The Measurement of Productive Efficiency." *J. Royal Stat. Soc.* 120(1957):253–81.
French, Ben C. "Fruit and Vegetable Marketing Orders: A Critique of the Issues and State of Analysis." *Am. J. Agric. Econ.* 64(1982):916–23.
Friedman, Milton. "The Methodology of Positive Economics." *Essays in Positive Economics,* ed. M. Friedman, pp. 3–43. Chicago: University of Chicago Press, 1935.
Gardner, Bruce. "Structuring Incentives for Change in U.S. Farm Programs." *Am. J. Agric. Econ.* 67(1985):336–40.
Gilder, George. *Wealth and Poverty.* New York: Simon and Schuster, 1979.
Goldberg, Victor P. "The Economics of Product Safety and Imperfect Information." *Bell J. Econ.* 5(1974):683–88.
Hicks, John R. "The Foundations of Welfare Economics." *Econ. J.* 49(1939):696–712.
Ippolito, Pauline, and Richard A. Ippolito. "Measuring the Value of Life Saving from Consumer Reactions to New Information." *J. Public Econ.* 25(1984):53–81.
Johnson, A. C., and E. V. Jesse. "Congress and the Capper-Volstead Act: Undue Price Enhancement." *Agric. Law J.* 3(1981):230–61.

Just, Richard E., Darrell L. Hueth, and Andrew Schmitz. *Applied Welfare Economics and Public Policy.* Englewood Cliffs: Prentice-Hall, 1982.

Kaldor, Nicholas. "Welfare Propositions of Economics and Interpersonal Comparisons of Utility." *Econ. J.* 49(1939):549–52.

Kelman, Stephen. "A Case for In-Kind Transfers, or: Policy Analysis, Meet Moral Philosophy." Kennedy School of Government, Harvard University, 1983.

Keynes, John Neville. *Scope and Method of Political Economy.* 4th ed. London: Macmillan, 1917.

Kilmer, Richard L., and Walter J. Armbruster. "Methods for Evaluating Economic Efficiency in Agricultural Marketing." *South. J. Agric. Econ.* 16(1984):101–9.

Kopp, Raymond J. "The Measurement of Productive Efficiency: A Reconsideration." *Q. J. Econ.* (1981):477–503.

Kuttner, Robert. *The Economic Illusion: False Choices Between Prosperity and Social Justice.* New York: Houghton Mifflin, 1985.

Ladd, George W. "Value Judgments and Efficiency in Publicly Supported Research." *South. J. Agric. Econ.* 15(1983):1–7.

Lang, Mahlon G. "Economic Efficiency and Policy Comparison." *Am. J. Agric. Econ.* 62(1980):772–77.

Leamer, Edward. "Let's Take the Con Out of Econometrics." *Am. Econ. Rev.* 73(1983):31–43.

Lerner, Abba P. "The Economics and Politics of Consumer Sovereignty." *Am. Econ. Rev.* 62(1972):261–68.

Little, I. M. D. *A Critique of Welfare Economics.* London: Oxford University Press, 1957.

Lovell, Michael C. "Data Mining." *Rev. Econ. Stat.* 45(1983):1–12.

McCloskey, Donald N. "The Rhetoric of Economics." *J. Econ. Lit.* 21(1983):481–517.

Mishan, E. J. "The Implications of Alternative Foundations for Welfare Economics." *De Economist* 132(1984):76–85.

Mueller, Dennis C. *Public Choice.* Cambridge, England: Cambridge University Press, 1979.

Murrell, Peter. "The Economics of Sharing: A Transactional Cost Analysis of Contractual Choice in Farming." *Bell J. Econ.* 14(1983):283–93.

Nagel, Ernest. "Preference Evaluation and Reflective Choice." *Human Values and Economic Policy,* ed. S. Hook, pp. 73–84. New York: New York University Press, 1967.

Ng, Yew-Kwang. "Quasi-Pareto Social Improvements." *Am. Econ. Rev.* 74(1984):1033–50.

Olson, Mancur. *The Rise and Decline of Nations.* New Haven, Conn.: Yale University Press, 1982.

Pareto, Vilfredo. *The Mind and Society.* New York: Harcourt, Brace, 1935.

Penn, J. B. "Agricultural Structural Issues and Policy Alternatives for the Late 1980s." *Am. J. Agric. Econ.* 66(1984):572–76.

Philbrook, Clarence E. " 'Realism' in Policy Espousal." *Am. Econ. Rev.* 43(1953):846–59.

Pokorny, D. "Smith and Walrus: Two Theories of Science." *Can. J. Econ.* 11(1978):475–90.

Pollak, Robert A. "A Transactions Cost Approach to Families and Households." *J. Econ. Lit.* 23(1985):581–608.

Posner, Richard A. *Economic Analysis of Law.* Boston: Little, Brown, 1973.

Rausser, Gordon C. "Political Economic Markets: PERTs and PESTs in Food and Agriculture." *Am. J. Agric. Econ.* 64(1982):821–33.

Robbins, Lionel. *An Essay on the Nature and Significance of Economic Science.* London: Macmillan, 1935.

Senauer, Benjamin. "Food Program Policy Initiatives in an Era of Farm Surpluses: Discussion." *Am. J. Agric. Econ.* 67(1985):354–55.

Smith, V. Kerry, William H. Desvousges, and A. Myrick Freeman, III. *Valuing Changes in Hazardous Waste Risks: A Contingent Valuation Analysis.* Vol. 1. Washington, D.C.: Draft Interim Report to the Economic Analysis Division, U.S. Environmental Protection Agency, Feb. 1985.

Sosnick, Stephen. "A Critique of Concepts of Workable Competition." *Q. J. Econ.* 72(1958):380–423.

Stigler, George J. "Comment." *Studies in Public Regulation,* ed. G. Fromm, pp. 73–77. Cambridge, Mass.: MIT Press, 1981.

Stuart, Charles. "Consumer Protection in Markets with Informationally Weak Buyers." *Bell J. Econ.* 12(1981):562–73.

Tarascio, Vincent J. "Paretian Welfare Theory: Some Neglected Aspects." *J. Pol. Econ.* 77(1969):1–20.

Thomson, J. A. K. *The Ethics of Aristotle.* New York: Penguin Classics, 1976.

Violette, D. M., and L. G. Chesnut. *Valuing Reductions in Risks: A Review of the Empirical Estimates.* Washington, D.C.: Report to the Economic Analysis Division, U.S. Environmental Protection Agency, June 1983.

Viscusi, W. K. *Risk by Choice: Regulating Health and Safety in the Workplace.* Cambridge, Mass.: Harvard University Press, 1983.

Von Weizsacker, C. Christian. "The Costs of Substitution." *Econometrica* 52(1984):1085–116.

Willig, Robert D. "Social Welfare Dominance." *Am. Econ. Rev.* 71(1981):200–204.

Wittman, D. "Efficient Rules in Highway Safety and Sports Activity." *Am. Econ. Rev.* 72(1982):78–90.

The Science and Art
of Efficiency Analysis:
The Role of Other
Performance Criteria

A DISCUSSION

Emerson M. Babb

MILON BEGINS by exploring the relationship between efficiency analysis and welfare economics. It is difficult to argue with his conclusion that "efficiency analysis is simply 'welfare economics' and that our interpretation of 'welfare' inevitably requires value judgments." We should heed his call to broaden our measurement of efficiency beyond commodity values. While other performance criteria and social objectives are mentioned, the focus of Milon's suggested changes relates to equity or distributional issues. It would be desirable to develop similar theoretical bases for other criteria, such as growth and quality, and to describe approaches to their measurement. This would facilitate the broadening of performance analysis.

Milon examines assumptions and value judgments inherent in conventional analyses of production, allocative, and economic efficiency. While much of this material is not new, it is an excellent summary of problems with efficiency evaluation. More specific suggestions about ways to expand the scope of efficiency analysis might have been mentioned. For example, ignoring external effects has been a major criticism of studies of production efficiency. It may be possible to use both private and public costs for such inputs as water in evaluating production efficiency. If we are mindful of the shortcomings of traditional efficiency analysis, we may avoid some of the justified criticism of our work and enhance its usefulness to the public.

Milon briefly mentions the need for disaggregated analysis in the context of better understanding distributional consequences. Too frequently we assume that transactions occur at a single point in space or time and ignore real temporal and spatial considerations. A finding of price discrimination in fact may be the result of our not including relevant

EMERSON M. BABB is professor, Department of Agricultural Economics, Purdue University, West Lafayette, Indiana.

transportation and storage costs. It would be useful to conduct research to provide guidelines about aggregation effects. How large do differences in demand and supply elasticities among regions or time periods have to be before one obtains significant biases from aggregation? What problems result from aggregating areas with different production, processing, marketing, and transportation costs? What biases might be associated with aggregating areas in which production or consumption densities are quite different? Aggregation could result in erroneous measurement of efficiency. Alternatively, our quantitative measure may be correct on average, but inaccurate for most regions or time periods. It should not be too difficult to gain better insights into the consequences of combining nonhomogeneous units through research on aggregation under conditions we might encounter.

We tend to choose optimization models for analysis. The difficulty of incorporating multiple objectives into such models may be one reason for the restricted scope of our efficiency analyses. We need to consider the gains and losses of using optimization procedures, in which typically a single objective is imposed, versus simulation, in which objectives do not have to be specified in advance. Simulation can be used to generate a wide array of policy consequences or performance criteria. Those affected can then evaluate choices on the basis of their own objective functions. The researcher does not have to determine weights to be assigned various objectives or use the defense that a policy is "good." This approach would permit us to be good economists without necessarily being good social philosophers. Greater use of simulation probably would produce results that would quantify more of the "other performance criteria" that are of interest to the public. Decision makers may be exposed to outcomes and criteria they had not considered previously. They may understand better the trade-offs among performance criteria. This may reduce suboptimization and increase the understanding of the position taken by competing interest groups. At a minimum, people will appreciate information that permits them to improve their welfare, even if utility or net income is not maximized.

Milon points out that there is less than complete agreement about the impacts of special interest groups. Regardless of our assessment of whether their actions have positive or negative value, they are not likely to disappear in the foreseeable future and they do influence policies. We should thus pursue some of Milon's research suggestions regarding interest groups. One approach to such research is that of experimental economics. A large literature on market experiments involving individual decision makers has emerged, but there is almost a complete void of research using competing groups as the unit of analysis. Many of the market experiments have used the prisoner's dilemma framework, which would be appropriate to model regulatory and legislative environments in which special interest groups compete. The prisoner's dilemma has only conceptual value for field research, but it can be used directly in experiments.

One experimental study, which used competing groups of subjects, analyzed bids for public goods (Quesnel et al. 1985). That study examined the effectiveness of demand revealing mechanisms in retarding free rider behavior among members of competing groups in which group size, rewards, and types of public good were varied. Similar research could be conducted that would compare behavior of competing groups with that of individual decision makers. Would public policies be different if there were no special interest groups? These behavioral comparisons could be analyzed under conditions in which factors such as levels of information, socioeconomic composition of the groups, and directness of rewards/penalties were varied. In fact, it would be useful to analyze the outcomes of decisions made by competing groups in more traditional experiments of market economies. Groups are often involved in choices made by firms, public agencies, and even households.

Milon's critique of efficiency analysis is especially valuable at a conceptual level. His introductory comment that he would address some basic changes in the scope and practice of efficiency analysis that would remedy problems related to assumptions and value judgments really got my attention. I expected too much. It was unreasonable to think that Milon would provide remedies for all the problems in analyzing efficiency that he described. The equivalent of several professional careers has been spent toiling in this vineyard. Milon's suggestions about distributional impacts and the comparison of gains and losses within income groups are important contributions to putting efficiency analysis on a less value-dependent footing. As we design research, interpret our findings, or examine the work of others, we need to keep Milon's comments in mind.

REFERENCES

Quesnel, F. N., E. T. Loehman, and E. M. Babb. *Factors Affecting Bidding for Public Goods by Competing Groups*. Dept. of Agric. Staff Paper 85-8, Purdue University, July 1985.

CHAPTER 4

Does the Concept of Economic Efficiency Meet the Standards for Truth in Labeling When Used as a Norm in Policy Analysis?

James D. Shaffer

ONE OF THE PROBLEMS in discussing economic efficiency is the different meanings implied by the way the term is used and measured. As used by economists, the term ranges in meaning from the seemingly simple notion of the ratio of output to input to the complex and esoteric notion of the maximization of total welfare allegedly flowing from an economy meeting the conditions of the perfect market ideal.

As generally used by economists, efficiency is a normative concept. It is posited as a measure of benefits to costs. It is set as a standard for performance. Failure to meet the standard is labeled inefficient. It carries the connotation of ought. The most efficient means, program, method, firm, or economy is implied to be the best. And efficiency is implied to be an objective measure, perhaps even scientific. While it is accepted that desiring to achieve the optimum allocation of resources or to minimize costs is a value judgment, and it is suggested that other goals may have merit, *it is not made clear that judgments about rights and equity are presumed in the measure of efficiency*.

I am not particularly concerned about the use of efficiency as a norm in informing private economic decisions, although the use of static efficiency concepts in a complex, dynamic, uncertain world may result in poor private advice. Important costs or outputs may be left out of the

JAMES D. SHAFFER is professor, Department of Agricultural Economics, Michigan State University, East Lansing. The following people provided useful comments on an earlier draft: Warren Samuels, Allan Schmid, Donald Ricks, John Staatz, and James Oehmke.

analysis. Minimum cost feed rations, minimum cost assembly routes, identification of potentials for profitable arbitrage and storage, optimum size and location of plants, etc., are based upon an efficiency concept and not only can serve the private advisee, but probably enhance the wealth of the nation, although we cannot be sure of the latter.

EVALUATING POLITICAL RIGHTS

My concern is rather with the use of economic efficiency norms in political discourse; that is, with the notion that an economist can offer objective professionally authoritative information in support of or in opposition to a particular definition of rights embodied in a regulation, policy, or program based upon an argument that such a definition of rights contributes to efficiency or inefficiency. What can economists legitimately say in informing policy based upon the economic concepts of efficiency? Would statements evaluating policy in terms of economic efficiency hold up in an evidentiary hearing involving careful cross-examination? Would the way we usually present our policy arguments meet the test of honesty in labeling?

I recall the response of a judge after cross-examination of an economist expert witness who had used the usual hypothetical supply and demand curves to make a point: "You mean you just made that up?"

My argument is elementary, fundamental, and generally accepted by economists, yet often ignored by economists in political discourse or in presenting policy-related analysis involving efficiency criteria. Simply put, the argument is that *the economic efficiency criterion of welfare economics, based upon the perfectly competitive model as a norm, is inappropriate for judging rights, including regulations, laws, policy, and public programs.*[1] The basis for such judgments does not exist within the theory. Efficiency criterion must assume certain rights as given. It is only on the basis of assumptions about whose interests count in determining costs and the definition of products that conclusions about economic efficiency can be made. It is simply not logical to assume selected institutions and an existing distribution of wealth as given, and then to use the perfect market norm to conclude that a particular change in rights, which affects that distribution, reduces welfare.[2] This is a judgment that one set of rights and one distribution of income is better than another. It is no different than arguing that economists have a superior capacity to decide on the proper distribution of income. In this respect it can be argued that, as a criterion for evaluating policy, economists have as much to say about equity as they do efficiency.

Pareto optimality, the criterion for judging a change in policy set forth in welfare economics, which argues that someone is made better off by an action while no one is made worse off, is a very strict one. Without passing this test we cannot be sure that the change resulted in an increase in the ratio of value of output to the cost of inputs. The problem is that Pareto optimality is so strict a test that it is difficult to find a significant policy change that could pass the test. Holding to this rule would simply support the status quo. Pareto-optimal changes generally can be accomplished through private negotiation. Politics deals with non-Pareto-optimal changes.

The notion that the test should be that those made better off be enough better off that they could compensate all losers to make them as well off as before the change is a ploy of little practical value. Surely it is meaningful only if the compensation is actually made. And the problems of assessing benefits and damages to individuals and the costs involved in making compensation transactions are both practically and conceptually difficult. How, for example, would the damages to individuals who lose jobs and the sense of self-worth as a result of the elmination of a trade barrier be determined? If we ask the loser, the incentive will be to exaggerate the value of the loss, and, without the self-report, an external subjective evaluation is required. Such a judgment can be made, but economists have no special basis to provide superior value judgments.

I assume that there are few economists who would claim that there is a basis within economic theory supporting or rejecting policies based upon their consistency with the characteristics of the perfect market ideal. In fact an economist would be hard pressed to describe the unique set of rights that is assumed as a precondition for the ideal market because the theory simply assumes an existing set of property rights to be given. Rights are a political problem.

OUTPUT/INPUT RATIO

If the efficiency criterion derived from the perfect market ideal is inappropriate for evaluating rights (i.e., policy), what can economists say about the seemingly simpler concept of efficiency as simply the ratio of output over inputs? If a change in policy can be shown to increase output at the same input or to produce the same output at a lower input, is not that evidence in favor of the change in policy?

Perhaps. However, most of the same problems exist as with the perfect market norm. If someone is harmed even though the ratio is increased, a judgment involving equity is required. But in this case can the economist inform policymakers of the magnitude of the efficiency gains or losses and the related changes in income distribution and let the political system decide the trade-offs between equity and efficiency? Probably not, since almost any policy relevant measure of efficiency is based upon a preexisting set of rights. To measure efficiency gains or losses requires the measurement of inputs and outputs. Economic relevance requires that analysis be in terms of value of output and costs of inputs. But rights determine costs, costs determine shares in income distribution, and income distribution is an important determinant of the value of output. The system of rights determines what is taken into account in determining costs and in counting and valuing output. Prices always reflect the rules of the game and efficiency measures require valuation. Thus it would seem we are back to a judgment that one set of rules or rights is better than another. But economists have opted out of that arena by arguing that rights are a political issue. Or have they done so when they use an efficiency measure to inform policy decisions? Truth in labeling requires that we not gloss over these difficulties in presenting analysis to inform policy.

RIGHTS VERSUS INTERVENTIONS

Let me extend the argument. While most economists would accept these basic notions, the economic literature is full of discussion of market distortions and inefficiencies caused by market interventions. Somehow a distinction is made between a set of rights taken as given, legitimate, or necessary for markets to work and those labeled as interventions. How are these different?

What, for example, is the fundamental difference between the set of rights that sanctions the corporation, including granting it the rights of a person in regard to the Fourteenth Amendment and stockholders' limited liability, and those establishing a marketing order that allows a group of growers to manage supply of a commodity they produce? The corporation is an institution of collective action that has enormous influence on the allocation of resources and the distribution of income and power. I have never seen the rights that sanction a corporation as a person referred to as a market intervention. Decisions by a corporation regarding how much to produce and at which price to sell are usually considered private decisions; to restrict the perceived private decisions is considered intervention. If the government specifies a price support or price control it is labeled a market intervention and is challenged as being inefficient.

By contrast, a marketing order with a supply management provision is perceived as a market intervention. If an estimate can be made of the amount by which the price exceeds that which would theoretically have resulted under perfect competition, then the extent of the inefficiency caused by the intervention is said to be measured. Can we say that any right that influences prices is a market intervention? If so, then the rights establishing corporations would clearly be market interventions, as would laws of liability, land ownership, etc. If there is another criterion, what is it?

Economically relevant rights affect what has to be taken into account in production and consumption—i.e., costs and prices. Are all economically relevant rights (regulations) market interventions? How are we to explain this selective perception so frequently practiced in policy discourse?

Some economists would like to separate equity and efficiency. But is that possible? The most important factor in costs and thus prices is payment of wages and salaries, which amount to more than 80 percent of payments to all factors of production in the U.S. economy. Would any economist argue that individual wages and salaries are measures of individual contributions to total output? Surely the output of an economy depends on the accumulated knowledge embedded in the workers, tools, and facilities as well as the organization of the economy, not simply on the uninformed effort of individuals. Note the output of workers in knowledge-poor countries. How is ownership of this accumulated knowledge determined? The rules for appropriation, use, and distribution of the benefits of this accumulated knowledge have a significant part in determining compensation, prices, and demand and thus the level and mix of output. The rules that sanction the corporation and marketing orders are only examples of a very large set. Clearly the rules determining shares in the output cannot be separated from the rules for resource allocation. They are the same rules.

Take, for example, a few of the rules that facilitate the claim of a young athlete for $30 million for five years of playing basketball. First is the height of the basket. I am reminded of the response of a local coach to the question of what rule change would make his team of short players competitive. He said the only thing he could think of was to move the basket down to the level of a hole in the floor. A rule specifies that a TV station does not have access to the images of the game by simply purchasing a ticket to the game, but must purchase the rights. And the TV stations have exclusive rights to a limited number of frequencies for transmitting the images. It is these and other rights that result in the $30 million offer and, in turn, influence demand and prices. Another set of rules, including those sanctioning the corporation, facilitated the appropriation of $100 million by the 170 top-paid executives in the U.S. auto industry in 1984. How do these rules differ from those establishing a marketing order? Shares determine costs and costs determine prices.

In *Equality and Efficiency—The Big Trade-off,* Arthur Okun (1975,

48), a liberal economist of high repute, makes a statement representing a belief not uncommon among economists as well as many others in our society: "Any insistence on carving the pie into equal slices would shrink the size of the pie. That fact poses the tradeoff between economic equality and economic efficiency." The argument is that in the pursuit of the equality goal, society would forego any opportunity to use material rewards as incentives to production. Okun continues, "And that would lead to inefficiencies that would be harmful to the welfare of the majority."

In this context what does efficiency mean? Surely to achieve equality in income distribution, a very different set of rights would be required than now exists. Is there anything in our theory to support the proposition that one of these sets of rights is superior to the other? Not in the pure theory of welfare economics. The conclusion derives from a pragmatic observation that material incentives are useful in promoting work and that well-being is related to what and how much is produced. Note that the argument is that the majority will be better off, not that all will be. It also implicitly recognizes the market as a system of discipline or coercion. As a disciplinary system, the market dispenses rewards and punishments as participants respond to preferences expressed through transactions in markets and through the political process. The market is an institution for blending preferences expressed politically in establishing rights with preferences expressed through market transactions in disciplining economic activity. Determining the mix of market and political processes for articulating preferences is central to the policy process. The pure theory of neoclassical microeconomics with its counterfactual assumptions cannot inform the decisions on the proper expression of political preferences in establishing rights. What would be useful in informing such decisions would be empirical evidence about the consequences of different patterns of rights that institute markets.

How could Okun's (1975) basic proposition be tested empirically? I would suggest that such a test is impossible in the context of neoclassical theory. It would be impossible to prove that an equal distribution of income would reduce welfare (i.e., would be less efficient) since we could not prove that any loss in physical output resulting from the loss of incentives would not be offset by the value of leisure or the pleasure of doing what one pleases with one's resources. Does the argument sound familiar?

I suggest that it would be more honest labeling to substitute some measure of output, such as GNP, for the term efficiency in Okun's (1975) big trade-off. The empirical problem then becomes more obvious. We know the GNP does not include all output and that valuing outputs through time and space has many measurement problems.[3] But at least it makes sense to talk of trade-offs between some measure of output. Comparisons could be made between situations with more and less equal distributions of income. And the logic of casual empiricism relating incentives to output makes sense.

PRAGMATIC POLITICAL ECONOMICS

It does not make sense to me to consider the trade-off between economic efficiency, meaning the optimum allocation of resources, and other goals. What is the meaning, for example, of the trade-off between the optimum allocation of resources and the level of unemployment? To me, you cannot have unemployment and an optimum allocation of resources. Important costs and benefits have not been counted in the efficiency measure!

So what are we to do? Thurow (1983), after reviewing the state of economics, recently called for a reconstruction of economics based upon an understanding of real world behavior and conditions. I agree. To contribute more effectively to the policy dialogue, I suggest we abandon the myth that economists have the formula for the optimum allocation of resources and help to develop a pragmatic political economics.

I believe we should make it clear that the analysis and presentation of evidence in political economics is more akin to the preparation of evidence in a legal hearing than the practice of science as described by logical positivists (see McCloskey 1983). The pretense of rigor is false labeling.[4] The appropriate role for economists in the policy process, in my opinion, would be to help sort out and display the probable substantive consequences of different patterns of institutions for organizing economic activity. As a behavioral discipline, economics would attempt to explain the relationships between institutions and incentives, behavior, output, demand, and the distribution of benefits. The inseparability of the distribution of benefits and resource allocation would be explicit.[5]

Perhaps this sounds like Don Quixote charging windmills or straw men. Some of the chapter titles suggest an interest in reconstructing economics or at least modifying the efficiency concepts to make them more applicable to the dynamic, uncertain, political, and confusing world we live in. Applied economists tend to be pragmatic in practice, embroiled as they are in real world problems. I hope that a more realistic and useful theoretical foundation to help structure analysis will evolve out of the work of applied economists. I expect this book to contribute to that objective.

What I am suggesting will not give the appearance of rigor. Nor, perhaps, does it have the persuasive power of labeling selected policies as contributing to economic efficiency. But it would come closer to meeting the standard for truth in labeling.

NOTES

1. For a more formal presentation of the argument see Lang (1980). Also see Schmid (1978) (especially Chap. 11, 210ff.) and Samuels (1981).
2. It may be argued that Pareto optimality is the criterion and that economists have developed the concept of and specified the conditions of the perfect market as the means of achieving optimum welfare. Economists then use the model as the norm.
3. See, for example, Abramovitz (1959) for a discussion of the problems in evaluating welfare consequences from changes in national income and output accounts.
4. This recognizes that we do not have evidence from controlled experiments, that human behavior is too dynamic and complex to predict with certainty, and that some important variables are unobservable.
5. See Bromley (1982) for an elaboration of this point.

REFERENCES

Abramovitz, Moses. "The Welfare Interpretation of Secular Trends in National Income and Product." *The Allocation of Economic Resources,* pp. 1–22. Palo Alto, Calif.: Stanford University Press, 1959.
Bromley, D. W. "Land and Water Problems: An Institutional Perspective." *Am. J. Agric. Econ.* 64(1982):834–44.
Lang, Mahlon George. "Economic Efficiency and Policy Comparisons." *Am. J. Agric. Econ.* 62(1980):772–77.
McCloskey, Donald. "The Rhetoric of Economics." *Rev. Econ. Lit.* 21(1983):481–517.
Okun, Arthur M. *Equality and Efficiency—The Big Trade-off.* Washington, D.C.: Brookings Institution, 1975.
Samuels, Warren J. "Welfare Economics, Power and Property." *Law and Economics,* ed. W. J. Samuels and A. A. Schmid, pp. 9–75. Boston: Martinus Nijhoff, 1981.
Schmid, A. Allan. *Property Power and Public Choice.* New York: Praeger Publishers, 1978.
Thurow, Lester C. *Dangerous Currents.* New York: Random House, 1983.

CHAPTER 5

Comments on Economic Efficiency

Ben C. French

THIRTY YEARS AGO the University of Kentucky hosted Marketing Efficiency in a Changing Economy, the first national conference on marketing efficiency. Sponsored by the Joint Land-Grant College/USDA Committee on Training, it was attended by representatives from many state universities, federal agencies, and some state agencies. To the best of my knowledge, the symposium on which this book is based is only the second national conference with that emphasis. It may be of interest, therefore, to compare the thinking in the earlier conference with the concepts that have evolved over the succeeding 30 years.

EVOLUTION OF CONCEPTS

Although the participants in the 1955 conference recognized that efficiency is a complex concept, they nevertheless adopted a rather simple definition. In the workshop report (USDA 1955, 180) efficiency was defined as simply "the ratio of ends to resources." It was viewed as a single concept, but with many applications: "What makes the strategic difference between the indiviual and the group is the differing content each might give to ends and to the resources concerned." In particular, it was noted that the ends and resources relevant to efficiency may differ for the total economy, for total agriculture, for the industrial agricultural subsector, for the firm, and for the individual consumer. Among the ends identified as relevant to the examination of efficiency were freedom, security, stability (political, income, price), growth, output of goods and services,

BEN C. FRENCH is professor, Department of Agricultural Economics, University of California, Davis.

composition of output, and the distribution of output and income. It was further recognized that the analysis of efficiency must take into account legal, political, technological, health, religious, and other constraints imposed by society generally, and that what may be regarded as efficient at one level may be inefficient at another.

An important characteristic of the thinking in the earlier conference was a sort of client orientation—a willingness to focus on efficiency within a particular sector or group with minimal consideration of spillover effects on other groups. Although recognized, these effects were either ignored or thought to be of no great consequence. This may be contrasted with the more global view of efficiency in this book wherein the focus has been on aggregate social welfare. As we have seen, this adds greatly to the difficulty of making efficiency comparisons.

The emphasis on sector or subgroup efficiency continued to be the primary research focus for most of the first two decades following the enactment of the Agricultural Marketing Act of 1946 that made cost reduction and productivity improvement in the marketing system official policy goals. The idea that increased productivity could involve significant social costs as well as benefits began to emerge with the landmark paper by Schmitz and Seckler (1970) on the mechanical tomato harvester. The study applied welfare analysis to evaluate the social cost of labor displacement as well as the gains to producers and consumers. The concerns with social costs of increased productivity passed well beyond the theoretical level when, in January, 1979, the California Agrarian Action Project, a nonprofit corporation, and several individual farmworkers brought suit against the University of California, charging the university with misusing public funds for research that benefited only large agricultural interests while displacing farmworkers and small farmers. These charges were not levied directly at studies that might lead to labor displacement in marketing firms. That may have been only because such studies were not thought to have much real impact or because the possible impacts were not recognized. The suit was brought to trial in 1984 and, after the expenditure of substantial sums of money and time, it is now in limbo awaiting rulings by a judge on some procedural issues. I shall return to this case later.

A second way in which the discussions in this book have differed from the 1955 workshop is in the emphasis on second-best rather than first-best solutions and, along with this, repeated rejection of the competitive model as an efficiency standard. It would be easy to infer from this that the competitive model is now passé, with no real role to play in efficiency analysis. That would be wrong. Two illustrations follow.

First, in spatially and temporally separated markets in which arbitrage is possible, it seems reasonable to expect that prices (or price differences) will approximate a competitive norm even though many market participants may be imperfect competitors in other respects. Actual prices may deviate at any time from the perfectly competitive equilibrium values because of time and information lags in adjusting to profit incentives, but the competitive norm still may serve as a useful underlying standard.

Second, if we wish to evaluate the effect of a market coordinating mechanism such as a bargaining association or a marketing order program, the appropriate comparison is without the program in effect. The "without" alternative may or may not involve competitive behavior on the buyer side but is most likely to be close to the competitive model on the grower side. When uncertainties and time lags in adjustments are involved the competitive model will not necessarily be preferred, but that does not remove it as an important component of the system structure.

Finally, the most important way in which the discussions in this book differ from the conference held 30 years ago is the association of efficiency with welfare measurement rather than only with costs and prices. Most of the welfare concepts discussed here were not well developed at the time of the first efficiency conference.

MEASURING WELFARE

The first four chapters provide excellent summaries of the major concepts, issues, and limitations involved in measuring welfare or welfare change. I have classified the comments as falling into five schools of thought.

1. Those in the first school, which I shall call the Pope school, feel that welfare issues can be approached by adapting conventional economic analysis.

2. Those in the second school, which I shall call the Just school, feel that the conceptual methodology for measuring welfare under complex market situations is fairly well developed, but recognize that the data requirements become very great when realistic assumptions are incorporated. The members of this school paint a bleak picture of our abilities to generate appropriate and useful welfare measures for the difficult issues of a complex, dynamic, uncertain, multimarket world.

3. Members of the third school, which I will call the Milon school, feel that conventional efficiency analysis has little to offer. They argue that the issues must be viewed in the much broader context of social philosophy. They place great emphasis on performance objectives other than efficiency.

4. The fourth school, which I shall call the Rausser-Perloff-Zusman

school, encompasses some of each of the three previous schools, but adherents feel there is an urgent need to clarify and focus our view of economic efficiency and the implied operational measures. Their evaluations to this point tend to be more proscriptive than prescriptive.

5. Members of the fifth school, which I shall call the Shaffer school, reject the notion that the analysis followed by any of the first four schools can be used as a basis for judging the efficiency of regulations, laws, policies, and public programs. They argue that these regulations and policies are rights granted by a government authority and must be assumed to be given.

With the possible exception of the Pope school, the outlooks reflected in the several schools of thought are somewhat discouraging. In fact, the more pessimistic views might suggest possible reduction in employment opportunities among agricultural economists.

Perhaps surprisingly, it may turn out that an extension of the Shaffer school holds the most promise of leading us out of the mire. It seems reasonable to assume that when rights are granted, such as the right to establish a marketing order, the granting agency may have a very imperfect perception of all the consequences of granting that right. An important task for economists is to provide information to right-granting authorities that may be useful in evaluating their decisions. The evaluation might use any of several approaches, including estimates of social surplus, to generate information. But in the Shaffer school it would not be claimed that the findings showed that the regulation or policy was or was not "efficient" or desirable in a real sense. That would be left to the right-granting authority to decide.

USEFUL ANALYSIS

Following the Shaffer school of thought, even if we accept the most pessimistic views of the several other schools concerning welfare analysis, economists may still be able to provide some very useful analysis pertaining to the effects of granting various rights to various groups. These fall into three classes.

1. The formulation of conceptual models and the identification of the dimensions of the problem and performance criteria may be very helpful to right-granting agencies, even though empirical measurements may be lacking. The chapters in this book suggest that we have made considerable progress along these lines.

2. Quantitative models (with all their econometric limitations) may

be used to generate time paths or scenarios for prices, costs, output, and the like, with and without the right in effect. Simulations of this sort may be very useful even though no efficiency measures (social surplus computations) are involved.

3. Finally, we still may be able to make some useful surplus calculations. Here sensitivity analysis may play an important role in tesing the robustness of estimates (i.e., how well they hold up under alternative behavioral assumptions). The results should be reported in a form that attempts to show how various market participants may be affected, but without any claims as to revealed efficiency.

I suggest three problem areas in which the research orientation outlined above seems especially applicable and promising. These areas are illustrative rather than all-inclusive.

1. One of the arguments of the plaintiffs in the farm-mechanization suit against the University of California was that the university should be required to make social impact studies before undertaking research pertaining to agricultural mechanization. Potentially, this could be extended to research that might affect employment or other resource use in the agriculture marketing sector as well. For obvious reasons, the university has strongly resisted the idea that social impact studies be a precondition for undertaking any kind of research. This clearly would be a very great constraint on academic freedom. However, while I would not want social impact studies to be a precondition for other research, studies that evaluate potential dynamic impacts of new production or marketing technologies may indeed be a promising direction for marketing efficiency research. It would involve some marriage of econometric modeling with cost analysis and market structure evaluation and then the development of various scenarios for dynamic time paths. The findings could be very useful in anticipating potential adverse effects and suggesting means for their mitigation.

2. In his 1982 American Agricultural Economics Association (AAEA) presidential address, Leo Polopolus (1982, 808) stated, "There is a special need to reacquaint ourselves with firm-level problems beyond the farm gate." He based this conclusion, in part, on the relatively larger size of the food system beyond the farm gate and relatively poor productivity performance of the food marketing system. To achieve his goals he emphasized the need to develop theoretical frameworks that depart from the perfectly competitive model and suggested a "system economics" approach. Some of the concepts and concerns advanced in the preceding chapters no doubt would be relevant to Polopolus's modeling suggestions. There are, however, two possible impediments to the achievement of

Polopolus's goals: (1) concern on the part of some of our profession and some government agencies (value judgments) as to the appropriateness of further public support of research in this area, and (2) the problem of needed access to data and cooperation from the increasingly large and complex firms involved in the marketing system. A resurrection of something like the old National Commission on Food Marketing on a sustained basis might be needed for this to have any real impact.

3. The final area involves the evaluation of alternative market coordination and exchange systems. This includes government-sanctioned market control programs, bargaining arrangements and thin-market problems associated with decreasing numbers of market participants, and increasing use of various contracting and integrating arrangements. While there are many difficult empirical problems, we have already made some progress and I believe the issues are within the scope of our ability to develop useful economic models and associated performance measures.

REFERENCES

Polopolus, Leo. "Agricultural Economics Beyond the Farm Gate." *Am. J. Agric. Econ.* 64(1982):803–10.
Schmitz, Andrew, and David Seckler. "Mechanized Agriculture and Social Welfare: The Case of the Tomato Harvester." *Am. J. Agric. Econ.* 52(1970):569–77.
U.S. Department of Agriculture. *Marketing Efficiency in a Changing Economy.* Washington, D.C.: USDA AMS-60, Sept. 1955.

PART II

Concepts for Evaluating Economic Efficiency

The Economic Efficiency of Alternative Forms of Business Enterprise

Ronald W. Cotterill

The firm as production function needs to make way for the firm as governance structure if the ramifications of internal organization are to be accurately assessed (Williamson 1981, 1539).

AGRICULTURAL ECONOMISTS have not spent a significant amount of research effort analyzing how economic efficiency, or other dimensions of performance, vary among alternative forms of business enterprise. At a glance, the task of analyzing the efficiency of alternative enterprise forms may appear to require only a straightforward comparison of different businesses' performance for some commonly accepted measures of economic efficiency. Although this approach yields answers, it provides little guidance for private or public decision makers who wish to improve efficiency.

There is need for a theory that (1) relates business enterprise form, commonly described as organizational structure in the organization theory literature, to economic efficiency, and (2) recognizes the impact of other factors, some considerably more important than organizational form, upon the efficiency of a business enterprise. Rather than being straightforward, the task is a very complex one, as attested by the recent array of surveys and essays on the theory of the corporation (Caves 1980; Marris and Mueller 1981; Williamson 1981).

Identifying differences in organization involves more than compar-

RONALD W. COTTERILL is associate professor, Department of Agricultural Economics and Rural Sociology and Department of Business Environment and Policy, University of Connecticut, Storrs.

ing organization charts of functional activities within a corporation. There is a great diversity of corporate organizational forms in the food system. Investor-owned firms (IOFs), cooperatives, vertically integrated firms, conglomerates, joint ventures, franchise organizations, chain retailers, voluntary wholesale affiliated groups of independent retailers, and multinational firms are a few. Why are firms in the food system organized as they are? Do they contribute to an economically efficient organization of the food system?

This chapter reviews efforts to develop a comprehensive theory of business enterprise organization. Work from organization theorists, business policy and management researchers, and economists does suggest a common conceptual framework for analyzing the economic performance of firms. Given the focus of this book the analysis will be devoted to economic efficiency, a major dimension of performance. By way of preview, the following points will be established:

1. There exists no single most efficient organizational form.
2. It is possible to identify the conditions that determine which organizational form is most efficient in a given situation.
3. The efficiency properties of an organizational form may depend upon interaction with other organizational forms. Consider, for example, the competitive yardstick theory of cooperatives.
4. In heterogeneous product markets two or more efficient organizational forms can exist in equilibrium. Consider, for example, the coexistence of chain supermarkets, voluntary wholesale affiliated independents, cooperative wholesale affiliated independents, unaffiliated independents, chain convenience store operators, and mom-and-pop grocers in the retail grocery industry. Michael Porter's theory of strategic groups is instructive on this point (Porter 1980).
5. Empirical research on the efficiency/performance properties of different organizational forms will be most successful if pursued within the industrial organization/strategic marketing/business policy framework. This framework can be used to analyze issues in corporate planning as well as public policy (Caves 1980; Porter 1980, 1985).

The next section contains an eclectic review of the economists' approach to efficiency comparisons among organizations. It illustrates a range of approaches. The third section develops a theoretical framework for efficiency analysis. Following the lead of Caves (1980), industrial organization theory is merged with the contingency approach to organization theory (Lawrence and Lorsch 1967; Thompson 1967). Since 1973 contingency theory has provided a general framework for what was, and some would say still is, a confusing and often conflicting array of organizational theories of firm. The resulting conceptual framework is used to determine how to evaluate economic efficiency. Finally, potential research opportunities are identified.

ANTECEDENT RESEARCH

When addressing efficiency issues in the food system, agricultural economists have tended to examine cost performance at the plant rather than the firm level. Moreover, studies at both levels have primarily focused upon short- and long-run economies of scale in production. Other dimensions of economic efficiency include technical X-efficiency, spatial (plant location and transport) efficiency, product market pricing (allocative) efficiency, dynamic efficiency in operations such as a pear packing plant during harvest season, and, more recently, efficiencies related to multiproduct operations (economies of scope—Baumol et al. 1982). The comprehensive surveys by French (1977) and Helmberger et al. (1981) cover efforts by agricultural economists to measure efficiency in all except the last of these various dimensions.

The issue at hand cuts across this literature in a novel fashion. Here the intent is to analyze the impact of the organizational structure of a business enterprise upon economic efficiency, however measured. The organization and tasks of management have commonly entered neoclassical economic theory only as a vague explanation for decreasing returns at high levels of output in one or more efficiency dimensions. The bend in the U-shaped average cost curve, for example, usually is justified with no more than a few words on the problems of management coordination at high levels of output (Marris and Mueller 1981).

Liebenstein (1966, 413) introduced the question of organization to economists in another fashion with his theory of X-efficiency. He described X-efficiency as:

> Firms and economies do not operate on an outer-bound production possibility surface consistent with their resources. Rather they actually work on a production surface that is well within that outer bound. This means that for a variety of reasons people and organizations normally work neither as hard nor as effectively as they could.

Others have described this condition as organizational slack (Cyert and March 1963). The relationship between inputs and output, commonly described by the marginal product of a neoclassical production function, is a function of motivation and other organizational traits (Liebenstein 1966).

In competitive economies Liebenstein hypothesized that the need to pass the "market test" would force firms toward zero slack. The opposite result can occur in noncompetitive market structures such as oligopoly and monopoly. Liebenstein's own research and that of others (e.g., Parker and Connor 1979) suggests efficiency losses are significantly understated when measured only by allocative inefficiency (pricing above unit costs).

The research on X-inefficiency cited here relies upon aggregated industry data and for this reason, along with others, has been rigorously questioned. Agricultural economists have also used two less aggregate approaches to identify X-inefficiency. Production economists have examined plant level data using frontier production function models to determine the boundary of the production set (Kilmer and Armbruster 1984). Actual observed performance deviates from this efficient frontier in most cases and the deviation is interpreted as the amount of X-inefficiency.[1] Farrell (1957) introduced the frontier production function approach in 1957; however, as Boles (1980) has noted, it has not been widely used. He suggests that the lack of specialized quantitative programming packages for this type of analysis may be the limiting factor. The fact that it requires very detailed cost and production data may also limit its uses. To my knowledge this data-intensive, microanalytic approach has not been used to analyze X-efficiency of nonfarm firms in the food system. Moreover, plant level analysis cannot capture firm level management efficiency deviations in areas such as marketing, distribution, investment planning, and coordination among several divisions, each possibly with several plants producing different products. Using the frontier production function methodology to analyze corporate level management performance of a large multidivisional company like Beatrice or R. J. Reynolds is inappropriate.

Kelton (1983) examines the X-efficiency hypothesis in a more aggregate fashion than Farrell-type studies but in a more directed fashion than the Liebenstein (1966)/Harberger (1954) monopoly loss studies. She analyzes the relationship between market structure, wage levels, and productivity growth for 59 five-digit classes in food and tobacco manufacturing (Standard Industrial Classification [SIC] groups 20 and 21). Kelton finds that more highly concentrated food and tobacco product classes pay higher hourly wages, and that there are no increases in labor productivity within the concentrated sector to justify higher wage rates. One of the conclusions of Kelton's (1983, 2) study is, "The higher wage rates may be indicative of operational slack or technical (X) inefficiency, since oligopolistic firms may be under less pressure to minimize costs than competitive firms." Of course this input-specific approach cannot identify X-inefficiency related to other aspects of the firms' activities, such as excess capacity due to overinvestment or plush office environs and other executive perks.

All three approaches to measuring X-efficiency suffer a common shortcoming. They tend to treat the firm as a black box. Nowhere are particular organizational structures analyzed and related to particular efficiency levels. Another general approach that underlies a wide array of studies does just that. Annual operating performance statistics for the retail and wholesale grocery industry as reported by Cornell University and the Food Marketing Institute (FMI), for example, are split into subsamples by organization type; therefore, chain stores can be compared to independents, etc.

A second example of explicit organizational comparisons is the set of studies on cooperatives and investor-owned agribusiness firms completed at Purdue University during the 1980s (Schrader et al. 1985). Detailed comparisons were conducted in several dimensions of performance that relate to overall economic efficiency. Those dimensions include technical efficiency, the level of prices, financial performance as measured by different profit ratios (percent of sales, assets, net worth), asset turnover, leverage ratios, growth of the firm, and services provided.

Although the results of these studies are important, for present purposes the research designs employed are most relevant. These studies generally produced more than FMI/Cornell-type average efficiency measures for subgroups. Economic models relating efficiency to underlying product, firm, or market characteristics are often developed and statistically tested with analysis of variance or multiple regression methods.

The model of agribusiness firm growth by Chen et al. (1985) is an example of the Purdue work that squares well with the strategic planning/ business policy approach of this chapter. They analyzed how growth in ·sales and assets varied between cooperatives and investor-owned firms (IOFs) from 1975 to 1980. Regression models were estimated for a sample that included 32 of the top 100 agricultural marketing cooperatives, and 35 IOFs from the top 200 food and tobacco processing firms. The independent variables employed to explain growth were: profitability, diversification, mergers and acquisitions, advertising, the leverage factor, and initial firm size.

The IOFs were larger on average than the cooperatives, but cooperatives grew more rapidly during the 1975–1980 period. Although the factors included in the strategic growth models accounted for more than half the variation in growth, they did not explain a major share of the difference in growth of cooperatives and IOFs. Chen et al. conclude that "obviously some major factors associated with firm growth are not included. These factors are likely to be intangible and difficult to measure such as managerial capacity, organizational structure, degree of ownership by managers, and goals of managers and owners."

This identifies the research frontier facing agricultural economists who wish to evaluate not only the growth performance of firms, but also numerous other components of economic performance including economic efficiency.

THEORIES OF THE STRATEGIC ANALYSIS
OF ENTERPRISE ORGANIZATIONS AND MARKETS

Economists are familiar with market-based analysis of economic activity, so this discussion focuses first upon organization theory, and then endeavors to merge it with more familiar economic theory. It follows the lead of Richard Caves (1980) whose comprehensive analysis of the link between the organzational structure literature and the industrial organization analysis of markets establishes the legitimacy of this approach.

Progress in developing a general theory of organizations has proceeded in a fashion almost identical to the development of industrial organization theory. There is no lack of deductive theory. Rather there is a large variety of specialized theories starting from different environmental assumptions and normative value sets. Just as the industrial organization framework expanded from Mason's (1939) original plan through comprehensive case studies of individual industries and cross-section analysis of markets, the general tenets of organization theory have emerged from empirical research rather than deductive theory (Caves 1980). Thompson (1967) and Lawrence and Lorsch (1967), classics in the organization theory literature, solidified the empirical tradition of the field. Miles and Snow (1978) and Schendal and Hofer (1979) are more recent works that are highly respected by business policy researchers.

The basic issue at hand is how to manage a firm. *Strategy and Structure,* Chandler's (1962) pioneering and now classic book, definitively established the proposition that corporate management centers upon a two-step procedure. First the firm determines its strategy. It defines the business that it is in and its goals and objectives in the areas of profitability, growth, market share, social responsiveness, etc. Then it builds an organizational structure that enables the firms to implement the strategic plan in a least cost fashion. Since the 1960s organization theorists have built upon Chandler's dictum: strategy determines structure.

There are several general concepts that provide management guidance in their effort, for a given corporate strategy, to minimize the adminstrative cost of attaining the desired objectives. Lawrence and Lorsch (1967) describe the optimum organizational structure as one that attains an economic balance between differentiation and integration. Differentiation is the division of the management team into departments that take advantage of task specialization and small group dynamics to improve management productivity. Integration is establishing effective communication channels and information flow among the different departments so that all aspects of a firm's activities economically contribute to the stated strategic goals. Inadequate integration can lead to suboptimization within the organization.

Broadly defined, management information systems are a critical component in any organizational structure. Information is defined as any piece of knowledge that may rationally be applied to a decision by a person who has the authority and responsibility to make that decision (McGosh et al. 1978). All employees do not need to know everything about the firm to perform their jobs effectively. From the administrative viewpoint, therein lies the economizing power of large-scale organizations.

Three other related concepts that provide insight into the design of an efficient organization are control loss, opportunism, and bounded rationality (Caves 1980, Williamson 1975). As the chain of command in a hierarchy lengthens from top to bottom, top management finds itself in a position of bounded rationality. It does not know all that it needs to know to make decisions because there is control loss. More levels of middle management in the chain of command mean that messages get garbled passing up and down the hierarchy. Opportunism defined by Williamson as "self-interest with guile" is one reason why messages get garbled. Individuals within the organization often pursue their own personal agendas at the expense of the organization's stated objectives.

Given these basic concepts and criteria, how have social scientists developed explicit theories of organization? Lawrence and Lorsch (1967) identify four major schools of thought: (1) the classical administrative process school, (2) the human relations participative management school, (3) the cognitive process decision-making school (the Carnegie-Mellon School of Simon, Cyert, and March), and (4) the bureaucratic school of Max Weber. Economists have developed at least two other general approaches. The managerial school stems from Berle and Mean's 1932 book and includes the works of such prominent economists as Galbraith and Marris. A recent variation of the management-owner control literature is the agency theory/contracts approach to corporate organization as typified by the recent works of Fama (1980) and Fama and Jensen (1983). A second set of economic writings on organization is based upon works by Coase (1937) and Williamson (1975) on neoinstitutional transaction cost theory of the firm.

Given so many schools of thought, how can we proceed? Lawrence and Lorsch (1967) focused upon the classical and human relations approaches to organization for the following reasons: (1) They were most widely used by businesses and comprised the core of the management curricula in the business schools at that time; and (2) They represent a middle level of abstraction that can be connected to the more complex theories of Weber and the Carnegie-Mellon School on the one hand, and to the practical affairs of managers, on the other.

This second reason has withstood the test of time. Since then such "middle level" theory has grown into an entirely new area, strategic management. If writing today, I doubt they would feel compelled to include the transactions costs approach, which reduces management analysis to cost accounting for specific transactions and provides less scope for a variety of insightful approaches from other social sciences. I think they would recognize the managerial control approach, and, especially, agency theory, a recent variation of it, as co-terminous with their middle level theory. Agency theory has been focused most acutely upon the stockholder/owner-management relationship whereas organization theorists' efforts are focused more directly upon the internal structure of management.

A brief summary of the basic approaches of the classical administrative process and human relations school can provide insights into the current research approach used by business policy and organization scholars.[2] Lawrence and Lorsch (1967, 163) introduce the classical school:

> The classical writers usually start their reasoning by using examples of very primitive organizations. One favorite, for instance, involves a man who wants to move a stone that is too heavy for him. So, of course, he arranges to secure the temporary services of a second or third man by offering a reward. When one pushes while another pulls, we have the beginning of a division of labor. When the first calls out the signal for a big heave, we have a primitive chain of command serving to integrate the differential parts of the system. From such simple examples evolves much of the final theory. They provide the rational basis for deducing many of the so-called "principles" that classical theorists' have stressed.

The five basic principles of the classical school are: (1) the scalar principle, (2) unity of command, (3) span of control, (4) organizational specialization, and (5) parity of authority and responsibility.

The scalar principle defines the hierarchical relationship between the top management and subordinates. It emphasizes the need for the flow of authority and responsibility from top to bottom in an unbroken chain through delegation.

Unity of command has the goal of avoiding dual subordination on specific tasks. No member should receive orders from more than one boss.

Span of control sets the limit on the number of persons one should effectively supervise. The limits specified by theorists vary from three at the top of the firm to six or more at the bottom. At the higher level, where responsibility is heavy, the span should be small, and at the lower level, where activities are repetitive, the span may be large.

Organizational specialization assumes that the tasks can be divided and performed effeciently. Specialization occurs through division of labor. The tasks of each department are grouped around some common base (e.g., products, process, functions, etc.). Parity of authority and responsibility recognizes that if a manager is assigned responsibility for task achievement, he needs to be given matching authority.

For an organization designed on these principles to work, all workers must be motivated to follow instructions from higher-ups in the hierarchy. The classical theorists assumed that the ability of top management to mete out rewards and punishments was a sufficient source of motivation to ensure performance.

The human relations school rejected this mechanistic and authoritarian approach to management. It is more than a coincidence that it became a major component of organization theory during the depression years of the 1930s. It gained acceptance at the same time that industrial unions and industrial psychology were coming of age. To attain an efficient management structure the human relations school generally advocates the use of a low-structure "organic" organization along with widely shared influence and open, confronting modes of conflict resolution (no authoritarian chain of command). It places most emphasis on realizing a high degree of integration, and definitely plays down the utility and importance of achieving the advantages of specialization through appropriate differentiation (Lawrence and Lorsch 1967).

Lawrence and Lorsch's main contribution to the organizational theory literature was to provide a broader conceptual framework that encompassed the classical and human relations theories as special cases. First they explicitly asserted the primacy of organizational structure over individual behavior. Changing structure can produce desired changes in individual conduct. Second, they broadened the definition of organizational structure to include more than the formal organizational chart suggested by the classical concepts previously enumerated. As a result, today's definition includes social and psychological features of an organization as well. Organizational structure can be defined as the combination of rules and procedures, roles of the members of the organization, and the relationships that exist between the members and also between the systems and subsystems of the organization (McGosh et al. 1981). Finally, following the lead of Chandler (1962), their own research, and the research of others—most notably Woodward (1980) as well as Burns and Stalker (1961)—they concluded that the search by organization theorists for the most efficient organization was misconceived and hopeless.[3] Within their contingency theory of organization, the most appropriate organizational structure depends upon the firm's chosen strategy and that, in turn, depends upon the firm's environment. Firm performance, and overall social welfare, depends upon the choices made at all stages in this causal sequence of management events.

Contingency theory as presented here is the basic building block for analyzing corporations that are considerably more complex than the proto-type firm that organization theorists usually analyzed prior to 1970. That firm is what Williamson (1975) has described as the unitary or U-form corporation, more generally called the functional type of corporation. The functionally specialized firm differentiates its activities into departments, each of which undertakes a distinctive function—production, finance, mar-keting, etc. Their heads report to a central executive staff whose responsi-bilities include the integration of all efforts to avoid suboptimization.

During the past 100 years, the growth of corporations from single-product, predominantly local businesses to very complex firms often en-compassing multiple product lines, vertical integration, and/or widespread geographic operations in several markets required a corresponding growth in organization toward more complex forms. Chandler (1962) identifies the holding company and the multidivisional forms as the two major alternatives for very large enterprises. The former is a legal con-struction that allows a parent company to control a subsidiary, usually through stock ownership and election of a board of directors. A holding company has no corporate staff actively engaged in the strategic manage-ment and coordination of its subsidiaries. Each is essentially independent of the others.

The multidivisional organizational structure, which Williamson (1975) calls the M-form organization, is generally credited to the genius of Alfred Sloan, head of General Motors during the 1920s. Its top man-agement is considerably more active than that of a holding company, and its primary organizational breakdown is into divisions assigned different activities or responsibility for supplying different markets. The secondary organizational breakdown is the differentiation of each division into an appropriate set of functional departments.

The M-form corporation establishes more than another layer of ad-ministration in the chain of command; it creates a completely new dimen-sion in organizational structure, the strategic dimension. Business can now consist of a single functional unit or a portfolio of many such busi-ness units. The strategic question, What business are we in? becomes more manageable. Organizational structure at the strategic level is differ-ent than at the business unit level because the tasks are different. None-theless, contingency theory and its basic concepts such as the need to balance between differentiation and integration can be applied to strategic organization issues (Lorsch and Allen 1973).

The final aspect of organization that deserves explicit comment is the ownership-management link. To the extent that the managerial theory of the firm focuses upon the analysis of stockholder and management perogatives, it focuses upon how one important aspect of the environment, the capital market, affects organization. Fama and Jensen (1983) have done the most recent theoretical work in this area. They have developed a managerial theory based on the concept of agency relationships. An organization is seen as a nexus of contracts among various economic agents (laborers, managers, materials suppliers, equity investors, bond holders, etc.) whose activities constitute the activity of the organization (Fama and Jensen 1983). Equity investors are residual claimants on the proceeds from economic activity. As the set of contractual relations is changed, the distribution of benefits to all agents, including equity investors, changes. No one "owns" the firm. It is a coalition of different groups with different power bases.

Although this theory can be applied to all aspects of organizational structure, it has primarily been used to analyze the performance of stockholder versus management-controlled firms. Fama (1980), for example, constructs a provocative argument for the economic efficiency of large corporations wherein stock ownership, which resides in the capital market, is completely separated from managerial control.

As residual claimants, equity security holders are the corporation's risk bearers. The capital market, which is presumably efficient, is a market for the "risk-bearing service." According to Fama (1980), if the firm does not adequately compensate its equity holders for the firm's level of risk, they will shift their investment to another firm. Moreover, he argues that investors hold diversified portfolios and really have no special interests in overseeing the detailed activities of any firm. Today's investment methods seem to imply a large degree of separation of security ownership from control of a firm's strategic and operational agenda. Entrepreneurs—those hands-on, risk-taking owner-managers—no longer exist in the corporate sector (Fama 1980).

With regard to managerial effectiveness, the compensation of executives in the long run, is determined in the executive labor market (Fama 1980). That market looks to the past performance of the firm when deciding how much to pay an executive being hired from that firm. Therefore an executive seeks out of self-interest to maximize the performance of a firm.

To date there is no empirical research on the validity of Fama's theory. Lest one find this Chicago-school paean to the power of unfettered markets and self-interest irresistable, consider the following joke attributed to James Tobin. Two Chicago economists Milton (Friedman) and Eugene (Fama) are walking down the street.

> *Milton:* "Isn't that a $20 bill I see on the sidewalk?"
> *Eugene:* "No, Milton, if it were it wouldn't be there."

Caveat emptor holds on all such reasoning.

HOSTILE TAKEOVERS ILLUSTRATE THE NEED FOR RESEARCH ON CORPORATE CONTROL AND EFFICIENCY

Fama's (1980) efficient capital market/managerial talent market model is a variation of the "market for corporate control" theory of managerial efficiency developed by Manne (1965) and by Alchian and Demsetz (1972). They assert that the threat of takeover ensures that all publicly held corporations will select optimal strategies and organizational structures. Empirical research, however, finds considerable slack and perverse behavior in the takeover mechanism. After reviewing this literature Marris and Mueller (1981) conclude, "Rather than deviant managerial behavior being driven out by stockholder-welfare maximizing behavior the so-called 'deviant' behavior has more likely driven out the other."

Recently, hostile takeover attempts on *Fortune* 500 firms have accelerated. The corporate raiders include T. Boone Pickens (attempted takeover of Gulf), Carl Icahn (takeover of TWA), James Goldsmith (attempted takeover of St. Regis Paper Corp.), and Irwin Jacobs (takeover of AMF). At the beginning of this century, financial entrepreneurs made great fortunes assembling large corporations, often forcibly, over the desires of owner-managers of the target companies. Today, corporate raiders are amassing large personal fortunes by doing the opposite, acquiring large corporations and restructuring or wholly dismembering them to sell component assets at a profit. One might call this industrial deconcentration "Republican style." Robert C. Clark, a Harvard law professor following the tradition of Berle and Means, argues that control of capitalist enterprises is fated to move from entrepreneur-founders through professional managers and finally to institutional investors. The raiders are catalyzing that change. According to Clark (1985, 81), "They are really breaking the vise of the managing class."

Others are not as sanguine as Clark. When confronted by a corporate raider, target companies often find it in the best interests of their stockholders to pay "greenmail" (buy back the block of stock owned by the raider at a price above the raider's purchase price) rather than succumb to the takeover attempt. As Sloan (1985, 137) puts it:

When the target company pays greenmail—and the raider, naturally, accepts it—it is the shareholders the raider professes to care about who ultimately pay the bill. If a company is taken over and liquidated at immense profit, didn't that profit belong rightly to its shareholders? The idea that most of these raiders are out to maximize value for anyone other than themselves is ludicrous.

The recent hostile takeover attempt at Uniroyal, a $2.1 billion diversified company with strong positions in the rubber and chemical industries (including agricultural herbicides and growth regulants), as described in the *Hartford Courant* (1985, C-1) illustrates the magnitude of the shift in corporate strategies and organizational structures that can be forthcoming.

Uniroyal Inc. announced . . . that stockholders had approved a $476 million leveraged buyout by a group of the company's managers and the New York investment firm Clayton & Dubilier Inc. . . . The buyout was agreed to on May 6 as Uniroyal sought to fend off a hostile takeover bid by investor Carl C. Icahn. Icahn agreed to accept a $5.9 million payment from Uniroyal in return for dropping his $18-per-share bid. The buyout makes Uniroyal a private company. Each current owner of Uniroyal's common stock will receive $22 per share in cash.

Shareowners also approved two other proposals. One authorized Uniroyal's directors to restructure the company into several wholly owned subsidiaries, making Uniroyal a holding company. The other amended Uniroyal's incorporation certificate and bylaws to permit stockholder action by written consent and to reduce the minimum number of Uniroyal directors from 11 to three.

Is this new organization more efficient than the old Uniroyal? It will be difficult to evaluate the performance of the new firm because it is not a public firm. Data will not be readily available.

The stock tender offer is the vehicle for hostile takeovers. Until recently there was what Andrew Sigler, chairman of the Corporate Responsibility Task Force of the Business Roundtable, C.E.O. and chairman of Champion Paper Co., and white knight (friendly acquirer) of thrice greenmailed St. Regis Paper Company, describes as "due process" in merger negotiations (Sigler 1985). A prospective acquirer approached the board of directors of their targeted company and proposed merger or acquisition terms for them to accept or reject. Raiders subvert "due process" by purchasing billion dollar blocks of stock and threatening takeover by displacing the board of directors rather than negotiating with them. Five recent developments have enabled them to do this:

1. An unexpected result of the 1981 Economic Recovery Tax Act has been that its accelerated depreciation provision increased the gap

between cash flows and reported earnings. According to Sloan (1985, 136):

> Because the extra cash wasn't reflected in earnings [the tax change] didn't give stocks an upward push. . . . [But] the tax act so increased corporate cash flows that many companies now sell at low multiples of their real cash flow and their ability to service debt. . . . They have substantial untapped borrowing capacity which allows acquirers to finance a substantial part of the acquisition price against the acquisition itself.

This also has been the source of leveraged buyouts such as the Uniroyal result described above and the recent acquisition of First National Stores Inc., one of the nation's top 20 food chains, by four of its top executives.

2. Financial deregulation has enabled banks to bankroll raiders almost overnight, and it has allowed large sums of money to be raised quickly in the commercial paper market by selling what the trade calls "junk bonds."

3. A glut of investment money has been available due to macroeconomic policies that have caused the value of the dollar to increase and real interest rates to remain high, relative to rates in other countries.

4. The institutional nature of the stock market facilitates purchasing large blocks of stock. Pension fund managers control some 60 percent of the stock on the New York Stock Exchange (Priest 1985).

5. The laissez-faire antitrust policy of the Reagan administration has given a green light to nearly all mergers.

Raiders pick targets by identifying companies whose assets are undervalued by the stock market. There is no lack of targets as Clark (1985, 83) points out:

> For the last decade or so, shares of the average U.S. public company have traded for about two-thirds to three-quarters of the value of the share's underlying assets. The gap has grown cavernous in industries where return on investment has not kept pace with the inflation-bloated liquidation value of hard assets. In the oil industry, to take one dramatic example, stocks have been selling at less than half the value of their underlying reserves. And in the spread between price and value, opportunity waits. The raiders have thrived essentially by acting as grand-scale arbitrageurs, exploiting the asset-value gap.

The hanging question remains. Even if hostile takeovers do not maximize shareholders' wealth, do they increase efficiency of the economic system and thus increase social welfare?

Chicago-school economists answer affirmatively. They point out that takeover attempts, whether consummated or ending in greenmail, and moreover the fear of takeover attempts, are resulting in the redeployment of assets into higher value uses. They see corporate raiders as the practitioners of hit-and-run ownership in a perfectly contestable market for corporate control. Managerial X-inefficiency is eliminated by the raiders. Any profits arising from the strong market position of the firm in product or input markets, however, are not reduced to the competitive (efficient) level.[4]

The Business Roundtable, an organization of the chief executive officers of the *Fortune* 200, see the situation otherwise, says Priest (1985, 4):

> Clearly, the effectiveness of the raiders' techniques has had a chilling impact on corporations. Many managers are loath to invest for growth when they know it means that their company's stock price will be battered and their company's rendered vulnerable to attack. Instead, they prefer to invest company money in areas where it will boost stock prices, even if the investment brings no new customers, no higher sales, or no better competitive position. Thus we see more top managers causing the buy back of their own companies' stock.

In testimony before Congress, on behalf of the Business Roundtable, Sigler (1984, 4) emphasized the financial legerdemain that raiders are forcing upon large corporations.

> Hostile takeovers create no new wealth. They merely shift ownership and replace equity with large amounts of debt. Thus, an increasingly inevitable component of the recent wave of hostile tender offers is, in the words of Chairman Shad of the SEC, "the leveraging of America" and the response of institutions and individuals to the lure of junk bonds.

> More and more companies are being pushed—either in self defense against the raiders or by the raiders once they achieve control—into unhealthy recapitalizations that run contrary to the concepts of sound management I have learned over thirty years. This type of leveraging exposes companies to inordinate risks in the event of recession, unanticipated reverses, or significant increases in interest rates.

The jury is still out on whether the strategic shuffling of business units among large corporations and other defensive strategic moves to bring short-run earnings in line with underlying asset values to stave off the raiders produces more wealth for stockholders and/or more efficient organization of the economy.

This area of industrial organization analysis—the analysis of the impact of capital markets and financiers upon shareholder welfare and the public's interest in maximum social welfare—might appropriately be labeled "Republican industrial organization theory." The issues that it analyzes are consonant with the Reagan administration's laissez-faire economic philosophy of minimal antitrust and regulatory intervention. Democrat industrial organization theory, typified by the topics covered in texts such as Scherer (1980), focuses relatively little attention upon the capital market and ownership, per se, of the firm. Moreover its analysis of the relationship between product market structure and economic performance serves as the basis for an active role by government in the antitrust and regulatory areas.[5]

A GENERAL FRAMEWORK FOR BUSINESS EFFICIENCY ANALYSIS AND OPPORTUNITIES FOR RESEARCH

In today's heterodox environment the opportunities for research to compare alternative theories and to evaluate the impact of organizational structure upon economic efficiency are numerous, and, I think, exciting. Given the recent wave of hostile takeovers, one may find ample evidence for rejecting Fama's (1980) assertion that the linkage between stock ownership and management is redundant. Fig. 6.1 can aid in the identification of other hypotheses and the formulation of models to test them. It summarizes the organizational structure analysis explained in this chapter and integrates it with the industrial organization framework to produce a general framework for analysis. Most of the framework comes from Scherer (1980) and from Porter (1980). The novel components that I have added are the capital market/ownership structure category in the environment stage, an organizational structure stage, and a firm-level performance category in the performance stage. Arrows indicate causality.

Another change is in the focus of the analytical framework. Traditionally the focus of the industrial organization was on the market rather than the firms selling in the market. Recently many economists, recognizing the interface with strategic marketing and business policy research, have shifted to the firm as the focal point. Hence the addition of the firm-level category in the performance stage. With the firm as the unit of analysis, it also is easier to introduce an input market (the ownership/capital market) as a new dimension of market structure. (I will finesse the issue of whether these are two separate markets.)

To some theorists it may seem objectionable to elevate one input market structure and not others to coequal status with product market structure. Notwithstanding the agency theory approach, most economists recognize the special role that the ownership/capital market plays in directing economic activity.[6] As documented previously, we need to think

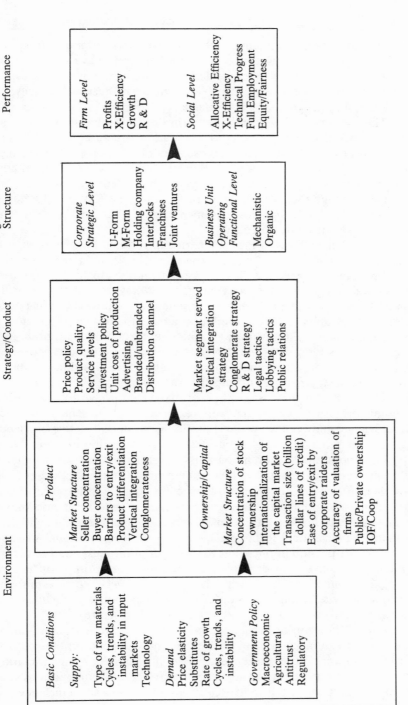

FIG. 6.1. A general framework for analyzing the determinants of economic performance, including efficiency.

more broadly because financial deregulation, laissez-faire competition policies, and changes in the capital market itself have loosened the bounds of behavior for financiers. The structure of the ownership/capital market has become a more central determinant of business strategy, organization, and, ultimately, performance.

The cooperative/investor-owned firm distinction has heretofore usually been included as a part of product market structure. Since cooperatives are user-owned and their equities are not traded on stock exchanges, there is good reason for doing so. Recent theories of cooperation, however, have stressed that they are a special type of tied-equity firm, and have used agency theory to analyze their strategies (Caves and Petersen 1983; Vitaliano 1985). For this reason co-ops are placed in the ownership/capital market structure category.

Two other features of Fig. 6.1 merit explanation. First, note that the amount of vertical integration and conglomeration in an industry is part of the product market structure. This measurement is distinctly different from the vertical integration and conglomeration *strategies* that the particular firm under analysis adopts, which determine the composition of its portfolio of business units. Second, interlocks (among the boards of directors of different companies), franchises, and joint ventures, three corporate-level intercompany strategic organizational structures not discussed above, are included at the organizational structure stage. This was done simply to show where such structures fit into the framework.

The particular dimension of performance that we wish to measure is economic efficiency. This social welfare concept is represented by allocative efficiency and X-efficiency in Fig. 6.1. Consider allocative efficiency. Fig. 6.1 illustrates how various business enterprise forms are related to it.

First note that different business enterprise forms are located at different stages of the theoretical framework. Cooperatives and other ownership forms are at the market structure stage; a firm's vertical integration and conglomerate strategy (its decision as to what portfolio of business units to hold) is at the business strategy/conduct stage; and management organizational forms are located at the organizational structure stage. This dispersion implies that the concept of business enterprise form is multidimensional. An example of a business enterprise form is a regional *cooperative* that strategically has *vertically integrated* in farm supply distribution by adopting a version of the *holding company organizational structure* (a federated as opposed to centralized structure).

Each dimension of organizational form can have a separate impact upon allocative efficiency, and that impact may depend on other factors in the framework. The presence of a supply cooperative in a market, ignoring for the moment the need to specify the other dimensions (i.e., not including them in the model), can improve allocative efficiency, not only by selling to its own patrons on a business-at-cost basis, but also by acting as a competitive influence (yardstick) upon other firms in the market. The industry would thus move toward a price-output policy more consistent with allocative efficiency. Yet this efficiency result depends upon the existence of a noncompetitive market structure. If the market is competitively structured the cooperative does not improve allocative efficiency.[7]

Another insight suggested by the general framework is that the impact of a particular organizational structure upon a performance measure (e.g., the M-form structure upon X-efficiency) depends upon the environment/business strategy configuration of the firm. In one such configuration the M-form may perform well, but in another it may be totally inappropriate.

It is also very possible that different organizational forms can coexist in a market and be efficient. Porter's theory of strategic groups predicts this result (Porter 1980). Firms in an industry may cluster around different modal strategies. One group of firms may target the high-quality, branded, highly promoted segment of the consumer market. Another may target the acceptable quality, lower priced, unbranded segment of the market. Given these different strategies, firms in the two groups may have different organizational structures. The brand product firms may be M-form, conglomerate, investor-owned firms. The unbranded firms may be U-form farmer cooperatives. Each may or may not operate in a fashion that produces X-efficiency and allocative efficiency.

Finally, consider the market for corporate control. If the theory explained above is valid, then businesses have strong incentives to set strategies and build organizations that are X-efficient and maximize the value of the firm to stockholders (i.e., maximize profits). Recall that this result is necessary but not sufficient for allocative efficiency. A monopoly with blockaded entry, for example, would not price in an allocatively efficient manner.

If the market for corporate control does not work as the theory predicts, which is the position of the Business Roundtable, then defensive strategy moves by firms to avoid corporate raiders and the restructuring of firms by successful raiders result in a misallocation of resources.

These examples illustrate how challenging it can be to specify a model that correctly identifies the impacts of different dimensions of enterprise organization upon any measure of performance, including efficiency. Multivariate econometric models are a necessity if one wishes to capture the multidimentional features of business enterprise forms.

Research using the general framework illustrated in Fig. 6.1 can do more than broaden our analysis of economic efficiency. Agricultural marketing economists have, for example, provided valuable assistance to farmer cooperatives and other agribusiness firms by evaluating plant-level economies, plant-location economies, and related transportation/distribution economies. Such studies will always be useful; however, today there is a critical need for strategic marketing and organizational research. This is especially true for farmer cooperatives, many of which are facing major reorganization in the near future because of the current crisis in agriculture. One might call this work quantitative institutional economics. It is the design of organizations to improve the performance of the system. Richard Caves's (1980, 88) comments on the role of economists in this area emphasize contributions that economists can make.

> I shall not let professional modesty blur an important conclusion: well-trained professional economists could have carried out many of the research projects cited in this paper more proficiently than did their authors, less effectively equipped by their own disciplines. . . . However economists preconceptions have steered them away from business strategy and organization as an area of research. Business organization involves in essense selecting the right point on a production function, but "production function" for the economist evokes only the harmonies of labor, capital, and land.

Hopefully this paper will help agricultural economists move into new and needed areas of research on business organization.

NOTES

1. Kilmer and Armbruster (1984) also describe a second approach that uses duality theory to estimate a "unit output profit model" that can then be used to measure X-efficiency.
2. See Lawrence and Lorsch (1967, Chap. 7) and McGosh et al. (1978, 17–23), for excellent, succinct explanations of them. The five classical principles are from the latter reference.
3. Woodward (1980) examined organization in English manufacturing plants that were classified into different groups depending upon the type of technology they used. She reported that organization varied between the groups and that firms within a group that conformed to the median organizational form of the group were most profitable. Burns and Stalker (1961) found that mechanistic classical theory explained the management organization of the stable textile industry well, and the more organic human relations theory best explained the management organization of the highly dynamic electronics industry.
4. Very few markets are perfectly contestable; however, with regard to X-efficiency, the ownership/capital market may very well be such a market. The hostile takeover issue and the contestability explanation also provide an important insight into the appropriateness of perfect contestability as a welfare norm. Just as perfect competition was rejected as a welfare norm and re-

placed by the concept of workable contestability, perfect contestability may lead to undesirable performance and need to be replaced by some sort of workable contestability. The concept of destructive competition is familiar to agricultural marketing economists who have designed marketing order, price stabilizing, and income policies for agricultural markets. It should surprise no one that there can be destructive contestability.

5. Some economic theorists may find it objectionable to label theories as Republican or Democrat, but economic policy analysts recognize that the research agenda is strongly influenced by political actions. Of course Democrats are interested in the corporate control issue and Republicans find much that is useful in Scherer (1980).

6. This viewpoint probably reached its zenith at the turn of the century in the Populist and Marxist economic literature. Rudolf Hilferdings, as explained in Sweezy (1942), is a classic example.

7. See Cotterill (1985, Chap. 2) for a comprehensive analysis of how different cooperative strategic choices and organizational structures influence market behavior. Not all variants produce a competitive yardstick result.

REFERENCES

Alchian, Armen A., and Harold Demsetz. "Production, Information Costs, and Economic Organization." *Am. Econ. Rev.* 62(1972):777–95.

Baumol, William, John Panzar, and Robert Willig. *Contestable Markets and Theory of Industry Structure.* New York: Harcourt Brace Jovanovich, 1982.

Berle, Adolph A., Jr., and Gardiner C. Means. *The Modern Corporation and Private Property.* New York: Macmillan, 1932.

Boles, James. "The Measurement of Productive Efficiency: The Farrell Approach." Giannini Foundation Agriculture Working Paper No. 157, University of California-Berkeley, 1980.

Burns, Tom, and G. M. Stalker. *The Management of Innovation.* London: Tavistock, 1961.

Caves, Richard E. "Industrial Organization, Corporate Strategy." *J. Econ. Lit.* 18(1980):64–92.

Caves, Richard E., and Bruce C. Petersen. "Cooperatives' Shares in Farm Industries: Organizational Policy Factors." Harvard Institute of Economic Research Discussion Paper No. 974, 1983.

Chandler, Alfred D., Jr. *Strategy and Structure: Chapters in the History of the American Industrial Enterprise.* Cambridge, Mass.: MIT Press, 1962.

Chen, Kwo-Shin, Emerson Babb, and Lee Schrader. "Growth of Large Cooperative and Proprietary Firms in the U.S. Food Sector." *Agribusiness* 1(1985):201–10.

Clark, Robert C. "The Raiders." *Business Week,* 4 March 1985, pp. 80–90.

Coase, Ronald H. "The Nature of the Firm." *Economica* 4(1937):381–405.

Cotterill, Ronald. "Agricultural Cooperatives: A Unified Theory of Pricing, Finance and Investment." University of Connecticut, Agric. Econ. and Rur. Soc. Staff Paper No. 85-8, 1985.

Cyert, Richard, and James March. *A Behavioral Theory of the Firm.* Englewood Cliffs, N.J.:Prentice-Hall, 1963.

Fama, Eugene F. "Agency Problem and the Theory of the Firm." *J. Pol. Econ.* 88(1980):288–307.

Fama, Eugene, and Michael Jensen. "Agency Problems and Residual Claims." *J. Law and Econ.* 26(1983):327–49.

Farrell, Maurice. "The Measurement of Productive Efficiency." *J. Royal Stat. Soc.* 120(1957):253–81.

French, Ben. "The Analysis of Productive Efficiency in Agricultural Marketing: Models,

128   II / CONCEPTS FOR EVALUATING ECONOMIC EFFICIENCY

Methods, and Progress." *A Survey of Agricultural Economics Literature.* Vol 1, *Traditional Fields of Agricultural Economics, 1940s to 1970s,* ed. L. R. Martin, pp. 94–208. Minneapolis: University of Minnesota Press, 1977.

Harberger, Arnold C. "Monopoly and Resource Allocation." *Am. Econ. Rev.* 44(1954):77–87.

Hartford Courant. "Uniroyal Buyout Voted." 24 Sept. 1985, p. C-1.

Helmberger, Peter, Gerald Campbell, and William Dobson. "Organization and Performance of Agricultural Markets." *A Survey of Agricultural Economics Literature.* Vol. 3, *Economics of Welfare, Rural Development, and Natural Resources in Agriculture, 1940s to 1970s,* ed. L. R. Martin, pp. 503–628. Minneapolis: University of Minnesota Press, 1981.

Kelton, Christina M. L. "Operational Efficiency in Food and Tobacco Manufacturing." Dept. of Agric. Econ. NC-117 Working Paper No. 72, University of Wisconsin, Sept. 1983.

Kilmer, Richard, and Walter Armbruster. "Methods for Evaluating Economic Efficiency in Agricultural Marketing." *South. J. Agric. Econ.* 1(1984):101–9.

Lawrence, Paul, and Jay Lorsch. *Organization and Environment.* Boston: Harvard University Press, 1967.

Liebenstein, Harvey. "Allocative Efficiency vs. 'X-Efficiency'." *Am. Econ. Rev.* 56(1966): 392–415.

Lorsch, Jay W., and Stephen A. Allen. *Managing Diversity and Interdependence: An Organizational Study of Multidivisional Firms.* Boston: Harvard University Press, 1973.

McGosh, Andres, M. Rahman, and Michael Earl. *Developing Managerial Information Systems.* New York: Macmillan, 1981.

Manne, Henry G. "Mergers and the Market for Corporate Control." *J. Pol. Econ.* 73(1965):110–20.

Marris, Robin, and Dennis C. Mueller, "The Corporation, Competition, and the Invisible Hand." *J. Econ. Lit.* 19(1981):32–64.

Mason, Edwin. "Price and Production Policies of Large Scale Enterprises." *Am. Econ. Rev.* 29(1939):61–79.

Miles, R. E., and C. C. Snow. *Organizational Strategy, Structure, and Process.* New York: McGraw-Hill, 1978.

Parker, Russell C., and John M. Connor. "Estimates of Consumer Loss Due to Monopoly in the U.S. Food Manufacturing Industries." *Am. J. Agric. Econ.* 61(1979):622–39.

Porter, Michael. *Competitive Strategy: Techniques for Analyzing Industries and Competitors.* New York: The Free Press, 1980.

———. *Competitive Advantage: Creating and Sustaining Superior Performance.* New York: The Free Press, 1985.

Priest, Alice L. "The Takeover Game." Report prepared for the Corporate Responsibility Task Force, the Business Roundtable, Washington, D.C., March 1985.

Schendal, D. E., and Hofer, C. W. *Strategic Management: A New View of Business Policy and Planning.* Boston: Little, Brown & Co., 1979.

Scherer, Frederick M. *Industrial Market Structure and Economic Performance.* 2d ed. Chicago: Rand McNally, 1980.

Schrader, Lee F., E. M. Babb, R. D. Boynton, and M. G. Lang. *Cooperative and Proprietary Agribusiness: Comparison of Performance.* Exp. Sta. Bull. 982, Purdue University, 1985.

Sigler, Andrew C. "Testimony before Hearings of the House Committee on Energy and Commerce." Report to the Business Roundtable, Washington, D.C., 23 May 1985.

Sloan, Allan. "Why is No One Safe?" *Forbes* 11 March 1985, pp. 134–40.

Sweezy, Paul. *The Theory of Capitalist Development.* New York: Modern Reader Paperbacks, 1942.

Thompson, James D. *Organization in Action: Social Science Bases of Administrative Theory.* New York: McGraw-Hill, 1967.

Vitaliano, Peter. "The Cooperative as an Economic Organization: An Institutional Analysis with Special Reference to Agriculture." Unpublished manuscript, Dept. of Agric. Econ., Virginia Polytechnic Institute, 1985.

Williamson, Oliver. *Market and Hierarchies: Analysis and Antitrust Implications.* New York: The Free Press, 1975.

————. "The Modern Corporation: Origins, Evolution, Attributes," *J. Econ. Lit.* 19(1981): 1537–68.

Woodward, Joan. *Industrial Organization: Theory and Practice.* 2d ed. New York: Oxford University Press, 1980.

The Economic Efficiency of
Alternative Forms
of Business Enterprise

A DISCUSSION

Lee F. Schrader

RON COTTERILL promised us a review of economists' approaches to efficiency comparisons, a theoretical framework for efficiency analysis, and a lesson in how to use the framework. The promises are in order of increasing difficulty and decreasing degree of delivery. He has pushed us in the direction of considering the firm and its internal organization as a factor in efficiency. He has also presented the argument that we should proceed to assess the efficiency of different organizational forms in an industrial organization/strategic marketing/business policy framework.

Ron has done an excellent job. It seems that I have a great deal of reading to do to comprehend fully the task that should be done to assess the efficiency of alternative internal firm structures. If we look back only a few years to remarks by Peter Helmberger (1968, 24) on O-efficiency (related to organization of firms and markets) we find, "While we are in considerable difficulty in detecting departures from the usual welare efficiency conditions, the prospects for accurate measurement of departures from O-efficiency appear downright dismal." We have made some progress. There is quantitative analysis of economies of scope, which moves us closer to an understanding of the boundaries of the firm as well as other empirical and conceptual work in the area. Incidentally, Helmberger's prescription for public policy was to let the market work. This is particularly interesting in light of the corporate raiders about which Cotterill seems to have some doubts. We will come back to that later.

I am a believer in X-inefficiency. Most of us are as lazy as we dare be. How many of us hold back just a little (budget, energy, etc.) for when the crunch comes. It is truly amazing how many fewer people were needed at all levels of firms during the recent recession. Even a university department absorbs a budget cut without cutting programs. In profitable

LEE F. SCHRADER is professor, Department of Agricultural Economics, Purdue University, West Lafayette, Indiana.

periods, plant managers let inventories climb to comfortable levels and offices get redecorated. Adversity brings on the serious search for efficiency within an organization. Perhaps we need to deal directly with the fact that there are elements of consumption in the process of production. The farmer's decision to trade equipment (in better times) includes a mix of wants and needs.

In the theoretical, perfectly competitive market there is no room for X-inefficiency. But all markets are to some extent noncompetitive. Even the farmer has some scope for decision. He can sell or not sell storable commodities on a given day. Clearly there is scope for inefficiency even in farming.

A recent analysis at Purdue of fertilizer retailer performance shows much less plant-to-plant variation in several performance measures in 1984 than in 1974 (Bullerdick et al. 1985). Today's environment tolerates much less inefficiency even as the number of firms has declined (increasing concentration).

I am much less ready to accept the notion that firms typically elect a strategy and then select an organizational structure to implement the strategy at least cost. I have little evidence except that it seems most firms have evolved without having a carefully defined strategy. It is not clear that it matters a great deal, they must still search for an organization to accomplish what they do. Clearly a balance between specialization and integration of functions is a primary factor in the selection of an organizational form. Organization to serve strategy is the logical sequence. I am arguing only that things are often not so logical.

I am impressed, time after time, with how many aspects of a firm are determined by tradition. "That's the way we do it" or "That's the way it is done in this industry" are typical statements. Few of us systematically question all we do until circumstances force us to do so.

Cotterill's view of the role of transactions costs is much narrower than mine. If one takes a broad view of transactions costs it includes some of what others might see as a part of contracts or the specialization/integration decision. Much of what some consider as transactions costs may be classified as uncertainty by others without recognizing its relationship to transactions.

I do appreciate the view that firm structure affects behavior. My direct experience involved one company employing a functional organization in which a manufacturing facility was a cost center and another company at which each plant was a profit center. In the first case, the plant would reject raw material of low quality regardless of its price because its use would increase plant cost. In the latter case, the plant would use anything it could clean up at a profit. The plant as a profit center was better able to integrate the decision in this instance. The profit center concept encouraged other less desirable behavior that will not be detailed here.

The ownership/management link is given prominent status in the proposed framework for analysis. We do need to know more about its impact on economic efficiency. The raiders role is an interesting subject. The individual stockholder is in a poor position to discipline management. Selling one's stock in an underperforming company is not a very attractive alternative. Why should one stockholder sell low to induce management to shape up for the benefit of those who do not sell? The outside buyer can perform a service for the stockholder. Whether that is the buyer's motive is of no relevance. If assets are worth more deployed elsewhere it is in the interest of efficiency to get them there. The measures taken to discourage or evade takeovers do appear to be largely wasted.

The popularity of start-up issues with no earnings at all seems to indicate that the market can take a long view. The market for land has typically taken a longer view, with prices seldom justified by current earnings.

Markets do provide discipline in the manufacturing and marketing dimensions. I am even willing to accept the consumer's preference for one brand of colored sugar water over another. Satisfaction is what you think it is in many respects. When someone gets too greedy people do adjust. Maybe the capital market is different. We should take it into account.

Tax policy is also clearly relevant. A single tax on corporate earnings, whether retained or paid out, would facilitate the redeployment of capital without the help of raiders. Some similarity between earnings for taxes and earnings for the financial statement could also facilitate adjustment in the capital markets.

Fig. 6.1 summarizes Cotterill's framework for analysis. I have some problem with the indicated causal relation from basic conditions to ownership/capital market structure. It seems a rather weak link. Perhaps a two-way relationship between product market structure and ownership/capital is more nearly to the point. Economies of size seem to be a major factor relating to the capital market, but I am not sure where they fit into the diagram. The organization structure block fits more easily into place.

We have been provided a challenge to improve our contribution to the analysis of the efficiency of alternative forms of business enterprise. The direction is worth a try. The data requirements are formidable, both for the measurement of efficiency and to quantify strategy. I hope that Cotterill will provide an example using his framework soon.

REFERENCES

Bullerdick, J., J. T. Akridge, and W. D. Downey. *The 1984 FRED (Fertilizer Retail Efficiency Data) Summary of Midwestern Fertilizer Plants.* Agric. Exp. Sta. Bull. No. 479, Purdue University, Oct. 1985.

Helmberger, P. "O-Efficiency and the Economic Organization of Agriculture." *Agricultural Organization in the Modern Industrial Economy,* ed. T. T. Stout, pp. 18–28. Columbus: Ohio State University, Dept. of Agric. Econ., April 1968.

CHAPTER 7

The Economic Efficiency of
Alternative Exchange Mechanisms

Richard L. Kilmer

EXCHANGE MECHANISMS are means by which buyers and sellers coordinate with one another to trade products and services. At the producer-first handler level, exchange arrangements include bargaining (cooperatively), formula pricing, administered pricing (milk marketing orders), private treaty (negotiation between two people), and central or auction markets (Tomek and Robinson 1981, 214). Although not an external exchange mechanism, vertical integration is also an alternative. These mechanisms differ by the amount of information, transaction costs, productive efficiency, risk, and market power allocated to buyers and sellers.

Above the producer-first handler level, central markets are less frequently observed. Mechanisms include the spot market, formula pricing, administered pricing, vertical integration, and contracting. Contractual alternatives include franchises, tying arrangements, output royalties, sales revenue royalties, and lump sum entry fees (Blair and Kaserman 1983).

Nonspot exchange predominates at all stages of the vertical system. The United States Department of Agriculture (USDA) estimated that the percent (dollar volume basis) of production and marketing contracts used in agriculture at the producer-first handler level has increased from 15.1 percent in 1960 to 17.2 percent in 1970 to 22.9 percent in 1980 (Sporleder 1983, 389). Vertical integration has increased from 3.9 percent in 1960 to 4.8 percent in 1970 to 7.4 percent in 1980. In total, nonspot coordination has increased from 19.0 percent in 1960 to 30.3 percent in 1980. This is not an astronomical increase since 1960; however, it does serve to show that nonspot coordination has been in existence for some time.

RICHARD L. KILMER is associate professor, Department of Food and Resource Economics, University of Florida, Gainesville.

Information is not as readily available concerning nonspot exchange downstream from the producer-first handlers. The expectation is that there is less nonspot exchange because of the large number of products that must be exchanged and the small number of buyers and sellers, particularly at the manufacturing and wholesale level. At the retail level, buyers are numerous but the number of products is also very large. Thus, administered pricing is frequently used. It would be very costly for buyers if they were required to attend an auction to buy groceries. This would require buyers to be at a particular location at a particular time. The administered pricing done by supermarkets places fewer constraints on the buyer's time and place, thus adding utility to the product purchased. The price discovery process may be slower than for the central market price for cattle because the supermarket manager receives information more slowly on the demand for products. The automated checkout provides the supermarket manager with information that has the potential of hastening the price discovery process.

Exchange mechanisms affect economic efficiency in two ways. First, the mechanisms influence the price that allocates resources. Second, as the characteristics of exchange are altered over time (e.g., quality becomes more variable), alternative mechanisms can be substituted for existing ones, which may allow fewer resources to be used in the exchange process.

Economic efficiency is defined as the allocation of consumption and production activities so any reorganization of resources cannot be accomplished without decreasing the utility of one or more individuals in an attempt to increase the utility of one individual. Society's resources are valued at the margin such that marginal benefits equal marginal costs. The pricing system that brings about these results is the perfectly competitive system.

Even though the perfectly competitive system does not exist in the real world, it is instructive to revisit the first order conditions. First, for the final goods markets to reflect an efficient price for all products in a two-consumer, two-producer, three-good world, the following must occur.

$$MRS_{ij}^1 = MRS_{ij}^2 = MRTF_{ij}^1 = MRTF_{ij}^2 \qquad (1)$$

where MRS is the marginal rate of substitution; ij represents the final goods i and j; and $MRTF$ is the marginal rate of transformation. The conditions must hold for every pair of final goods. This suggests that the relative benefit between the two goods must equal the relative cost of transforming one good into another. The price ratio that will allocate resources in an economically efficient manner is the one that equals the marginal rate of substitution.

Consumers in this economy can also consume the factors of production or release them for use in making the final goods previously discussed. In a two-consumer, two-producer, three-factor of production world in which the consumers own the factors of production, the following first order conditions must be satisfied.

$$MRS^1_{kl} = MRS^2_{kl} = MRTS^1_{kl} = MRTS^2_{kl} \tag{2}$$

where $MRTS$ represents the marginal rate of technical substitution; kl represents the k and l factor of production. This condition must hold for every pair of production factors. Thus, the relative benefits from consuming the factors of production must equal the relative cost of using l instead of using k.

Lastly, the final coordination brought about by the consumer involves the use of factors of production in producing the final goods. Specifically,

$$MRS^1_{ki} = MRS^2_{ki} = MP^1_{ik} = MP^2_{ik} \tag{3}$$

where all terms are as previously defined and (3) must hold for every final good-factor of production combination.

This perfectly competitive system has a number of assumptions:

1. Consumers' desires are paramount in the system.
2. Perfect information is required.
3. Producers interact with consumers directly.
4. Consumers own the factors of production.
5. Efficient prices are implicit in the barter system.
6. No resources are used to establish equilibrium.
7. Producers are assumed to be technically efficient.
8. Buyers and sellers experience no risk.

Agricultural economists have conducted a significant amount of research on real world markets in an attempt to evaluate the impact on market performance of the violation of the eight assumptions. Even though the model detailed above is not attainable in the real world, it serves as a standard of comparison. The model results in the marginal benefit of the last unit equaling the marginal cost of the last unit. This allocative rule seems reasonable in any type of market in which market failure is not a problem.

EXCHANGE MECHANISMS AND ECONOMIC EFFICIENCY

The extent to which the perfectly competitive assumptions are violated is influenced by exchange mechanisms. Exchange mechanisms influence (1) the amount of information available to buyers and sellers, (2) transaction costs, (3) productive efficiency, (4) buyer and seller risk, and (5) the market power of the buyers and sellers.

INFORMATION

First, perfect information results in price determination in the perfectly competitive model. The price discovery process is nonexistent. However, without perfect information, the price discovery process is predicated on the information available to the exchangers, the type of coordinating mechanism used, the number of buyers and sellers, and the economic environment. The speed of adjustment through disequilibrium to equilibrium is important in the resource allocation process. The rapid adjustment to a new equilibrium can cause unnecessary haste or hesitancy on the part of exchangers because of the price risk involved in an exchange. This will cause an adjustment in demand or supply depending on the risk behavior of the participants.

An efficient market, as defined by Fama (1970), makes no reference to the fact that the resulting price is a competitive price (Buccola 1984, 712). An efficient market is one that arrives at a price over time in a random walk fashion. Thus, an efficient market could result in a monopoly price because of the structure of the market. An efficient market may result in an efficient price if it is further assumed that the buyers and sellers have equal bargaining power, equal information, equal bargaining ability, and the absence of collusive behavior (Buccola 1984, 714).

Gordon (1981) discusses the stickiness of administered prices. He attributes the slow speed of adjustment to adjustment costs and incomplete information. Gordon maintains that the reason that there can exist an auction market and a price setting market is the heterogeneity in the quality and type of products and in the location and timing of transactions. "Heterogeneity would create overwhelming transactions costs for an economy that insisted on determining every price in an auction market. This is easiest to see if we imagine the obstacles to selling by auction in the aisles of a supermarket" (Gordon 1981, 517–18).

TRANSACTION COSTS

The type of exchange mechanism also influences the transaction costs associated with exchange. Such costs can be divided into two categories. First, there are costs associated with the price discovery process, which include (1) the costs associated with the buyer and seller obtaining information on the supply and demand conditions, (2) the buyers searching for the best price, (3) the sellers establishing a price that allows them to maximize profits, and (4) the buyer and seller negotiating an exchange price. Second, the costs of bringing about the exchange include (1) the cost associated with the building and the operation of the exchange, (2) the cost of advertising the exchange, (3) the cost of bringing the product to the market, (4) the cost of grading the product, (5) the cost of packaging the product, (6) the cost of drawing up the contract, (7) the cost of enforcing the contract, and (8) the wages of the people involved in the exchange process.

Williamson (1971, 1973) has done extensive work in this area and evaluates the cost of using the market mechanism based on environmental and human factors. Environmental factors include uncertainty and the small number of buyers and sellers. Human factors include bounded rationality and opportunism. Bounded rationality relates to the limited ability of humans to deal with uncertainty. Humans are assumed to act in a rational manner given the limitations on information and analytical abilities. Opportunism refers to an individual taking advantage of a situation that is in the best interests of the buyer or seller but not both.

When environmental uncertainty increases, the cost of using the market mechanism increases because of the limited ability of humans to handle uncertainty. When the number of buyers (sellers) decreases, the buyers (sellers) encounter more opportunities to take advantage of sellers (buyers).

PRODUCTIVE EFFICIENCY

The type of exchange mechanism also influences the productive efficiency of buyers and sellers. For example, the buyer (seller) can gain additional control over factor inputs (outputs) by decreeing when the product is to be delivered, in what quantity, what quality, the location, and mode of transport. This control can be attained by using a contract in lieu of the spot market. This can decrease the buyers (sellers) costs and increase the demand (supply) for the product.

Agricultural economists have researched this area extensively. French (1977) details the post–World War literature and has a bibliography of 763 publications through the early 1970s.

RISK

Risk is another assumption that if violated can be influenced by exchange mechanisms. Risk goes hand in hand with productive efficiency in that the uncertainty associated with quality, quantity, etc., decreases the demand (supply) of a buyer (seller). There are real resource costs associated with this type of risk. If the exchangers are also risk averse, demand (supply) decreases as a result.

MARKET POWER

Finally, an exchange mechanism can also influence the market power of the exchanger. For example, tying arrangements, output royalties, sales revenue royalties, and lump sum entry fees can improve the market power of the seller. Successive monopoly provides an incentive for the upstream and downstream monopolist to vertically integrate. It can be shown that the upstream monopolist can increase profits by vertically integrating (under a fixed proportions technology) (Blair and Kaserman 1983, 31–35). Output also expands, thus increasing efficiency by decreasing the monopoly elements in the vertical system. The price of the final product will be lower and the output quantity will be higher.

It can be shown that an input monopolist can increase profits by buying the downstream competitive firms who face highly elastic demands and then discriminate on the basis of price. Thus the monopolist can increase the price charged to the downstream firms with an inelastic demand (Blair and Kaserman 1983, 120–24). This results in an increase in output from the firms purchased by the monopolist and a decrease in the output from the firms not purchased. Thus, the welfare effect cannot be established on a priori grounds.

A COSTLY EXCHANGE MODEL

Most of the research on pricing mechanisms has focused on the impact of violating one assumption of the perfectly competitive model on one dimension of market performance. The model in this section assumes that an individual can classify exchange mechanisms with respect to the impact on transaction costs, productive efficiency, and risk. Then, the impact of alternative exchange mechanisms on pricing efficiency, productive efficiency, the distribution of total receipts, and economic surplus is analyzed. The lack of perfect information is not analyzed and is handled by Antonovitz and Roe (See Chap. 9).

The costly exchange model is used to evaluate the effect of alternative exchange mechanisms on market performance. To determine the impact of alternative exchange mechanisms on economic efficiency, the model by Allen (1962) and by Hicks (1963) and more recently used by Floyd (1965) and by Gardner (1975) will be utilized here. This model differs from that used by Gardner only in that Gardner's retail demand is quantity dependent demand. The model in this chapter has been altered to a price dependent demand. Whereas most conventional supply and demand models assume a costless exchange, the model to be presented here assumes a costly exchange.

MODEL

The exchange function, which includes transaction costs, will be quantified through an intermediary (Ulph and Ulph 1975, 360) in the form of

$$X = f\{A, B\} \qquad (4)$$

where X is the exchanged product; A is the product before exchange; and B represents the units of transaction inputs. The production function is assumed to possess constant returns to scale.

The market demand function is

$$P_x = D\{X, N\} \qquad (5)$$

where P_x is the output price of X; X is the quantity of product (not transformed); and N represents a productive efficiency index that captures the impact on demand made by alternative exchange mechanisms and affects P_x as $(\partial P_x / \partial N) > 0$.

The firms involved in the exchange function between the buyer and seller are assumed to be profit maximizers such that

$$Z = P_x X - P_a A - P_b B \qquad (6)$$

where Z equals the aggregate profit from performing the exchange function; P_a and P_b are the prices of inputs A and B. Profit maximization requires that

$$P_x f_a = P_a \qquad (7)$$

$$P_x f_b = P_b \qquad (8)$$

where f_a and f_b are marginal products.

To complete the vertical system, the input market supply equation for exchange services is

$$P_b = G\{B, T\} \qquad (9)$$

where T represents an index of transaction costs such that $(\partial P_b/\partial T) > 0$. The input market supply equation for the exchanged product is

$$P_a = H\{A, W\} \tag{10}$$

where W is an index of productive efficiency and $(\partial P_a/\partial W) < 0$.

The supply and demand equations for the three markets can now be solved for equilibrium. Equilibrium in the market for X is (4) and (5)

$$P_x = D\{f(A, B), N\}, \tag{11}$$

equilibrium in the market for A, (7) and (10), is

$$P_x f_a = H\{A, W\}, \tag{12}$$

and equilibrium in the market for B, (8) and (9), is

$$(P_x)(f_b) = G\{B, T\}. \tag{13}$$

The impact of N or T or W on the equilibrium values of A, B, and P_x can be determined by taking the total derivative of (11), (12), and (13) with respect to one of the exogenous shifters (N, T, or W) at a time. Then all derivatives are changed to elasticities. The three equation system of elasticities can be solved simultaneously to determine the impact of an exogenous variable on the equilibrium values of the quantities A and B and the price of X. The performance of alternative exchange mechanisms can be analyzed from this system of equations and the shocks to the system provided by the exogenous shifters.

PERFORMANCE DIMENSIONS

The performance dimensions include pricing efficiency, productive efficiency, the distribution of total receipts, and the change in economic surplus (consumer and producer surplus). Pricing efficiency is measured by the ratio P_x/P_a. An improvement in relative pricing efficiency occurs when the ratio decreases. Thus, when N increases toward 1, for example, a decrease in the ratio indicates that the exchange mechanism with the higher N results in improved pricing between the two exchange mechanisms. The two mechanisms can also be compared with a third mechanism that has costless exchange and a ratio value of 1.

The second performance dimension is productive efficiency. Productive efficiency is measured as the change in P_a and A for sellers and the change in P_x and X for buyers. If P_a decreases for a given level of A

following an increase in W, then the sellers are productively more efficient as a result of using an alternative exchange mechanism that allowed the sellers to improve productive efficiency. Likewise, if P_x increases for a given level of X, then the alternative exchange mechanism allows the buyer to improve productive efficiency (assuming that the output price of the buyer remains constant).

The third performance dimension is the distribution of total receipts among the intermediaries (providers of input B) and the sellers. The ratio $(P_aA)/(P_xX)$ represents the relative share of the seller (S_a). An increase in the relative share (S_a) means an increase for the seller. The ratio has an upper limit of 1 and a lower limit of 0. An increase in this ratio does not necessarily indicate an increase in total dollars.

The final dimension is the economic surplus of the buyers and sellers. This is measured by the ratio P_x/P_a and the level of A. For example, if the ratio decreases and A increases, this indicates that the economic surplus increases because the ratio P_x/P_a moves closer to 1 where $P_x = P_a$, which would represent the maximum economic surplus (the demand curve for X and the supply curve for A are assumed to be income compensated curves). The net change is positive among the three participants even though the intermediaries are likely losing economic rent.

Economic surplus can also increase when the ratio P_x/P_a does not decrease even though A increases. This can occur when the demand curve shifts to the right or when the supply curve shifts to the right. These shifts occur when the productive efficiency of the buyers and sellers improves as a result of using an alternate exchange mechanism.

RESULTS

Transaction Costs. The pricing efficiency associated with transaction cost (T) is evaluated with respect to (A8) in Appendix 1 which is

$$E\{(P_x/P_a), T\} = \langle\langle\langle\langle\{-e_t * (1/N_p)\} * [\{(S_b ** 2/Sigma)$$
$$+ (S_b/e_a)\} + \{(S_b * S_a)/Sigma\}]\rangle/Det\rangle$$
$$- \langle[(-S_b * e_t) * \{(1/Sigma) + (1/N_p)\}]/Det\rangle \qquad (14)$$
$$* (1/e_a)\rangle$$

where E is total elasticity; e_t is the partial elasticity of P_b with respect to T; N_p is the partial price elasticity of demand; S_b is the relative share of the intermediaries; $Sigma$ is the elasticity of substitution between A and B; e_a is the partial elasticity of supply for A; S_a is the relative share of the sellers; Det is a determinate as defined in Appendix 1 (A15); e_b is the partial elasticity of supply for B. The elasticity in (14) is evaluated over the following variable values: $e_t = 1$; $S_a = .1$ to 1; $S_b = 1 - S_a$; $Sigma = .1$ to 1.9; $e_a = .1$ to 1.9; $e_b = .1$ to 1.9; $N_p = -.1$ to -1.9. The total elasticity was found to be positive in all cases ranging from .005 to 3.15 percent. In general, small positive values are associated with large values of *Sigma*. Thus, an increase in T is associated with a decrease in pricing efficiency.

The next performance dimension is the distribution of total receipts. The total elasticity of S_a with respect to T is (A10) in Appendix 1 which is

$$E\{S_a, T\} = \langle\langle\langle[(-S_b * e_t) * \{(1/Sigma) + (1/N_p)\}]/Det\rangle$$
$$* (1/e_a)\rangle\rangle - \langle\langle\{-e_t * (1/N_p)\} * [\{(S_b ** 2/Sigma)$$
$$+ (S_b/e_a)\} + \{(S_b * S_a)/Sigma\}]\rangle/Det\rangle \quad (15)$$
$$+ \langle S_b * \langle\langle[(-S_b * e_t) * \{(1/Sigma) + (1/N_p)\}]/Det\rangle$$
$$- \langle[e_t * \{(S_a/N_p) - (S_b/Sigma) + (1/e_a)\}]\rangle/Det\rangle\rangle$$

where all variables are as previously defined and the equation is evaluated over the previously stated ranges. The total elasticity of (15) is found to range from a -2.83 to .41, which indicates that the sellers are impacted differently depending upon variable values. When *Sigma* equals 1 then $E\{S_a, T\}$ equals 0.

The final performance dimension is economic surplus. (14) was found to be positive for all values. However, the impact of an increase in T on the quantity of A has yet to be analyzed. This total elasticity is defined as

$$E\{A, T\} = \langle[(-S_b * e_t) * \{(1/Sigma) + (1/N_p)\}]/Det\rangle \quad (16)$$

where all variables are as previously defined and the equation is evaluated over the ranges previously stated. The total elasticity of A with respect to T was found to vary from a $-.77$ to .77. Therefore, when positive or negative values of (14) are associated with positive values of (16), then total buyer and seller surplus has increased. If the total elasticity of A with respect to T (16) is negative, then total buyer and seller surplus has decreased irrespective of the sign of (14).

In summary, an increase in T worsens pricing efficiency and may or may not improve economic surplus and the total distribution of receipts to sellers.

Buyer Productive Efficiency. Mechanisms can influence the supply and demand behavior of sellers and buyers and the cost of exchange. The change in demand behavior is simulated through the exogenous variable N (buyer productive efficiency) that initially shocks the system of equations by shifting the demand function (5) such that P_x changes by 1 percent as N changes by an arbitrary 1 percent for a given X. The performance of the two exchange mechanisms can be compared by determining the total elasticity of each of the performance dimensions with respect to N.

The 1 percent increase in N does influence exchange performance. First, the impact on pricing efficiency is measured by the total elasticity (A5) in Appendix 1 which is

$$
\begin{aligned}
E\{(P_x/P_a),N\} = \langle\langle\langle -N_n * \langle\{(S_b/Sigma) * (S_a/Sigma)\} \\
- [\{(1/e_b) + (S_a/Sigma)\} * \{(S_b/Sigma) \\
+ (1/e_a)\}]\rangle\rangle/Det\rangle - \langle\langle\langle N_n * [\{(1/e_b) \\
+ (S_a/Sigma)\} + (S_b/Sigma)]\rangle/Det\rangle * (1/e_a)\rangle\rangle
\end{aligned}
\tag{17}
$$

where N_n is the partial elasticity of P_x with respect to N and all other variables are as previously defined. (17) is evaluated over the previously stated ranges. The total elasticity in (17) went from -2.84 to $.84$. This indicates that pricing efficiency first improves then worsens. In general, the negative total elasticity is associated with an inelastic supply for A and an elastic supply for B.

The next performance dimension is productive efficiency. Productive efficiency is defined relative to the sign of

$$
\begin{aligned}
E\{P_x,N\} = \langle -N_n * [\{(S_b/Sigma) * (S_a/Sigma)\} \\
- \{(1/e_b) + (S_a/Sigma)\} * \{(S_b/Sigma) \\
+ 1/e_a\}]\rangle/Det
\end{aligned}
\tag{18}
$$

where all variables are as previously defined and the equation is evaluated over the value of the variables as previously stated. By definition, an increase in N is an increase in the productive efficiency of the buyer. However, (18) gives the total elasticity of P_x with respect to N, which will differ from the partial elasticity of P_x with respect to N. The total elasticity ranged from $.05$ to $.95$ percent.

The next performance dimension is the distribution of receipts among the intermediaries and the sellers. This is defined as (A7) in Appendix 1 which is

$$E\{S_a, N\} = \langle\langle\langle N_n * [\{(l/e_b) + (S_a/Sigma)\} + (S_b/Sigma)]\rangle/Det\rangle$$
$$* (1/e_a)\rangle - \langle\langle -N_n * \langle\{(S_b/Sigma) * (S_a/Sigma)\}$$
$$- [\{(1/e_b) + (S_a/Sigma)\} * \{(S_b/Sigma)$$
$$+ (1/e_t)\}]\rangle\rangle/Det\rangle + \langle S_b * \langle\langle\langle N_n * [\{(1/e_b)$$
$$+ (S_a/Sigma)\} + (S_b/Sigma)]\rangle/Det\rangle - \langle\langle N_n$$
$$* [\{(S_b/Sigma) + (1/e_a)\} + (S_a/Sigma)]\rangle/Det\rangle\rangle\rangle$$

(19)

where all variables are as previously defined and evaluated as previously mentioned. The total elasticity in (19) ranged from $-.75$ to 2.56 with a large range of the parameters yielding 0 elasticity. An increase in the elasticity of B from 1 to 1.9 causes an increase in the total elasticity from .64 to 2.55. In general, an increase in N results in a decrease or very small increase in S_a.

The final performance dimension used to evaluate an increase in N is that of economic surplus. This dimension is defined with respect to the total elasticity of P_x/P_a given a percentage change in N (17). The total elasticity was both positive and negative.

The total elasticity of A with respect to N must also be evaluated to analyze economic surplus. This elasticity is defined as

$$E\{A, N\} = \langle\langle N_n * [\{(1/e_b) + (S_a/Sigma)\}$$
$$+ (S_b/Sigma)]\rangle/Det\rangle$$

(20)

where E is the total elasticity of A with respect to N and the other variables are as previously defined. The total elasticity of A with respect to N was always positive. The elasticity ranged from .01 to .95. Thus, an improvement in N always leads to an increase in the quantity of A traded. This indicates that, whether the total elasticity of the price ratio was positive or negative, economic surplus increased in all cases.

In summary, an increase in N was associated with an increase in productive efficiency and an increase in economic surplus. Pricing efficiency was ambiguous but improvement in pricing efficiency was associated with an inelastic supply for A and an elastic supply for B. A worsening in pricing efficiency is associated with an elastic supply for A and an inelastic supply for B. The distribution of total receipts was also ambiguous with no or little improvement over the parameter ranges.

Seller Productive Efficiency. The next characteristic that may differ among exchange mechanisms is the productive efficiency of sellers

W. As alternative mechanisms are used by sellers, W influences the performance of the market. The pricing efficiency associated with W is evaluated by using the total elasticity (A11) in Appendix 1 which is

$$
\begin{aligned}
E\{(P_x/P_a), W\} = \langle\langle\{-e_w * (1/N_p)\} * [\{(S_a/e_b) \\
+ (S_a ** 2/Sigma)\} + \{(S_a * S_b)/Sigma\}]\rangle/Det\rangle \\
- \langle\langle\langle e_w * [(S_b/N_p) - \{(1/e_b) \\
+ (S_a/Sigma)\}]\rangle/Det\rangle/\langle\langle(N_p * Sigma) \\
+ [e_b * \{(S_a * N_p) - (S_b * Sigma)\}]\rangle \\
/\{e_b + (S_a * Sigma) - (S_b * N_p)\}\rangle\rangle
\end{aligned}
\tag{21}
$$

where all terms and ranges are as previously defined. The pricing efficiency was found to worsen in all cases, $E\{(P_x/P_a), W\} > 0$. The elasticity ranged from .005 to .93.

The next performance dimension is productive efficiency which is evaluated by (A12) in Appendix 1 which is

$$
\begin{aligned}
E\{P_a, W\} = \langle\langle\langle e_w * [(S_b/N_p) - \{(1/e_b) + (S_a/Sigma)\}]\rangle/Det\rangle \\
/\langle\langle(N_p * Sigma) + [e_b * \{(S_a * N_p) \\
- (S_b * Sigma)\}]\rangle/\{e_b + (S_a * Sigma) - (S_b * N_n)\}\rangle\rangle
\end{aligned}
\tag{22}
$$

where all terms and ranges are as previously defined. Productive efficiency improves by definition whenever W increases $E\{P_a, W\} < 0$. The improvement ranges from $-.05$ to $-.95$ percent.

The next performance dimension is the distribution of total receipts. The total elasticity of S_a with respect to W is (A14) in Appendix 1 which is

$$
\begin{aligned}
E\{S_a, W\} = \langle\langle\langle\langle e_w * [(S_b/N_p) - \{(1/e_b) + (S_a/Sigma)\}]\rangle/Det\rangle \\
/\langle\langle(N_p * Sigma) + [e_b * \{(S_a * N_p) - (S_b * Sigma)\}]\rangle \\
/\{e_b + (S_a * Sigma) - (S_b * N_p)\}\rangle\rangle - \langle\{-e_w * (1/N_p)\} \\
* [\{(S_a/e_b) + (S_a ** 2/Sigma)\} + \{(S_a * S_b)/Sigma\}]\rangle\rangle \\
/Det\rangle + \langle S_b * \langle\langle\langle e_w * [(S_b/N_p) - \{(1/e_b) + (S_a/Sigma)\}]\rangle \\
/Det\rangle - \langle[(-e_w * S_a) * \{(1/Sigma) + (1/N_p)\}]/Det\rangle\rangle
\end{aligned}
\tag{23}
$$

where all terms and ranges are as previously defined. The total elasticity is found to be both positive and negative with a value of 0 when *Sigma* equals 1. The elasticity ranges from $-.84$ to .41.

The last performance dimension is the change in economic surplus when W increases. The total elasticity is defined as

$$E\{A, W\} = \langle\langle e_w * [(S_b/N_p) - \{(1/e_b) + (S_a/Sigma)\}]\rangle/Det\rangle \qquad (24)$$

where all terms and values are as previously defined. (24) is positive for all parameter values. The results indicate that an increase in W increases P_x/P_a (21) and the level of A. Therefore, total buyer and seller surplus increases. The elasticity ranges from .05 to .95.

In summary, an increase in W will worsen pricing efficiency, improve productive efficiency, improve economic surplus, and alter the distribution of total receipts by decreasing S_a when *Sigma* is less than 1 and increasing S_a when *Sigma* is greater than 1.

Risk. The last characteristic that may differ among alternative exchange mechanisms is that of risk. The model is altered to include risk by redefining N and W as indices of risk. The partial elasticity of P_x with respect to N (N_n) is negative. N will now be redefined as N^* and the partial elasticity as N_n^*. A 1 percent increase in N^* will initially decrease $P_x(N_n^*)$ by an arbitrary 1 percent. The impact of a riskier exchange mechanism on the performance dimensions is exactly opposite of that discussed in (17) through (20). Positive values become negative values and negative values become positive values with the same magnitudes. Thus, an increase in buyer's risk will worsen productive efficiency and decrease buyer and seller surplus. Pricing efficiency was ambiguous but the worsening of pricing efficiency was associated with the elastic supply for A and the inelastic supply for B. An improvement in pricing efficiency is associated with an inelastic supply for A and an elastic supply for B. The distribution of total receipts is also ambiguous.

Seller risk can be operationalized in this model by redefining W as an index of risk, W'. The partial elasticity of P_a with respect to W' is positive ($e_w > 0$). The impact of a riskier exchange mechanism on the sellers can be evaluated by looking at (21) through (24).

In summary, an increase in W' will improve pricing efficiency, worsen productive efficiency, worsen economic surplus, and alter the distribution of total receipts from an increase in S_a when *Sigma* is less than 1 and decrease S_a when *Sigma* is greater than 1.

SUMMARY

Being able to classify exchange mechanisms into components that can be analyzed has been a major stumbling block to evaluating the influence of exchange mechanisms on economic efficiency. The components include (1) the amount of information available to buyers and sellers, (2) transaction costs, (3) productive efficiency, (4) buyer and seller risk, and (5) the market power of the buyers and sellers. This chapter evaluates the impact of alternative exchange mechanisms on (1) pricing efficiency, (2) productive efficiency, (3) the distribution of total receipts, and (4) the change in economic surplus. In general it was found that an increase in transaction costs worsens pricing efficiency, and may or may not improve economic surplus and the total distribution of receipts to sellers. An increase in buyer productive efficiency improves economic surplus, but the effects on pricing efficiency and the distribution of total receipts to sellers are ambiguous. An increase in seller productive efficiency worsens pricing efficiency, improves economic surplus, and the effect on total receipts is ambiguous. An increase in buyer's risk improves pricing efficiency, decreases productive efficiency, decreases economic surplus and the distribution of total receipts to sellers is ambiguous. Finally an increase in seller risk decreases productive efficiency, decreases economic surplus, and the effects on pricing efficiency and the distribution of total receipts to sellers are ambiguous.

The shortcomings of the model include (1) the assumption of perfect information, (2) the model is not dynamic, (3) market power is not analyzed, and (4) the exchange function is performed by an intermediary rather than the firms themselves. Further research remains to be done.

APPENDIX 1

The derivation of the total elasticities (14) through (24) relied upon the following relationships.

$$f_{ab} = (f_a * f_b)/(Sigma * X) \text{ (Allen 1962, 343)} \tag{A1}$$

$$f_{aa} = -(B/A) * [(f_a * f_b)/(Sigma * X)] \text{ (Allen 1962, 343)} \tag{A2}$$

$$f_a = P_a/P_x \text{ (Eq. 7)} \tag{A3}$$

$$f_b = P_b/P_x \text{ (Eq. 8)} \tag{A4}$$

$$E\{(P_x/P_a),N\} = E\{P_x,N\} - E\{P_a,N\} \text{ (Gardner 1975, 408)} \tag{A5}$$

$$E\{P_a,N\} = E\{A,N\}/e_a \text{ (Gardner 1975, 408)} \tag{A6}$$

$$E\{S_a,N\} = E\{P_a,N\} - E\{P_x,N\} + S_b[E\{A,N\} - E\{B,N\}] \tag{A7}$$
$$\text{(Gardner 1975, 409)}$$

$$E\{(P_x/P_a),T\} = E\{P_x,T\} - E\{P_a,T\} \text{ (Gardner 1975, 408)} \tag{A8}$$

$$E\{P_a, T\} = E\{A, T\}/e_a \quad \text{(Gardner 1975, 408)} \tag{A9}$$

$$E\{S_a, T\} = E\{P_a, T\} - E\{P_x, T\} + S_b[E\{A, T\} - E\{B, T\}] \tag{A10}$$
$$\text{(Gardner 1975, 409)}$$

$$E\{(P_x/P_a), W\} = E\{P_x, W\} - E\{P_a, W\} \quad \text{(Gardner 1975, 409)} \tag{A11}$$

$$E\{P_a, W\} = E\{A, W\}/E\{A, P_a] \quad \text{(Gardner 1975, 409)} \tag{A12}$$

$$E\{A, P_a\} = [(N_p * Sigma) + e_b * \{(S_a * N_p) - (S_b * Sigma)\}] \tag{A13}$$
$$/\{e_b + (S_a * Sigma) - (S_b * N_n)\} \quad \text{(Floyd 1965, 153)}$$

$$E\{S_a, W\} = \{P_a, W\} - E\{P_x, W\} + S_b[E\{A, W\} - E\{B, W\}] \tag{A14}$$
$$\text{(Gardner 1975, 409)}$$

$$DET = \langle -[(S_a/N_p) * \{(1/e_b) + (S_a/Sigma)\}] - [(S_b/N_p) * \{(S_b/Sigma)$$
$$+ (1/e_a)\}] - \{(S_b/Sigma) * (S_a/Sigma)\} + [\{(1/e_b)$$
$$+ (S_a/Sigma)\} * \{(S_b/Sigma) + (1/e_a)\}] \tag{A15}$$
$$- \{(S_b/Sigma) * (S_a/N_p)\} - \{(S_a/Sigma) * (S_b/N_p)\}\rangle$$

REFERENCES

Allen, R. G. D. *Mathematical Analysis for Economists*. New York: Macmillan, 1962.

Blair, Roger D., and David L. Kaserman. *Law and Economics of Vertical Integration and Control*. New York: Academic Press, 1983.

Buccola, Steven T. "Pricing Efficiency and Information Use in Risky Markets." *Am. J. Agric. Econ.* 66(1984):711–16.

Fama, E. "Efficient Capital Markets: A Review of Theory and Empirical Work." *J. Fin.* 25(1970):383–417.

Floyd, John E. "The Effects of Farm Price Supports on the Returns to Land and Labor in Agriculture." *J. Polit. Econ.* 73(1965):148–98.

French, Ben C. "The Analysis of Productive Efficiency in Agricultural Marketing: Models, Methods, and Progress." *A Survey of Agricultural Economics Literature,* vol. 1, ed. L. R. Martin, pp. 93–206. Minneapolis: University of Minnesota Press, 1977.

Gardner, Bruce L. "The Farm-Retail Price Spread in a Competitive Food Industry." *Am. J. Agric. Econ.* 57(1975):399–409.

Gordon, Robert J. "Output Fluctuations and Gradual Price Adjustment." *J. Econ. Lit.* 19(1981):493–530.

Hicks, J. R. *The Theory of Wages*. New York: St. Martin's Press, 1963.

Sporleder, Thomas L. "Emerging Information Technologies and Agricultural Structure." *Am. J. Agric. Econ.* 65(1983):388–94.

Tomek, William G., and Kenneth L. Robinson. *Agricultural Product Prices*. Ithaca, N.Y.: Cornell University Press, 1981.

Ulph, A. M., and D. T. Ulph. "Transaction Costs in General Equilibrium Theory—A Survey." *Economica* 42(1975):355–72.

Williamson, Oliver E. "The Vertical Integration of Production: Market Failure Considerations." *Am. Econ. Rev.* 61(1971):112–23.

———. "Markets and Hierarchies: Some Elementary Considerations." *Am. Econ. Rev.* 63(1973):316–25.

The Economic Efficiency of
Alternative Exchange Mechanisms

A DISCUSSION

William G. Tomek

RICHARD KILMER points out that exchange mechanisms affect economic efficiency in two ways: (1) through their influence on price behavior, and (2) through their own use of resources. Thus, an efficient exchange mechanism is the least cost method of generating competitive prices. Kilmer's paper is mainly about the first component, namely the influence of pricing mechanisms on price behavior. My discussion emphasizes that the minimization of transactions costs is important in understanding the evolution of pricing mechanisms. The first section, however, outlines a few quibbles about minor points in Kilmer's paper. Then, the second section characterizes his model, and the third section discusses the importance of transactions costs as a basis for explaining the development of pricing mechanisms.

MINOR QUIBBLES

Kilmer singles out "too rapid" adjustments in prices as a potential problem of pricing mechanisms. This is a bit puzzling because the perfect competition model used by Kilmer implies instantaneous adjustments of prices. Perhaps the definition of an efficient pricing mechanism should include an optimal adjustment path, but this notion needs to be defined more precisely. Imperfections in price adjustments can be of two types: price continuity (prices underadjust initially to new information) and price reaction (prices overadjust initially to new information).

In addition, I found the discussion of competition, efficiency, and random walks in prices a bit confusing. With perfect competition, current price reflects all existing information, and prices adjust instantly to new information. Since truly new information occurs randomly, this imparts a random component to price changes. But competitive spot prices have systematic components as well. Clearly, for example, the competitive spot

WILLIAM G. TOMEK is professor, Department of Agricultural Economics, Cornell University, Ithaca, New York.

market for potatoes would generate a price series with a seasonal component. Monopoly prices are administered and hence are sticky. Thus, it seems unlikely that changes in administered prices are random. In sum, an efficient price need not be a random walk, and a monopoly price is neither a random walk nor efficient.

KILMER'S MODEL

The major part of Kilmer's paper is devoted to a model of competitive equilibrium that is used to analyze the consequences of alternative exchange mechanisms for economic efficiency. The model closely parallels Gardner's (1975) marketing margin model. This model includes a production function for food with farm and marketing inputs, a retail demand function for food, supply functions for each of the two inputs, and conditions for a competitive equilibrium under profit maximization. The retail demand function and the two supply functions each contain an exogenous variable, and the effects of changes in these variables on the marketing margin are analyzed.

Basically, Kilmer substitutes exchange mechanisms for the marketing inputs of Gardner's (1975) model. In this transformation of the model, the exogenous variables in the demand and supply functions are related to the various exchange mechanisms. Thus, the level of buyers' demand depends on the type of exchange mechanism, and the supply of exchange services depends on an index of transaction costs. Likewise, the productivity of sellers is made dependent on the type of exchange mechanism.

Consequently, a subtle difference exists between Gardner's (1975) and Kilmer's use of the one-product, two-input model. In the Gardner application, the shifters in the demand and supply functions clearly are exogenous to the market; they are such variables as population and a tax on marketing inputs. Since, in the Kilmer specification, the exogenous variables depend on the exchange mechanism and since, whether or not a particular mechanism is used depends on these same variables, the exogenous variables are better viewed as endogenously determined in a larger system. This does not change the mathematics of the analysis, but it does raise a question about the practicality of applying the model.

I also have some difficulty with using the notion of a supply schedule for exchange services. I can accept the concept of a supply of exchange services that is a function of a price of exchange services (i.e., an equation derived from the underlying marginal cost function for a particular mechanism). This function, however, may differ from one pricing mechanism to another, and little basis exists for postulating the slopes or elasticities of the supply functions for the alternative pricing mechanisms.

This lack of information about the parameters of the model is important, because the model is intended to answer questions about the economic efficiency of alternative mechanisms. Merely indicating how efficiency will vary as parameters and "exogenous" variables change is not very interesting unless these changes can be associated with a particular pricing mechanism.

Thus, several difficulties exist in applying the model. First, the variables being used in the analyses are, in a sense, endogenous to a larger system that explains the adoption of the mechanism. Second, as one switches mechanisms, the parameters are likely to change, but little or no basis exists for making good (useful) guesses about these parameters. Thus, while the model can answer general questions about efficiency, it cannot explain why a particular mechanism was adopted nor can it compare specific mechanisms.

Of course, the Gardner-Kilmer approach could be used to analyze the effects of truly exogenous variables on a particular pricing system. This also would require that reasonable conjectures about the parameters of the model be available, but in this case the consequences of alternative parameters for a given mechanism are being appraised.

TRANSACTIONS COSTS

Assessing the factors that explain changes in pricing mechanisms is not easy, but by using Williamson's (1981) analysis of modern corporations, a case can be made that shifts and innovations in pricing systems are influenced importantly by incentives to economize on transactions costs. (Williamson discusses other variables as do Tomek and Paul 1979.) The nature of transactions costs helps explain why some economic activity takes place within firms while other economic decisions are best mediated by markets (Coase 1937). Similar forces presumably shape the institutional arrangements within markets.

Transactions costs must be broadly conceived. As Kilmer mentions, they include the costs of search among buyers and sellers, the cost of obtaining information, the physical costs of trade such as operating an exchange or drawing up a contract, and the efficiencies (or inefficiencies) associated with the location and timing of transactions. Transactions costs also depend on how flexible the system is in adapting to unforeseen circumstances and how important and costly this flexibility is to obtain (i.e., the nature of the demand for flexibility and the cost of providing it). A liquid futures market, for example, allows a firm to enter and leave a forward contract at low cost. In addition, the probability of default on a futures contract is nil. In contrast, a forward contract on a spot market is not liquid and has a higher risk of default. But futures contracts are homogeneous and cannot be adapted easily to specialized circumstances. For example, the need to specify a particular delivery schedule from a grower to a processor makes a forward contract more useful than a futures contract.

Naturally in a dynamic economy, the relative costs of alternative mechanisms can change. Exogenous changes in the relative prices of capital and labor can occur. Perhaps more important, a revolution is occurring in the technology of communicating and computing, and this surely has implications for transactions costs. Also, changes in technology are making many agricultural commodities less perishable and more transportable. At the same time, price risk has tended to increase in some agricultural product and input markets, though the degree of price risk in given markets changes with the passage of time.

Kilmer's model helps provide a general understanding of the consequences of changes in pricing mechanisms, but it does not identify the sources and strengths of the factors causing shifts in pricing mechanisms. It is important, in my view, to try to understand these forces. Markets and their associated pricing mechanisms may be trending toward more monopolistic structures and toward more decisions being made within firms. If these trends are thought to be undesirable, then the question arises of whether public policy can influence the trends, and I doubt that the one-product, two-input model can address this fundamental issue.

In sum, Kilmer's paper deals with one piece of a complex puzzle. It is too much to ask any single paper to deal with the entire puzzle, but the big picture must be kept in mind as we deal with the pieces.

REFERENCES

Coase, R. H. "The Nature of the Firm." *Economica* 4(1937):386–405.
Gardner, Bruce L. "The Farm-Retail Price Spread in a Competitive Food Industry." *Am. J. Agric. Econ.* 57(1975):399–409.
Tomek, William G., and Allen B. Paul. "Coordination and Exchange Influences on Farm Structure." In *Structure Issues of American Agriculture.* Washington, D.C.: USDA ESCS Agric. Econ. Rep. 438, pp. 235–40. Nov. 1979.
Williamson, Oliver E. "The Modern Corporation: Origins, Evolution, Attributes." *J. Econ. Lit.* 19(1981):1537–68.

Economies of Scope, Contestability Theory, and Economic Efficiency

James M. MacDonald

TRADITIONAL APPLICATIONS of microeconomic theory to industrial organization often encounter two related sources of theoretical dispute stemming from traditional theory's reliance on polar cases. Each affects a traditional component of efficiency measurement. The first source arises in the area of pricing, where traditional theory offers the clean predictions of pure monopoly and perfect competition, but a frustrating multiplicity of special cases where oligopoly exists. The second is traditional theory's reliance on single product cost functions in a world of highly diversified firms whose products may be closely related on the production side.

Contestability theory directly takes on the first area of dispute and attempts to move away from associating competitive outcomes with the number of competitors (because of the multiplicity of potential outcomes under oligopoly) by describing markets in which the number of firms is irrelevant to performance. In brief, contestability attempts to specify the conditions under which natural oligopolies (markets in which scale economies are large enough to ensure a small number of sellers) achieve perfectly competitive results and, therefore, allocative efficiency. Purely contestable markets, like perfectly competitive markets, are abstractions without real world counterparts, and the importance of contestability theory depends upon the degree to which results are robust to small changes in market conditions. I will emphasize the robustness issue in my discussion.

JAMES M. MACDONALD is an agricultural economist with Economic Research Service, USDA, Washington, D.C.

The second source of dispute is under attack from several directions. First, recent developments in data bases and econometrics have allowed for the statistical investigation of multiproduct production. Second, theorists have begun to develop new concepts of costs for multiproduct firms and have related these concepts to the ideal (least cost) industry structure and to the theory of contestability. One of these concepts, economies of scope, refers to cost complementarities among separate outputs, and in its ambitious form relates product diversification to contestability, economies of scope, and productive efficiency in an analogy to the link between productive efficiency, economies of scale, and natural monopoly.

The terms "contestability" and "economies of scope" were coined and popularized by William Baumol, John Panzar, and Robert Willig (1982, 1983) in a series of papers, and the terms have achieved a wide, if sometimes inappropriate, usage.[1] I will outline the theories in the sections that follow. Each has important precursors in industrial organization and I try to place the theories in the context of those developments.

Contestability theory has attracted a considerable amount of comment already. For that reason, my section on contestability will review the theory and the major criticisms without breaking new ground, and I will try to assess the contribution of contestability in light of the current criticism and the considerable amount of previous research.

Scope economies have yet to receive the close scrutiny given contestability; most commentaries have been descriptive. Therefore, I will try to provide a thorough discussion of several weaknesses in the emerging literature that I think must be resolved if the ideas are to prove useful. The weaknesses, which result from the poorly understood nature of the sources of economies, attenuate the welfare implications of scope economies and the relevance of empirical tests.

CONTESTABILITY THEORY

The best way to approach the idea of contestability is to think of it as a generalization of perfect competition, and therefore to proceed with a comparison of the two and a description of the points of departure.

Perfect competition is feasible under a set of well-known conditions. Among them, profit maximization, perfect information, and the absence of externalities are also assumed to hold for perfect contestability. More important, perfect competition requires constant or diminishing returns to scale, or scale economies that are quite small in relation to the size of the market. The scale economy assumption allows for a large number of competitors, which removes the incentives for strategic behavior and allows firms to be price takers. Price taking, in turn, leads to desirable welfare outcomes (prices equal to marginal and average costs) and precise predictions about the behavior of firms and industries in response to changes in external conditions.

Problems arise when scale economies become important. With few sellers, firms must take account of each other's reactions; with such strategic behavior comes a multiplicity of potential equilibria, welfare outcomes, and firm and industry responses to changed external conditions.[2]

Contestable market theory applies directly to a world of scale economies. It is analogous to perfect competition in that it locates a welfare optimum (prices equal to marginal and average costs under constant returns, and optimal "Ramsey prices" under increasing returns) under conditions of scale economies and identifies industry characteristics necessary for that optimum. In short, contestable market theory tries to provide a welfare standard that is more robust than that of perfect competition, because of the relaxation of the assumption of many sellers.

Now recall that in the theory of perfect competition the assumption of nonincreasing returns leads to large numbers of sellers and price-taking behavior, which in turn leads to the welfare optima. With scale economies and small numbers in the theory of contestability, optimal performance is assured, not by large numbers of sellers, but by the threat of entry, which takes a prominent role in all analyses of contestability.

ENTRY IN CONTESTABILITY THEORY

In perfect contestability, free entry, which Shepherd (1984) calls "ultra-free" because of its stringent requirements, exists when for any single seller there are potential competitors(s) with the same cost function as the seller, who can enter and leave the market before the incumbent can react to that entry by changing price. While this is clearly an extreme assumption, recall that the authors are providing a normative standard, just as in the theory of perfect competition. We will consider the robustness of the theory to modest changes in assumptions in later sections, but for now we will consider "free entry" more closely.

The first part of the definition, identical cost curves, can hardly be a controversial theoretical position. It follows from a standard, perfect information assumption, and is akin to Stigler's (1968) conception of barriers to entry, wherein a barrier imposes costs on an entrant that are not borne by the incumbent. That is, scale economies do not pose a barrier to entry in contestable markets.

The second part of the definition is the critical one and is essentially a statement of the degree to which capital must be committed to a market or "sunk." The idea can best be described with an example, and proponents of contestability theory often use the example of airlines.[3]

Most airline markets (defined as city pairs) are served by a small number of carriers and sometimes only a single carrier. However, monopoly power can still be constrained because of the ease of entry into a specific market (after deregulation and with no landing slot constraints at airports). The entrant, assumed to be an existing airline serving other markets, must commit some aircraft to the market. Although aircraft are expensive, the investment is not sunk with respect to any specific market since the aircraft can be flown to other markets if the firm decides to exit. Some ground-level investment in crew and equipment must be made, but that investment is small and much of it can be moved. In short, very little of the investment must be committed to the specific city-pair and so there is little entry risk; an entrant can easily reverse its decision and exit the market without losing capital.

Large fixed costs (such as the outlay for aircraft), which give rise to downward sloping short-run average cost curves, do not serve as barriers to entry. Rather, sunk costs are the critical determinant.

By way of contrasting example, consider railroad service between two cities. A considerable amount of capital (right-of-way, trackage, and facilities) must be committed to the market (sunk) and cannot be directed to other markets if the investment turns sour (rolling stock, of course, is not sunk since it can be rolled elsewhere). As a result, there is considerable entry risk in a railroad market and sunk costs can serve as real barriers to entry.

If there are no sunk costs, then entry will be profitable as long as price exceeds the incremental costs of providing service. If an incumbent seller sets a price above incremental costs, an entrant (who has an identical cost function) can enter the market, slightly undercut the price of the incumbent, and attract all of the buyers while making a profit. Incumbents are assumed to be unable to cut price during the time it takes for this to occur.

The threat of this "hit-and-run" entry, given zero sunk costs, leads to perfect contestability. As long as the market is perfectly contestable, the incumbent's best strategy will be to set price equal to incremental costs; consequently, prices and market structure will mirror the least cost structure of production, and monopoly or oligopoly will not present a welfare problem.

The theory of contestability emphasizes the role of entry barriers in the determination of industry performance, consistent with common practice in the empirical literature of industrial organization. However, the use of entry barriers, in the theory developed thus far, can be at variance with common interpretations in the empirical literature. First, the threat of entry is the key disciplining factor in perfect contestability. Actual entry, because it is consistent with an excess of price over incremental costs, becomes evidence against perfect contestability in markets with a small number of sellers. Second, in the context of structure-performance studies, we may try to treat markets as if they were generally contestable if we find no contemporaneous association between concentration and price levels or properly defined profits. This is a stringent requirement since the "pro-competitive" criticisms of structure-profit studies follow a different approach. For example, Peltzman (1977) as well as Demsetz (1973) argue that large firms in concentrated markets are more efficient than their competitors. While entirely possible, that position is inconsistent with contestability's emphasis on identical cost functions. Alternatively, Brozen (1971) argues that positive concentration-profits relationships are temporary phenomena, as entry erodes monopoly power over time. Again, that position, while an attractive possibility, is inconsistent with contestability theory, in which ease of entry leads to no contemporaneous relation between profits and the number of sellers.[4]

Is the Theory Robust?

No one treats perfectly contestable markets as faithful reflections of real markets. Perfect contestability has two functions. First, it serves as a normative welfare standard, as does perfect competition. Second, there is a tradition in industrial organization, and in applied microtheory generally, that takes the position that we can map small changes in industry conditions into small changes in the predicted performance of firms and industries, and that for many purposes we can proceed "as if" many markets were perfectly competitive and use the competitive model to analyze the effects of cost changes resulting, for example, from shifts in taxes or input prices on output price changes.[5] For contestability to be useful, it must also give promise of being robust in the sense of mapping small changes in the sunkenness of costs into small changes in performance. Recent criticism of contestability focuses on these issues.[6]

To consider the robustness issue, return to the definition of free entry in contestable markets: free entry exists when there is a potential entrant, with costs which match the incumbents, who can enter and leave within the time frame required for incumbents to change prices.

Note, first, that buyers are presumed to react instantaneously to entrant price changes, while rival sellers respond only with a lag. There is further reason to criticize the incumbent's pricing lag that is assumed in the definition, since it essentially serves to assume away any conjectural interactions (rivalous price or output behavior) among the firms, and conjectural interactions are the essence of oligopoly modeling. Baumol et al. (1982, 1983) respond that in reality price changes are costly and therefore take some finite amount of time to carry out; the pricing lag is an innocuous assumption because, without sunk costs, firms can instantaneously enter and leave markets.

They also hold that contestability should be robust. That is, for modest amounts of sunk costs, the threat of entry will keep incumbent's prices close to competitive levels. Prices diverge from incremental costs only when sunk costs are large and sellers are few. It is this position that Schwartz and Reynolds (1983, 1984) attack. They define sunkenness as the proportion of fixed costs that cannot be recovered after operation for some specified time period (the incumbent's pricing lag). For various combinations of discount rates, pricing lags, and degrees of sunkenness, they argue that the optimal strategy for an incumbent with small sunk costs is to charge the monopoly price and invite entry. As a result, they argue, contestability theory has limited relevance as a theory of the pricing behavior of firms since perfect contestability is unlikely to be realized and small departures from perfect contestability do not necessarily map into small changes in pricing. It may be rational for incumbents to price like monopolists in some "almost contestable" markets.

The popularity of contestability theory may not be much affected by disputes over the robustness of its pricing predictions. It seems to me that for many economists the term has come to represent a metaphor for any market with low or nonexistent entry barriers. Among specialists in empirical industrial organization, I suspect that there is wide support for the proposition that, absent entry barriers, monopoly power cannot be sustained.[7] Along with the associated proposition that regulation serves principally to protect politically powerful groups, that proposition underlies economists' support for deregulation of airlines, trucking, and, to a lesser extent, telecommunications; it also provides the basis for skeptical views of the importance of predatory pricing. Finally, the proposition underlies treatment of corporate mergers. However, note that scale economies are not generally assumed to be an essential factor in any of these cases, while they form the basis of the theoretical analysis of contestable markets. In short, contestable market theory has been far more influential as a metaphor than as a theory with specific predictions.

ECONOMIES OF SCOPE AND CONTESTABILITY THEORY

Most large firms in the United States and in other industrialized countries are highly diversified. They manufacture products in a variety of different industries; many of their industries appear to be closely related in raw materials, production characteristics, or demand, but others appear to be entirely unrelated.[8]

Leading industrial firms also are active in a wide variety of transportation, service, agricultural, and mining activities. There is no reason to believe that a firm's costs of producing one of its products are entirely unaffected by the nature and scale of output of its other products, so there has been considerable interest in the development of cost concepts for multiproduct firms. Ideally, such concepts can help us understand why integrated, diversified corporate structures have developed, and they can help in ascertaining the costs and benefits, both private and public, of corporate mergers, vertical integration, diversification, and foreign investment.

Industrial diversification, as generally understood, is not the only phenomenon generating interest in multioutput production and cost functions; indeed, it may not even be the primary source. There are many industries within which a given firm produces a variety of products. For example, a railroad usually hauls a variety of commodities, and rail services may be further characterized according to length of haul, speed of shipment, the likelihood and cost of damage to the product, and the size of the shipment. Changes in speed or size of shipment of one commodity likely affect the nature of transport costs for other commodities, and empirical analyses seek to account for these interrelationships. Similarly, trucking, hospitals, and telecommunications all involve a variety of distinct products with interrelated costs.

While there has been widespread interest in the analysis of multioutput firms in recent years, fundamental disagreements about the nature of the phenomenon have channeled that interest into several quite distinct analytical paths. The path most familiar for economists essentially argues that technological relationships have evolved in such a way as to make multioutput production the least cost, most efficient way of organizing production. This variant of a standard neoclassical view sees competition driving producers to adopt the most efficient technology at any time while technologies evolve in an essentially autonomous fashion. Empirical practitioners along this path use the assumption of competition, along with rigorous econometric techniques, to "uncover the structure of production," a clear statement of the vision that fundamental technological forces underlie firm and market structure.[9]

Many specialists in industrial organization and finance approach the issue along a second path, emphasizing the analysis of transactions costs. Typically neoclassical in many respects, they are comfortable with the idea that competition among firms provides a spur toward adoption of efficient technologies, which are in turn important determinants of firm and market structure.[10] However, they argue that the purely neoclassical approach of the first group offers no explanation for the existence of firms, and therefore offers weak explanations for multioutput production. They find that relatively high costs of market exchange lead firms to internalize certain transactions and that certain comparative institutional advantages, held by firms over markets, account for multiproduct production.[11]

A third path, which reflects a rapidly growing Marxian literature on the subject, has some close associations with the transactions cost analyses of the second path, and is distinguished by the view that technology is neither autonomous nor efficient. Relatively high-cost technologies may be initiated by firms if they have advantages in the control of the workplace (Bowles 1985).

Much of the empirical and theoretical work on economies of scope follows the first approach. The development of the theory and empirical analyses and criticisms of them can best be understood in terms of the fundamental differences in approach of these groups.

EMPIRICAL ANALYSES OF SCOPE ECONOMIES

Early production function studies of multiproduct industries took the approach of aggregation; the various outputs were combined into a single measure of aggregate output, and the analyst then proceeded as one would with a single product industry. Aggregation of output imposes a number of strict assumptions upon the production function, which are unlikely to be met in practice.

Beyond that, aggregation avoids some of the most interesting questions in multiproduct cost functions: How are product X's costs affected by changes in the output level of product Y? Are scale economies specific to a product, or do they act jointly among a set of products? Is the set of products more efficiently produced by a set of specialized firms, a set of diversified firms, or a single diversified firm? Later econometric studies took explicit account of the multioutput nature of production and sought to identify cost linkages among outputs explicitly.

The most popular approach to this issue has been to specify a flexible cost function, such as the translog

$$\log C = a_o + \sum_{i=1}^{m} b_i \log Y_i + \sum_{j=1}^{n} C_i \log P_j$$

$$+ \frac{1}{2} \sum_{i=1}^{m} \sum_{k=1}^{m} d_{ik} \log Y_i \log Y_k$$

$$+ \frac{1}{2} \sum_{j=1}^{n} \sum_{k=1}^{n} e_{jk} \log P_j \log P_k \tag{1}$$

$$+ \frac{1}{2} \sum_{i=1}^{m} \sum_{j=1}^{n} f_{ij} \log Y_i \log P_j$$

where C is total (enterprisewide) costs, Y_i is output of the ith product, and P_j is the price of the jth input. Additional terms may be entered to account for technological change. In this framework, cost complementarities (or economies of scope) are said to exist for two outputs i and k if

$$b_i b_k + d_{ik} < 0 \tag{2}$$

or, alternatively, if

$$|d_{ik}| > b_i b_k \text{ and } d_{ik} < 0 \tag{3}$$

This general approach is taken in several recent empirical studies.[12] The authors are generally quite cautious in their interpretation of their results. For example, they carefully point out that the test of scope economies implied in (2) and (3) is carried out at a point of approximation, usually the mean value of the variables, and so it may not tell us much about the relative advantages of specialized and diversified production at extreme firm sizes. Furthermore, the translog cannot be applied to cases of zero output (since the log of $Y_i = 0$ is undefined), so it cannot be used directly in comparisons of specialized versus diversified firms.[13] However, in reviewing the studies, I am struck by a common omission in the discussion of the models and the results. Even though they typically deal with a single industry, multioutput cost analyses rarely have anything to say about the sources of economies of scope.[14] At least in part, this is due to a focus on other issues, such as economies of scale, the appropriate statistical tests, or presentation of the methodology.

Nevertheless, the omission is striking; the analysts depend entirely on (3) to identify the existence and importance of scope economies. Moreover, estimation of equations like (3) often involves a large-scale specification search as a variety of variables and data sources are experimented with before an acceptable result is reported (see Friedlaender et al. 1983, for a forthright discussion of a typical search). One rarely finds a discussion of the "engineering" characteristics of the production process that gives rise to this result.

This common practice imposes severe pressures on the data and the model. The econometric approach to the analysis of cost functions aims to estimate the parameters of the long-run cost function. To do so, we first need proper data on output. We never have ideal measures of output, and the best measures are usually found in regulated industries, which is why most cost function analyses are applied to such industries. However, we cannot comfortably use the assumption of competition to enforce least cost production techniques in those industries. More important, it is quite difficult to measure capital services in multiproduct industries, or to account for variations in the flow of services relative to capital stocks. This is especially important for multioutput industries, since excess capacity is often advanced as a cause of firm expansion into new products.[15] Excess capacity in some input, whether physical capital stock, management, or marketing organization, implies a very low (and possibly zero) opportunity cost of that input. If excess capacity really does serve as a source of diversification, then the relevant input prices in (1) should be adjusted to reflect true opportunity costs. A failure to adjust input prices can lead to systematic biases in coefficient estimates and specious estimates of economies of scale and of scope. In short, statistical cost functions are subject to a variety of data and specification problems, which means that the results of such estimates must be interpreted with care. They cannot be expected to provide reliable information on economies of scope in the absence of other evidence.

My criticisms of the implications to be drawn from analyses of multioutput cost functions mirror those made about analyses of single output cost functions. Empirical estimates of scale economics in single product cost functions rarely provide specific discussions of the technological sources of scale advantages (see McGee 1983; Scherer 1980; or Gold 1981). Analysts often face difficulties in separating the effects of technological changes, short-run demand shifts, and economies of scale, due to weaknesses in the data, ignorance of industry history, or uncertainties of functional form.[16]

This is not to say that multioutput cost functions are of no use; when interwoven with a careful discussion of industry production practices, they can provide us with valuable information and with checks on our suppositions. For example, Friedlaender and Spady (1980) on railroads, and Caves et al. (1984) on airlines, do statistical cost analyses that distinguish between effects of economies of density (the density of use of an existing route network) and economies of scale (changes in the size of a network). Their results are relevant to policy and help to explain railroad and airline behavior. Density analyses are relatively simple, however, and their approaches were directed at intensively studied industries with reasonably well-known and measurable production techniques. Economies of scope are a far more slippery concept, and it is still far from clear whether cost function exercises will help in illuminating them.

THE THEORY OF SCOPE ECONOMIES

While applied econometricians attempted to adapt various flexible function forms to statistical cost analyses, other economists were developing a theoretical apparatus for the analysis of multioutput industries. They found that single product cost concepts (such as economies of scale or marginal costs) could not be readily extended to the multiproduct case; they had to devise new concepts. There were close connections between the empirical and theoretical approaches, since each was spurred by developments in regulated industries (especially transportation and telecommunications), and the development of each fed off the other. In particular, applied econometricians quickly adopted the concept of "economies of scope" developed by Baumol et al. (1982), along with their suggested tests for its existence.[17]

According to Panzar and Willig (1981), economies of scope are said to exist if the cost of producing outputs 1 and 2 jointly is less than the total cost of separate production, that is, if

$$C(Y_1, Y_2) < C(Y_1, 0) + C(0, Y_2) \tag{4}$$

where Y_1 is the output level of product 1 and Y_2 is the output level of product 2. A general measure of the extent of scope economies derives directly from (4)

$$S_C = \frac{C(Y_1, 0) + C(0, Y_2) - C(Y_1, Y_2)}{C(Y_1, Y_2)} \tag{5}$$

Thus S_C is positive if economies of scope exist, and negative if there are diseconomies. If scope economies exist, then for a given mix and level of output, firms with diversified product mixes will tend to have lower total costs than specialized firms. Therefore, for any two products 1 and 2, each produced at output levels of 100, measures of scope economies aim at the cost changes realized from combining production 1 and 2 in a single firm, while measures of scale economies aim at the cost changes of an expansion of output from 100 to, say, 200. The term suggests an analogy to economies of scale, especially in the presumption that technological factors are the essential determinants of each.

Scope economies, when combined with contestability, have an important role to play in the Baumol et al. (1982, 7–8) welfare analyses. Specifically, in contestable markets, Baumol argues that the most efficient [least cost] industry structure must emerge "as the industry structure selected by market behavior." For markets that are not perfectly contestable, he asserts that "my guess is that there are no sharp discontinuities here, and that while the industry structures which emerge in reality are not always those which minimize costs, they will constitute reasonable approximations to the efficient structures." Baumol's views here are, of course, not unusual; they likely accord with the mainstream of industrial organization specialists, and they clearly reflect the "first path" to multi-product analyses described above, in which statistical cost analyses seek to "uncover the structure of production." Empirical evidence in favor of the position arises from two sources. First, industry structures (the size distribution of plants and firms) tend to be quite similar across countries. That is, automobile and cigarette production, for example, tend to be highly concentrated industries in all countries, while agriculture and apparel, to take two other examples, are unconcentrated. Since we normally assume that technology is mobile across countries, it follows that technology, rather than nation-specific factors, must be a major determinant of industry structures. Second, technological and market factors (such as measures of scale economies and industry size) seem to do a reasonably good job of accounting for measures of the concentration of firms in an industry. Baumol cites these widely known pieces of evidence, but, curiously, these are measures based on single product industries, and do not tell us about the typical structures of firms. That is, they explain the distribution of plants and firms within an industry, but do not explain the distribution of industries occupied by firms. If multiproduct cost functions were technologically given and markets were approximately contestable, then we should see clusterings of firm structures. That is, we should see groups of firms engaging in broadly similar activities, and these clusterings should hold across countries. Now, it is fairly clear that diversification and vertical integration do not occur at random; firms active in the same industry do often tend to diversify in broadly similar directions.[18] However, the term "broadly" should be understood cautiously. As one who has done empirical work in this area, I can attest to the enormous variety of firm structures, even among firms primarily located in the same industrial grouping. If competition combines reasonably well with technology to generate observed industry structures (defined as the size distribution of plants and firms within a four-digit SIC industry), there is as yet no strong evidence that competition and technology combine to generate observed firm structures.

It seems to me a theory of multioutput production must account for the structure of firms, since the common "stylized facts" cited above do not obviously account for the pattern of firm structures, and econometric analyses rarely provide information on the sources of estimated economies of scope, which might then provide a basis for observed firm structure. Baumol et al. (1982, 75–79) provide a lengthy analysis of abstract cost concepts for multiproduct firms and the nature of linkages among their concepts. However, they devote but four pages to a discussion of the sources of economies of scope. Two of the pages are devoted to Marshallian joint production, with the authors then concluding that "however, cases of joint production processes do not seem sufficiently common to account for the near universality of multiproduct firms, many of which presumably enjoy economies of scope." They then go on to attribute economies of scope to indivisibilities in inputs that can be applied to a variety of outputs. They conclude that their discussion "may not exhaust the possible sources of economies of scope. It has been intended to show only that they can be attributed to phenomena which have appeared before in the literature, and about which there need be little mystery."

That is a very strange passage. First, the literature that they cite (Clemens 1950; Hicks 1935) consists of quite general statements in theoretical tracts, with no specific examples of scope economies. Second, although there is a tradition of attributing scale economies to indivisibilities, this is a deus ex machina that is both inconsistent with the usual theoretical approaches and subject to strong criticism on grounds of realism and practicality (see Gold 1981). Third, even if one takes the indivisibilities argument seriously, it implies an inverse cross-section association between firm size and diversification, and predicts that multiproduct production should decline over time, as firms grow larger. Neither prediction is generally true.[19] As a result, there indeed is a mystery concerning the source of long-run (all inputs variable, no indivisibilities), technologically given, economies of scope.[20] That is, excess capacity may be a perfectly good explanation of diversification, but it cannot be a cause of productive efficiency in the usual neoclassical welfare analyses. The mystery represents a serious obstacle for the theory, which seeks to influence policy and which links, through analogy, economies of scope to economies of scale. Furthermore the linkage conveys the implication that scope economies are, like scale economies, technologically given and socially desirable. Yet neither the empirical nor the theoretical literature provides a persuasive documentation of the sources of economies of scope, so that one may directly assess their technological determinance.

The issue is important for its own sake and because there is an alternative explanation for multiproduct production, which emphasizes the costs of market exchange rather than technology.

MULTIOUTPUT PRODUCTION AND
TRANSACTIONS COST THEORY

Baumol et al. (1982) agree with the users of econometric cost functions on the "technological" argument for firm structure. That argument essentially states that economies of scope, operating through workable contestable markets, account for the diversified (multiproduct) organization of firms. The transactions cost argument, as presented by Teece (1980, 1982), asserts that, while economies of scope may explain joint production, they do not explain why joint production must be organized within a multiproduct enterprise. Rather, "joint production can proceed in the absence of multiproduct organization if contractual mechanisms can be devised to share the inputs which are yielding the scope economies" (Teece 1980, 40). In other words, Teece argues that there is no necessary reason the benefits of joint production and scope economies cannot be realized by independent firms through contractual agreements.

Several examples suffice to illuminate Teece's position. Baumol et al. (1982) offer, in description of scope economies, the Marshallian wool and mutton example (sheep produce both wool and mutton); they argue that it is clearly more efficient for single enterprises to produce both wool and mutton rather than have separate wool enterprises and mutton enterprises. Yet a closer look at sheep farming reveals that the organization structure is not so clear; some enterprises produce the common input (the sheep), while often other separate enterprises shear the wool, and still other separate enterprises slaughter the animals and process the meat. That is, it is not obvious that joint production leads to a multioutput organization of the enterprise.

Teece (1980) offers another example involving sheep. In orchards, space is left between trees to facilitate tree growth and the movement of machinery among trees. The space can, of course, be planted in grass, and sheep may graze in the intervening pasture. Economies of scope exist in such a case, with land as the common input. However, one does not need a diversified enterprise to gain the advantages of scope economies, since the orchardist may lease the land to the sheep farmer. Under the leasing alternative, economies of scope exist but do not imply multioutput enterprises.

Next, consider developments in the meat-packing industry. In 1950, according to data collected in a special Federal Trade Commission survey of distribution of shipments by the 1000 largest manufacturers, meat packers were highly integrated into byproduct processing. They produced fertilizers, chemicals, leather, animal oils and fats, and pharmaceuticals, using animal byproducts. According to company annual reports and industry histories, they had been integrated at the turn of the century.

After 1950, the meat packers turned away from integration so that, by 1975, most byproducts were sold to independent firms for further processing. It is not clear what technological changes could account for the shift; after all, there were still byproducts. The transactions cost approach emphasizes the development of markets in this case, rather than technology. That is, the early meat packers introduced major innovations with the early application of byproducts. There were no independent processors with the skills and knowledge to develop applications, and if any appeared, they might become monopsonist buyers. Thus meat packers integrated to gain returns on their knowledge of applications and to avoid monopsony. As the industry matured over time, knowledge became widespread and a competitive processing industry developed, making integration a less attractive alternative. This view is clearly consistent with Stigler's (1951) early theory of vertical integration. In sum, integration did not result from efficient technology so much as it reflected the development of markets for byproducts.

Finally, take another leasing example. Brand names are often asserted to be a potential source of economies of scope (see, for example, Klein and Leffler 1981). A firm with a particularly valuable brand name may diversify into another industry and use the brand in the new industry. That is, the brand may have certain "public good" characteristics for the firm. Examples of such shifts are Carnation Breakfast Bars and Pepperidge Farm frozen entrees. Such a move is risky, since errors in the new industry may hurt the brand's value in the old; such risks account for the relative paucity of such moves and the likelihood that diversifying firms will introduce new brands in new industries. More important for our purposes, however, is the contractual alternative represented by two recent transactions. One now sees Seagram's ginger ale and mixers in supermarkets; however, the beverages are manufactured and distributed by Coca-Cola Bottling Company of New York, which leases the brand name from the Seagram Company. Similarly, vegetables with the Libby brand are now produced by independent canners who lease the Libby name. Further, mass merchandisers (such as Sears, Safeway, or L. L. Bean) often apply their label to a variety of products manufactured under contract by a large number of independent manufacturers. In short, even where a valuable brand name may generate economies of scope through application as a common input to several products, the "economies" may be obtained through contractual arrangements and do not require the enterprise to diversify.

As the examples imply, the key factor in the transactions cost view of multioutput production is the cost of market transactions relative to administrative reallocation of assets (within the firm).[21] That is, firms are assumed to have, or to generate, assets that can be used in a variety of markets. The assets can be physical, such as structures and equipment, or human, such as managers, salespersons, engineers, or other key operatives. Production may or may not be joint (i.e., the assets must be applicable to more than one industry), but it does not matter whether they are applied to one or several at a time.

The firm presumably will seek to assign the asset to its most profitable use. However, the firm does not have to do so internally; it may sell or lease the asset to producers who are already in the new industry. In fact, this would seem to be the most profitable method of reallocation, since incumbent producers are more likely to have achieved any scale economies that exist, and they are also more likely to have realized any learning-related advantages of specialization. In an economy with no transactions costs, sale or lease of the asset should be preferred to internal reallocation. However, where there are costs to using markets, internal reallocation and multioutput production may be the low-cost, more profitable alternative. The task that transactions costs theorists set for themselves is to identify cases in which market transactions costs are relatively high, and thus to explain the existence, size, and scope of firms and the directions in which they grow through diversification, vertical integration, foreign investment, and home industry expansion. For transactions cost theorists, transferable assets and the relative advantages of markets and bureaucracies, rather than the technology driven "structure of production," account for the structure of enterprises.

As might be expected, research on the analysis of transactions costs centers on a specification of cases in which market exchange might be subject to relatively high transactions costs (absent transactions costs, market exchange will be preferred to internal reallocation). Generally, the costs of exchanging information in a market underlie all of the specific analyses.

Market exchange of information is subject to a variety of problems. The first is the appropriability problem. It is difficult for transactors to agree on the value of a piece of information because the buyer does not know the information and, if the seller reveals it, the buyer will have no incentive to purchase it (since he already knows the information). Since the value of the information (to the seller) is destroyed by revelation of content, the seller will have difficulty in appropriating the returns to an investment in new information. Furthermore, even though the seller knows the content of the information, he may not be certain of its value. The prospective buyer will use it in conjunction with a variety of other inputs, and its relative contribution will be hard for an outsider to discern. Information is typically idiosyncratic because it is not auctioned in a market with a large number of buyers whose competing bids provide evidence of value. As a result, buyer and seller will each be uncertain of the value of information and, especially where exchanges are nonrecurrent, will each have an incentive to misrepresent what they do know about the information's value. The alternative, internal allocation, may reduce informational uncertainty on both sides and may allow for the suppression of misrepresentation.

Where are information problems likely to be prevalent? The initial analyses in the area, not surprisingly, concerned research and development (R&D) investments, whose goal is the production of new knowledge.[22] Later analyses broadened the conception to include organizations within the firm whose members held considerable amounts of specific knowledge; the knowledge could not be appropriated by the firm through sale (since it resided in the organization), and since the organization itself was indivisible it could not be simply split up, with part sold. To appropriate the returns to the organization's skills, firms have diversified into related industries. Recent empirical work has concentrated on R&D and marketing organizations, while Williamson (1975) has emphasized the firm's financial organization (working as a minicapital market) in his discussions.[23] Several analyses have focused directly on markets with a variety of exchange arrangements (across companies or products) and have looked more closely at the informational characteristics associated with the choice of exchange arrangement.[24] Finally, the transaction cost approach posits that demand disturbances also affect firm structures, since slow growth in existing industries may generate excess capacity.[25]

The transactions cost approach is not without its problems. The theoretical background exists, but is still in its infancy. Consequently, there is always a danger that transactions costs analyses will slip over into tautology, imputing a new transaction cost to any perceived failure of market exchange. Of more immediate importance, categories of transactions costs often have no clear empirical analogues, with the result that empirical analyses often proceed with crude or ad hoc measures (of course, it is not unusual to have slippery connections between theoretical concepts and data; for example, the outputs of a multioutput industry are usually defined to be whatever exists in the data). The importance of the transactions cost approach is, first, that it offers some sound criticisms of the theory underlying economies of scope and, second, that it offers an alternative explanation—one whose empirical validity is not clearly inferior—for the existence of multioutput firms.

CONCLUSIONS

Econometric analyses of scope economies have yet to sort out a number of important issues concerning functional form, the selection of variables, and the design of statistical tests. I have tried to point out some more fundamental issues in the interpretation of such analyses. In general, I do not think that one can yet base welfare analyses of productive efficiency on current concepts of economies of scope. Nevertheless, statistical analyses of production have become more rigorous, and transactions cost analysts have also begun the necessary work of statistical explorations of their general framework. There is a great deal of intellectual excitement concerning these issues, since the two approaches seem to generate a large number of fundamental, precise, and testable research questions. The study of the nature of multioutput production is still in its infancy (note that the vast preponderance of work has only appeared since 1980), and research in the area shows a great deal of promise. In many respects, the competing analyses of multioutput production are real departures from previous thinking. Prior to their appearance, there was little rigorous analysis of multiproduct cost concepts, for example, or of the nature of firms as alternatives to market exchange. By contrast, the theory of contestable markets represents a more precise statement of an idea that goes back at least to J. B. Clark's analysis of trusts in the 1880s, the doctrine of potential competition. Most economists will agree that potential competition can restrain the exercise of monopoly power. The real questions at present concern the extent of barriers to entry and to exit. Contestable markets theory, through the analysis of the role of sunk costs, offers an interesting addition to current discussions of barriers, but does not fundamentally alter that discussion. More important, the empirical relevance of contestable market theory, in its strong form, remains open to considerable doubt.

NOTES

1. The standard citation is now the book by Baumol et al. (1982). Sharkey (1982) provides a useful summary of many of the issues. Baumol's (1982) American Economics Association (AEA) presidential address heralded the theories as an "uprising," if not quite an intellectual revolution. The theories have been the subject of two review articles (not reviews) in the *Journal of Economic Literature* (Bailey and Friedlaender 1982; Spence 1983).
2. How important are scale economies? Many empirical analyses in the industrial organization literature find constant returns to scale to be the norm (see for example, Scherer's 1980 discussion). However, these studies focus on fairly broad industries. For more narrowly defined product classes, scale economies may be important and prevalent. Dixit (1982) gives a lucid overview of recent game-theoretic approaches to the modeling of strategic behavior in oligopoly.
3. Much of the new theory arises from regulatory problems investigated by the authors, especially airline deregulation (contestability) and telecommunications (sustainability and economies of scope).

4. The theory's wide impact should also be viewed in the context of the explosion of work in theoretical industrial organization. Contestability gives precise conclusions in an area (small numbers competition) that has traditionally yielded a wide array of results and models. Harold Demsetz's (1968) article on franchise bidding in public utilities as a substitute for regulation mirrors in important respects the approach taken in contestability theory. Later comment on that article (Williamson 1975; Goldberg 1976) emphasized the degree to which experience (which lowered incumbents' costs) and sunk costs attenuated the argument for franchise bidding by reducing the contestability, to use the current term, of the franchise.
5. The best example of such a mapping is the Cournot oligopoly model, in which the difference between market price and the competitive price is a function of the number of firms.
6. See the comment on Baumol's AEA address by Schwartz and Reynolds (1983), the reply by Baumol et al. (1983), and the recent Schwartz and Reynolds paper (1984). Shepherd (1984) implicitly pursues the same criticism.
7. Note also, however, that contestability theory offers little that is new in the definition and measurement of entry barriers. Further, the emphasis on the irrelevance of scale economies is misleading, since the capital that generates scale economies is usually sunk capital.
8. See MacDonald (1985b) for a discussion of the patterns of diversification in U.S. manufacturing.
9. It is probably fairer to say that approaches along the "technology-driven" path think of it as a useful working assumption, and seek to determine the consequences of the application of the assumption. The quote, "uncovering the structure of technology," is quite common in applied econometric work.
10. The "technology-driven" group assumes competition in both of Stigler's (1957) conceptions: competitive behavior among firms, and smoothly functioning markets. Transactions cost analysts accept the first but question the second.
11. Coase (1935), Caves (1971), and Williamson (1975, 1982) originated much of this literature.
12. See Fuss and Waverman (1981); also Evans and Heckman (1984) for telecommunications; Cowing and Holtmann (1983) for hospitals; Sing (1984) on electric and gas utilities; Friedlaender et al. (1983) on automobiles; Harmatuck (1981) as well as Wang Chiang and Friedlaender (1984) on trucking; Kellner and Mathewson (1983) on life insurance; and Baumol and Braunstein (1977) on journal production.
13. Other flexible functional forms, such as a hybrid translog or a linear quadratic form, avoid this problem. See Sing (1984) or Baumol et al. (1982).
14. Sing (1984) does briefly discuss the possibility of assigning service and central office functions to gas and electricity distribution, but notes that these functions hold very small shares of total cost. Friedlaender et al. (1983) test for economies of scope in auto production, but provide no discussion of the reasons for them. Similarly, Evans and Heckman (1984) and Fuss and Waverman (1981) test for the existence of scope economies in telecommunications without explaining their source. Similar procedures are followed by Cowing and Holtmann (1983) for hospitals, and Baumol and Braunstein (1977) for academic journal production. Wang Chiang and Friedlaender (1984) do discuss some potential sources of their large estimated scope economies in trucking (between long and short hauls), but also note that the observed technol-

ogy may not have been "least-cost," but may rather have been imposed by entry regulation. In other words, the "structure of production" may not have been uncovered.

15. See Penrose (1959) or Baumol et al. (1982). I will discuss the role of excess capacity in more detail in a later section.

16. In a fascinating article, Ball and Chambers (1982) interweave a post-war historical overview of the meat-packing industry with an empirical cost-function analysis to account for three anomalies of the cost function estimates. First, capital structures were estimated to be inferior goods. Ball and Chambers (1982) argue that technical changes in cattle raising and cattle feeding reduced peak load capacity demands in meat-packing and made structures appear inferior due to excess capacity. Second, large estimates of unrealized economies of scale appeared for the 1970s, but the authors argue that excess capacity (due to unexpected demand declines) shifted many plants to the downward-sloping portion of short-run cost functions. The analysis also finds evidence of labor-saving technological change, which reflects the structural change in the industry away from skilled labor and toward assembly line techniques using unskilled labor. The Ball-Chambers approach is illuminating in several respects. First, their statistical analysis yields unexpected anomalies, which the authors seek to explain. Anomalies are more often dealt with through manipulation of the data or the functional form (data mining) until the expected coefficient values show up. Second, they try to interpret the driving forces behind their expected coefficient values, rather than simply report the results ("economies of scale," "labor-saving technical change").

17. I will concentrate on scope economies in this discussion. Bailey and Friedlaender (1982) summarize other cost concepts.

18. Food manufacturers, for example, tend to diversify across other food manufacturing industries, other consumer products such as toiletries or apparel, and food wholesaling or food services, while avoiding other manufacturing (MacDonald 1985a). Firms from "hi-tech," R&D intensive industries are more likely to diversify toward other R&D intensive industries, while firms with intensive advertising backgrounds diversify into other advertising intensive industries (Lemelin 1982; MacDonald 1985b; Stewart et al. 1984). While these results are statistically significant, they still leave large amounts of diversification unaccounted for; that is, a large amount of diversification does appear to be statistically random in analyses performed to date.

19. The predictions are spectacularly false for manufacturing, but are consistent with the evidence in agriculture. Historically, the farmer's time, and that of his family, has been a major indivisibility in agriculture. Farmers diversified by, for example, raising hogs to take up slack time from crop production, by working off the farm, or by raising broilers. Over time, large-scale specialization became more important in livestock production, and large-scale enterprises tend toward specialization (Schertz 1979).

20. Bailey and Friedlaender (1982) do provide a listing of specific examples. However they consist largely of asserted indivisibilities, short-run excess capacity, and regulatory impositions.

21. The principle outlines of the transaction cost approach may be found in Coase (1935); Caves (1971); Williamson (1975, 1982); Klein et al. (1978); and Teece (1980, 1982).

22. Most of the early work consisted of case studies, theory, and speculative essays. More recently, however, Mowery (1983) completed several statistical

investigations of the rise of industrial research labs in the United States, and one was specifically concerned with the contractual provisions for sale of research output. It appears that contract research, whose outputs were sold to independent firms, concentrated on less complex analyses, such as standard chemical analyses. Over time, intrafirm research departments grew to eclipse independent organizations as generators of new research. In other words, the cost of market exchange of new R&D results led to reliance on vertical integration.

23. R&D and marketing organizations should influence the extent and the directions of diversification. Lemelin (1982); MacDonald (1985b); and Stewart et al. (1984) have all found evidence of directional effects of R&D and marketing investments. Such variables are also used to account for the directions (industrial and national) and extent of foreign investment.

24. Monteverde and Teece (1982) have looked at automakers' decisions to buy or make various components. Purchase is more likely where components are technologically simpler, where they are not specific to the auto manufacturer, and where they can be produced by a variety of sellers. Masten (1984) has investigated a similar set of choices for airplane manufacturers. In a series of papers, Wiggins and Libecap (1985a, 1985b) have looked directly at transactions costs in the process of oil field unitization. Unitization raises fieldwide rents by reducing costs, yet private market forces have not led to universal unitization. The success of unitization appears to have been more likely where information problems, in the form of dispersed ownership and valuation opinions and incentives for misrepresentation, were less severe.

25. That is, relatively poor prospects in an industry provide an incentive for diversification. Therefore, entrants to an industry may not necessarily be the least cost producers, but will also include those with excess capacity in human and physical capital as well as cash, which may in turn include relatively inefficient producers. See LeCraw (1984) for a recent empirical analysis.

REFERENCES

Bailey, Elizabeth E., and Ann F. Friedlaender. "Market Structure and Multiproduct Industries." *J. Econ. Lit.* 20(1982):1024–48.

Ball, V. Eldon, and Robert G. Chambers. "An Economic Analysis of Technology in the Meat Products Industry." *Am. J. Agric. Econ.* 64(1982):699–709.

Baumol, William J. "Contestable Markets: An Uprising in the Theory of Industry Structure." *Am. Econ. Rev.* 72 (1982):1–15.

Baumol, William J., and Yale M. Braunstein. "Empirical Study of Scale Economies and Production Complementarities: The Case of Journal Publication." *J. Polit. Econ.* 85(1977):1037–48.

Baumol, William J., John C. Panzar, and Robert D. Willig. *Contestable Markets and the Theory of Industry Structure.* San Diego, Calif.: Harcourt Brace Jovanovich, 1982.

———. "Reply." *Am. Econ. Rev.* 73(1983):491–96.

Bowles, Samuel. "The Production Process in a Capitalist Economy." *Am. Econ. Rev.* 75(1985):16–36.

Brozen, Yale. "Bain's Concentration and Rates of Return Revisited." *J. Law and Econ.* 14 (1971):351–69.

Caves, D. W., L. R. Christensen, and M. W. Tretheway. "Economies of Density versus Economies of Scale: Why Truck and Local Service Airline Costs Differ." *Rand J. Econ.* 15(1984):471–89.

Caves, Richard E. "International Corporations: The Industrial Economics of Foreign Investment." *Economica* 38(1971):1–27.

Clemens, E. "Price Discrimination and the Multiple Product Firm." *Rev. Econ. Studies* 19(1950):1–11.

Coase, R. H. "The Nature of the Firm." *Economica* 4(1935):386–405.

Cowing, Thomas G., and Alphonse G. Holtmann. "Multiproduct Short-Run Hospital Cost Functions: Empirical Evidence and Policy Implications from Cross-Section Data." *South. Econ. J.* 49(1983):637–53.

Demsetz, Harold. "Why Regulate Utilities?" *J. Law and Econ.* 11(1968):55–65.

———. "Industry Structure, Market Rivalry, and Public Policy." *J. Law and Econ.* 16(1973):1–10.

Dixit, Avinash. "Recent Developments in Oligopoly Theory." *Am. Econ. Rev.* 72(1982): 12–17.

Evans, David S., and James J. Heckman. "A Test for Subadditivity of the Cost Function with an Application to the Bell System." *Am. Econ. Rev.* 74(1984):615–23.

Friedlaender, Ann F., and Richard H. Spady. *Freight Transport Regulation: Equity, Efficiency, and Competition in the Rail and Trucking Industries.* Cambridge, Mass.: The MIT Press, 1980.

Friedlaender, Ann F., C. Winston, and K. Wang. "Costs, Technology, and Productivity in the U.S. Automobile Industry." *Bell J. Econ.* 14(1983):1–20.

Fuss, Melvyn A., and Leonard Waverman. "Regulation and the Multiproduct Firm: The Case of Telecommunications in Canada." *Studies in Public Regulation,* ed. G. Fromm, pp. 277–313. Cambridge, Mass.: The MIT Press, 1981.

Gold, Bela. "Changing Perspectives on Size, Scale, and Returns: An Interpretative Survey." *J. Econ. Lit.* 19(1981):5–33.

Goldberg, Victor P. "Regulation and Administered Contracts." *Bell J. Econ.* 7(1976):426–48.

Harmatuck, Donald J. "A Motor Carrier Joint Cost Function: A Flexible Functional Form with Activity Prices." *J. Trans. Econ. and Pol.* 15(1981):135–53.

Hicks, J. R. "Annual Survey of Economic Theory-Monopoly." *Econometrica* 3(1935):1–20.

Kellner, S., and G. Frank Mathewson. "Entry, Size Distribution, Scale and Scope Economies in the Life Insurance Industry." *J. Bus.* 56(1983):25–44.

Klein, Benjamin, R. A. Crawford, and A. A. Alchian. "Vertical Integration, Appropriable Rents, and the Competitive Contracting Process." *J. Law and Econ.* 21(1978):297–326.

Klein, B., and K. Leffler. "The Role of Market Forces in Assuring Contractual Performance." *J. Polit. Econ.* 29(1981):615–41.

LeCraw, Donald J. "Diversification Strategy and Performance." *J. Ind. Econ.* 33(1984): 179–97.

Lemelin, Andre. "Relatedness in the Patterns of Diversification." *Rev. Econ. and Stat.* 64(1982):646–57.

MacDonald, James M. *Product Diversification Trends in U.S. Food Manufacturing.* Washington, D.C.: USDA ERS Agric. Econ. Rep. 521, March 1985a.

———. "R&D and the Directions of Diversification." *Rev. Econ. and Stat.* 67(1985b):583–90.

McGee, John. "Economies of Size in Auto Body Manufacture." *J. Law and Econ.* 16(1973):248–53.

Masten, Scott. "The Organization of Production: Evidence from the Aerospace Industry." *J. Law and Econ.* 27(1984):403–18.

Monteverde, K., and D. J. Teece. "Supplier Switching Costs and Vertical Integration in the Automobile Industry." *Bell J. Econ.* 13(1982):206–13.

Mowery, David C. "The Relationship Between Interfirm and Contractual Forms of Industrial Research in American Manufacturing, 1900–1940." *Explor. in Econ. Hist.* 20(1983):351–74.

Panzar, John C., and Robert D. Willig. "Economies of Scope." *Am. Econ. Rev.* 71(1981): 268–72.

Peltzman, Sam. "The Gains and Losses from Industrial Concentration." *J. Law and Econ.* 20(1977):229–63.

Penrose, Edith T. *The Theory of the Growth of the Firm.* London: Basil Blackwell, 1959.

Scherer, F. M. *Industrial Market Structure and Economic Performance*. Chicago: Rand McNally, 1980.

Schertz, Lyle. *Another Revolution in U.S. Farming?* Washington, D.C.: USDA ECS Agric. Econ. Rep. 441, Dec. 1979.

Schwartz, Marius, and Robert J. Reynolds. "Contestable Markets: An Uprising in the Theory of Industry Structure: Comment." *Am. Econ. Rev.* 73(1983):488–90.

– ——. "On the Limited Relevance of Contestability Theory." Washington, D.C.: Econ. Policy Office Disc. Paper 84-10, Antitrust Division, U.S. Department of Justice, 1984.

Sharkey, William W. *The Theory of Natural Monopoly*. London: Cambridge University Press, 1982.

Shepherd, William G. " 'Contestability' vs. Competition." *Am. Econ. Rev.* 74(1984):572–87.

Sing, Merrile. "The Cost Structure of the Gas Distribution and Electricity Industries." Ph.D. diss., University of Wisconsin, 1984.

Spence, Michael. "Contestable Markets and the Theory of Market Structure: A Review Article." *J. Econ. Lit.* 21(1983):981–90.

Stewart, John F., Robert S. Harris, and Willard T. Carleton. "The Role of Market Structure in Merger Behavior." *J. Ind. Econ.* 32(1984):293–312.

Stigler, George J. "The Division of Labor is Limited by the Extent of the Market." *J. Polit. Econ.* 59(1951):185–93.

——. "Perfect Competition, Historically Contemplated." *J. Polit. Econ.* 65(1957):1–17.

——. *The Organization of Industry*. Chicago: University of Chicago Press, 1968.

Teece, David J. "Economies of Scope and the Scope of the Enterprise." *J. Econ. Behav. and Organ.* 1(1980):223–47.

——. "Towards an Economic Theory of the Multiproduct Firm." *J. Econ. Behav. and Organ.* 3(1982):39–63.

Wang Chiang, Judy S., and Ann F. Friedlaender. "Output Aggregation, Network Effects, and the Measurement of Trucking Technology." *Rev. Econ. and Stat.* 66(1984):267–76.

Wiggins, Steven N., and Gary D. Libecap. "The Influence of Private Contractual Failure on Regulation: The Case of Oil Field Unitization." *J. Polit Econ.* 93(1985a):690–714.

——. "Oil Field Unitization." *Am. Econ. Rev.* 75(1985b):368–85.

Williamson, Oliver E. *Markets and Hierarchies*. New York: The Free Press, 1975.

——. "The Nature of the Corporation: Origins, Evolution, Attributes." *J. Econ. Lit.* 19(1982):1537–70.

Economies of Scope,
Contestability Theory,
and Economic Efficiency

A DISCUSSION

Timothy G. Taylor

ANY DISCUSSION of the broad implications for the general theory of industry, or perhaps market, structure raised by the notions of contestable markets, economies of scope, and multiproduct production as discussed by MacDonald would require that I, as a production economist, step somewhat outside my area of expertise. However, there is, I believe, a significant issue raised both implicitly and explicitly by MacDonald that not only falls within the domain of production economics, but also merits additional discussion.

To be more specific, the concept of economies of scope in contestable market theory, while being of central importance, seems not only to be poorly understood as to its sources, but also a potential source of confusion in determining the precise meaning of some of the basic definitional elements of the theory. MacDonald explicitly recognizes the former problem, pointing out that while the existence of multiproduct firms is argued to be largely a result of firms capturing scope economies, there seems to be little discussion as to the precise sources of such economies. The latter problem is implicitly raised by MacDonald's definition of a contestable market and the ensuing discussion. It is upon this potential for the concept of scope economies to foster such confusion in contestable market theory that I shall focus my discussion.

The potential of scope economies to cause confusion in defining the basic elements of contestable market theory can be demonstrated by comparing the definition of a contestable market as given by Baumol (1982, 3–4) with that given by MacDonald. Baumol defines a contestable market as, "one into which entry is absolutely free, *and exit is absolutely costless.* We use 'freedom of entry' in Stigler's sense, not to mean that it is costless or easy, but that the entrant suffers no disadvantage in terms of production technique or perceived product quality relative to the incum-

TIMOTHY G. TAYLOR is assistant professor, Food and Resource Economics Department, University of Florida, Gainesville.

bent." MacDonald, in defining a perfectly contestable market, follows Spence (1983, 982) who defines a contestable market as one in which "entry is free in the sense that there are potential competitors with the same cost function, who can enter and leave without loss of capital." The key element in these two definitions is that the term "suffers no disadvantage in terms of production technique" has been translated into "the same cost function."

Now, in a world populated by industries composed of firms producing a single homogeneous product, these definitions are, of course, the same. Firms producing the same product will adopt the same "most efficient" technology. And, since the production technology is the primary determinant of the structure of the cost function, the firms will necessarily have the same cost function. However, in a world populated by firms each producing a possibly different, but nondisjoint, multiplicity of goods and services, these two definitions are not, in the absence of additional assumptions, equivalent. The difference is the presence of economies of scope and the technological effects that the presence of such economies have on the cost function of these firms. Given that the structure of the production technology dictates the cost structure of the firm, in a multiproduct setting and in the presence of economies of scope, the only way in which firms could have the same cost function would be to produce the same multiplicity of products.

That this implied difference in these definitions is nontrivial in defining additional elements of the theory is perhaps best demonstrated by considering the concept of sustainability. Let y^i be the output vector of firm i with corresponding price vector, p, m denotes the number of firms and $Q(p)$ is the industry multiproduct demand. Drawing on Spence (1983, 982–83), an industry configuration $(m; y^1, \ldots, y^m; p)$ is feasible if

$$\sum_{i=1}^{m} y^i = Q(p)$$

$$p \cdot y^i - C(y^i) \geq 0 \text{ for all } i \text{ and } y^i > 0.$$

Further, an industry configuration is sustainable if it is feasible and if

$$p^e \cdot y^e \geq C(y^e) \text{ for all } p^e \geq p$$

and

$$y^e \geq Q(p^e).$$

Although not explicitly stated, a sustainable industry configuration also implicitly requires that scale and scope economies be exhausted as well. It is the need to exhaust scope economies that creates problems.

If one defines the notion of multiproduct firms narrow enough to equate the definitions of a contestable market as given by Baumol (1982) and by Spence (1983), all firms would have to produce the same multiplicity of products. Indeed, in the absence of additional assumptions regarding the ranges of products over which economies of scope extend, it seems that such narrowness of definition is required to meaningfully define precisely what constitutes a multiproduct industry and its sustainable configuration. In contrast, if one takes Baumol's definition of a contestable market and a world populated by multiproduct firms producing nondisjoint sets of products, in the absence of additional assumptions concerning the nature and causes of scope economies, one can argue that the only sustainable "industry" configuration is a single mega-industry comprising one group of firms producing all products.

There is, of course, a moral to this rather brief discussion: economies of scope are perhaps of a more fundamental importance to the theory of contestable markets than MacDonald or even Baumol et al. (1982) lead one to believe. It is clear in the theory that economies of scope are to be considered as the primary reason for the existence of multiproduct firms, and for this reason alone a more complete understanding of what are the sources of scope economies is needed.

The existence of scope economies moves the concepts of multiproduct production structures and production theory to a very prominent role in the study of industry structure, and requires that great care be used in building contestable market theory. This discussion is intended to demonstrate that, from a technical point of view, a vague treatment of scope economies and its technological implications has resulted in two different definitions of precisely what constitutes a contestable market. These two definitions, in turn, lead to two quite different notions as to what constitutes a sustainable industry configuration and, for that matter, precisely what constitutes a multiproduct industry.

One can use a multiproduct analogue of a single product industry and define a multiproduct industry as one composed of firms producing the same multiplicity of products. However, such a definition is much too narrow to be a part of a general theory of industry structure. At the other extreme, however, if economies of scope are sufficiently pervasive, the only sustainable "industry" configuration is composed of a single mega-industry with each firm producing all products.

If the theory of contestable markets is to achieve the uprising in the theory of industry structure of which Baumol, its chief architect, speaks, it seems that the causes and role of economies of scope must be more clearly understood. Indeed such an understanding seems essential if some of the basic elements of the theory, such as the definitions of a contestable market, multiproduct industry, and sustainability, are to have clear and unambiguous meaning.

REFERENCES

Baumol, W. J. "Contestable Markets: An Uprising in the Theory of Industry Structure."
    Am. Econ. Rev. 72(1982):1–15.
Baumol, W. J., J. C. Panzar, and R. D. Willig. *Contestable Markets and the Theory of
    Industry Structure.* San Diego: Harcourt Brace and Jovanovich, 1982.
Spence, M. "Contestable Markets and the Theory of Industry Structure: A Review Arti-
    cle." *J. Econ. Lit.* 21(1983):981–90.

Economic Efficiency and Market Information

Frances Antonovitz and Terry Roe

STIGLITZ (1985) points out that the assumption of perfect information is critical in the development of the theory of efficient markets. In the absence of perfect information many of these results no longer hold. If the problems of adverse selection and moral hazard are pervasive in the economy, a market economy may no longer be Pareto-efficient. The result from traditional competitive analysis of decentralization of efficient resource allocations is no longer valid, and efficient resource allocations may not be achieved without government intervention (such as subsidies, taxes, or provision of information by government sources). Governments, however, face the same problems of adverse selection and moral hazard so that second-best instruments may be required to induce "signaling" of the targeted groups (e.g., taxing those commodities with high income elasticity of demand because it is not in the interests of the wealthy to reveal their income). Moreover, markets may no longer be characterized by market clearing at a single price for a homogeneous commodity. With imperfect and costly information, the most efficient markets may no longer have some of the characteristics of perfectly competitive markets.

Clearly, how information is processed and conveyed is of key importance in the study of marketing efficiency. Unfortunately, as Stiglitz (1985) points out, the traditional competitive equilibrium paradigm is not robust to slight alterations in the informational assumptions upon which it is based. Alteration of these assumptions amounts to the construction of a new paradigm. Consequently, the traditional concepts of efficiency may no longer be valid to serve as a standard, at least without qualifications,

FRANCES ANTONOVITZ is assistant professor, University of California, Davis. TERRY ROE is professor, University of Minnesota, St. Paul.

when the process by which information is processed and conveyed in an economy is omitted from the analysis. This, of course, magnifies the task at hand and requires that we narrow our focus to selected topics.

OVERVIEW

It is useful to illustrate some implications of accounting for information in economic models by focusing on a class of models that share a common approach. In its simplest form, the decision theory approach (e.g., Marschak and Miyasawa 1968; Nermuth 1982) is illustrated by defining a set $e \epsilon E$ of possible states of the world where the element e is an event describing one state. Information consists of another set of events, referred to as signals, $s \epsilon S$. A stochastic transformation $f(e,s)$ is assumed to exist between the set S of possible signals and events E. Essentially, this transformation serves to forecast events; it assigns a probability that signal s is observed given that state e prevails. The triple (f, E, S) is called an information structure with state space E and signal space S.

An agent is viewed as facing the problem of choosing an action a from a set A of possible actions to maximize expected utility, denoted by the von Neumann-Morgenstern utility function $U[p(a,e)]$, of net returns p. The choice of a must be made prior to the occurrence of an unknown event. The agent is assumed to possess prior beliefs regarding the possible occurrence of e. These beliefs are described by a prior probability density function $f_1(e)$. Uncertainty is summarized by the agent's subjective distribution over the possible states e. This approach clearly distinguishes between risk attitudes and uncertainty.

The agent faces two problems. First, prior to obtaining a signal, the agent does not know which signal $s \epsilon S$ he will obtain. Moreover, the signals can be viewed as a distorted or incomplete picture of reality so that they only provide imperfect information about E. The signals may be incomplete for reasons of adverse selection and moral hazard. Hence, the agent must decide upon the choice of whether to receive a signal without knowing for certain how the signal will affect his expected welfare (because he does not know which signal he will receive).

There are numerous insights provided by this approach. For example, an *ex ante* measure of the value of information can be determined rather than an *ex post* measure, which is obtained after the agent has realized the consequences of the choice. Also, under certain assumptions, Hess (1982) has shown that the value of information increases with either an increase in Rothschild-Stiglitz or in Diamond-Stiglitz risk.

In this elementary form, the major weakness of the approach is that the process generating signals is exogenous to actions. This weakness is addressed, but not eliminated, in models of dynamic systems with adaptive control (see Kendrick 1982 for an example). In these models, actions influence signals. If information is valuable, the potential for learning affects the choice of actions. While complex, with seemingly strong conditions required for existence and convergence, the application of these models should provide insights into the economic effects of how information is produced and possibly conveyed in environments such as imperfect competition and in other adverse selection and moral hazard problems.

For the most part, the literature on search follows the basic structure of the previous approach. Following the path-breaking article by Stigler (1961), the numerous articles in this area (McCall 1971) have established that a sequential search process, in which the stopping rule is to accept an offer if the price is superior to a predetermined reservation price, is generally superior to taking a sample of given size. The reservation price is dependent on earlier observations and the cost of search. The cost of search in turn can be thought of as depending on the structure of the event space E.

Equilibrium in markets with positive search costs, however, provides a stark contrast to the traditional model. Stiglitz (1979) shows that in a model of a market with a large number of homogeneous firms and consumers and a homogeneous commodity with infinitesimal search costs, a single price will prevail. Because there is no price dispersion and price is below the monopoly price, it would pay any firm to raise its price by an amount less than the magnitude of search costs for the individual with the lowest search cost. For then it would not pay any customer to leave the given store and go to another. But this implies that all firms can raise their prices also. The price that prevails is the monopoly price. In the case of a large number of firms, no single firm has any effect on the search behavior of individuals. Hence, as Stiglitz points out, if a group of firms can get together, they can, by lowering their price, induce individuals to search to find one of the members of the low price chain.

In markets with search costs, a distribution of market prices can be reestablished if noise is introduced and/or if search costs (e.g., the opportunity cost of leisure) are not uniform among consumers. Product variety, quality, and advertising (which serves to alter search costs) relate to the value of information and can be shown to give rise to a distribution of prices in markets with search costs.

Grossman and Stiglitz (1976) in their article on the impossibility of informationally efficient markets show that traders can earn a return on their activity of information gathering if they can use their information to take positions in the market that are "better" than the positions of uninformed traders. However, if anybody obtains information, prices will perfectly reflect the information so that the individual who expends resources to obtain information is no better off than the individual who does not. Hence, when information is costly, prices in "efficient markets" do not reflect all of the information and, hence, the impossibility of informationally efficient markets.

While these models are based on the reasonably sound postulates of expected utility optimization, the fundamental implication is that the monotonicity and convexity assumptions upon which the competitive model under perfect information is based are, in reality, violated (Stiglitz 1985). Hence, while weights, measures, grades, and standards serve to reduce costs of adverse selection, many other attempts at consumer protection and notions of market efficiency need to be examined carefully to assure that type 1 errors are not made.

While information may have private value, it does not necessarily have social value (Hirshleifer 1973). For information to have social value in pure exchange, the requirement is essentially that the preposterior expected utility function (defined formally below) over possible actions a associated with the signals $s \epsilon S$ must be equal to or exceed the expected utility of an action in the absence of signals for all agents. For this situation to arise, Hankansson et al. (1982) show that, for the two-period model they posit, the presence of signals must give rise to nontrivial trades. An important sufficient condition for nontrivial trades to occur is essentially that, in the absence of contingency markets for each possible state of nature $e \epsilon E$, signals must give rise to posterior beliefs that differ from prior beliefs, but the difference must be such that the ratio of prior to posterior beliefs is not equal for at least any two agents. Otherwise, the revised probabilities do not alter the ratio of prior probabilities associated with the marginal rates of substitution of wealth between any two states and any two agents. This analysis does not consider the mechanism of how information is produced and conveyed. Thus, no insights are provided as to whether a system exists to provide signals and, if resources were consumed in this process, whether the signal in this case would be socially profitable.

Models of search and learning can be viewed as specifying the mechanism that gives rise to the value of information, its acquisition and, through Bayes's rule, its role in affecting actions. Nevertheless, even within the confines of this approach, numerous issues are deserving of further consideration. We are unaware of efforts to modify these models to include other possible sources of information that may serve to substitute for search and learning. For example, publicly supported and private research including consultants and advertisements at various levels in vertical and horizontal markets have never been included. Moreover, the welfare analysis of the social value of information treats information as a private good. Yet, information relating to many problems of adverse selection and moral hazard have properties of public goods in the sense that the use of information by a single agent does not reduce its consumption by other agents. This raises the question as to what are the appropriate welfare measures when information is not freely available.

THE VALUE OF INFORMATION TO AN INDIVIDUAL

The value of information to an individual consumer or producer may be measured using various methods. In the spirit of the above discussion, the Bayesian approach is used here. We begin by presenting the measures of the value of information to an individual firm or producer and then briefly examining the consumer or household.

A THEORETICAL BAYESIAN MODEL

Consider a producer or firm that must choose to take an action (perhaps how many resources to allocate in a production process) when some event (such as output price) is unknown. The firm is assumed to have a von Neumann-Morgenstern utility function u, which is a continuous and differentiable function of profit, π with $u'(\pi) > 0$ and $u''(\pi) < 0$. The firm's goal is to maximize the expected utility of profit. Let

$e =$ the random variable or event, $e\epsilon E$
$f_1(e) =$ the agent's prior probability density function (p.d.f.) over e
$s =$ signals received by the producer giving additional information about e, $s\epsilon S$.
$f_2(s) =$ p.d.f. over $s\epsilon S$
$f(e,s) =$ joint p.d.f. over e and s
$a =$ the nonstochastic action taken by the firm, $a\epsilon A$
$g(e|s) =$ conditional p.d.f. of e given s
$\theta_e =$ vector of moments of $f_1(e)$
$\gamma_e(s) =$ vector of moments of $g(e|s)$, i.e.,
$\gamma_e(s) = [e(s), \sigma_e(s), \ldots]$

If the firm does not obtain a signal providing it with additional information about the uncertain event, let $a^o = a(\theta_e)$ denote the value that maximizes the expected utility of profit

$$\int f_1(e)u[\pi(a^o,e)]de = \max_a \int f_1(e)u[\pi(a,e)]de \qquad (1)$$

where $u[\pi(a^o, e)]$ and $u[\pi(a, e)]$ are the indirect and direct utility functions of profit, respectively. Suppose that the firm decides to purchase a signal but is uncertain exactly which signal it will receive. To choose its optimal action, the firm uses preposterior analysis and maximizes its expected utility

$$\iint f_2(s)g(e|s)u[\pi(a^P, e)]deds = \int f_s(s)\left\{\max_a \int g(e|s)u[\pi(a,e)]de\right\}ds$$

(2)

where the conditional distribution $g(e|s)$ is the firm's posterior p.d.f. of e obtained by updating $f_1(e)$ by Bayes's rule with the information contained in the signal, and $a^P = a[\gamma_e(s)]$ is the action the firm would take given that it has received a particular signal s.

Suppose that signal $\tilde{s}$ has been observed. The firm still does not know which event will occur but revises its prior beliefs about e with the information contained in the signal in a Bayesian manner. Let $\tilde{a} = a[\gamma_e(\tilde{s})]$ denote the value that maximizes expected utility after signal $\tilde{s}$ has been observed

$$g(e|\tilde{s})u[\pi(\tilde{a}, e)]de = \max_a \int g(e|\tilde{s})u[\pi(a,e)]de.$$

(3)

Instead of receiving signals giving additional information about e, suppose that the firm receives a signal indicating exactly which event will occur. The expected utility of perfect information

$$\int f_1(e)u[\pi(a^*, e)]de = \int f_1(e)\left\{\max_a U[\pi(a,e)]\right\}de$$

(4)

where $a^* = a(e)$ represents the optimal action when the firm knows that e will occur with certainty. If the firm had already received the signal indicating the exact event that would occur, say $\tilde{e}$, it would choose the action maximizing its expected profit since no uncertainty remains

$$\pi(\tilde{a}, \tilde{e}) = \max_a \pi(a, \tilde{e})$$

(5)

where the optimal action is represented by $\tilde{a} = a(\tilde{e})$, and $\pi(a, \tilde{e})$ and $\pi(a, e)$ are the indirect and direct profits, respectively.

In the preceding discussion, it is clear that there are varying degrees of information that could be received, and, hence, each would have a different value to the firm. Furthermore, for the approach used here, either a compensating or equivalent variation type of measure could be used to determine a money metric of the value of information. We choose, as do most other authors, to use the compensating variation measure that indicates how much profit or income must be taken away from the firm after it has received the information so that it will have the same expected utility as when it did not have the information.

The *ex ante* value of obtaining a signal, VI_1, can be determined from (1) and (2):

$$\iint f_2(s)g(e|s)u[\pi(a^p,e) - VI_1]deds = \int f_1(e)u[\pi(a^o,e)]de. \qquad (6)$$

If signal $\bar{s}$ is obtained but the event is still unknown, the "quasi" *ex ante* value of information, VI_2, can be found from (1) and (3)

$$\int g(e|\bar{s})u[\pi(\tilde{a},e) - VI_2]de = \int g(e|\bar{s})u(a^o,e)de. \qquad (7)$$

If the firm knew it would receive perfect information, the *ex ante* value, VI_3, can be determined from (1) and (4)

$$\int f_1(e)u[\pi(a^*,e) - VI_3]de = \int f_1(e)u[\pi(a^o,e)]de. \qquad (8)$$

If event $\bar{e}$ actually occurs, the *ex post* value of information, VI_4, is simply the difference in realized profits since there is no longer any uncertainty about the event

$$VI_4 = \pi(\tilde{a},\bar{e}) - \pi(a^o,\bar{e}). \qquad (9)$$

Clearly, the value of information to the firm, and implicitly to the market, depends on when the evaluation is taken (before the signal is observed, afterwards, or after the event occurs) and on the information and decision structure $\{f(e,s),u[\pi(a,e)]\}$. (See Nermuth 1982.)

A very similar framework can be used to analyze the value of information to the consumer or household.[1] Utility is a function of both the consumer's actions or decisions to purchase various bundles of commodities and the random event e, which might be interpreted most easily as income. When consumption choices in the current period are made (i.e., purchases of durables, automobiles, or housing) the possibility of unemployment, the wage rate, the return on assets, etc., and, hence, the future income stream may not be known with certainty. Signals might include factors such as labor contracts, forecasts on the strength of the economy, and so forth.

Following the results presented for the firm, let $a^o = a(\theta_e)$ denote the value that maximizes expected utility when the household does not obtain a signal

$$f_1(e)u(a^o,e)de = \max_a \int f_1(e)u(a,e)de. \qquad (10)$$

If the household decides to purchase a signal but is uncertain exactly which signal it will receive, it will choose its optimal action, $a^p = a[\gamma_e(s)]$, using preposterior analysis

$$\iint f_2(s)g(e|s)u(a^p,e)deds = \int f_2(s)\left[\max_a \int g(e|s)u(a,e)de\right]ds \qquad (11)$$

The *ex ante* value of obtaining a signal, VI_1, can be determined from (10) and (11)

$$\iint f_2(s)g(e|s)u[a^p,(e - VI_1)]deds = \int f_1(e)u(a^o,e)de. \qquad (12)$$

Other *ex ante* and *ex post* measures can be derived in a manner similar to those of the firm.

Nermuth shows how this approach can be extended to assess the circumstances under which one information structure is "more informative" than another. Consider an information structure $[h_1(e,s_1),E,S_1]$. Although the agent is unable to observe the true event $(e \epsilon E)$ that will occur, information about e, although imperfect, can be obtained through observation of $s_1 \epsilon S_1$. Consider another information structure, $[h_2(e,s_2),E,S_2]$, which has the same state space E and is related to $[h_1(e,s_1),E,S_1]$ in the following way. Instead of observing $s_1 \epsilon S_1$, the agent observes signal $s_2 \epsilon S_2$ that is generated from S_1 by a stochastic transformation from S_1 to S_2 represented by a Markov kernel $m(s_2|s_1)$ such that[2]

$$g_2(s_2|e) = \int g_1(s_1|e)m(s_2|s_1)ds_1. \qquad (13)$$

Intuitively, the observation of $s_2 \epsilon S_2$, generated by such a double randomization and called a garbled signal, gives less (or at least not more) information about the true state $e \epsilon E$ than a signal $s_1 \epsilon S_1$ that is not garbled. In fact, Blackwell's theorem indicates that signal space S_1 is more informative and more valuable than the garbled signal space S_2. To express this mathematically, we need to define

$k_1(s_1)$ = p.d.f. over s_1
$k_2(s_2)$ = p.d.f. over s_2
$l_1(e|s_1)$ = conditional p.d.f. of e given s_1
$l_2(e|s_2)$ = conditional p.d.f. of e given s_2
$\delta_e(s_1)$ = vector of moments of $l_1(e|s_1)$
$\delta_e(s_2)$ = vector of moments of $l_2(e|s_2)$.

Because S_1 is more informative than S_2, expected utility (using preposterior analysis) will be greater when a signal from S_1 is observed rather than from S_2

$$\iint k_1(s_1)l_1(e|s_1)u[\pi(a^{s_1},e)deds_1 \geq \iint k_2(s_2)l_2(e|s_2)U[\pi(a^{s_2},e)]deds_2$$

(14)

where $a^{s_1} = a[\delta_e(s_1)]$ and $a^{s_2} = a[\delta_e(s_2)]$ are the actions the agent would take given that it has received a particular signal s_1 or s_2 respectively. The *ex ante* value of obtaining a signal from S_1, VI^{s_1}, can be determined in a manner similar to (6)

$$\iint k_1(s_1)l_1(e|s_1)u[\pi(a^{s_1},e) - VI^{s_1}]deds_1 = \int f_1(e)u[\pi(a^o,e)]de \quad (15)$$

and the *ex ante* value of obtaining a signal from S_2, VI^{s_2} is

$$\iint k_2(s_2)l_2(e|s_2)u[\pi(a^{s_2},e) - VI^{s_2}]deds_2 = \int f_1(e)u[\pi(a^o,e)]de \quad (16)$$

where the right hand sides of both equations are the expected utility when no signal is obtained. Given the results of (13) through (16), it is clear that $VI^1 > VI^2$ or that the garbled signal is less valuable than the signal that is not garbled.

IMPLICATIONS TO INDIVIDUAL SUPPLY FUNCTIONS

Suppose that the uncertain event is output price. If the agent's utility function exhibits constant absolute risk aversion (Pope et al. 1983) or the utility function is separable in the sense defined by Pope (1978), the risk averse supply function can be derived from expected utility as

$$\partial EU(\pi^*)/\partial \bar{e} = q \quad (17)$$

where q is supply, $\bar{e}$ is expected output price, and $EU(\pi^*)$ is the indirect expected utility function. When no signal is received, supply can be determined from (1)

$$\partial EU(\pi^*)/\partial \bar{e} = \int \{\partial U[\pi(a^o,e)]/\partial \bar{e}\} f_1(e)de = q^{NB}. \tag{18}$$

Supply after a signal $s \epsilon S$ is received can be determined in a similar manner

$$\partial EU(\pi^*)/\partial \bar{e} = \int \{\partial U[\pi(a^p,e)]/\partial \bar{e}\} g(e|s)de = q^s. \tag{19}$$

Expected supply before the signal from S has been received can be expressed as the mean of planned supply over all signals

$$\iint \{\partial U[\pi(a^p,e)]/\partial e\} g(e|s) f_2(s)deds = E(q^s). \tag{20}$$

In the next section, we aggregate over individual supply functions to derive market supply.

IMPLICATIONS OF THE THEORY

The Bayesian model of the value of information to the individual agent indicates how much the agent would be willing to pay to obtain additional information. This, of course, does not tell us whether the agent will purchase the signal. The purchase decision depends on the cost of the signal relative to the *ex ante* value to the agent given in (6). In addition, as Hess (1982) points out, an agent may be more likely to purchase information when the distribution of events is more risky in the Rothschild-Stiglitz sense, because under certain assumptions about the utility function the agent may have a higher value of information. The process $f(e,s)$ by which the signal is produced and conveyed is largely exogenous to this analysis.

The model presented here considers the situation in which the agent may have the opportunity to observe only one signal before taking an action. The analysis could easily be extended to allow the agent to observe multiple signals in either a sequential or nonsequential manner. Kihlstrom (1974), for example, examines a nonsequential sampling process for information about product quality. If the signals are actual realizations of the event and the agent is trying to obtain a high or low value of the event, this is generally referred to as search theory.

Models of agent behavior in the presence of forward markets (e.g., Holthausen 1979; Feder et al. 1980, as well as others) imply that the presence of these markets may eliminate the need for information on spot market prices since the agent can use the certain futures price rather than the stochastic price to determine the optimal level of production. However, these models contain rather stringent assumptions such as no basis risk (i.e., perfect hedge), nonstochastic production, and allowing agents to take either long or short positions in the futures market. Signals on spot market prices, however, do affect hedging strategy. If production is stochastic, it can be seen from Turnovsky (1983) that information that reduces the difference between planned and realized production for producers in a market can in turn influence the futures price that determines planned production. If participants in the futures market are allowed to hedge but not speculate, Antonovitz and Roe (1986) and Hildreth (1984) show that production may be based on expected spot price and, hence, the signals about spot market prices are valuable. However, even if all the assumptions of Holthausen (1979) or Feder et al. (1980) hold, Arrow (1981) points out that resource allocations based on futures prices may be inefficient because futures prices may be based on other expected prices for which futures markets do not exist.

The value of information is also an important issue in models of adverse selection, in which there is imperfect information about what is being bought or sold in the market, and in models with moral hazard, in which actions of individuals may be uncertain to market participants. The actions of firms (a product guarantee) or of individuals (the amount of insurance purchased or level of education) may provide signals to market participants in models of adverse selection. Whereas, in models with moral hazard, if the relationship between market participants is long-term, the payments (such as those made by employers or insurance companies) may be made contingent upon signals received at earlier dates. Clearly, the model presented here suggests a way in which the value of these signals could be measured.

Signals about product quality can be provided by advertising, labeling, grades, and standards. The Bayesian model presented can be used to measure the value of information each of these types of signals provides. Examples of *ex post* empirical analyses of product labeling are provided by Senauer et al. (1984) as well as by Sexton (1981).

THE VALUE OF INFORMATION TO THE MARKET

In the previous section, a methodology for measuring the *ex ante* value of a signal to an individual agent was suggested. To determine the value of information to all producers in the market, one of the supply functions in (18) through (20) (depending on exactly which value of information is being obtained) can be aggregated over all agents. Producer and consumer surplus triangles based on expected prices obtained from the aggregate demand and risk averse supply functions can then be used to obtain a money metric of the value of information to all market participants.

We could measure the value of information to market participants under a number of different scenarios. The one suggested here is common in agricultural applications and will correspond to the empirical example that will be presented later. It should be kept in mind, however, that other situations can be analyzed using this type of producer and consumer surplus analysis.

Suppose that production decisions must be made in advance of the time the commodity will be marketed. (Planting decisions or purchases of feeder livestock are typical examples.) Production is assumed to be non-stochastic, while demand is not known with certainty when production decisions are made. Although the information provided in signals may take a variety of forms, we will assume that the producer receives information on the mean and other moments of the distribution of output price.

To measure the *ex ante* values of obtaining signals that are garbled and not garbled, consider Fig. 9.1. First assume that all producers receive exactly the same signal. Since the prior mean of a distribution is identical to the preposterior mean,[3] expected demand, $E^o D$, would be exactly the same regardless of whether the signal is garbled or no signal is received. Even though production is not stochastic, producers may supply different quantities depending on exactly which signal is received. Let $E^o S^{NG}$ be the expected risk averse supply when producers anticipate receiving signals that are not garbled, with EQ^{NG} denoting the corresponding expected quantity supplied.[4] The expected price is represented by $E^o(P^{NG})$. If producers instead received a garbled signal, the expected risk averse supply curve, $E^o S^G$, should lie to the left of $E^o S^{NG}$ since garbled signals contain more uncertainty and, hence, are more risky than signals that are not garbled. The expected quantity supplied with a garbled signal is EQ^G and expected price is $E^o(P^G)$. Similarly, risk averse supply when no signal is received should lie to the left of $E^o S^G$, since there is even more risk when no signal is received. The corresponding quantity supplied would be Q^{NS} with expected price $E^o(P^{NS})$.

It is now possible to evaluate the values of each of these signals to the entire market. From the given assumptions, it follows that the *ex ante* expected value of a garbled signal (the expected deadweight loss) is given by the triangle $a + b$; while for a signal which is not garbled, the value is $a + b + c + d + e + f$. The difference, $c + d + e + f$, is what it would be worth to both producers and consumers to have a signal that is not garbled. Clearly, the expected *ex ante* value of each of these signals could have been decomposed for consumers or for producers.

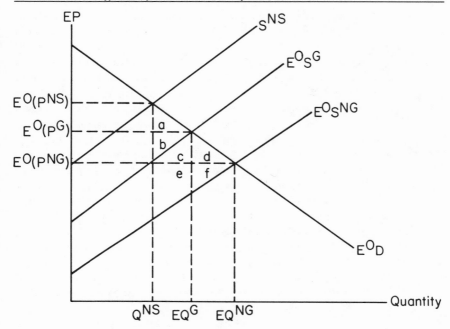

FIG. 9.1.   Value of garbled and not garbled signals.

These ideas will be examined next when "quasi" *ex ante* and *ex post* measures are discussed.

Suppose that all producers in the market have received a particular signal *s,* but actual price has not been observed. Fig. 9.2 is to be used to examine the "quasi" *ex ante* value of this signal. This value corresponds to (3) and (7) for the case of the individual agent. Let expected demand be represented by E^sD, which is unlikely to be the same as the preposterior expected demand E^oD. After the signal is observed but before the event occurs, the risk averse supply is represented by S^s with quantity supplied Q^s and expected price $E^s(P^s)$. In the absence of signals, let Q^{NS} be the quantity producers would have produced with $E^s(P^{NS})$ the expected price based on E^sD. The expected deadweight loss (the "quasi" *ex ante* market value of information) is given by the triangle $f + g + i + j + n$. The expected value of this signal to consumers in the market is given by the area $c + d + e + f + g$. The gain or loss to producers is given by the change in producer surplus $i + j + n - (c + d + e)$.

It is also possible to measure the *ex post* value of the signal to the market after the commodity has been marketed and actual demand has been observed. In Fig. 9.2, realized demand is depicted by RD, and realized prices from production choices Q^{NS} and Q^s are given by P^{NS} and

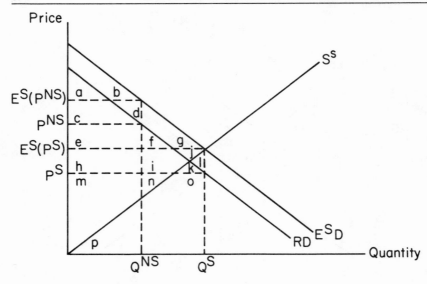

FIG. 9.2.   "Quasi" *ex ante* and *ex post* values of a signal.

P^S, respectively. The *ex post* value of information to the market is given by $f + i + n - l$, which can be negative depending on the magnitude of the triangle l. The *ex post* change in consumers' surplus is the area $e + f + h + i + k$, while for producers it is $n - (e + h + k + l)$. The departure of the "quasi" *ex ante* measure from the *ex post* measure over a large number of observations suggests that it is not a reliable estimate of the value of the forecast.

It should be noted that the "quasi" *ex ante* value of the signal to the market will always be positive (see Roe and Antonovitz 1985). Hence, the entire market can expect to gain from any signal received although either producers or consumers (but not both) may expect to lose. The *ex post* value may, on the other hand, be negative.

AN EMPIRICAL EXAMPLE FOR FED BEEF

Feedlot operators typically purchase feeder cattle and feed five to eight months in advance of selling finished cattle. Thus, the price that will be received for fed cattle is unknown when the inputs are committed to production, while production uncertainty is quite small for feedlot operations. Hence, data from the fed cattle sector were used to provide an empirical application of the theoretical framework. Antonovitz and Roe (1984) use this model to estimate the "quasi" *ex ante* and *ex post* values of a forecast for the fed cattle market, and the results will be briefly summarized here.

The key assumptions employed to obtain measures of the market value of a rational expectations forecast are: (1) all producers are identical, exhibiting constant absolute risk preferences, so there is no aggregation problem in deriving market supply; (2) the forecast is given as a distribution of output price; (3) all producers in the market adopt the forecast as their conditional distribution, $g(e|\bar{s})$ in equation (3); (4) all exogenous variables whose values are unknown at the time the forecast is formulated are assumed to follow stable stochastic processes; and (5) the agency providing the forecast is assumed to know the parameters of the model. Given these assumptions, a forecast provided by a government agency might be considered as one of the least garbled signals to a market. With other price forecasts or signals, the variance of the forecast may be larger for a number of reasons. If all producers do not adopt the same forecast there may be more uncertainty in predicting producers' supply after the signal is received. Also, larger forecast variance could result if the provider of the forecast was uncertain of the parameters of the demand and supply equations. Thus, the "quasi" *ex ante* value of the forecast reported below may give an upper bound to the value of a price forecast to the market.

It is further assumed that the distribution of output price can be expressed in terms of its first two moments. From assumption (1), the farm level market supply in time period t is an aggregation of the individual supply functions (19), and can be stated as

$$S_t^s = S[E^s(p_t), \sigma_t^s] \tag{21}$$

where $\sigma_t^s = E^s [P_t - E_s(P_t)]^2$. The expressions $E^s(P_t)$ and σ_t^s are the first two moments of the distribution of market price. Expectations are taken with respect to the conditional p.d.f. of P given the rational expectations forecast s defined below. The exogenous variables normally appearing in (21) are omitted for convenience since their values are assumed to be known when producers make production commitments.

Let

$$P_t = D(Q_t^d, \vec{Z}_t) \tag{22}$$

denote the inverse farm level demand function where Q_d^t denotes the quantity demanded and $\vec{Z}_t$ denotes a vector of random exogenous variables.

The model is closed by assuming that in each period the price equilibrates quantity demanded and quantity supplied. Thus, market price can be determined by using (21) and (22)

$$P_t = D\{S[E^s(P_t), \sigma_t^s], \vec{Z}_t\}. \tag{23}$$

Because the public forecast is assumed to be a rational expectations forecast, expected price is determined by taking the conditional expectation of (23). Depending on the form of the supply and demand functions, the rational expectations forecast can be stated as

$$E^s(P_t) = F[\sigma_t^s, E(\vec{Z}_t)] \tag{24}$$

where σ_t^s is defined by (25) and $E(\vec{Z}_t)$ is the expected value in a period previous to t of the vector of exogenous variables, which by assumption (5), follow stable stochastic processes.

The rational expectations variance of market price is

$$\sigma_t^s = E^s[P_t - E^s(P_t)]^2. \tag{25}$$

The quantity supplied can be determined by substituting (24) and (25) into (21), which gives

$$\begin{aligned} S_t^s &= S\{F[\sigma_t^s, E(\vec{Z}_t)], \sigma_t^s\} \\ &= S\{G[\sigma_t^s, E(\vec{Z}_t)]\}. \end{aligned} \tag{26}$$

Aggregate bimonthly data on cattle slaughter between 1970 and 1980 were used to estimate linear demand and supply (22) and (26). The input prices included in the supply equation were feeder cattle, corn, and soybean meal. It was assumed that producers were not using rational expectations forecasts of the mean and variance of market price. An Auto-Regressive Integrated Moving-Average (ARIMA) (2,1,0) model was used to estimate, three to four bimonths in advance, the mean and variance of the aggregate subjective distribution of fed cattle price. The producer's price forecast can be viewed as corresponding to either the conditional p.d.f. $g(e|\bar{s})$ in (3), or, with no forecast, to the prior $f_1(e)$. The empirical forecasting model, however, is not derived from Bayes's rule. The exogenous variables used to estimate the bimonthly farm-level demand for fed cattle included per capita disposable income and a farm level index of other meats. Parameter estimates for supply and demand equations appear in Tables 9.1 and 9.2.

The mean and variance of the rational expectations forecast are conceptually based on (20) and (21) and are empirically based on the estimates of supply and demand in Tables 9.1 and 9.2. The "quasi" *ex ante* and *ex post* value of information to the market are determined from

TABLE 9.1. Parameter estimates of the market risk averse supply function of fed cattle production, bimonthly from 1970 to 1980

Independent variables	Coefficient estimates
Constant	92,235,000.**
Corn price	−7,522,300.*
Soybean meal price	16,428.
Feeder cattle price	−1,501,900.**
Mean fed cattle price	1,041,700.**
Variance of fed cattle price	−481,220.*
R^2 is .81	
First order autocorrelation coefficient is .45606	
Variance of the estimate corrected for first order autocorrelation is 5.0921×10^{12}	

  * Indicates significance of a two-tailed t-test at the .05 percent level.
  ** Indicates significance of a two-tailed t-test at the .01 percent level.
  The corn price was the average price received by farmers in Iowa. Soybean cake and meal price, 44 percent protein, bulk in Decatur was used. Feeder cattle price was determined by averaging 400–500 pound and 600–700 pound choice feeder steers in Kansas City. All input prices were divided by the USDA's index of prices paid by farmers. The ARIMA forecasts of the mean and variance are of the deflated average fed cattle price received by farmers in the U.S. Estimates of fed cattle production were obtained from the USDA's bimonthly commercial cattle slaughter. All prices were in 1972 dollars.

TABLE 9.2. Parameter estimates of the inverse market farm level demand function of fed cattle, bimonthly from 1970 to 1980

Independent variables	Coefficient estimates
Constant	2.973×10
Quantity of fed cattle	3.0895×10^{-7}**
Per capita disposable income	6.2023×10^{-3}
Farm-level index of other meats	2.798×10*
R^2 is .86	
First order autocorrelation coefficient is .84449	
Variance of the estimate corrected for first order autocorrelation is 2.6776	

  * Indicates significance of a two-tailed t-test at .05 percent level.
  ** Indicates significance of a two-tailed t-test at the .01 percent level.
  Estimates of fed cattle production were obtained from the USDA's bimonthly commercial cattle slaughter. Per capita disposable income and average fed cattle price received by farmers in the U.S. were deflated to 1972 dollars. The farm level index of other meats was determined as follows

$$I_t = \frac{\Sigma P_{it} Q_{it}}{\Sigma P_{it} Q_{it} + P_{Bt} Q_{Bt}}$$

where the P_i and Q_i are the farm level prices and quantities of chicken and pork, and P_B and Q_B are for beef.

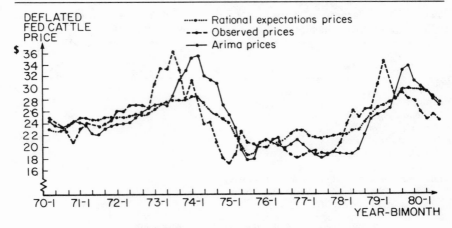

FIG. 9.3.   Rational expectations forecasts of, ARIMA forecasts of, and observed fed cattle prices.

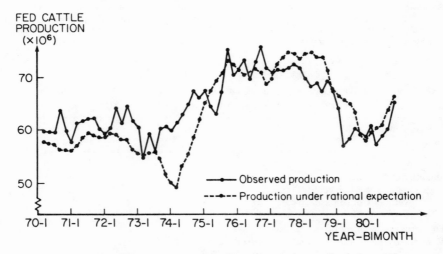

FIG. 9.4.   Fed cattle production observed and under rational expectations.

the consumer and producer surplus triangles given in Fig. 9.2. Results are presented in Figs. 9.3 through 9.6.

The mean deflated fed cattle price given by the rational expectations forecast, the ARIMA forecast, which represents the aggregate subjective deflated mean of output price, and the deflated observed prices are contrasted in Fig. 9.3. It is interesting to note that the rational expectations forecasts exhibit a discernable cycle but that price variance and amplitude

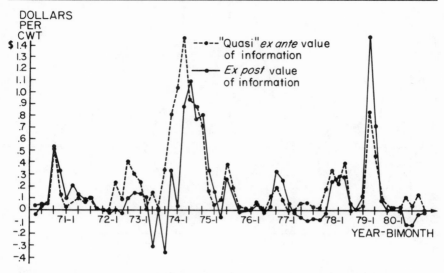

FIG. 9.5. "Quasi" *ex ante* and *ex post* values of a rational expectations forecast.

of the cycle are much smaller than either the observed or ARIMA prices. ARIMA forecasts are noted to lag observed prices and have a similar variance.

Production under the rational expectations forecast is shown in Fig. 9.4. Production based on the rational expectations forecast exhibits fewer peaks and troughs than observed production, although it too exhibits a cycle. The largest departure from observed production occurred in 1974 and 1979, years in which the world economy also suffered shocks. However, the model suggests that overall the adoption of a rational expectations forecast would have only a small effect on fed cattle production. For the period from 1970 to 1980, the mean of the expected bimonthly production when all producers are assumed to adopt the rational expectations forecasts is 98.32 percent of the mean bimonthly production levels actually produced.

The "quasi" *ex ante* value of information to the market is given in Fig. 9.5. The mean bimonthly value of information for the 1970–1980 period was $.21 per cwt of production or, in total value terms, a mean of approximately $13.3 million per bimonth. These estimates range in value between virtually zero to a maximum of $1.47 per cwt; the minimum value occurred in the fifth bimonth of 1979, while the maximum value occurred in the second bimonth of 1974. The "quasi" *ex ante* value of information increases when the ARIMA forecasts diverge from the ra-

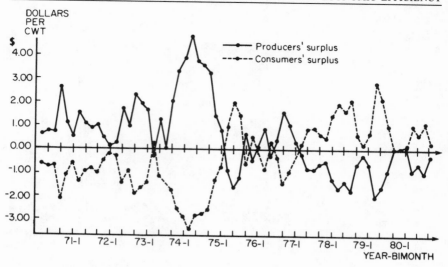

FIG. 9.6.   Expected value, *ex ante*, of information to fed cattle producers
and consumers.

tional expectations forecasts depending on the relative variances of the
forecasts. This divergence tends to occur at turning points in the ARIMA
price series in which prices differ from those of the rational expectations
price series.

Also appearing in Fig. 9.5 are the *ex post* estimates of the value of
information to the market that provide insight into the validity of the
"quasi" *ex ante* estimates. It is encouraging to note how closely the
"quasi" *ex ante* value follows the *ex post*. The mean bimonthly value of
this *ex post* measure is approximately $.15 per cwt, ranging from −$.37 to
$1.45. Of the 64 bimonthly estimates obtained, negative values, although
small, were reported 36 percent of the time. Hence, the adoption of the
forecast by producers would have resulted in a "realized" welfare loss to
the market 36 percent of the time. Nevertheless, the gains still out-
weighed these losses.

Fig. 9.6 gives the *ex ante* expected producer and consumer gains and
losses from adopting rational expectations forecasts. The bimonthly mean
value of information to producers of fed cattle during 1970 to 1980 was
estimated to be $.49 per cwt, ranging from a minimum of −$2.04 to a
maximum of $4.76. On average, consumers lose $.28 per cwt from the
adoption of the rational expectations forecast by producers. The range in
consumer gains and losses is from a high of $2.86 to a low of −$3.35.
Expected gains to producers are positive when the expected quantities
produced under the rational expectations forecast are less than the quan-

tities actually produced. The converse relationship holds for expected gains to consumers.

CONCLUSIONS

In this chapter we attempt to provide selected general and specific insights into questions of economic efficiency and information. An attempt is also made to illustrate how the informational efficiency of markets might be empirically estimated by fitting a restricted version of a Bernoullian decision theory model of the firm to time series data at the market level.

From the work of Stiglitz (1979, 1985), we point out that the economic efficiency implications drawn from the traditional neoclassical paradigm of competitive markets are not robust to slight alterations in the informational assumptions upon which the theory is based. Hence, perfect information is a critical assumption in many models of market efficiency. If problems of adverse selection and moral hazard are pervasive in an economy, a market economy can no longer be assumed to be Pareto-efficient so that government intervention may serve to increase efficiency.

In the case of adverse selection, examples are grades and standards, weights and measures, the reporting of spatial prices, and the provision of price forecasts. Taxes and subsidies may also be warranted. Whenever there is imperfect information, individuals or commodities that are in fact different will tend to be grouped together so that prices reflect their average quality. Hence, the more desirable commodities are taxed while the less desirable are subsidized. The distortion associated with this tax can be reduced in principle by imposing other taxes and subsidies that increase the supply of the taxed commodity. In some respects, the Commodity Futures Trading Commission can be viewed as supporting the functioning of futures markets, the existence of which can be viewed as alleviating, to some degree, the temporal dimension of the adverse selection problem. Cooperatives, marketing orders, and marketing agreements that, among other functions, tax members for purposes of providing market information, research, and the imposition of quality controls, also perform activities that seek to address problems created by imperfect information.

To obtain insights into how information is processed and conveyed in an economy, models must be constructed in which information is continuously being processed and decisions are continuously made. The models briefly reviewed in this chapter, for the most part, fall short of this objective. Yet, they do provide sufficient insights to suggest that attempts at consumer protection, from, for example, increasingly concentrated in-

dustries, and notions of market efficiency need to be examined carefully
to assure that actions taken do not lead to greater inefficiencies.

To provide specific insights into some of the issues of determining
the value of information to the individual, a Bernoullian model of the
firm was presented wherein information could be obtained in the form of
signals. Essentially, signals were treated as exogenous to the model.
Agents were assumed to determine whether to obtain a signal on the
basis of its expected value in utility terms. Agents could use the signal to
update their prior notions about an uncertain event in a Bayesian manner. The value of this signal could then be measured *ex ante* (before the
signal is received), "quasi" *ex ante* (after the signal is received but before
the event is observed), and *ex post* (after the event is observed). This
framework was then illustrated by an empirical example of the fed cattle
market with "quasi" *ex ante* and *ex post* measures of a rational expectations forecast provided by a public agency.

It is pointed out that the desirable measure is the *ex ante* value.
However, this measure, in the absence of primary data, would seem
difficult to obtain. In any case, the *ex post* measure is based on numerous
assumptions that are not likely to hold so that the estimated values are
only approximate.

Much theoretical work still needs to be done to update the many
existing neoclassical models to include the possibility of imperfect information and its effect on marketing efficiency. Insights into how public
policy might be designed to influence the generation and processing of
information should be one of the important outcomes of additional work
in this area.

NOTES

1. For a review of this literature, see Lippman and McCall (1981). An empirical
   illustration appears in Roe and Graham-Tomasi (1985).
2. Essentially, $m(s_2|s_1)$ is the conditional distribution of s_2 given s_1. (See Mar-
   schak and Radner 1972, 64–67.)
3. Although this may not be intuitively obvious, the proof is straightforward.
   The preposterior mean of the uncertain event e is given by

$$\iint ef_2(s)g(e|s)deds = \int e\left[\int f_2(s)g(e|s)ds\right]de.$$

By definition of conditional probability

$$g(e|s) = f(e,s)/g_2(s).$$

Substituting into the above equation

$$\int e\left[\int f(e,s)ds\right]de = \int ef_1(e)de.$$

The right hand side is the mean of the prior distribution.
4. Problems of aggregation are ignored in the derivation of market supply.

REFERENCES

Antonovitz, Frances, and Terry Roe. "The Value of a Rational Expectations Forecast in a Risky Market: A Theoretical and Empirical Approach." *Am. J. Agric. Econ.* 66(1984):717–23.
———. "Hedging and the Competitive Firm Under Price Uncertainty: Theoretical and Empirical Considerations." *J. Futures Mark.* Forthcoming.
Arrow, Kenneth J. "Futures Markets: Some Theoretical Perspective." *J. Futures Mark.* 1(1981):107–16.
Feder, Gershon, Richard E. Just, and Andrew Schmitz. "Futures Markets and the Theory of the Firm Under Uncertainty." *Q. J. Econ.* 94(1980):317–28.
Grossman, Stanford J., and Joseph Stiglitz. "Information and Competitive Price Systems." *Am. Econ. Rev.* 66(1976):246–53.
Hankansson, Nils H., J. Gregory Kunkel, and James A. Ohlson. "Sufficient and Necessary Conditions for Information to Have Social Value in Pure Exchange." *J. Fin.* 37(1982):1169–81.
Hess, James. "Risk and the Gain from Information." *J. Econ. Theory* 27(1982):231–38.
Hildreth, Clifford. "Qualitative Analysis of Production and Hedging." Dep. Agric. and Appl. Econ. Working Paper P83-4, University of Minnesota, revised 1984.
Hirshleifer, J. "Where Are We in the Theory of Information?" *Am. Econ. Rev.* 63(1973):31–39.
Holthausen, Duncan M. "Hedging and the Competitive Firm Under Price Uncertainty." *Am. Econ. Rev.* 69(1979):989–95.
Kendrick, David. "Control Theory with Applications to Economics." *Handbook of Mathematical Economics,* ed. K. Arrow and M. Intriligator, pp. 111–58. Amsterdam: North Holland, 1981.
Kihlstrom, Richard. "A General Theory of Demand for Information About Product Quality." *J. Econ. Theory* 8(1974):413–39.
Lippman, Steven A., and John J. McCall. "The Economics of Uncertainty: Selected Topics and Probabilistic Methods." *Handbook of Mathematical Economics,* ed. K. Arrow and M. Intriligator, pp. 211–84. Amsterdam: North Holland, 1981.
McCall, John J. "Probabilistic Microeconomics." *Bell J. Econ. Manage.* 2(1971):403–33.
Marschak, Jacob, and Koichi Miyasawa. "Economic and Comparability of Information Systems." *Int. Econ. Rev.* 9(1968):137–74.
Marschak, Jacob, and Roy Radner. *Economic Theory of Teams.* Cowles Foundation of Res. in Econ. Monograph 22, Yale University, 1972.
Nermuth, Manfred. "Information Structures in Economics." *Lecture Notes in Economics and Mathematical Systems.* Monograph 196, ed. M. Beckman and H. P. Kunzi, pp. 12–44. Berlin: Springer-Verlag, 1982.
Pope, Rulon D. "The Expected Utility Hypothesis and Demand-Supply Restrictions." *Am. J. Agric. Econ.* 62(1978):619–27.
Pope, Rulon, Jean-Paul Chavas, and Richard E. Just. "Economic Welfare Evaluations for Producers Under Uncertainty." *Am. J. Agric. Econ.* 65(1983):98–107.
Roe, Terry, and Frances Antonovitz. "A Producer's Willingness to Pay for Information Under Price Uncertainty: Theory and Application." *South. Econ. J.* 52(1985):382–91.
Roe, Terry, and Theodore Graham-Tomasi. "Yield Risk in a Dynamic Model of the Agricultural Household." Econ. Growth Center Paper 479, Yale University, 1985.

Senauer, Ben, Jean Kinsey, and Terry Roe. "The Cost of Inaccurate Information: The Case of the EPA Mileage Figures." *J. Consum. Aff.* 18(1984):193–212.

Sexton, Richard. "Welfare Loss from Inaccurate Information: An Economic Model with Application to Food Labels." *J. Consum. Aff.* 15(1981):214–31.

Stigler, George. "The Economics of Information." *J. Polit. Econ.* 69(1961):213–25.

Stiglitz, Joseph E. "Equilibrium in Product Markets with Imperfect Information." *Am. Econ. Rev.* 69(1979):339–45.

———. "Information and Economic Analysis: A Perspective." *Econ. J.* 95(Supplement 1985):21–41.

Turnovsky, Stephen J. "The Determination of Spot and Futures Prices with Storable Commodities." *Econometrica* 51(1983):1363–87.

Economic Efficiency
and Market Information

A DISCUSSION

Dennis R. Henderson

ANTONOVITZ AND ROE (AR) present an interesting theoretical analysis on the value of information to market participants. They also make a useful application of their analytical framework in determining the amount of welfare loss in a market subjected to less than perfectly forecasted information. This they did with sufficient mathematical sophistication to confound my sometimes prosaic turn of mind and to the point that at least some, and perhaps most, of the presumed theoretical richness of their analysis was lost to this reviewer.

Indeed, I find little with which to take issue. I suggest their conclusions are consistent with the teachings of generally received microeconomic theory. Thus, the point of my discussion is not to revisit the AR analysis, but to raise some questions about the necessary conditions for information to play a positive role in obtaining an efficient market outcome. By efficient market outcome, I mean the market's ability to generate trading that closely approximates the volume and price outcome theoretically expected at equilibrium under perfectly competitive conditions. I take this to be consistent with Pareto optimality in a welfare sense.

I pursue this approach because logic and observation suggest that at least part of the value of information to individual market participants rests on their ability to gain advantage over their competitors, trading partners, or both. By this I refer to their use of superior information to obtain a trading outcome that is supracompetitive in terms of their individual profit account. The existence of any such trade, I contend, is evidence of some inefficiency in the market, and the more such trades that occur in any given market, the greater the magnitude of the inefficiency. My perspective is, therefore, that the value of information in terms of obtaining an efficient market stems from the ability of that information to reduce, if not eliminate, supraprofitable trading opportunities for individual traders. In essence, this suggests that information with the greatest social value, in a welfare optimization sense, is that

DENNIS R. HENDERSON is professor, Department of Agricultural Economics and Rural Sociology, Ohio State University, Columbus.

which has the least value to individual traders in terms of creating extraordinary profit opportunities.

I have been involved in a large number of pricing experiments in a laboratory setting during the past few years. While I recognize the legitimate debate over the generalizability of results in laboratory experiments to the general population, they do offer one particularly attractive feature for inquiring into the nature of factors that can influence marketing efficiency. This is, the efficient market outcome can be fixed by the experimenter and thus is known with certainty a priori. Trading can then occur among subjects under a wide variety of conditions and the outcome, in terms of individual transaction prices and quantities traded, can be compared with the theoretically efficient objective. By varying the conditions under which the laboratory trading occurs, the experimenter gains insight into the impacts of various factors on market efficiency.

Our results, in general, have been very instructive. Consistent with the findings reported by Vernon Smith (1982) and others, we have been able to closely approach competitive equilibrium market outcomes when we structure a competitive market using at least four buyers and four sellers and conduct transactions through a double auction procedure. By like token, we have been able to approximate monopoly equilibrium market outcomes when we structure markets with one buyer and utilize posted prices. We have also consistently found appreciably less-than-competitive outcomes when using other than double auction pricing procedures even with competitively structured markets. Further, we have been able to approach competitive equilibrium in monopolistically structured markets using a double auction.

These results set us to pondering the ways of the marketplace. Why, for example, does the double auction generate market outcomes close to the competitive equilibrium even when the market is not competitively structured? Why does a competitively structured market deviate from the competitive equilibrium when prices are posted rather than auctioned?

After observing several hundred trading sessions in the laboratory, some things become apparent. For example, much information floats around in the market when a double auction is in progress—information on unfilled bids, unaccepted offers, completed transactions, and the like. To what extent, we wondered, is the information generated by the double auction procedure responsible for the more efficient market results? To try to answer that question, we designed a series of trading experiments using a competitively structured market with price posting. In one laboratory we provided traders with no information on their competitors' bids or offers, on the number of completed transactions, or on the prices at which trades occurred. In another laboratory, we provided all of this information on an ongoing basis. If it was the informational content of

double auctions that was primarily responsible for their improved performance, we posited, then the posted market with information should out-
perform the one without.

The results were surprising. Deviations in market outcomes from
the efficient, competitive equilibrium solution were *greater* in the setting
with market information. This again prompted us to ponder, why? Revis-
iting the experiments, we observed something else. While all of the inefficient markets with information stopped trading short of reaching the
equilibrium quantity, some traded predominantly above equilibrium price
and others predominantly below. Further, individual transaction prices in
those markets trading above equilibrium tended to trend upward, while
those in markets trading below frequently trended downward. That is to
say, information often appeared to cause these markets to perform increasingly poorly over time.

Closer observation suggested that, surprise of all surprises, not all
traders are created equal! In some markets, buyers were apparently
dominating; in others, sellers were dominant. Even when using professional agricultural marketing economists as subjects, we found dominant
personalities! And, such dominant personalities tended to bias the market
outcome. Technically, this is called subject bias. One might argue that if
there were equally dominant personalities on each side of the market they
would be offsetting, but we have not yet determined how to test such a
supposition.

To further evaluate the "personality factor," we returned to the
laboratory and to the double auction. This time we compared trading
results using computerized double auction with those in an oral version of
the same pricing procedure. Trading rules were essentially the same, but
personality could be a factor in the oral auction while the electronic
system essentially homogenized personalities. The computerized system
achieved more nearly efficient results. One could debate whether personality dominance was the most significant difference here, but it is a tempt-
ing conclusion.

Our experiments generate observations that strongly suggest that
market information does not always lead to improved market efficiency.
This is not inconsistent with the AR findings of the occurrence of both
some deadweight loss and income redistribution associated with market
information in the cattle feeding industry. Such observations seem contrary to theoretical expectations. However, those expectations are formed
on the basis of the assumption of not only perfect information but numerous other conditions of perfect competition. Take away one or more of
the other conditions and it may no longer be valid to conclude that there
is a positive relationship between market information and market efficiency. While this may be no more than an obvious second-best state-

ment, at the least the question deserves to be examined in more detail as part of determining the appropriate role for publicly supported market information services.

REFERENCES

Smith, Vernon L. "Microeconomic Systems as an Experimental Science." *Am. Econ. Rev.* 72 (1982): 923–55.

CHAPTER 10

Comments on Concepts for Evaluating Economic Efficiency

Ronald W. Ward

THIS CHAPTER attempts to provide some added perspective relating to what has been covered in the chapters dealing with evaluating economic efficiency—a broad topic that is relevant to every phase of economic activity. Likewise, the range of empirical efforts dealing with efficiency issues is diverse, sometimes tentative, and frequently inadequate. Even with these limitations, progress has assuredly been made in the last several years. Progress is reflected through advances in the theory, through econometric and other modeling methods, and through a clearer understanding of the problems.

I will first restate the concept of efficiency and then identify particular areas of concern relevant to agricultural marketing. Finally, I will give a few observations about the four chapters dealing with the concepts of efficiency.

BASIC PREMISE AND SETTING

As each author deals with the issues of economic efficiency, there are three basic underlying premises that give rise to the problems. First, there exist demands for products that may be market or nonmarket goods, and the demands may be reasonably static or highly dynamic. The more dynamic the demands, the more difficult it is to deal empirically with many of the social issues relating to efficiency. Second, there exist alternative structures and/or organizational arrangements used to pro-

RONALD W. WARD is professor, Department of Food and Resource Economics, University of Florida, Gainesville.

duce, distribute, and facilitate the marketing of the goods demanded. Finally, uncertainty exists with both the physical characteristics and subsequent supplies and demands as well as with the quality of information available about the good today and for future periods.

Demands for characteristics exist, and methods have been devised to change the characteristics of the product demanded as well as change the demand for a fixed set of characteristics (product). Likewise, a wide range of exchange methods, ownership and managerial systems, and transformation services have been adopted as these products pass through the vertical market system from the producer to the final consumer. Lastly, methods for forward transactions in the face of uncertainty have taken a number of alternative forms.

As we view the complex marketing and distribution system, questions of economic performance are of particular importance. Performance is generally stated in terms of efficiency, equity, and other criteria such as freedom, security, and satisfaction. This book emphasizes the first of these, economic efficiency. Efficiency is probably the only dimension among the three that can be dealt with in an economic framework without being value-laden.

The chapters have dealt with basically three types of efficiencies. *Internal efficiency* is attained when firms manufacture and distribute their products using the minimum resources necessary. Internal efficiency can be expressed in terms of X-inefficiency or the degree that actual cost of transformation exceeds the minimum possible cost of achieving the transformation. When these costs do not differ, society obtains the maximum output from its limited resources.

Allocative efficiency relates to the allocation of resources across markets. It occurs when the marginal conditions are met for all products across all markets. Allocative inefficiency represents the positive differential attributed to a reallocation of resources from the existing arrangement to the efficient alternative.

Finally, one can discuss *dynamic efficiency,* which deals with the optimal allocation of resources over time. This aspect is particularly difficult to evaluate since by its very nature the optimal level is changing as technologies change.

The achieved performance or level of efficiency is clearly a constrained solution. Both technical and pecuniary externalities will affect consumption and/or production. These externalities can create social inefficiencies even with private efficient criteria met. The initial resource endowment may be inequitable. Allocative efficiency may be achieved without assuring any degree of fairness (i.e., a redistribution of initial resources). Technical changes across markets may lead to considerable differences among markets, depending on whether the technical change is external or in response to allocative changes within a market. The ability of producers to influence consumers' preferences via advertising and other persuasive means changes the entire concept of allocative efficiency. This dimension is particularly important to agricultural marketing with the increased emphasis on generic promotion. Finally, the other performance criteria directly serve to constrict the range of allocative decisions. Reallocation cannot be achieved at the cost of complete loss of freedom.

AGRICULTURAL MARKETING ISSUES

Efficiency is of paramount importance to both private and public policies relating to agricultural marketing. I have identified a number of agricultural marketing efficiency issues of particular importance, and while this list is likely incomplete, it should encompass most of the more immediate issues:

1. Are the appropriate market signals being generated within the marketing system to achieve the desired (or at least conjectured to be desired) product mix expressed by consumers?

2. Do existing distribution systems operate efficiently?

3. Do existing industry and firm structures achieve cost economies? Are prices elevated above the theoretical competitive levels? What about thin markets?

4. Are institutions that provide forward pricing functions fully reflecting existing information (e.g., how efficient are commodity futures markets)?

5. How do governmental or quasi-governmental structures alter the industry efficiency levels (i.e., marketing orders, allotments, price controls, and tariffs)?

6. How do public or quasi-public information sources impact both static and dynamic efficiency (e.g., what is the role of USDA crop forecasts, weather reporting, public research and education, and trade statistics in changing allocative efficiency)?

7. What is the impact of collusive efforts, joint ventures, and cooperative efforts?

8. How do alternative exchange functions alter the pricing process (auctions, electronic exchanges, administrative pricing, and formula pricing)?

9. What is the social impact of cooperative generic advertising versus brand advertising?

10. Do the current marketing systems encourage market development, especially for foreign markets?

The preceding chapters do not deal explicitly with these topics, but they do provide useful input to developing a conceptual framework and alternative methods for dealing with the questions.

CONCEPTUAL APPROACHES

The four chapters by MacDonald, Kilmer, Cotterill, and Antonovitz and Roe, respectively, deal with important conceptual problems for evaluating efficiency and there is complementarity among them. Specific applications to marketing issues noted above are not that direct, however, and there is a considerable gap between the theory and operationalizing the evaluation of efficiency. At the risk of considerable omission, I will provide some summary comments on these chapters.

Cotterill addressed efficiency issues under alternative forms of business enterprise. He recognizes that firms are driven by an array of decision-making units that may not have the same objective function. Frequently firms, especially large corporations, are driven by controls over information flows. Information is power within the internal structure of corporations and is used for personal advancement that, hopefully and possibly secondarily, directs the organization toward X-efficiency. Often, control of information and the methods for decision making are major sources of firm inefficiencies. X-inefficiency is probably the more important problem relative to allocative inefficiencies.

Cotterill provides an interesting perspective on the role of enterprise efficiency, and his arguments contribute to our understanding of the broad efficiency problem area. His analysis gives less guidance when attempting to operationalize and measure the extent of the problem within firms.

MacDonald addresses issues relating to structural differences across markets in terms of market power. He deals with the concepts of "contestable markets," which are basically an extension of Bain's (1972) original work dealing with barriers to entry and entry forestalling prices. The essence of the conceptual framework is that prices can be elevated above the competitive levels if barriers to entry exist. These barriers arise out of product differentiation, small and large scale economies, and absolute differences in cost. There are always potential entrants, and, as such, firms with considerable market power are limited by the possibility of attracting potential entrants into the market place. Given that existing firms do have economic advantages over potential entrants, prices can and will be raised above the competitive levels. However, in contestable markets one may see the observed price near the competitive price even with high concentration levels, thus implying allocative efficiency in a less than competitive market structure.

The concepts of contestable markets and Bain's entry forestalling pricing provide a very meaningful conceptual model for understanding performance. It helps us explain why competitive (or nearly competitive) pricing may exist in an oligopolistic market. Similarly, the existence of prices above the competitive levels in the face of minimal entry barriers can be addressed. Operationalizing the theory into a framework for dealing with specific food marketing issues is some distance away. But there is little doubt that the contestable market literature has changed the hypothesis when attempting to link performance to definable market structures in the traditional sense.

While Cotterill and MacDonald deal with the horizontal structure, Kilmer turns more to the vertical market system and how changes in vertical arrangements can impact pricing. His model shows how exchange mechanisms differ in terms of relative cost and other measures of industry performance, control over pricing, and ability to impact consumption. Kilmer simulates the impact of altering the exchange arrangement under a number of supply and demand conditions (i.e., changing elasticities). His conceptual mechanism is still abstract and one must know how effective the exchange mechanism is in its ability to change cost, impact consumption, etc. Once these initial parameters are known, the impacts of alternatives can be used to show relative prices. This conceptual model is built on several prior models and it should be useful for studying an array of alternative mechanisms. As in the other chapters, operationalizing the model has considerable limitations at the present stage of development.

Finally, Antonovitz and Roe deal with the problem of information and its impact on the pricing system. Information is essential to production decisions relative to expected demands for the goods. They derive the conditions under which the *ex post* value of the signal is positive. This area of research is extremely important in that much of the effort of public institutions is in the business of providing information. Measuring the value of information, which Antonovitz and Roe addressed, has two important dimensions. First, the value should depend directly on the quality and accessibility of the information. Second, the information may be of high quality and extremely accurate, but of lesser value because of limitations of the potential user. This second dimension makes evaluating information much more suspect simply because the same information will clearly have different values among user groups.

While the measured benefits are extremely important, I do have questions relating to their calculation of the benefits of the information in their applied example. They essentially build a rational expectation model and an Auto-Regressive Integrated Moving-Average (ARIMA) model to forecast market prices and calculate consumer and producer surpluses from the differences in prices generated. Obviously, the conclusions are restricted by the limitations of the econometrics.

These four chapters dealt with pieces of a complex area with each contributing to the broader issues of efficiency. The analyses by Kilmer as well as by Antonovitz and Roe come close to providing empirical methods for measuring the economic gains for some dimensions of the marketing function. However, these chapters alone cannot be expected to provide the complete conceptual framework for addressing efficiency in a broader context. Although each chapter makes a contribution to developing a conceptual framework, we are not yet there.

REFERENCES

Bain, Joe S. *Essays on Price Theory and Industrial Organization.* Boston: Little, Brown, 1972.

PART III

Economic Efficiency,
Public Programs,
Private Activities

Economic Efficiency
and Marketing Orders

Edward V. Jesse

FEDERAL MARKETING ORDERS were first authorized by Congress in the 1933 Agricultural Adjustment Act (AAA) as part of a legislative package designed to improve the financial situation of farmers through price and supply controls. Reauthorized in the Agricultural Marketing Agreement Act (AMAA) of 1937, federal orders remain as potentially powerful tools of market control with resulting significant potential effects on economic efficiency.

Through referenda, producers approve the use of marketing orders containing regulations binding on handlers. Marketing cooperatives are usually instrumental in the process of documenting the need for orders and developing order proposals.

Regulatory provisions differ between the two classes of commodities for which federal orders are authorized, milk and specified fruits, vegetables, and specialty crops. Milk orders permit classified pricing and pooling. Minimum prices for fluid-eligible (Grade A) milk are set according to whether the milk is used by handlers for fluid milk or for manufactured products. Total market receipts based on these class prices and handler utilization are pooled and producers delivering milk to regulated handlers receive a common, or blend, price.

Fruit and vegetable marketing orders permit a variety of tools, distinguished by their degree of control over marketings. Three broad categories are quantity controls, quality controls, and market support activities. Quantity controls, representing the strongest form of regulation permitted under fruit and vegetable orders, include producer allotments, market

EDWARD V. JESSE is professor and chairman, Department of Agricultural Economics, University of Wisconsin, Madison.

allocation and reserve pools, and intraseasonal volume controls. Producer allotments restrict the amount handlers may acquire from individual growers. Market allocation restricts the amount of handler sales in designated primary market outlets. Reserve pools function as a form of market allocation, the distinction being that restricted quantities are stored for subsequent sale in either primary or secondary markets. Intraseasonal controls affect the temporal distribution of shipments through shipping prohibitions (shipping holidays) or assignment of weekly shipping allotments (handler prorates). Where shipping allotments are used for all or most of the season, they are functionally equivalent to market allocation.

Quality controls set minimum standards for grade or size, enforced by mandatory USDA inspection. For specified commodities, imports must meet the same standards as those imposed by the orders. Market support activities, which do not directly affect quantity or quality, include pack and container standards and authority to assess handlers for research and promotion.

Marketing order provisions that set prices and restrict marketings represent clear departures from perfectly competitive price and output determination. Hence, marketing orders suggest the theoretical likelihood of efficiency losses unless their use is a response to market failures.

Much attention has been devoted to identifying the nature and magnitude of marketing order efficiency losses during the last ten years. The USDA (1981, 1984) conducted mandated reviews of marketing orders for milk and for fruits and vegetables, both of which have been thoroughly digested and debated.[1] These reviews followed and were partly influenced by analyses conducted by the U.S. Federal Trade Commission (1975) and the U.S. Department of Justice (1977), analyses that were sharply critical of orders because of asserted negative economic efficiency effects. More recently, the American Agricultural Economics Association (1984) sponsored a special review of milk marketing orders. Numerous other research efforts have addressed orders and their efficiency effects.[2]

Given the extensive literature, it would seem that little more needs to be said about marketing orders and economic efficiency except to summarize where consensus and disagreement lie. This can be done briefly. Milk marketing orders result in efficiency losses to the extent that classified pricing represents price discrimination.[3] Excessive Grade A milk production may be induced by "supracompetitive" blend prices. Classified pricing may contribute to inefficient milk processing plant locations and inefficient fluid milk trade patterns. Order pricing restrictions on reconstituted milk (fluid milk made from condensed milk or dry ingredients) elevate the cost of providing fluid milk to consumers distant from major milksheds.

Fruit and vegetable marketing orders permitting producer allotments may restrict entry, causing deficient resources to be devoted to production. Orders using market allocation may perpetuate surpluses, thus contributing to excess resources. Market allocation and continuous use of prorates may distort firm growth incentives and reduce competition among handlers. Quality controls may reduce the range of quality available to consumers. To the extent volume controls successfully reduce marketings in the short run, they elevate consumer prices.

Where efficiency gains to marketing orders have been identified, they are usually attributed to price and output stabilization (French 1982; Gardner 1984). However, there is considerable disagreement about how much stability is provided by marketing orders. The state of knowledge is confounded by a lack of a reference base (i.e., an appropriate historical period or comparable commodity for making comparisons) (see Jesse and Johnson 1981). Causing even more discord is a debate over whether the type of stabilization provided by marketing orders is socially beneficial, with some arguing that marketing orders are, in fact, destabilizing (Masson et al. 1978). Other efficiency benefits of marketing orders are related to their role in improving the quantity and quality of marketing information.

Analysts willing to assume perfect competition in the absence of marketing orders have found negative net efficiency effects (see, for example, Lenard 1975). Those conceding possible order benefits have equivocated, declining to apply the subjective weights to costs and benefits that would be necessary to draw definitive conclusions about net efficiency (Jesse 1982).

This paper might terminate abruptly here but for two related questions concerning economists' appraisals of the efficiency effects of marketing orders. The first question is in reference to how economic efficiency has been defined and measured in evaluating orders: Has efficiency been interpreted broadly enough to encompass socially desirable performance? The second question relates to the usefulness of research findings to the USDA in its marketing order oversight and administration roles: Should the Secretary of Agriculture use economic efficiency as the sole criterion for assessing order performance?

ON ECONOMIC EFFICIENCY

Economists have long wrestled with definitions and measurements of economic efficiency. The terminology is confusing. Some definitions disaggregate *economic* efficiency into components consisting of *technical* efficiency (or, alternatively, *productive* efficiency or *operational* efficiency) and *pricing* efficiency (or *allocative* efficiency or, sometimes, *economic* efficiency). Other definitions equate economic efficiency with maximum social welfare, employing various notions of what constitutes social welfare.

The feasibility of measuring economic efficiency and the means of measuring it vary according to definition and also according to the level of aggregation at which it is to be measured. In discussing the conclusions of a national marketing workshop, Kohls (1956, 71) notes that:

> . . . efficiency is a single concept defined as the ratio of ends to resources. The ends are to be considered in the broadest or the narrowest sense depending on the particular problem at hand.
>
> If the problem is one of firm or intrafirm efficiency, the formulation of the ends in measurable terms may be relatively simple. If the problem is one concerning efficiencies of the whole marketing system, the framework of the ends must be worked through giving explicit consideration to all the value judgments involved. At this level, quantification of the ends may be impossible. This means that the difficulty of giving definitive answers to such broad issues is acknowledged rather than avoided through the process of whittling the concept down to where something can be said that is not relevant to the total problem.

If economic efficiency is equated with net social welfare, then measurement must rely on concepts of social utility. Because these are nebulous, the tendency has been to measure economic efficiency in terms of producer and consumer surplus. Where economic costs of marketing orders have been quantified, they have been expressed in terms of deadweight losses relative to a perfectly competitive price and output solution.

Conceptually, this is a fine approach. There is a certain analytic comfort gained from making welfare appraisals on the basis of supply and demand equations. In the harsh light of reality, measuring social welfare gains and losses by integrating areas bounded by price lines and supply and demand curves is akin to counting angels waltzing on pinheads. This futility is partly related to our inability as economists to accurately measure supply and demand or to forecast market structure and behavioral and institutional changes in the absence of marketing orders. But more importantly, social welfare consists of far more than what can be derived from supply and demand diagrams.[4]

ON ADMINISTERING MARKETING ORDERS

The USDA is responsible for administering federal marketing orders. The Secretary of Agriculture holds the ultimate authority to approve new orders, to propose amendments, and to terminate or suspend existing orders. The USDA plays an active role in administering milk marketing orders through its market administrators. Its role in administering fruit and vegetable orders is more passive, involving evaluating and passing judgment on the regulatory recommendations of industry committees.

The AMAA contains only broad guidelines for marketing order administration and oversight. Orders should establish and maintain orderly marketing conditions that will, in turn, establish parity prices to farmers and avoid unreasonable fluctuations in supplies and prices. Parity prices should be approached gradually, the speed of adjustment conditioned by demand conditions and the public interest.[5]

These imprecisely defined legislative objectives are devoid of reference to consumer surplus, producer surplus, and net social welfare.[6] One might interpret this to mean that orders are to be used to benefit producers as long as they do not hurt consumers too much. Alternatively, the AMAA's objectives might refer to a broader social performance goal, one that includes equity and orderliness as well as more conventional indicators of social welfare.

I submit that this broader notion of what orders should accomplish is the proper interpretation of legislative intent. This interpretation has important implications for the USDA in administering marketing orders, suggesting that in appraising orders the Secretary must use economic performance criteria that transcend common definitions of economic efficiency. A narrow focus on economic efficiency measures that involve producer and consumer surplus is inappropriate, since intangible measures of social welfare referenced by legislative intent would not likely be included in these measures.

A semantic distinction may be at issue here. If economic efficiency is defined as maximum net social welfare, then perhaps imprecise concepts like orderly marketing can be made integral components of that definition. I would not quarrel with using such a broad definition in guiding marketing order evaluation, but performance seems a more fitting criterion. Performance includes a broader spectrum of economic attributes than efficiency. Further, using performance as an evaluative guideline avoids a tendency to concentrate on efficiency indicia that are easily measurable.

The remainder of this paper endeavors to provide a broader framework for evaluating marketing orders; one that focuses on performance measures beyond economic efficiency. Some specific performance criteria are identified, and some general guidelines for evaluation are discussed.

ON EVALUATING MARKETING ORDER PERFORMANCE EFFECTS

Measuring performance is certainly no less a precarious undertaking than measuring efficiency (Jesse 1978). However, there seems to be fairly broad agreement on performance *elements*. For purposes of identifying marketing order performance criteria, I will employ a list of elements used by Brandow (1977) in discussing food industry performance (Table 11.1).

TABLE 11.1.   Elements of market performance

1. Returns to Factors of Production
2. Stability of Prices, Output, and Employment
3. Fair Conduct
4. Price Coordination
5. Product Characteristics
6. Efficiency
7. Progressiveness
8. Selling Costs
9. Externalities

Brandow's list is quite general including, explicitly or implicitly, performance elements suggested by most others. Definitions and performance norms are apparent in most cases, but there are some exceptions. Conduct is not the industrial organization concept of firm behavior; it is more related to exploitation, whether firm or labor. Price coordination refers to the level and rigidity of marketing margins. Product characteristics include quality, healthfulness, and safety as well as packaging. Efficiency is narrowly defined as technical efficiency. Selling costs refer to advertising expenditures.

Some of these performance elements relate directly to economic efficiency (product characteristics, efficiency, progressiveness, and selling costs). The relationship is more indirect in the case of others (returns to factors of production and price coordination). Other elements appear to be unrelated to common definitions of economic efficiency (fair conduct and externalities). And stabilization is noted independently as a performance element, not as it influences efficiency.

The list of elements can be split into two groups: (1) elements that orders are intended to *positively* influence, and (2) elements that orders are not intended to influence, but that orders should not *negatively* influence. This categorization is illustrated in Tables 11.2 and 11.3, which also show specific marketing order performance criteria related to the elements.

The first four performance elements noted in Table 11.1 relate specifically to orderly marketing concepts as these are referenced in the AMAA. Order evaluation using the associated performance criteria first should ascertain whether industry conditions absent marketing orders would produce undesirable performance. These conditions might include imperfect competition on the buyer sides of markets, inherently unstable supply or demand, or other market imperfections. If these are present, then evaluation would proceed to an assessment of how effectively orders contribute to achievement of the performance objectives.

Some guidelines and comments about this second phase of order evaluation are:

TABLE 11.2.   Performance element subset I: Desirable performance that marketing orders should enhance

Performance element	Marketing orders should encourage:
Returns to factors of production	Producer and handler profits consistent with changing market conditions
Stability of prices, output, and employment	Elimination or amelioration of industry overadjustments in resource use
Fair conduct	Equitable treatment among and between handlers and producers
Price coordination	Transmission of price signals that reflect supply conditions and consumer preferences

TABLE 11.3.   Performance subset II: Desirable performance that marketing orders should not inhibit

Performance element	Marketing orders should not discourage:
Product characteristics	Enhanced food safety
Efficiency	Least-cost production and marketing practices
	Least-cost regional production, processing, and distribution patterns
Progressiveness	Rapid adoption of cost-saving technology
Selling costs	Information/educational promotional efforts
Externalities	Elimination, reduction, or internalization of externalities

1. "Reasonable" profits to all producers may be inappropriate if these prevent or postpone necessary industry adjustments. Orders should not attempt to maintain or elevate grower returns at the expense of contributing to chronic excess or deficit productive capacity.

2. Evaluation of the benefits of price and output stabilization is extremely complex. Brandow's (1977, 91) admonition that "an industry should not itself be a source of instability" seems apropos here. That is, marketing orders should address socially costly cyclical production patterns induced by product perishability and imperfect information. Of questionable value is the use of orders to reduce price and output variability resulting from exogenous forces such as exchange rate fluctuations.

3. French (1982) notes important distinctions among types of marketing order stabilization that are important in evaluating performance. *Pure* stabilization, exemplified by reserve pool provisions that augment short crops with supplies withheld from large crops, is preferable to *monopoly* stabilization that permanently diverts supplies from primary markets during years of large crops. And monopoly stabilization that cuts only extreme peaks in supply is preferable to regular use of diversion, which may indicate a chronic surplus problem that marketing orders cannot adequately address.

4. One of the primary justifications for marketing orders is to assure "fair" treatment of producers, especially with respect to market access. Fairness has usually been interpreted as equality. All Grade A milk producers shipping to plants pooled under a marketing order receive equal prices (adjusted for butterfat content and farm location). California orange growers are assured equal access to the regulated market irrespective of other marketing opportunities.

But equality is not equity. It is not equitable for dairy farmers whose milk is never needed for fluid use to receive the same price as farmers who regularly supply fluid markets. It is not equitable for orange growers who can sell much of their fruit in unregulated markets at prices comparable to those in regulated markets to be granted equal marketing rights to regulated sales vis à vis growers who do not enjoy that advantage.

5. Little research has been directed toward the effects of marketing orders on marketing margins. Logic suggests that fluid milk margins would tend to be smaller with administered pricing, since handlers face equivalent raw product costs. Similarly, intraseasonal stabilization of shipments might be expected to reduce produce distributor margins. These hypotheses have not been well tested.

The last five elements in Table 11.1, reproduced in Table 11.3, relate to aspects of economic performance that marketing orders are not intended to influence. The associated criteria reflect generally desirable performance, not necessarily goals of orders. But orders should not operate so as to prevent achievement of the goals. Thus, order performance evaluation should focus on negative order effects.

Some comments on these elements of performance and how they are or may be affected by marketing orders follow:

1. Marketing orders have no effect on food safety, but some fruit and vegetable order provisions influence food quality, variety, and packaging. Performance evaluation should consider whether order quality standards or pack/packaging requirements reflect consumer preferences or those of growers, handlers, or distributors.

2. Milk orders effectively prohibit the sale of reconstituted milk through pricing penalties. This has negative efficiency implications (elevating balancing and transportation costs), but also limits the range of fluid milk products available to consumers. Although some claims about potential consumption of reconstituted milk are exaggerated, there is little doubt that some consumers would purchase the product at some cost-justified discount from whole milk prices. The issue of order pricing of reconstituted milk goes well beyond producer-consumer trade-offs. It is becoming a source of interregional friction in the dairy industry. The intensity of the debate is not likely to subside, and the USDA needs to take prompt and assertive action to prevent further discord and to reaffirm the integrity of the milk marketing order system.

3. To the extent that marketing orders achieve intended performance goals (competitive returns to factors of production, price and output stability, fair conduct, and coordinated prices), they promote an environment conducive to farm-level investment. Thus, the technical efficiency of producers should be enhanced. Because we lack a reference base, we have not been able to empirically document or refute such potential efficiency gains. In contrast to amorphous and speculative gains, efficiency losses are glaring: Class I utilization rates in some markets that are less than 25 percent; cheese factories located in the heart of fluid milk supply areas; qualification fees paid by pooled milk manufacturing plants for the "privilege" of hauling milk to high-utilization handlers and then back home again; and surplus lemons left unharvested to qualify for "on-tree certification." Some of these clear efficiency losses may be inevitably associated with attaining primary marketing order goals. Others can be avoided without materially affecting order achievements. Order performance evaluation must address this important distinction.

4. Generic promotion has become big business in agriculture. Many programs are funded by handler assessments under fruit and vegetable marketing orders. Whether economic performance is improved by generic advertising is not clear. Neither is whether producers benefit from such programs. Order performance evaluation should consider the magnitude

of promotion expenditures relative to sales, the general thrust of promotion efforts (i.e., educational vs hype), and the manner in which the effectiveness of promotion is documented.

THE NEED FOR ORDER PERFORMANCE CRITERIA

A recent General Accounting Office (GAO) report on fruit and vegetable marketing orders (U.S. General Accounting Office, 1985) commented on USDA's administrative and decision-making roles. The report noted that the department often failed to articulate rationale for marketing order decisions or was inconsistent in specifying reasons. GAO recommended that USDA develop explicit performance criteria and reference these in supporting department decisions to initiate, amend, and terminate orders. In responding to the report, USDA recognized the need for performance criteria and promised to continue efforts to develop them.

Recently, a number of decisions regarding marketing order amendments, suspensions, and termination and the application of authorized tools have been politicized. This emphasizes the need for performance guidelines. While USDA cannot prevent individual legislators, other government agencies, or the White House from intervening in order decision making, it might minimize such intervention by employing a well-publicized set of performance standards in discharging its oversight responsibilities.

Performance criteria would also provide clearer guidance to producers, handlers, and marketing order administrative committees. Groups petitioning USDA for amendments or a new order would be made aware of performance expectations.

The performance criteria would incorporate concepts of efficiency, both directly and indirectly, as indicated earlier. While efficiency would be important in the performance criteria, the broader coverage specifying elements expected to be positively influenced and those that should not be negatively influenced would be quite useful in order administration.

NOTES

1. The USDA study on milk orders was mandated in the Agriculture and Food Act of 1981. The fruit and vegetable study was conducted at the request of Vice President Bush's Task Force on Regulatory Relief.
2. See Dash and Sommer (1984) for an annotated bibliography of milk order studies; U.S. GAO (1985) for fruit and vegetable order studies.

3. This is a sharply debated issue. Milk order opponents argue that the entire difference between Class I (fluid) prices and Class II (manufacturing) prices represents price discrimination, since the product (Grade A milk) is homogeneous. Order proponents argue that the product is inseparable from the bundle of services provided, and that fluid milk prices reflect costly services, such as weekly and seasonal balancing of supply and demand, that are equal in value to the price difference between fluid and manufacturing milk.
4. Fred Waugh (1954, 127) suggests that inefficiency may be tolerated to achieve other social objectives:

> . . . actually, the public may prefer to keep some known inefficiencies rather than adopt new methods—especially if the prospective improvements in efficiency might reduce employment, decrease price competition, or lead to greater concentration of economic power.

5. This paper ignores the economic implications of the parity price goal, since parity has been nearly universally rejected as an appropriate price standard.
6. The assumption of equal marginal utility of money necessary to calculate net social welfare by netting producer and consumer surplus seems inappropriate in light of the AMAA's clear intent to transfer income from consumers to producers.

REFERENCES

American Agricultural Economics Association Policy Task Force on Dairy Marketing Orders. *Federal Marketing Orders: A Review of Research on Their Economic Consequences.* Ithaca, N.Y.: Report prepared for the AAEA Policy Task Force on Dairy Marketing Orders, July 1984.

Brandow, George E. "Appraising the Economic Performance of the Food Industry." *Lectures in Agricultural Economics,* ed. James Sayre, pp. 81–100. Washington, D.C.: USDA, June 1977.

Dash, Suzanne L., and Judith Sommer. *Recent Dairy Policy Publications With Selected Annotations.* Washington, D.C.: USDA ERS Staff Rep. AGES840417, Apr. 1984.

French, Ben C. "Fruit and Vegetable Marketing Orders: A Critique of the Issues and State of Analysis." *Am. J. Agric. Econ.* 64(1982):916–23.

Gardner, Bruce L. "Price Discrimination or Price Stabilization: Debating with Models of the U.S. Dairy Industry." *Am. J. Agric. Econ.* 66(1984):763–68.

Jesse, E. V. "Measuring Market Performance: Quantifying the Non-Quantifiable?" Madison: University of Wisconsin, N. C. Project 117 WP-15, Mar. 1978.

———. "Costs and Benefits of Marketing Orders." *Fruit Situation.* Washington, D.C.: USDA ERS TVS-22, Mar. 1982.

Jesse, E. V., and A. C. Johnson, Jr. *Effectiveness of Federal Marketing Orders for Fruits and Vegetables.* Washington, D.C.: USDA ESS Agric. Econ. Rep. 471, June 1981.

Kohls, R. L. "Towards a More Meaningful Concept of Economic Efficiency." *J. Farm Econ.* 38(1956):68–73.

Lenard, T. *Government Regulation of Milk Markets.* Washington, D.C.: Discussion paper prepared for the Council on Wage and Price Stability, 1975.

Masson, Alison, Robert T. Masson, and Barry C. Harris. "Cooperatives and Marketing Orders." *Agricultural Cooperatives and the Public Interest.* Proceedings of the North Central Regional Research Committee 117, Monograph 4, ed. B. C. Marion, pp. 187–218. Madison: University of Wisconsin, 1978.

U.S. Department of Agriculture. *A Review of Federal Marketing Orders for Fruits, Vegetables, and Specialty Crops: Economic Efficiency and Welfare Implications.* Washington, D.C.: AMS Agric. Econ. Rep. 477, Nov. 1981.

U.S. Department of Agriculture. *Review of Existing and Alternative Federal Dairy Programs.* Washington, D.C.: ERS Staff Rep. AGES840121, Jan. 1984.

U.S. Federal Trade Commission. *A Report on Agricultural Cooperatives.* Washington, D.C.: A report prepared by the Bureau of Competition, Sept. 1975.

U.S. General Accounting Office. *The Role of Marketing Orders in Establishing and Maintaining Orderly Marketing Conditions.* Washington, D.C.: GAO/RCED-85-57, July 1985.

Waugh, F. V., ed. "Efficiency." *Readings on Agricultural Marketing.* Ames: Iowa State University Press, 1954.

A DISCUSSION

Mary C. Kenney

IN HIS CHAPTER, Jesse maintains that efficiency, as reflected by consumer and producer surplus, is too narrow an indicator for evaluating marketing orders. He is concerned about the correspondence between the specification of supply and demand functions for purposes of welfare measurement and marketplace behavior. One can hardly claim that the effects of marketing orders can be portrayed by noting the difference in consumer and producer surplus under these institutions and in their absence. The chapter notes the difficulty of postulating a reasonable set of prevailing conditions in the absence of marketing orders for commodity markets directly influenced by the presence of those regulations for decades. Jesse sensibly argues that the assumption of perfect competition is suspect. For these reasons, he proposes that "performance," a notion of broader scope than efficiency, be adopted for purposes of analyzing the effectiveness of marketing orders. The chapter goes on to suggest some appropriate standards for consideration, such as price and output stability, fair conduct, and returns to factors of production consistent with changing market conditions.

Records pertaining to the enactment and subsequent amendment of legislation authorizing marketing orders provide little guidance by way of articulating goals that are both unambiguous and relevant today. Hence, lacking other information, a broad social performance goal for marketing orders as proposed by Jesse is as sensible an interpretation of legislative intent as any other.

I would like to propose that the concept of efficiency as it relates to marketing orders not be discarded so hastily. I believe that by emphasizing economic efficiency, in the sense of the least cost approach to attaining a well-defined goal, economists can confine their role to tasks that they have a history of doing well, that is, measuring the relative cost effectiveness of alternative means to a given end. In the process, they may avoid making pronouncements in a murky and troubled area, that of establishing "appropriate" societal goals.

At the time of the conference, MARY C. KENNEY was staff economist, Agricultural Marketing Service, USDA, Washington, D.C.

We in the economics community must look to other disciplines for guidance. We should encourage greater cooperation with political and other social scientists so that appropriate methods will be developed for translating the expressions of participants in the relevant political arena into food and agricultural policy goals for heuristic purposes. With such tools available, marketing orders and other forms of government intervention could be evaluated according to their ability to meet established societal goals.

In such a setting, pricing efficiency has a pivotal role in evaluating cash costs associated with marketing orders and with alternative means of addressing an agricultural policy problem. Economic efficiency as it relates to consumer and producer losses and gains would figure prominently.

Let us say, for example, that there is general agreement that it is in the best interests of society to ensure the vitality of midsize farming operations, a reasonable goal in today's agricultural economy. The questions for economists become (1) whether there is a need for government involvement, and, if there is a need, (2) what public policy measures can be undertaken to promote the viability of these units? Prior to proposing policy and program alternatives for addressing the situation, economists usually attempt to understand the origin of the perceived problem. In our example, one would want to explain why the number of farmers earning between $40,000 and $200,000 annually is declining in absolute and relative numbers and in share of total agricultural output. Then, policy and program alternatives to stem the exit of the targeted group from agriculture could be developed. Finally, objective analysis of alternative solutions would be made available to policymakers.

For producers of commodities operating under marketing orders, the analysis should include the costs of marketing orders in sustaining this targeted group of farmers. There is some evidence that the size distribution of fruit, vegetable, and specialty crop growers may be maintained through marketing orders. It is believed that fewer smaller producers may leave the industry as their ability to share in higher priced primary markets increases through marketing order provisions such as reserve pools and prorates. Marketwide quality standards also assist the small grower who does not have the ability to differentiate his product.

Under my proposal, efficiency losses and gains from marketing orders would be compared with the costs of alternative means of preserving the viability of the middle income group in affected industries. Jesse is correct in insisting that subjective weights would have to be applied. Presumably, the articulation of a consensual goal prior to the cost comparison of alternatives would contribute to the development of appropriate weights for groups of affected individuals.

CHAPTER 12

Economic Efficiency Issues
of Grading and
Minimum Quality Standards

Nancy E. Bockstael

THIS CHAPTER considers the economic efficiency of two closely related, but institutionally differentiated, agricultural marketing practices—grading and standards. While the term *standards* is frequently used in conjunction with grades to denote the boundaries of grades, it is used here in a more specialized fashion. Throughout, standards will refer to minimum quality standards such as those set forth in agricultural marketing orders. Even though grades and standards so defined are implemented under different authorities and for different purposes, they are closely related conceptually because they both relate to the quality dimension of a commodity. Interestingly, the euphemisms "orderly marketing" and "price enhancement" have been associated with both.

The literature provides a surfeit of articles of all varieties, sizes, and maturities on topics related to grading and minimum standards. Yet, despite the impressive number of papers, no simple consensus exists on the assessment of these practices. Most of the literature, although excellent in its discussion, is not highly analytical. The number of dimensions to grading and standards questions make them difficult to model analytically. In an attempt to provide marginally more decisive answers, this chapter restricts the dimensions of the grades and standards problems to be considered. For one thing, it is limited to agricultural products that are marketed in unprocessed form. Additionally, as the title suggests, the focus is economic efficiency considerations.

NANCY E. BOCKSTAEL is associate professor, Department of Agriculture and Resource Economics, University of Maryland, College Park.

There is a second reason why economists have been unable to present a united and unambiguous evaluation of grading schemes and minimum quality standards. The objective of grading and standards is quality, and classical economic theory is not particularly facile at handling quality as a dimension of demand. Even when relevant approaches to the treatment of quality can be identified, theoretical results on grading and standards are conditional on the amount and type of information about quality held by all parties and on the market structure of the industry.

In the next section the general agricultural literature on minimum quality standards and grading is reviewed, and the apparent controversies highlighted. In the following two sections, several strains in the literature are pulled together and an analysis of grading and standards is presented for the case in which product quality is known with certainty and in which there exists uncertainty about quality. In these sections an attempt is made to integrate relevant analyses from both the agricultural and mainstream economics literature and to determine what, if any, decisive theoretical results exist.

While it takes a slightly different perspective, this chapter is similar to previous literature in that it is more of a discussion than an analytical piece. Yet it attempts to provide new insights into old questions and offers a hypothesis that it is hoped will stimulate some empirical research. In the final section the possibility is explored that industry structure may affect the evaluation of grades and standards as potentially efficient practices.

REVIEWING THE ARGUMENTS

Although both grading and minimum quality standards relate to the concept of product quality, their respective places in the literature are quite distinct. Minimum quality standards have received the most attention by virtue of their regulatory-restrictive nature and because of the recent attention directed to agricultural marketing orders by consumer groups and federal agencies.

In contrast, the literature on grading has been less abundant and less controversial. In addition to papers published in the 1950s and 1960s that described the functions of grades (see, for example, Mehren 1961; Shaw 1961) and that analyzed the effects on specific industries of grading changes (Fienup 1961; Purcell and Nelson 1976), there are only a few papers that have discussed the benefits and costs of grades, what grades should do, or how they should be set.

The best general discussion of grading can be found in Nichols et al. (1983). These authors stress the confusion that exists over the objectives of grading. The enabling legislation gives no clear indication for whom the grades are to be devised. The many potential functions of grades can really be grouped into those that facilitate handling and long-distance trade and those that serve to label and differentiate products at the consumer level.

Dalrymple (1968), presuming the former function to be dominant, attributes the paucity of economic analysis on produce grades to the rather mundane motivation for their existence, the practical need for a standard of identity for trading purposes at the wholesale level. In truth, this is probably the most important reason for the advent of grades—to facilitate trade between two distant points when physical inspection of goods by the buyer would require expensive travel. This role of grading is somewhat akin to the provision of standard weights and measures for orderly commerce. Even so, this function of grades is not completely innocuous and can be the source of controversy when changes in grading schemes have distributional implications among producers, handlers, shippers, etc. While this is clearly a critical role of grades and is of some importance in our discussions, the emphasis will be on the potential effect of grading schemes on consumers. For unprocessed agricultural commodities, there is no obvious reason why a quality characteristic should matter to handlers and wholesalers if it does not matter to final consumers.

Except for meat, however, much of the grading that takes place does not carry over to the consumer level. Nonetheless, many have argued that if graded products are to be consumed directly or in relatively unchanged form, then factors that relate to consumers' preferences for quality should be taken into account in establishing grading schemes. This theme is prevalent in a number of articles recognizing that if consumer demand is a function of quality, the way in which grade boundaries are set will affect revenues to producers. Of course, grade boundaries will also affect consumer benefits, but much of the discussion of optimal grading schemes appears to be aimed at maximizing producer returns (Rhodes and Kiehl 1956; Zusman 1967; Spriggs 1979; Matsumoto and French 1971).

The rigorous analysis of grading by Berck and Rausser (1980) is motivated by a desire for proper econometric modeling. While their analysis provides some interesting conclusions, it draws on and extends the literature on product differentiation and monopolistic competition. As such, the theoretical approach is more appropriate to processed agricultural products in which product differences are not associated with different processors and are not necessarily ordinally ranked by consumers. Nonetheless, the discussion of grading in the next two sections incorporates elements from Berck and Rausser and from the product differentiation literature and outlines the distinction in the character of the two problems.

Turning to the issue of quality standards, the literature is far more extensive. In addition to the discussions of marketing orders emanating from the academic ranks, from the early insights of Sidney Hoos (1978) to the recent and excellent ones of Ben French (1982), each administration since that of President Johnson has seen fit to mandate a study of the role of marketing orders. It was not until the 1970s that the need for understanding the welfare effects of market orders became most pressing, however. Since the mid 1970s there have been four Government Accounting Office (GAO) publications on the topic, two interagency or external reviews sponsored by United States Department of Agriculture (USDA), and a number of papers authored by economists at the Department of Agriculture and the Department of Justice.

There is no doubt among the authors of these reports that the original intent of marketing orders was to enhance producer returns, although other more ambiguous goals, such as "orderly marketing," have also been mentioned. In fact the intent of some of the early literature (e.g., Price's 1967 paper on minimum quality standards) was to illustrate how marketing orders could be used to increase revenues.

Only a few papers in the 1960s, including Jamison's (1966) work and Farrell's report for the National Commission on Food Marketing (1966), raised social welfare considerations. These rumblings were followed in the 1970s by a full-fledged controversy between consumer interests and inflation-fighting federal agencies on the one hand and marketing order proponents on the other. Of the many evaluations that were spawned by this controversy, those condemning the orders and those defending them were equally vehement and convincing. More recent reports have recognized the inconclusive evidence (both of a theoretical and an empirical nature) and provided more evenhanded assessments, although no more satisfying for those seeking definitive answers. What follows is a summary of the arguments that can be found in these reports about the quality control provisions of the orders.

The popular rationale for minimum quality standards is that by excluding low-quality produce, standards assure the consumer a high-quality product, which in turn enhances demand and raises the price of the remaining produce. Thus, it is frequently claimed that quality standards "work in the interest of both consumers and and producers." Few have been so naive as to ignore the quantity control dimensions of standards, however. In fact French et al. (1978) stated forthrightly what many have argued implicitly: "quality controls are really disguised volume controls." Marketing orders have been implicitly accused of harming consumers, but the 1976 GAO study (U.S. Comptroller General) attempted to demonstrate explicitly that consumers pay appreciably higher prices for some commodities because of quality provisions of marketing orders. Others have questioned the consumer welfare implications of the trade restrictions implicit in quality controls. Some marketing order standards apply to imported produce as well as domestic produce and have been accused of being implemented precisely to exclude certain foreign imports (e.g., Mexican tomatoes and Turkish raisins).

In defense of marketing orders, several studies were launched to respond to these accusations. Jesse and Johnson (1981) attempted to empirically test whether commodities under marketing orders tended to exhibit higher or more stable prices than commodities not covered. They found no significant difference between groups but recognized that (1) such patterns were difficult to test for, and (2) there may be an inherent self-selection bias among marketing order commodities. Others attempted to argue a logical defense against the accusation of price enhancement. Studies such as the USDA (1975) report on price impacts of orders reasoned that if quality controls were being used in effect as quantity controls, then we should observe variation in minimum quality standards between years of gluts and scarcities. They found no such variations, although a later USDA report (1981) appeared to find evidence of variation for some crops. The same 1975 study argued that the presence of competing commodities (identical commodities from other geographic areas not under orders or commodities that were close substitutes) would prevent appreciable price impacts from quantity reduction. In fact, many reports argued that since there were no entry restrictions for most of these products, entry would tend to drive down prices in the long run.

I think it is worth recounting this debate. What strikes one immediately is the emphasis on "price enhancement." Justifiably or not, the intent of the orders was to increase producer revenues, and yet the defense of marketing orders has come to rest on proof that they have not increased prices. Since quality controls are unlikely to increase volume, they must necessarily increase price if they are to achieve the objective of increasing producer revenues.

The emphasis on price ehhancement in this debate is misplaced. There are several claims that minimum quality standards improve economic efficiency (U.S. Comptroller General 1985). To do this they must address a market failure. The 1981 Review of Federal Marketing Orders (USDA 1981, 19) was very clear on this point:

> In reassessing the need for marketing orders, a critical question is: Does an economic rationale exist for considering any form of governmental action in the industries involved? More specifically, are there reasons to expect that free competition among private entrepreneurs will not lead to efficient resource allocation and an appropriate income distribution? If governmental intervention in the industry cannot even potentially improve social welfare, such intervention is clearly inappropriate.

The question is: Under what conditions is social welfare improved? In this case, it is probably safe to rephrase the question as, Under what conditions could producers and consumers both benefit or at least producers benefit without consumers being hurt?

Recognizing that this was the issue, Jesse (1979) attempted to characterize the gains and losses to producers and consumers in a graphic analysis. Unfortunately he was able to deduce very little. At the heart of his difficulty was his inability to characterize the effects of standards on either producers or consumers in a manner representative of the nature of the problem yet not fettered by arbitrary restrictions such as functional form. Hoos (1978, 7) captured the dilemma agricultural economists have faced in evaluating standards when he said, "The ambiguous status of the quality provisions derives in large part from the lack of attention given in economic theory to the subject of quality."

In a paper that makes more explicit the nature of quality in consumer and producer decisions, Bockstael (1984) asks Jesse's questions and reaches some definitive conclusions for the case in which quality characteristics are observable. While it is useful to analyze this case, it is by no means the most interesting. As we shall see, the most convincing argument for standards can be made when consumers have uncertainty about quality characteristics. This idea is not new (see USDA 1981; French 1982). However, a more rigorous discussion, drawing on some of the work on quality and uncertainty (e.g., Akerlof 1970; Leland 1979), is presented later in this chapter.

In what follows, the relevance of existing literature will be assessed in structuring a discussion of the efficiency of grades and standards in agricultural markets. A focal point will be the popular belief, expressed in the 1985 U.S. Comptroller General's (1985, 38) report that, "Quality control [and market support tools] are generally less controversial than quantity controls because of the resulting 'public good' that comes from high quality products." It will become obvious that a meaningful assessment of the "public good" aspect of quality controls requires more than a superficial understanding of the nature of the product in question and the structure of the market.

THE ROLE OF GRADES AND STANDARDS
WITH QUALITY CERTAINTY

In this section, we address the role of grades and minimum quality standards when the quality characteristic of interest is easily observable. While this is not the most interesting case, it is the most prevalent. Minimum quality standards are defined for size, grade, and maturity, where all but the latter are directly observable. Grades are also generally defined on characteristics that can easily be discerned, although meat grading may be an exception. In addressing the observable quality case, we also set the stage for the more interesting results of the next section.

On a conceptual level, grading identifies ranges of quality for which different prices and therefore different markets (albeit interrelated) will exist. Minimum quality standards specified under fruit and vegetable marketing orders define those that are prohibited from being marketed. Standards do not always prohibit marketing of lower qualities entirely but often divert this produce into noncompeting uses.

The usual argument for minimum quality standards is that they maintain the integrity of the product so that the commodities' overall quality image is not diminished by a low quality sample. Additionally standards are deemed desirable because they prevent the shipment of valueless produce. Neither argument can logically be sustained when every party to the exchange is assumed to observe the quality characteristic before purchase. With perfect information, worthless produce would not be shipped and consumers would perfectly perceive the quality of the commodity and make purchases accordingly. This is not a sterile theoretical argument. Much evidence exists that, with or without standards, handlers and shippers are aware of quality levels that are unacceptable to consumers. They do not generally find it profitable to ship everything (U.S. Comptroller General 1985; Armbruster and Jesse 1983).

It has appeared obvious to some (see French 1982) and has been demonstrated analytically elsewhere (Bockstael 1984) that minimum quality standards cannot be Pareto-efficient when relevant quality characteristics are observable by all parties. The result that net social benefits decline when minimum quality standards are applied to perceivable quality characteristics holds, whether producers can control quality and whether the substandard produce is diverted to a secondary market (Bockstael 1984). At the heart of the analysis is the simple economic concept that restrictions on behavior are constraints on utility maximization that generally lead to reduced welfare levels. Explicit in the analysis is the elimination of a market for lower quality produce at a presumably lower price.

While the analysis as it stands is sound, it makes an implicit assumption that is a key one in modeling interrelated markets for quality. The assumption is that the market makes a distinction among all qualities, so that every product with a different set of perceivable quality characteristics sells at a different price.

In a smoothly functioning, perfectly competitive, auction-type market, different prices would arise for different qualities of a commodity. The Rosen model of hedonic markets is a representation of this phenomenon. Rosen (1974) argues that individuals will offer higher bids for commodities with higher valued characteristics and a continuum of prices will arise. In most actual markets (apart from the housing and job markets to which Rosen's model has most frequently been applied), transactions costs prevent this perfect quality discrimination. Even when all parties are completely informed, the costs of exercising different markets for every perceptibly different quality of product would be astronomical. This would be especially true for agricultural produce that has a high frequency of purchase and where no two units are identical.

Where product quality is continuous, grading schemes are a means of establishing different prices for different classifications of quality. This is an important yet frequently ignored aspect of grading. Consumers will not need grades to provide information about quality, if quality can be observed. But grades can provide a means of product differentiation. They can determine what quality ranges will be sold at different prices. In examining the economic efficiency of grading schemes, it would be desirable to determine the nature of an optimal classification scheme. Additionally it would be interesting to know (1) whether classification schemes would tend to develop without government intervention, and (2) the conditions under which optimal (or near optimal) classification schemes would arise.

The researcher seeking answers to these questions in the existing literature encounters frustration. There are a few papers specifically directed to the question of determining grading schemes for agricultural products, but some are not well formulated and all choose producer profits as the objective function. More recent papers (such as Dixit and Stiglitz 1977; Spence 1975; and Berck and Rausser 1980) are expositions of the related topic of product diversification in monopolistically competitive or monopolistic markets for branded consumer products. While this market characterization may be appropriate for the processed food industry, it is less relevant for unprocessed agricultural products.

In the product diversification literature referred to above, firms and quality differentiated commodities are assumed to have a one-to-one matching. That is, increased product diversification is linked with entry of new firms and optimal diversification is tied with industry size. This is clearly not an apt characterization of variety in agricultural produce. Each grower does not produce a completely homogeneous product and does not intentionally differentiate his product from that of the rest of the industry.

A second property of the product diversification literature is that it presumes there is social value to diversity per se. Product diversification in these models is stimulated by consumers' desires for variety. This view of quality is formalized by incorporating into the analysis utility functions with the property that if an individual were indifferent between two units of A and two units of B (quality differentiated commodities), he would necessarily prefer to either of these one unit each of A and B. For the sorts of characteristics that are the objects of grades and standards in agriculture (e.g., maturity, size, external blemishes), ordinal and consistent rankings of quality characteristics are likely. Large grapefruit are preferred to small, sweet oranges to bitter, and unblemished apples to bruised. Diversity for the sake of variety is less frequently observed.

There is a final distinction between the agricultural marketing and the monopolistically competitive product diversity problems. In the latter, variation exists across classes but not within. Each diversified product is itself homogeneous. In agricultural marketing, a product class will potentially include a range of qualities. This poses problems for analysis since conventional economic paradigms describe markets for identical goods. Berck and Rausser (1980) deal with the dilemma by assuming the quality composition of any purchased bundle is fixed even though the bundle is not homogeneous. The consumer is assumed to be unable to choose the composition of quality in the bundle, he merely knows it. In the unprocessed agricultural produce market, it is likely that consumers can choose the composition of their bundles. One pictures the individual choosing a preferred bundle from a bin of varying quality but identically priced produce. Time or shopping expertise rather than price may ration the better quality items. In such cases, a market clearing price would need to be low enough to clear the lowest quality of the commodity in each pricing classification. This kind of a market would be exceedingly difficult to model.

Alternatively, let us consider the proposition that producers can control the quality of the commodity. In agriculture this would never be completely true. However, there is ample evidence that growers can respond to economic signals or regulations and alter the quality (distribution) of their crop. Changing pruning practices can alter the size of a harvested commodity; spraying can affect appearance, etc. Consider the polar case in which producers can completely control the quality of the commodity. Then output within each classification would become standardized at the lower quality boundary. This is because it would be in no producer's interest to produce a higher quality item to be sold at an identical price. If growers have some control over quality, produce will tend toward the lower boundary of each classification.

How many grades should be established? Suppose for a moment that quality is discrete, not continuous, and there are obvious quality categories that could potentially be supplied. This is the problem addressed by Matsumoto and French (1971), who offer an approximate solution when the objective function is producer profits. The objective function can easily be changed to consumer and producer surplus maximization. However the problem with either objective function is not as simple as it seems, since it involves corner solutions. If the categories are already determined, we need only answer how much should be produced of each potential grade, but the optimal amount in some grades will be zero. Calculus is relatively ineffectual for this problem and recourse must be made to more complex models such as those proposed by Hanemann (1982).

In truth the problem is even more complicated, because quality is generally continuous and thus the bounds of the grades must be determined as well. The real question, then, is, How many grades do we offer and with what lower boundaries? One could write the problem as

$$g_1, \overset{\max}{\cdots} g_s, J \int_{p_1(g)}^{\bar{p}_1} \cdots \int_{p_J(g)}^{\bar{p}_J} \sum_{i=1}^{J} f_i(p) dp_i + \int_{\hat{p}_1(g)}^{p_1(g)} \cdots \int_{\hat{p}_J(g)}^{p_J(g)} \sum_{i=1}^{J} v_i(p, J) dp_i \quad (1)$$

where J is the number of grades and g_i is the lower boundary of grade i. The function f_i is the demand for quality of grade i and is a function of all prices. The function v_i is the supply of grade i produce and is a function of all prices and the number of grades that reflects grading and sorting costs. The $\bar{p}_i$ are prices, $\bar{p}_i$ is the price of the ith grade, which drives that demand to zero, $\hat{p}_i$ is the cut-off price for grade i in production. This expression is exceedingly complex to maximize with respect to the g_i and J. Nonetheless simplifications could be posed that argue the solution sequentially: e.g., we could begin with one grade and add grades incrementally.

Clearly the solution, even to an approximation of (1), depends on factors that can only be determined empirically. We can expect, for example, that there will be more room for profitable grades the more variant are consumers' preferences. That is, variation in consumers' quality and price elasticities will encourage quality diversity.

There is no obvious reason why a perfectly competitive industry with perfect information would not supply the optimal amount of grading. This result is consistent with Zusman (1967). The difficulty, as Zusman sees it, is the perfect information requirement. Somehow, appropriate signals about consumer preferences for quality must be transmitted through all levels of the marketing system. One imagines retailers, most aware of consumer preferences, sending information by way of premiums etc., to earlier marketing stages, with growers and handlers responding accordingly. Yet the process would appear to require more complex information than generally assumed necessary for the functioning of a market, or at least an order of magnitude increase in the number of iterations necessary to reach a solution.

A logical consequence of the need for extensive information and iteration is that the more cooperation within the industry, or alternatively, the more concentrated the industry, the more rapid the convergence to a grading scheme. This result might argue for grading schemes designed by grower-handler committees such as those that administer marketing orders. Unfortunately, any producer group that colludes to set grades and takes into account its own welfare, but not that of consumers, will establish too few grades.

In concluding this section, we can say (on the basis of previous results) that when quality is observable by all parties, there is no theoretical justification for implementing minimum quality standards. It is worth noting that marketing orders allow standards for size, grade, and maturity, and all but the latter are generally observable characteristics. Of course, it is possible that minimum quality standards may serve simply to formalize rules that are common knowledge among experienced marketing agents, if the standards automatically divert produce that would not be marketed by knowledgeable handlers because it is of too low quality to be profitable. Nonetheless, marketing orders facilitate the cooperation of growers and handlers, providing the opportunity (whether or not it is exercised) to collude to set standards too high.

Grading schemes are more difficult to evaluate. Clearly, markets cannot develop for every conceivable quality level. When producers have control over the quality that is produced, product quality will cluster at the lower boundaries of every grade classification. Theoretically, the number of grades set in a competitive market would appear to be optimal, but the actual process of optimal grading may require extensive iteration. The more the industry cooperates, the faster the grading scheme is likely to converge. However, when producers collude to set grades, the market is likely to have too few grades and too much standardization.

THE CASE OF QUALITY UNCERTAINTY

Uncertainty about quality has received a good deal of attention in the literature that considers product liability and safety issues and debates the welfare implications of advertising. One common theme in these articles is that quality uncertainty is more prevalent and more expensive to remedy than the price uncertainty so frequently modeled.

Of all the articles written on the topic of quality and uncertainty, perhaps the most relevant is the work by Akerlof (1970) and by Leland (1979). Akerlof demonstrates that when suppliers can determine quality by incurring greater costs, but consumers cannot observe quality before purchase, then bad goods will tend to drive out good. This is because consumers will purchase the product according to their perceived expectations of quality (average quality determined from past experience and hearsay), but with undifferentiated products it will be in no producer's interest to provide better-than-average produce to improve those expectations. In fact, it is in his selfish interest to provide inferior quality, for his returns are linked to the average quality of the industry's output, but his costs are a function of his own output's quality. Leland's article confirms the result that an open market with asymmetric information will under-provide quality relative to the social optimum. The result that quality will be lower when there is uncertainty seems to be a ubiquitous finding in all studies incorporating uncertainty (see, for another example, Shapiro 1981).

It was previously argued that so long as all parties have certain knowledge of quality, minimum quality standards are either superfluous or harmful. Consistent with these results, it is difficult to find justification in the mainstream economics literature for quality regulations. However, when there is asymmetry of information, there may exist a case for quality standards.

The key point is: Information asymmetry induces market failure. Here, for the first time in our discussions, we find a justification for government intervention on the grounds of economic efficiency. Only when a market failure can be identified can intervention be demonstrated to be Pareto-efficient.

Leland (1979) shows that while minimum quality standards are not a perfect corrective action, they do offer a potential improvement. Standards will inhibit the deterioration of quality and have the potential for raising social welfare. Leland argues that they will be more advantageous (1) the more sensitive consumers are to quality variation; (2) the more inelastic is demand; (3) the lower the marginal cost of improving quality; and (4) the lower the value placed on the lowest quality product. The principle unobservable dimension of agricultural produce is maturity, where (1) and (4) may be very applicable. Immature fruit may be completely worthless to the consumer and his purchases may be very sensitive to his expectations about this characteristic.

Minimum quality standards have the potential for improving welfare when quality is uncertain, but this is conditional on the optimal choice of the standard. Leland (1979) reaches one final conclusion of particular interest in assessing minimum quality standards in agricultural marketing. If the industry colludes to set standards, they will tend to set them too high. Under a marketing order system that allows growers and handlers to cooperate in the formation of quality standards, this result gives cause for concern.

Imposing optimal minimum quality standards may be preferable to no action at all, but clearly the optimal solution would be the provision of perfect information. Leland (1979) recommends standards when it is more practicable and least expensive to screen up front than to provide quality labeling. However, public provision of information, if its costs are warranted, has been justified on the basis that information about quality is a public good. This information may be expensive to discover, but once revealed it can serve to inform all interested parties at no extra cost. Here is our first indication of the presence of a public good. Quality per se cannot be deemed a public good, but information about it can be.

In the previous section, in which quality was assumed observable, our discussion of grading schemes focused on the market differentiating aspects of this activity. But surely in this context, if grades are defined on characteristics that are of value to consumers but unobservable to them, grading can convey information that will enhance economic efficiency.

What is the optimal grading scheme under uncertainty? Well, it is not obvious that the conditions are any different from those suggested in the last section. Growers and handlers will have no incentive to produce anything but the lowest level of quality in each grade, and so to the extent possible, quality within each grade will tend to become standardized at the lower end of the quality range. New grades will be socially desirable only if the increased benefits exceed the costs of production, labeling, and sorting. The one difference is that the costs of grading are likely to be much higher for unobservable characteristics than for size, external blemishes, etc. As a result, the optimal number of grades may be smaller when characteristics are expensive to assess.

ECONOMIC EFFICIENCY AND MARKET STRUCTURE: SOME IRONIES

The last two sections have presented as coherent an assessment of grades and standards as could be extracted and assembled from the various strains in the literature. A few decisive results exist; others are merely suggestive.

Rather than seek an elusive mathematical model of grades and standards, a proposition is presented that derives in part from the results of the previous section and in part from empirical evidence. If accepted, this proposition might suggest a redirection for future research in this area.

The proposition is:

1. Minimum quality standards in some circumstances and grading in most circumstances can be socially desirable.

2. If the industry colludes to set standards or define grades, they will tend not to be set optimally.

3. Industries that are already highly concentrated (both horizontally

and vertically) are likely to develop alternatives (not necessarily optimal) to both standards and grading.

4. Current organizational mechanisms (e.g., marketing orders) that facilitate the implementation of grades and minimum standards have the potential to increase concentration in the industry.

In the discussion of the previous sections, market structure played a subtle role; in the above proposition, market structure is central. We noted earlier that minimum quality standards were not warranted when quality was observable, and at best they may serve to reaffirm what informed market agents would know about consumer preferences (i.e., the level of quality so low as not to be profitably shipped). But when are we likely to have informed producers? Generally, information is most quickly disseminated in concentrated industries with few firms. One might make the argument, then, that standards serving to inform all parties of the lowest grade that is profitable to ship are most needed when growers (and possibly handlers) are highly competitive. "Innocuous" standards of this sort should be less important in industries with fewer firms and more vertical integration.

When quality is not observable, a case can be made for minimum quality standards. In the absence of either minimum standards or information, quality will tend to deteriorate, possibly so much as to eliminate the market altogether. Here information is the first-best solution, but in its absence standards will offer a Pareto improvement.

It is interesting to note that the information void may be filled by private actions. There is a clear incentive for firms or cooperatives to brand when consumers are uncertain about quality. Branding has been recognized as a means of product differentiation, particularly effective under conditions of quality uncertainty (Berck and Rausser 1980; Rozek 1982). The brand offers a means to differentiate a good from the average in its grade and thus can be used to certify that the branded goods are better than the average quality otherwise available in the grade. The Sunkist, Sun Maid, Ocean Spray, and Blue Diamond labels offer evidence that product differentiation of this kind can be supported in fresh produce markets.

Branding is only feasible, however, if the branded product controls a perceivable share of the relevant market. Thus product differentiation offers an incentive for firms to cooperate and provides rewards for market concentration. Mueller and Rogers (1980), among others, have found a significant correlation between branding and market concentration. Branding, as a form of product differentiation, is also a barrier to entry.

Ironically, unconcentrated industries have the most need for standards, but the authority to implement these standards conveys with it a certain amount of market power. Minimum quality standards can potentially serve a useful purpose, particularly when the industry structure is a many-firm, competitive one. However, quality standards are implemented through marketing orders that rely on administrative boards to set minimum standards. These grower-handler boards will have the incentive to set standards too high, to use standards as a means of diverting more than a socially optimal amount of produce to a secondary market. This will tend to occur whether standards are used for observable or unobservable characteristics.

The fact that marketing orders may alter the market power at different levels of the marketing chain has been recognized by some as a prevalent consideration. Farrell (National Commission on Food Marketing 1966) suggested that this was the very intent of marketing orders—to provide growers with increased market control vis à vis buyers. The idea that orders offer producers an opportunity to alter aspects of market structure was suggested earlier by Townsend-Zellner (1961). As evidence, he recounted the story of the raisin industry, which actually became more concentrated both at the grower and handler levels subsequent to their marketing order. In a later paper, Shafer (1968) encountered a different but related phenomenon. When minimum quality standards were imposed on Texas carrots, no appreciable effect was noticed at the consumer level, but Texas growers gained considerable market power relative to middlemen. The marketing order, in Shafer's estimation, served to unite and inform Texas growers. In essence, the order encouraged cooperation among growers, a form of countervailing power.

There is no way to discuss market structure and marketing orders without mentioning cooperatives. Some (e.g., Masson 1975; Masson et al. 1978) have argued that in industries where collusive forces already exist in the form of cooperatives, marketing orders have facilitated the preservation or spread of market power. Masson suggests that cooperatives have been able to build a dominant position where marketing orders have been in place.

The investigations by Shafer (1968) and by Masson (1975) present two examples of a similar phenomenon operating in different environments. Marketing orders can provide a means of industry collusion. In a market in which growers are numerous and unorganized, but intermediaries are reasonably concentrated, orders may provide a basis for countervailing power at the grower level (perhaps leaving consumers relatively unaffected). In an already cooperating industry in which grower organizations are dominant, orders (particularly the "less controversial" quality provisions) may provide a disguise for other actions. Quality standards, theoretically desirable or not, may be used in such cases as screens for policies of collusion.

In fact, the debate over minimum quality standards is parallel to that over cooperatives. The latter have been justified as a means of providing countervailing power in the face of a highly concentrated processing sector. Allowing growers to unite diminishes socially undesirable monopsonistic power. Eisenstat and Masson (1978) take the position that the horizontal market power acquired by cooperatives is a "positive economic force" as long as it merely "countervails" buyers' powers. It is undesirable if it leads to supracompetitive pricing. Like cooperatives, minimum quality standards cannot be evaluated without considering the context in which the market power is acquired.

A superior alternative to minimum quality standards can be found in publicly supplied information, if the costs of information are warranted. Grading is a form of information that could potentially reduce uncertainty about quality. Whether quality is observable or not, grades serve the purpose of defining the quality differentiated products that will be offered at different prices. Once again, the public provision of grading schemes is likely to be most compelling in industries made up of many small firms in which information about consumer preferences is difficult to disseminate and convergence to a standard system of product differentiation slow. However, some have argued that grading services may encourage concentration by facilitating shipping from distant points and thus expanding the size of the market to which any handler can sell.

Conversely, industry concentration could facilitate the formation of a standard classification scheme. Vertical integration hastens the flow of information from consumer to grower and horizontal integration can speed the convergence process. However, if sufficient market power exists, firms or cooperatives will more likely attempt to diversify their products through branding rather than developing an industrywide grading scheme.

It is interesting to look at our actual experiences with grading in unprocessed agricultural markets. Grading is generally accomplished by the first handler of the produce, and for many fruits and vegetables, grades are used by packers and shippers and dispensed with at the consumer level. In fact for much, although not all, fresh produce a limited variety of quality is sold and only one grade (i.e., no grading) offered.

This is in the face of decades of arguments that grades should be established with consumer preferences in mind and that grades can provide information and thus reduce uncertainty. Grades function to some extent in this capacity for meat but rarely are they supplied for fresh produce. Is this because there is neither uncertainty about quality nor variation in quality for fruits and vegetables? (If so, why do we have standards?) Or is it because providing more product variety or reducing quality uncertainty to consumers would not be advantageous to producers? Presumably, depending on the level of concentration, there can be forces at both the grower-handler and the retail levels in whose interests it would be to minimize such practices.

Where branding is prevalent among producer cooperatives (e.g., citrus, nuts, etc.) grading reduces the latitude for profitable branding and is likely to be discouraged. An example of this is the lamb market in which national packers who utilized branding opposed grading that reduced their profitable product differentiation (Fienup 1961). In any event, the point is that grading can have different distributional implications within the structure of an industry.

For many fruits and vegetables, neither grading nor branding is prevalent at the consumer level, yet variation in quality can exist. In such cases, consumers may be forced to rely on retailers' reputations. Retailers may use uncertainty about quality to their own advantage. When the store name is the only source of information, this is a form of branding in its own right.

Theory has less to add to this discussion than empirical work. This is because, in questions of market structure or industrial organization, empirical work often "out performs" theoretical analysis. Yet scant empirical work on the interaction of market structure and behavior on the one hand and quality standards and grading on the other has surfaced.

The absence of empirical work is most striking when we attempt to document consumers' reactions to quality differences in agricultural produce markets. Every bit of analysis of grading and standards presented above and every argument in defense of the quality provisions of marketing orders presupposes that consumer demand is an increasing function of the quality characteristic in question. However, empirical evidence of demand shifts in response to the implementation of standards, or of varying demand for differing quality levels of the same commodity, are difficult to unearth. In fact we know very little about the actual effects of standards at the consumer level. Those studies that debate the price enhancement capabilities of marketing orders have targeted producer prices. When extrapolation to retail prices is attempted, existing margin relationships are assumed.

We also know little about the levels of concentration at grower and intermediate market levels for many of the agricultural commodities of interest. Information on concentration ratios is hard to get. Perhaps it is in these directions that further research is warranted.

CONCLUSIONS

It is not at all surprising that a fair amount of confusion exists over the role of grades and standards in the market. In the literature of the

1950s and 1960s we find a number of papers whose apparent intent is to convince growers of the price-enhancing capabilities of marketing orders and grading schemes. This emphasis is not at all surprising given that it accords with the initial intent of the Agricultural Marketing Agreement Act of 1937. The 70s, however, brought a wave of consumer activism and with it a concerted attempt to deny the price-enhancing capabilities of orders. This defensive response is, in retrospect, a questionable one, for it provokes the unaffected bystander to ask, "If the orders do not achieve price enhancement, then why bother with them at all?"

Some of these arguments are just simply off base. They attempt to prove that only a small percentage of a marketed commodity is covered by orders and thus orders cannot have a price-enhancing effect. Surely, if this is true, then the intent of publicly enforcing cooperative orders is defeated. For example, quality standards are imposed ostensibly to ensure that substandard produce does not find its way to the market and destroy consumer confidence. If only some producers are subject to the order, what is the point? Surely, marketing orders have more pervasive effects on the market than these proponents would have us believe, or the orders are not addressing their objectives.

Clearly the first issue of real concern is whether quality standards or grading schemes can serve to correct market failures. Do they have the potential to increase both consumer and producer benefits and thus improve economic efficiency? The third and fourth sections of this chapter address this question and come to the conclusion that grades have a place in the marketing system and that socially optimal grading schemes can be devised. Additionally, minimum standards established under marketing orders, while generally either undesirable or innocuous, can potentially be justified on economic efficiency grounds when quality is unobservable.

The ultimate and unfortunate conclusion of these sections and the subsequent one is that grading and standards can be potentially beneficial, but they also can be used to accomplish socially undesirable ends. It may be that if left to well-organized, cooperating bodies of growers and handlers, standards and grades will be set suboptimally and may screen collusive type behavior. Alternatively, if provisions for grading and setting of standards are granted to unorganized, highly competitive growers, they may serve to improve information flow and combat marketing power of the middleman. Our frustration stems from our search for a definitive evaluation of provisions that can only be interpreted in the context of the individual markets in which they are practiced.

REFERENCES

Akerlof, George A. "The Market for 'Lemons': Quality Uncertainty and the Market Mechanisms." *Q. J. Econ.* 84(1970):488–500.

Armbruster, Walter J., and Edward V. Jesse. "Fruit and Vegetable Marketing Orders." *Federal Marketing Programs in Agriculture: Issues and Options,* ed. W. J. Armbruster, D. R. Henderson, and R. D. Knutson, pp. 121–58. Oak Brook, Ill.: Farm Foundation, 1983.

Berck, Peter, and Gordon C. Rausser. "Consumer Demand, Grades, Brands, and Margin Relationships." *New Directions in Economic Modeling and Forecasting in U.S. Agriculture,* ed. G. C. Rausser, pp. 99–129. New York: North Holland, 1980.

Bockstael, N. E. "The Welfare Implications of Minimum Quality Standards." *Am. J. Agric. Econ.* 66(1984):466–71.

Dalrymple, Dana. "On the Economics of Produce Grading." *J. Farm Econ.* 50(1968):157–59.

Dixit, A. K., and J. E. Stiglitz. "Monopolistic Competition and Optimum Product Diversity." *Am. Econ. Rev.* 67(1977):297–308.

Eisenstat, Philip, and Robert T. Masson. "Cooperative Horizontal Market Power and Vertical Relationships: An Overall Assessment." *Agricultural Cooperatives and the Public Interest.* Proceedings of the North Central Regional Research Committee 117, Monograph 4, pp. 281–91. Madison: University of Wisconsin, 1978.

Fienup, Darrell. "Economic Effects of Recent Changes in Lamb Standards." *J. Farm Econ.* 43(1961):1388–96.

French, B. C. "Fruit and Vegetable Marketing Orders: A Critique of the Issues and State of Analysis." *Am. J. Agric. Econ.* 64(1982):916–23.

French, Ben C., Niniv Tamimi, and Carole F. Nuckton. *Marketing Order Program Alternatives: Use and Importance in California, 1949–1975.* Giannini Foundation Information Series 78-2, Bulletin 1890. University of California-Berkeley, May 1978.

Hanemann, W. Michael. "Quality and Demand Analysis." *New Directions in Econometric Modeling and Forecasting in U.S. Agriculture,* ed. Gordon C. Rausser, pp. 55–98. New York: North Holland, 1982.

Hoos, Sidney. "U.S. Marketing Agreements and Orders: A Retrospective View." Dept. Agric. Res. Econ. Processed Paper, University of California-Berkeley, 1978.

Jamison, S. A. "Marketing Orders, Cartels, and Cling Peaches." Food Res. Inst. Studies 6, 1966.

Jesse, E. V. *Social Welfare Implications of Federal Marketing Orders for Fruits and Vegetables.* Washington, D.C.: USDA ESCS Tech. Bull. 1608, July 1979.

Jesse, E. V., and A. C. Johnson, Jr. *Effectiveness of Federal Marketing Orders for Fruits and Vegetables.* Washington, D.C.: USDA ESS Agric. Econ. Rep. 471, June 1981.

Leland, Hayne E. "Quacks, Lemons, and Licensing: A Theory of Minimum Quality Standards." *J. Polit. Econ.* 87(1979):1328–46.

Masson, A. "The Economic Effects of Marketing Orders." *A Report on Agricultural Cooperatives,* ed. B. C. Marion, pp. 137–80. Washington, D.C.: Federal Trade Commission, 1975.

Masson, Alison, Robert T. Masson, and Barry C. Harris. "Cooperatives and Marketing Orders." *Agricultural Cooperatives and the Public Interest.* Proceedings of the North Central Regional Research Committee 117, Monograph 4, ed. B. C. Marion, pp. 187–218. Madison: University of Wisconsin, 1978.

Matsumoto, Masao, and Ben C. French. "Empirical Determination of Optimum Quality Mix." *Agric. Econ. Res.* 23(1971):1–12.

Mehren, G. L. "The Function of Grades in an Affluent, Standardized-Quality Economy." *J. Farm Econ.* 43(1961):1377–84.

Mueller, W. F., and R. T. Rogers. "The Role of Advertising in Changing Concentration of Manufacturing Industries." *Rev. Econ. Stat.* (1980):89–96.

National Commission on Food Marketing. "Marketing Orders and Agreements in the U.S. Fruit and Vegetable Industries." *Organization and Competition in the Fruit and Vegetable Industry.* Tech. Study No. 4, pp. 287–359. Washington, D.C.: U.S. Government Printing Office, 1966.

Nichols, John P., Lowell D. Hill, and Kenneth E. Nelson. "Food and Agricultural Commodity Grading." *Federal Marketing Programs in Agriculture: Issues and Options,* ed. W. J. Armbruster, D. R. Henderson, and R. D. Knutson, pp. 59–90. Oak Brook, Ill.: Farm Foundation, 1983.

Price, David. "Discarding Low Quality Produce with an Elastic Demand." *J. Farm Econ.* 40(1967):622–32.

Purcell, Wayne D., and Kenneth E. Nelson. "Recent Changes in Beef Grades: Issues and Analysis of the Yield Grade Requirement." *Am. J. Agric. Econ.* (1976):475–84.

Rhodes, V. James, and Elmer R. Kiehl. "On Consumer Grades for Foods." *J. Farm Econ.* 38(1956):44–61.

Rosen, Sherwin. "Hedonic Prices and Implicit Markets: Product Differentiation in Pure Competition." *J. Polit. Econ.* 82(1974):34–55.

Rozek, Richard. "Brand Identification and Advertising: The Case of a Generic Trademark." *Appl. Econ.* 14(1982):235–48.

Shafer, Carl. "The Effect of a Marketing Order on Winter Carrot Prices." *Am. J. Agric. Econ.* 50(1968):879–84.

Shapiro, Carl. "Consumer Information, Production Quality and Seller Reputation." *Bell J. Econ.* 13(1981):20–35.

Shaw, Seth T. "A Merchandiser's View of the Function of Grades." *J. Farm Econ.* 43(1961):1399–1404.

Spence, A. Michael. "Product Selection, Fixed Costs and Monopolistic Competition." *Rev. Econ. Studies* 43(1975):217–36.

Spriggs, John. "Quality Choice in a Product Market." Paper presented at the annual meeting of the AAEA, Pullman, Wash., 29 July–1 Aug. 1979.

Townsend-Zellner, Norman. "The Effect of Marketing Orders on Market Structures and Some Consequent Market Developments." *J. Farm Econ.* 43(1961):1357–65.

U.S. Comptroller General. *Marketing Order Program—An Assessment of Its Effects on Selected Commodities.* Washington, D.C.: GAO ID-76-26, Apr. 1976.

U.S. Comptroller General. *The Role of Marketing Orders in Establishing and Maintaining Orderly Market Conditions.* Washington, D.C.: GAO/RCED-85-57, 31 July 1985.

U.S. Department of Agriculture. *Price Impacts of Federal Market Order Programs.* Washington, D.C.: Farmer Coop. Spec. Rep. 12, Jan. 1975.

U.S. Department of Agriculture. *A Review of Federal Marketing Orders for Fruits, Vegetables and Specialty Crops: Economic Efficiency and Welfare Implications.* Washington, D.C.: AMS Agric. Econ. Rep. 477, Nov. 1981.

Zusman, Pinhas. "A Theoretical Basis for Determination of Grading and Sorting Schemes." *J. Farm Econ.* 49(1967):89–106.

Economic Efficiency Issues
of Grading and
Minimum Quality Standards

A DISCUSSION

John P. Nichols

NANCY BOCKSTAEL contributes to the discussion of economic efficiency and marketing through a focus on the role of grades and standards in the agricultural and food marketing system. Her primary emphasis is on the relationship between efficiency and minimum quality standards under varying conditions of certainty. An additional focus is also provided in relating market structure to economic efficiency and grades and standards. The emphasis on these areas provides useful insights into the traditional debate about the role of grades and standards in agricultural and food marketing systems. In doing this, however, some of the original thinking with regard to the role of grades and standards in improving information throughout the marketing system is neglected. My comments will be directed at identifying some of these oversights and also providing examples that support Bockstael's observations relating to her main points.

To my way of thinking, the paper really starts with the section, "The Case of Quality Uncertainty." Earlier materials help to set the stage but are available in other published work by Bockstael (1984). It seems to me that the issue of quality uncertainty and information is what grades and standards are all about.

For the purpose of this book I think it is a distortion to dwell on the case of quality certainty and minimum standards. "Grade standards" should be recognized as a much broader concept than just "minimum standards." There are many examples in which the lowest useful grade is not excluded from the market. Much of this early discussion belongs in other chapters on marketing orders.

The primary purpose or role of agricultural grades and standards has long been debated. At least three types of considerations have been cited: (1) to facilitate trading through the establishment of identifiable

JOHN P. NICHOLS is professor, Department of Agricultural Economics, Texas A & M University, College Station.

homogeneous groupings of product; (2) to facilitate the flow of information regarding end-use value; and (3) to enable improved price reporting for agricultural commodities. In the evolution of grades and standards for different commodities, the emphasis on each has been different depending on the circumstances.

Early in the paper Bockstael refers to the conventional wisdom that the rather mundane motivation for the existence of grades has led to a lack of interest in economic analysis of their effects. The mundane purpose referred to is the need for a standard of identification for trading purposes at the wholesale level. She acknowledges this as "probably the principal reason for the advent of grades," but chooses in her paper to de-emphasize this role. Instead, she focuses on differentiating products at the consumer level and the potential effect of grading schemes on consumers. For purposes of this book, the review could have taken a more balanced approach to the multiple objectives of grades and standards.

One of the points that could have been made is the fact that having commonly accepted standards or language of trade has permitted adjustments and more efficient resource use at the production level. Why else would we see the production of produce shift to lower cost producing regions as technology changed? There is a need to sort out the various effects of technology in transportation and processing from the effects of grading systems. There are also some clearly structural implications that could be tied back in with her discussion later in the paper. In short, I object to her giving such short treatment to what is potentially the greatest contribution of grades and standards to marketing efficiency.

QUALITY UNCERTAINTY

As noted earlier, the real contribution of this paper begins with the discussion of the case of quality uncertainty. The discussion of work by Akerlof (1970) and Leland (1979) is appropriately incorporated into this analysis. The idea is that when consumers cannot observe quality before purchase then bad goods will tend to drive out good. This is a significant problem, for example, with the early harvest of immature produce to "beat the market." Although it is true that grades do not usually incorporate direct maturity measures, the general concept is valid. Trading at a distance where wholesalers cannot observe the quality of the product they are ordering introduces this type of uncertainty.

I have often thought that from the collective producers' perspective it would be useful to view the market as a resource, a common property resource. That in fact is how individual producers act when they attempt to "beat the market." The deterioration of a market resulting from shipping uneven or poor quality produce impacts the group but no individual producer has an incentive to incur the grading or quality control costs necessary for market maintenance. This is a classic common property problem from the producer's point of view. Collective action by producers in a defined region, often through marketing orders, is designed to deal with this problem.

Bockstael makes the key point that information asymmetry induces market failure and where a market failure exists it is rational to consider whether public intervention is appropriate on the grounds of economic efficiency. It seems to me that we should direct attention to identifying how prevalent these conditions are in agricultural commodity markets. Where does quality uncertainty and an asymmetry of information exist? I suspect that such circumstances are found in many areas of commodity marketing. The inclusion of these concepts of information asymmetry, market failure, and public goods is a useful contribution.

STRUCTURAL IMPLICATIONS

The structural implications discussion is another valuable contribution of this paper. There is increasing interest throughout the profession, both applied and methodological, in gaining a better understanding of true economic and behavioral relationships among economic agents in the marketing channel.

The relationship of grades to structure at early stages of this channel is an important one. The use of minimum quality standards may well be a source of countervailing market power for producers who are otherwise relatively large in number and small in size facing a much more concentrated industry at the wholesale level. Is there anything wrong with this? It becomes a question of dividing the rent more equitably between producers and wholesalers. It does not mean that marketing efficiency for the entire system has been improved or that consumers are any better off.

Bockstael notes that in different settings, grading can have different distributional implications within the structure of an industry. There are also distributional effects on a regional basis. Production in certain regions can be favored by an inflexible grading system because quality attributes are typically affected by different growing conditions. The controversy over changing technology for measuring attributes that are important in cotton grading and classing is an example in which regional effects might be unequal.

In the interest of proving that minimum quality standards as used by marketing orders are bad, Bockstael has concentrated on the literature dealing with the grading of horticultural crops. There are other commodity situations that also deserve attention. The beef industry affords interesting examples, some of which support her ideas while others do not.

Beef offers an example of research done on consumer response to quality grades. Rhodes et al. (1955), Branson (1957), and others studied this issue in the 1950s and early 1960s. Branson et al. (1986) have recently reported on current work in this area.

One of the more interesting things about beef grades is that there is a growing awareness that the traditional preference ranking among grades might be changing. Because of changing consumer preferences, we can no longer be sure that choice grade is preferred to good grade. Bockstael contrasts the theoretical treatment of brands and that for grading agricultural commodities. It is noted that agricultural commodity grading is different because the characteristics used are typically ordinally ranked. Beef may be emerging as an exception to this. Diet and health consciousness is changing the structure of demand for beef even though the producing industry has been slow to recognize the change or figure out what to do with it. There are some tremendous regional implications in this, and they are clearly being felt in the recent battle over proposed grade changes. If these changes in demand are real it may lead us away from beef grading toward a product differentiation emphasis or branding. Those involved in the management of United States Department of Agriculture grading programs might be relieved at this prospect.

Beef also provides a good example of the tendency for producers to collude to reduce the number of grades available. The recent grading controversy has been centered primarily on widening the tolerances for what can be called "choice" grade beef. The result would be to effectively reduce the number of meaningful grades available.

Bockstael laments the lack of empirical work to document consumer's reactions to quality differences. While I think she missed a few items, the criticism is probably valid. The expense of conducting research in a controlled market environment tends to be prohibitive.

It occurs to me that this area is ideal as an application of experimental economics methods. Over the past decade, experimental economics has made great strides in developing manageable methods and testing their validity. The economics literature in this field has literally exploded. Buccola (1985) reported recently on an application in agricultural marketing, and Colling and Sporleder (1986) have completed a study in which they evaluate the effect of reputation on the auction and bidding process. I think there is fertile ground here for some carefully constructed experiments designed to study consumers' reactions to quality and grades for specific agricultural products. The hypotheses of risk and uncertainty could be tested and consumer response to perceived quality delineated.

In summary, I found this chapter to be interesting and informative.

Key points are introduced regarding the role of grades when quality is uncertain and the relationship between grades and market structure. Bockstael's chapter does not provide a detailed treatment of some of the traditional literature regarding the economic rationale for grades and standards or a complete discussion of all aspects of the topic as it relates to economic efficiency and this book's objectives. However, the role and purposes of grading in agricultural markets have long been recognized as confusing and often conflicting. No single chapter is likely to sort out and lay to rest all of the important issues. This paper does a good job of addressing many of them.

REFERENCES

Akerlof, George. "The Market for 'Lemons': Quality Uncertainty and the Market Mechanism." *Q. J. Econ.* 84(1970):488–500.

Bockstael, Nancy E. "The Welfare Implications of Minimum Quality Standards." *Am. J. Agric. Econ.* 66(1984):466–71.

Branson, Robert E. *The Consumer Market for Beef.* Agric. Exp. Sta. Bull. 856, Texas A & M University, Apr. 1957.

Branson, Robert E., H. R. Cross, J. Savell, G. C. Smith, and R. A. Edwards. "Marketing Implications from the National Consumer Beef Study." *W. J. Agric. Econ.* 11(1986): 82–91.

Buccola, Steven T. "Pricing Efficiency in Centralized and Noncentralized Markets." *Am. J. Agric. Econ.* 67(1985):583–90.

Colling, Phil L., and T. L. Sporleder. "Reputation Trading in Commodity Markets: An Experimental Economics Approach." Paper presented at the annual meetings of the American Agricultural Economics Association, Reno, Nev., July 27–30, 1986.

Leland, Hayne E. "Quacks, Lemons, and Licensing: A Theory of Minimum Quality Standards." *J. Polit. Econ.* 87(1979):1328–46.

Rhodes, V. James, E. R. Kiehl, and D. E. Brady. *Visual Preferences for Grades of Retail Beef Cuts.* College of Agric. Res. Bull. 583, University of Missouri, June 1955.

Sporleder T. L., and P. L. Colling. *An Empirical Evaluation of Trader Reputation and Market Structure on Market Efficiency and Price in Commodity Markets.* Agric. Exp. Sta. Bull., Texas A & M University, forthcoming.

CHAPTER 13

Futures Markets and Intertemporal Commodity Pricing

Anne E. Peck

BY THEIR VERY NAME, futures markets bespeak the intertemporal nature of commodity pricing. Futures markets provide today's quotation of a commodity's value, both for the present and also for successive future dates. The simultaneous quotation of relative values can be expected to affect production, consumption, and marketing decisions of the firms that comprise the commodity system, thereby affecting the course of actual market prices over time. Futures markets affect the intertemporal pricing of commodities precisely because they are commercial markets.

At the same time, futures markets are also speculative markets. Speculation on commodity prices occurs without futures markets; commodity ownership, either actual or prospective, is speculative. Nevertheless, futures markets facilitate speculation through the centralization and standardization of trading and their performance-guarantee system. The costs of market participation are thereby reduced and the efficiency of price discovery is improved. Efficiency in speculative markets is defined relative to market information. Future prices should not be profitably predictable from past prices (weak-form efficiency), publicly available information (semistrong-form efficiency), or all public and private information (strong-form efficiency).

Although these views are not contradictory—futures markets are both commercial and speculative markets—they have led to dichotomous lines of investigation into market performance issues. One focuses on direct measures of the effects of changes in allocation decisions, while the other seeks to identify the efficiency (or inefficiency) of the

ANNE E. PECK is associate professor, Food Research Institute, Stanford University, Stanford, California.

price-formation process. As will be seen, the empirical results are not totally consistent even within the separate lines of investigation. More important, the results have at times been contradictory. This chapter summarizes the results and explores the contradictions. I confess at the outset that the dichotomy described above is not absolute. For example, a reduction in seasonal price variability could arise from either or, as is most likely, both improved information content of prices or altered storage decisions. Nevertheless, I think the dichotomy is useful in highlighting areas that need additional research.

ECONOMIC EFFECTS OF COMMERCIAL USE

Tomek and Gray (1970) identify the two main effects of commercial use of futures markets as inventory allocation and forward pricing. Both occur with storable commodities. For purely nonstorable commodities, futures markets can only affect prices through their influence as forward prices on the basic production and consumption decisions. Because of the historical dominance of futures trading in markets for storable commodities, most arguments focus on the effects of futures markets on storage decisions and on prices through the reallocation of inventories.

INVENTORY ALLOCATION

Simply stated, futures markets facilitate storage decisions by providing a reliable estimate at the time the storage decision is made of the return that can be expected from that storage.[1] Further, the reliably predictable return varies in a stabilizing way, encouraging storage in periods of surplus and discouraging storage in periods of shortage. Together, these relations imply an improved allocation of commodity stocks over time.

The most direct evidence of the effects of futures markets on storage decisions comes from analyses of seasonal price volatility before and after the introduction of futures trading in a market. Working (1960) demonstrated that the period of futures trading was associated with greatly reduced average seasonal price changes in the onion market. Price variations within each month declined as well. Gray (1963) updated the analysis with data from a period of years after the futures market had been closed and established that the onion market returned to its earlier prefutures pattern of seasonal volatility. In a reexamination of these data and the addition of data from several more postfutures years, A. C. Johnson (1973) found the results to be very sensitive to the selection of years to be included in the analyses. He concluded there was no effect of futures trading on seasonal volatility of onion prices. Empirical confirmation is evidently not as straightforward as the hypothesis suggests.

In the only comparable analysis for storable commodities, Tomek (1971) reexamined Boyle's (1922) 80-year record of monthly wheat prices from 1841–1921, a period that spanned the development of the wheat futures market. Boyle had found a significant reduction in seasonal price variation after futures markets became active and Tomek found marked declines in the monthly range of prices as well. In a similar vein, Emery (1896) examined the annual trading range of cotton and wheat prices before and after futures trading and found that a diminished trading range was apparent in the periods associated with futures trading.

Taylor and Leuthold (1974) extended the analysis to live cattle. Although cattle are not storable, feedlot placements and even marketings can respond to short-run price incentives, and thus futures markets might be expected to influence relatively short-run volatility in a way similar to that for the storable commodities. They examined annual, monthly, and weekly price variation in the live cattle market from periods before and after the introduction of futures trading. Both monthly and weekly prices showed significant declines in volatility. Annual variation declined as well, although not significantly.

Obviously, these before and after comparisons do not establish causality, a point that all the authors emphasize. Other elements of the marketing system are normally changing at the same time futures markets are introduced, and any observed changes in price volatility may be due to these other changes. The *ceteris paribus* assumption is particularly difficult to make for the markets in which futures trading originated and probably explains why there is not more direct evidence on changing seasonal volatility from these markets. However, the consistency of the evidence among commodities and time periods is reassuring. At least, there is no instance when the introduction of futures trading in an agricultural commodity was associated with increased price volatility.[2]

It is even less straightforward to evaluate the effects of futures markets on storage adjustments and on price variation between years. Futures markets provide forward prices as well as indications of storage returns and also influence prospective production and consumption decisions. Their effects on year-end storage levels are thus not separable from simultaneous supply and demand adjustments and any effect on annual price stability is a joint effect. The difficulty in evaluating directly the between-year storage effects of futures markets seems perverse. The supply-of-storage curve itself is usually estimated using year-end stocks data and thus directly reflects the price responsive variability in year-end stocks, which is the primary source of price stabilization in markets for storable commodities.

The clear responsiveness of U.S. stocks to prices of storage led Working (1928) to compare the responsiveness of storage to prices in the United States to that in other countries where there were no futures markets. He concluded that nearly one-half of the year-to-year changes in U.S. production of wheat were absorbed in changes in year-end stocks. By contrast, the other major wheat exporting countries exported most of their production variability with stock adjustments of only minor importance. Comparable analyses (Josling and Barichello 1984; Peck 1982) of more recent data from the wheat markets show similar contrasts in the storage responsiveness of the major exporters. The more recent comparisons, however, do not derive solely from futures markets and are as much reflections of contrasts in government policies. However, combined with Working's evidence from the earlier period (a period during which government interventions were not significant) the evidence is again very suggestive. If permitted to do so, storage responds to prices in a way that stabilizes markets and the response is particularly impressive in the presence of futures markets.

Forward Pricing

The examination of the role of storage between crop years is only a partial analysis of the effects of futures markets. In addition to the stock's response, the additional crop year means there will be new production and the prospect of substantially revised consumption needs. In this context, futures markets can be said to perform a forward pricing role. For a purely nonstorable commodity, this is their only role and evidence from these markets is considered first.

Conceptually, the role of futures markets for a nonstorable commodity is simple—to reflect, in prices, anticipated supply and demand. In the absence of a futures market, producers must form an independent expectation of what prices at harvest will be at the time they make their production decisions. Numerous studies of producers' supply response have found that producers form their expectations of next year's price on the basis of current and past prices. Perhaps the most widely and successfully used model of the decision is Nerlove's (1958) adaptive model, although a variety of approaches have been employed to extrapolate expected prices from past prices. The essential point is that all such models assume that current and past prices are used to formulate expected prices.

As Johnson (1947) noted nearly 40 years ago, resources will be significantly misallocated when producers' forecasts are retrospective and the degree of social loss and unnecessary price instability are directly related to the difference between the retrospective expectation and a rational forward price (i.e., one that reflected the prospective actions of producers and consumers). The question then is: To what extent are futures prices rational forward prices, and hence (to use Stein's distinction), eliminate *ex ante* social losses? *Ex post,* as Stein (1981) also notes, there still may be losses if demand shifts or if yields are not as expected, but these losses cannot be reduced by planting-time adjustments of producers and are not attributable to inappropriate forward prices.

A particularly clear example of the effects of a futures market on this process comes from the potato market and Maine potato futures trading. Prior to futures trading, a Nerlove-type adjustment model explained some 75 percent of annual acreage planted, and both past prices and acreage were significant explanatory variables (Simmons 1962). The retrospective supply response combined with stable and inelastic demand produced a nearly classic cobweb pattern of feast or famine in annual prices.

In the late 1940s, a futures market in Maine potatoes began on the New York Mercantile Exchange, becoming an active market in the early 1950s. Futures contracts for each prospective crop traded well in advance of producers' production decisions and continued trading over the growing period. For example, the first new crop future (the November contract) began trading in the preceding November or December, well in advance of the April planting decision. Tomek and Gray (1970) analyzed the preplanting quotations of the November futures and compared them with the eventual harvest prices. The results are shown in Fig. 13.1 (taken from Gray's 1972 extended analysis of their earlier findings). On the horizontal axis is the preplanting (February 28) quote of the November future, while the final closing price is on the vertical axis. The data, taken from 1953–1971 crop years, form a nearly vertical line—the preplanting futures price was a virtual constant from year to year, approximately the long-run price. Actual prices at harvest varied from year to year causing the vertical scatter of observations in the diagram.

The effects of this market-determined forward price on Maine potato producers' decisions were dramatic. Gray's (1972) reestimates of the supply relation with data from the period of futures trading found that neither lagged price nor lagged acreage coefficients were significant explanatory variables and, overall, the regression explained only 7 percent of Maine producers' decisions. Maine acreage planted to potatoes had virtually stabilized. The rational, if constant, futures prices had eliminated completely the retrospective responses and consequent *ex ante* social losses of Maine growers.

A natural extension of the analysis of the data in Fig. 13.1 is to consider, as Tomek and Gray (1970) did, the regression of the springtime futures price on the harvest-time price, a test of so-called forecasting

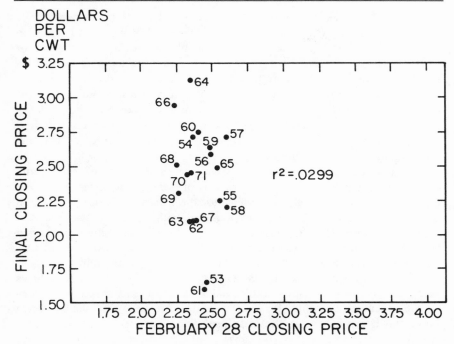

FIG. 13.1. February 28 and final closing prices of November potato futures, deflated by annual index numbers of prices received for all farm products, 1953–1971. Source: Gray (1972, 324).

performance. With the potato data, such a regression shows the futures prices did not explain the subsequent harvest prices, even though the two prices are the same on average. In view of this result, futures prices are useless "forecasts" of subsequent spot market prices.

There have been a number of evaluations of the "forecasting" performance of futures prices on other markets. Such comparisons are clearly relevant to the question at hand, although their interpretation is not always straightforward. In the simplest system, futures prices were useless "forecasts"; nevertheless, the futures prices were rational and optimal in a welfare sense. Martin and Garcia (1981), extending earlier work by Leuthold (1974), provide comparative analyses of the forecasting performance of cattle and hog futures prices. In both markets and over almost all forecast horizons (one to eight months prior to maturity of each future), futures prices were found to be unbiased estimates of the eventual cash prices. Their degree of predictability, however, declined markedly with distance to maturity.

The possibility of storing a commodity between production periods adds an additional dimension to the preceding discussion. Storage serves to absorb current excesses and cushion current shortages, and prices in current and subsequent years are inextricably linked. The linkage is, of course, not equally effective in shortage situations as it is in surplus situations. The amount current stocks can be drawn down is limited, whereas the amount of possible increase is nearly limitless. Futures prices reflect this asymmetry in the strongly nonlinear character of the price-of-storage relation. Carrying charges reflect current surplus and are limited to the amount of full storage costs; inverse carrying charges reflect current shortage and are unbounded.

Storage and the consequent linking of prices between crop years implies that rationality in forward prices is of even greater consequence in these markets. In their absence, misallocation occurs in both production and storage decisions, thereby compounding welfare losses relative to the nonstorable case. The empirical question is thus the extent to which futures prices for storable commodities are rational. Two sorts of evidence are available on rationality—biasedness and predictability.

There is an extensive literature on the question of bias in futures prices, although the question traditionally has been considered in the context of speculative profits. It is sufficient to note here that the evidence shows bias is not characteristic of futures prices. Biases have been found, but they appear to reflect particular market circumstances or time periods and not general tendencies.[3] Tomek and Gray (1970) provide evidence on the degree of predictability in futures prices for two storable commodities (corn and soybeans) for precisely the period of interest, planting to harvest. Their evidence shows no significant difference on average between the preplanting and expiration quotes of the respective futures. While the more general bias evidence includes all futures, Tomek and Gray's evidence shows the new crop futures in particular are unbiased.

In addition, the preplanting prices are shown to be both just as variable from year to year and good predictors of the postharvest prices. Just and Rausser (1981) show that futures prices predict subsequent prices as well as the forecasts of several of the well-known forecast firms. These results are in sharp contrast to the results from the potato market, a reflection of the contrasting nature of rational forward prices in the two types of markets. With truly nonstorable commodities, there is no link between production periods; what transpires this period will have no effect on decisions or prices next period (except insofar as a current change is a permanent change in a demand or supply relation). In contrast, current market events do influence next period prices and vice versa when the commodity is storable, precisely because it is storable and rational forward prices for storable commodities are as variable from year to year as are the subsequent, realized market prices.

Taken together, the evidence supports the view that futures markets in agricultural commodities have dampened both within- and between-year price variability in ways consistent with extensive commercial use of the markets. The evidence is not, however, as robust as it might be. Before and after comparisons are especially problematic for some of the largest futures markets because they are also the oldest markets. Their evolution in the last half of the 19th century corresponds to a period of profound changes in production, processing, and marketing as well. Finally, the evidence on crop year linkages and the contrasting performance of futures prices for storable and nonstorable commodities has raised pricing efficiency concerns worth further discussion.

A curious quirk in the literature is its exclusive focus on temporal stabilization. Storage hedging is, of course, temporal arbitrage. However, virtually none of this hedging occurs at delivery locations. One reflection of the spatial dimension of pricing coincident with futures markets is the very large set of analyses of location specific basis patterns. Another is the set of studies of producer hedging strategies, each of which is location specific. All of them clearly recognize the temporal and spatial aspects of typical commercial uses of futures markets.

Nevertheless, no one has examined the effects of the introduction of futures trading on price variation between regions.[4] Characteristic commercial uses certainly suggest that one might expect futures markets to be associated with improved spatial arbitrage and hence to reduce interregional price variability in much the same way as reduced intertemporal variability is expected. Indeed, a more consistent effect might be expected since all agricultural commodities for which there are futures markets involve regionally dispersed pricing. By contrast, strictly temporal analyses must distinguish between storable and nonstorable commodities as they relate to the potential effects of futures trading. Thus, analyses of the spatial integration of prices in the "before and after" framework of the price volatility studies would add significantly to the present evidence.

PRICING IN EFFICIENT SPECULATIVE MARKETS

Futures markets are also speculative markets. Compared to trading in the underlying physical markets, futures markets have offered standardized contract terms, centralized trading, and a sophisticated system of guaranteeing contract performance. All serve to reduce the costs of market participation and facilitate trading among strangers. They thereby increase speculation.[5] If speculation is efficient, futures prices ought to fluctuate randomly within the bounds established by transaction costs.

In its weakest form, efficiency requires that price changes should be a random walk (or martingale), and a fairly extensive literature has developed testing futures prices for deviations from randomness. For present purposes, suffice it to summarize the results as generally showing prices are random.[6] In a stronger form, efficiency requires that prices reflect publicly available information. Some evidence is available.

So-called efficient market concerns are not frequently linked to questions of intertemporal allocation and Stein (1981), for example, argues that weak-form efficiency is irrelevant to the welfare effects of futures markets. However, two areas of pricing efficiency are directly related to a concern with the intertemporal effects of futures markets. The first is cash market pricing efficiency, the extent to which futures trading affects the efficiency of pricing in the cash market. The second is the concern with semistrong-form efficiency, the extent to which publicly available information is reflected in prices. Both areas of study bear on the question of the effects of futures markets on the intertemporal allocation of commodities.

Cash Markets

Efficiency applied to the underlying cash prices is not so demanding as when applied to futures prices; structural dependencies such as those associated with storage or seasonality more generally are permitted. With a storable commodity, past prices will continue to relate to current prices in a systematic way (Samuelson 1965; Cox 1976; Stein 1981). If, however, futures markets improve the informational efficiency of price formation, one would expect a similar improvement in cash price formation. Tomek (1979–80) argues that futures trading could influence both the systematic and random components of cash prices. For example, the evidence in the prior section suggested that systematic seasonal variation may be reduced. Efficiency tests have the advantage, however, of not specifying exactly the source of the pricing improvement and can accommodate changes in the underlying structure.

Cox (1976) and Powers (1970) both utilized different techniques to isolate the systematic components, but their results are consistent. Powers found that marked declines in the random component of cash prices were associated with the introduction of futures trading in live cattle and pork bellies. Cox examined the systematic influence of past weeks' prices on the current price for periods before futures trading in six commodities (onions, potatoes, pork bellies, hogs, cattle, and frozen concentrated orange juice). Then, applying the models to cash prices from periods after the introduction of futures, he found current prices were uniformly much less dependent on past prices (the entire set of coefficients for prices lagged more than one week was no longer significant in each case) and the unexplained residual was reduced. Both authors took the evidence as indicative of improved information in markets associated with the introduction of futures trading.

Recently, Tomek (1979–80) reexamined the evidence from the cattle and hog markets. He used both the Cox (1976) and the Powers (1970) techniques to isolate systematic and random elements, as well as a third technique designed specifically to isolate seasonal elements. A much longer data series from the period postdating the introduction of futures in each market was also available to Tomek. With each technique, he found that on average no improvement in the information content of prices could be associated with the longer period of actively trading futures markets. Thus, although early evidence was as hypothesized, more recent evidence suggests a great deal of additional work could profitably be devoted to the links between cash prices, information, and futures prices.

FUTURES MARKETS

Finally, the question whether futures prices are themselves informationally efficient has been the focus of a great deal of research and the results are very mixed. Informational efficiency is related to the allocative processes discussed in the preceding section, and it is in that relationship that difficulties occur. Semistrong-form efficiency requires that futures prices reflect all publicly available information. Rationality in futures prices often requires that they cannot reflect that same information.

The tests have examined the behavior of futures prices in relation to a specific information series or to forecasts derived from several fundamental series. Conklin (1983), for example, examined changes in grain futures prices relative to the weekly release of export sales information and concluded that market prices were efficient with respect to this information. By contrast, Gray (1972) showed that new crop potato prices could be forecast effectively with past prices and that substantial trading (selective producer hedging) profits were possible based on this inefficiency. Earlier, Gray (1962) had shown significant profits were to be had in trading wheat futures in relation to the publicly announced support prices associated with the wheat market loan program.

Using more formal modeling techniques, Leuthold and Hartmann (1979, 1980) compared hog futures prices with forecasts derived from a simple, recursive prediction model and showed substantial profits could be made trading on the model's predictions. They concluded that the hog market was inefficient with respect to fundamental supply and demand information. In an analysis of pricing in the soybean complex, Rausser and Carter (1983) developed a model based on fundamental information that consistently outperformed futures prices. The authors also concluded that futures markets in the soy complex did not completely reflect all available information.

Of course, information is costly to acquire and process in these models, and speculation on futures prices is itself not costless. Nevertheless, the authors argue convincingly that costs do not explain the apparent inefficiencies. With the possible exception of the Rausser and Carter (1983) model, the comparative forecasting models were kept purposefully simple and demands on data as well as quantitative technique were minimal.

A second line of explanation derives from Working's (1949) earlier assertion that futures markets are mediums for rational price formation and not forecasting agencies. Tomek and Gray (1970) develop the argument for rationality, further noting that a rational forward price for potatoes could not at the same time be an informationally efficient forecast; if it were a forecast, it would be self-defeating. Similarly, Gray (1962) argues that for wheat futures prices to have reflected the announced support rates prior to wheat actually moving into the loan program would have been self-defeating. In the present context, the argument clearly implies that rational futures prices will not always be informationally efficient. And, heresy of heresies, the evidence is clear for potatoes at least that the observed information inefficiencies were optimal in a welfare sense!

The dichotomy between rational pricing and information efficiency does not at present explain all the documented inefficiencies. Thus, a particularly fruitful area for research is additional empirical analysis of the efficiency/rationality dichotomy. Is the dichotomy restricted to non-storable commodities? The weight of the contradictory evidence, coming as it does from the hog, cattle, and potato markets, suggests a strong connection. It would be imprudent, however, in the face of the inefficiencies found in the soybean markets as well, simply to assert that all futures prices are rational prices and therefore socially optimal.

CONCLUSIONS

Few if any of us doubt the fundamental proposition that futures markets facilitate the intertemporal pricing of agricultural commodities. Storage decisions are both more predictable in their returns and more responsive to prices. Production and consumption decisions are visibly coordinated in forward prices that typically span time periods long enough to accommodate substantial adjustments in both. Similarly, none of us questions the notion that futures trading improves the informational efficiency of commodity prices.

It may be somewhat surprising then that the empirical evidence is not as strong as it might be. Evidence from individual markets will never be convincing by itself because of the necessary caveats that attach to all such before and after studies. Evidence from additional markets needs to be developed. Totally absent is evidence on the effects of futures markets on spatial aspects of pricing, an absence particularly curious in light of the large number of studies examining location-specific hedging strategies.

Finally, the development of information-specific market efficiency analyses has raised more questions than it has answered. Early efficient market work was largely devoted to weak-form tests and generally confirmed the efficiency hypotheses. Its expansion to stronger tests and in particular to forecasting questions has not confirmed the efficiency hypothesis but has raised profound questions. Is optimal intertemporal allocation inconsistent with information efficiency in some or all markets? An agenda for future research is clearly defined.

NOTES

1. Hedging is required to obtain the reliability in storage return. For example, Working (1953) found that the September 1 difference between cash and (the December) wheat futures prices in Kansas City predicted some 70 percent of the change in their difference from September 1 until December. That is, the September 1 basis predicted the return to hedged storage with a 70 percent degree of reliability. Returns to hedged wheat storage over the May-July interval were predicted with 95 percent accuracy by the basis on May 1. Heifner's (1966) comparative results for corn storage are more dramatic. He found that the current basis predicted virtually none of the return to unhedged storage but very high percentages of the return to hedged storage.
2. Similar results would clearly not be expected in several of the nonagricultural futures markets and they illustrate various dimensions of the *ceteris paribus* caveat. Prior to active futures trading, the copper market was highly concentrated and prices were largely controlled by the major producers. Futures trading coincided with some lessening of the degree of concentration in the market and market prices are more variable than were controlled prices. Similar changes accompanied the introduction of petroleum-based futures. The introduction of interest rate futures coincided with a major change in monetary policy that led to significant increases in interest rate volatility.
3. The literature on bias in futures prices largely ignores both the inventory allocation and forward pricing implications of bias. The search for bias is usually traced to Keynes (1930) and the exchange between Telser (1960) and Cootner (1960a, b) exemplifies the difficulties of empirical verification. Gray (1961, 1963) summarizes much of the evidence and, on the basis of additional findings, argues for market and circumstance specific explanations of identified biases.
4. The single study of the effects of futures trading on spatial pricing is Culbertson's (1978) study of regional mortgage rates.

5. See Telser (1981) for a discussion of the specific role of margins in facilitating trading.
6. See Irwin and Uhrig (1983) for a recent summary of this literature. Departures from randomness have been found, but the major inefficiencies appear to be largely time period specific. Irwin and Uhrig's trading system tests illustrate the sensitivity of results to pricing characteristics in specific years.

REFERENCES

Boyle, J. E. *Chicago Wheat Prices for Eighty-one Years.* Ithaca, New York: Copyrighted by author, 1922.
Conklin, N. C. "Grain Exports, Futures Markets, and Pricing Efficiency." *Review of Research in Futures Markets,* vol. 2, no. 1. Chicago: Chicago Board of Trade, 1983.
Cootner, P. "Return to Speculators: Telser versus Keynes." *J. Polit. Econ.* 68(1960a):396–404.
———. "Rejoinder." *J. Polit. Econ.* 68(1960b):415–18.
Cox, C. C. "Futures Trading and Market Information." *J. Polit. Econ.* 84(1976):1215–38.
Culbertson, W. P., Jr. "GNMA Futures Trading: Its Impact on the Residential Mortgage Market." *International Futures Trading Seminar Proceedings.* Chicago: Chicago Board of Trade, 1978.
Emery, H. C. *Speculation on the Stock and Produce Exchanges of the United States.* New York: Columbia University, 1896.
Gray, R. W. "Characteristic Bias in Some Thin Futures Markets." *Food Res. Inst. Studies* 1(1960):296–312.
———. "The Search for a Risk Premium." *J. Polit. Econ.* 69(1961):250–60.
———. "The Seasonal Pattern of Wheat Futures Prices Under the Loan Program." *Food Res. Inst. Studies* 3(1962):23–34.
———. "Onions Revisited." *J. Farm Econ.* 45(1963):273–76.
———. "The Futures Market for Maine Potatoes: An Appraisal." *Food Res. Inst. Studies* 11(1972):313–41.
Heifner, R. G. "The Gains from Basing Grain Storage Decisions on Cash-Future Spreads." *J. Farm Econ.* 48(1966):1490–95.
Irwin, S. H., and J. W. Uhrig. "Statistical and Trading System Analysis of Weak Form Efficiency in U.S. Futures Markets." Dept. Agric. Econ. Stat. Bull. 421, Purdue University, 1983.
Johnson, A. C. *Effects of Futures Trading on Price Performance in the Cash Onion Market, 1930–68.* Washington, D.C.: USDA ERS Tech. Bull. 1470, 1973.
Johnson, D. G. *Forward Prices for Agriculture.* Chicago: University of Chicago Press, 1947.
Josling, T. E., and R. Barichello. "International Trade and World Food Security: The Role of the Developed Countries since the World Food Conference." *Food Policy* 9(1984):317–27.
Just, R. E., and G. C. Rausser. "Commodity Price Forecasting with Large-Scale Econometric Models and the Futures Market." *Am. J. Agric. Econ.* 63(1981):197–208.
Keynes, J. M. *A Treatise on Money.* New York: Harcourt, Brace, 1930.
———. "Some Aspects of Commodity Markets." *Manchester Guardian Commercial* March 29, 1923, pp. 784–86.
Leuthold, R. M. "The Price Performance on the Futures Market of a Non-Storable Commodity: Live Beef Cattle." *Am. J. Agric. Econ.* 56(1974):271–79.
Leuthold, R. M., and P. A. Hartmann. "A Semi-Strong Form Evaluation of the Hog Futures Market." *Am. J. Agric. Econ.* 61(1979):482–89.
———. "A Semi-Strong Form Evaluation of the Hog Futures Market: Reply." *Am. J. Agric. Econ.* 62(1980):585–87.
Martin, L., and P. Garcia. "The Price-Forecasting Performance of Futures Markets for Live Cattle and Hogs: A Disaggregated Analysis." *Am. J. Agric. Econ.* 63(1981):209–15.

Nerlove, M. "Adaptive Expectations and Cobweb Phenomena." *Q. J. Econ.* 72(1958):227–40.

Peck, A. E. "Futures Markets, Supply Response and Price Stability." *Q. J. Econ.* 90(1976):407–23.

———. "Futures Markets, Food Imports and Food Security." Agric. Rep. Div. Working Paper No. 43. Washington, D.C.: The World Bank, 1982.

Powers, M. J. "Does Futures Trading Reduce Price Fluctuations in the Cash Markets?" *Am. Econ. Rev.* 60(1970):460–64.

Rausser, G. C., and C. Carter. "Futures Market Efficiency in the Soybean Complex." *Rev. Econ. and Stat.* 65(1983):469–78.

Samuelson, P. A. "Proof that Properly Anticipated Prices Fluctuate Randomly." *Ind. Manage. Rev.* 6(1965):41–49.

Simmons, W. M. "An Economic Study of the U.S. Potato Industry." Washington, D.C.: USDA Agric. Econ. Rep. 6, 1962.

Stein, J. L. "Speculative Price: Economic Welfare and the Idiot of Chance." *Rev. Econ. and Stat.* 63(1981):223–45.

Taylor, G. S., and R. M. Leuthold. "The Influence of Futures Trading on Cash Cattle Price Variations." *Food Res. Inst. Studies* 13(1974):29–36.

Telser, L. G. "Returns to Speculators: Telser versus Keynes—Reply." *J. Polit. Econ.* 68(1960):404–15.

———. "Margins and Futures Contracts." *J. Futures Markets* 1(1981):225–54.

Tomek, W. G. "A Note on Historical Wheat Prices and Futures Trading." *Food Res. Inst. Studies* 10(1971):109–13.

———. "Futures Trading and Market Information: Some New Evidence." *Food Res. Inst. Studies* 17(1979–80):351–59.

Tomek, W. G., and R. W. Gray. "Temporal Relationships Among Prices on Commodity Futures Markets: Their Allocative and Stabilizing Roles." *Am. J. Agric. Econ.* 52(1970):372–80.

Working, H. "Disposition of American Wheat Since 1896, with Special Reference to Changes in Year-End Stocks." *Food Res. Inst. Studies* 4(1928):135–80.

———. "The Theory of the Price of Storage." *Am. Econ. Rev.* 39(1949):150–66.

———. "Hedging Reconsidered." *J. Farm Econ.* 35(1953):544–61.

———. "Price Effects of Futures Trading." *Food Res. Inst. Studies* 1(1960):3–31.

Futures Markets and Intertemporal
Commodity Pricing

A DISCUSSION

Sarahelen Thompson

I WILL DISCUSS two points raised by Peck. First, I will briefly comment on her suggestion to investigate the effects of the introduction of futures trading on price variation between regions. I will then direct my comments to the expectational role of futures prices and Peck's statement that rationality in futures prices often requires that they cannot reflect all publicly available information.

SPATIAL PRICE INTEGRATION

I am not as enthusiastic as Peck about the role futures markets per se play in improving spatial price integration. However, I do believe that her suggested "before and after" studies would likely reveal improvements in spatial price efficiency for many commodities with new futures markets. These improvements in spatial price integration would not be directly attributable to the intertemporal nature of futures trading. Instead, they would simply reflect the introduction of an organized central market. The attractions of futures trading may be responsible for attracting a wide range of commercial and speculative interests to the futures trading pit, thereby improving the liquidity and informational content of futures prices. This alone should reduce interregional price variation as would the institution of a highly liquid, organized central cash market.

The local basis (i.e., the difference between the nearest futures price, or the cash price at the delivery location, and the local cash price) is an appropriate measure of spatial price behavior. The relationship between local prices or local bases may become more stable with the introduction of futures trading as local prices are quoted as a local basis (i.e., specifically in terms of futures prices). As price discovery improves on futures markets, so should the determination of local cash bids as long as local bases are well arbitraged and integrated with the futures market

SARAHELEN THOMPSON is assistant professor, Department of Agricultural Economics, University of Illinois, Urbana.

delivery locations. It should be noted, however, that the introduction of futures may have a destabilizing effect on local bases if fixed premiums or discounts are set for delivery at alternate delivery locations. The fixed local basis implied by a fixed premium or discount may differ from a market determined local basis. Price relationships and commodity flows may then become inefficiently distorted from those that would prevail if there were no futures market.

EXPECTATIONS AND RATIONALITY

Peck raises some important questions about the informational content of futures prices and how their forecasting ability relates to the efficiency of a futures market. Similar questions have been raised before by a number of authors mentioned by Peck as well as recently by authors of the rational expectations school (Grossman 1981; Bray 1981). Peck uses Johnson's (1947) concept of a rational forward price as one that reflects the prospective actions of producers and consumers. In the case of some commodities (potatoes and other nonstorable commodities in particular) Peck states that there may be a conflict between rational prices and informationally efficient prices. A rational price, one that is optimal in a welfare sense, according to Peck as well as Tomek and Gray (1970), may not be a good forecast because a good forecast would be self-defeating. For some commodities, like potatoes, a poor forecast may serve some greater efficiency goal such as improved supply response or market stability.

How do Peck's rational prices relate to the rational expectations prices so popular now in economic literature? Are futures prices rationally expected, self-fulfilling prices? That is, do they, on average, prevail because everybody (or those people who matter) expect them to prevail? Or, put another way, is the futures price always equivalent to expected price, or should it be? Are they rationally expected prices for some commodities (e.g., storable) and not for others (e.g., nonstorable)? Perhaps it would be illuminating to understand more formally the pricing process in futures markets to gain insights into how publicly available information that would improve the forecasting performance of futures prices could be kept out of a futures price.

If futures prices are not in all cases rational expectations prices, is it because people do not have rational expectations, or is it instead because in some instances the primary role of a given futures market conflicts with reflecting expected price? I suspect the latter explanation will prove more useful or holds more promise in explaining divergences between futures prices and expectations. In some markets, the fulfillment of certain resource allocating functions such as hedging may prevent the fulfillment of the subsidiary forecasting function of reducing uncertainty about cash prices. However, I do not yet understand the mechanics of this. Moreover, does not a "good" forecast generally allocate resources better than a poor forecast? In this vein I agree with Peck; it would be a fruitful area of research to investigate under what circumstances are informational inefficiencies in futures prices optimal in a welfare sense for the sake of resource allocation. It would be worthwhile to research the circumstances under which futures prices reflect expectations of eventual cash market prices as well as provide a guide for resource allocation. I would also ask what would a conflict between informational efficiency and resource allocation imply about the relationship between expectations and output? If a rational expectations price is self-defeating, is it really a rational expectations forecast? I do not think so.

I have made a preliminary investigation of the relationship between expectations and futures prices for corn, a classic storable commodity. Data on farmer expectations of December 1983 cash prices for corn in Chicago were taken from a survey of Illinois Farm Business Farm Management Association (FBFM) farmers conducted by Sonka and Garcia (1983) in April of 1983. These data are summarized in Table 13.1.

Compare the expectations with the realized cash and futures prices presented in Table 13.2.

It is remarkable how close the average December futures price in April is to the average expectation of the most likely price. Either FBFM farmers in Illinois are, on average, listening to the markets at noon and believing futures prices represent the most likely prices in December, or the futures market for corn does a superb job of reflecting the average FBFM farmer's expectation of December prices. In either case, this evidence does not refute the notion that futures prices represent a rational expectations forecast. It is also interesting to note the very narrow average range between the highest and lowest possible expected price. The actual average price was slightly higher than this average range, owing to the unanticipated severe drought of 1983 coupled with the PIK program.

These preliminary findings provide a simple framework for evaluating empirically the extent to which, and the circumstances under which, futures prices reflect expectations or vice versa. It would be interesting and useful to compare storable versus nonstorable commodities in this manner, as well as to investigate if there is a particular type of market participant whose expectations are most closely reflected in futures prices. While this avenue of analysis will not answer the question of the informational efficiency of futures prices, it will address the more fundamental question: Are the price signals provided by futures markets a forecast of, or a guide for, later events, or something else?

TABLE 13.1. Farmer expectations of cash prices for corn in Chicago, December 1983

	Expected Price		
Statistics	Highest possible	Lowest possible	Most likely
Average price ($/bu.)	3.3315	2.6975	3.0118
Standard deviation	.3518	.2994	.2793
Number of farmers	163	153	155

Source: Sonka and Garcia, 1983.

TABLE 13.2. Realized cash and futures prices

Apr. 1983 Futures		Dec. 1983 Cash[a]	
Date	*Price ($/bu.)*	*Date*	*Price ($/bu.)*
Mar. 31	3.0250	Dec. 1	3.4650
Apr. 7	3.0425	Dec. 8	3.3675
Apr. 14	3.0300	Dec. 15	3.3175
Apr. 21	2.9900	Dec. 22	3.1475
Apr. 28	2.9900	Dec. 29	3.3650
Average	3.0155	Average	3.3865
Standard deviation	0.0241	Standard deviation	0.0564

[a] 15-day delivery in Chicago.
Source: USDA-AMS *Grain Market News*, various issues.

REFERENCES

Bray, M. M. "Futures Trading, Rational Expectations, and the Efficient Market Hypothesis." *Econometrica* 49(1981):575–96.

Grossman, S. J. "An Introduction to the Theory of Rational Expectations Under Asymmetric Information." *Rev. Econ. Studies* 98(1981):542–59.

Johnson, D. G. *Forward Prices for Agriculture.* Chicago: University of Chicago Press, 1947.

Sonka, S. T., and P. Garcia. "Farm Panel Survey of Price Expectations, Marketings, and Intentions." Unpublished data. University of Illinois, Department of Agricultural Economics, Winter 1983.

Tomek, W. G., and R. W. Gray. "Temporal Relationships Among Prices on Commodity Futures Markets: Their Allocative and Stabilizing Roles." *Am. J. Agric. Econ.* 52(1970):372–80.

USDA-AMS *Grain Market News.* Various issues.

CHAPTER 14

Efficiency in Commodity Storage

Bruce Gardner

EFFICIENT means least cost, so efficiency in commodity storage means least-cost storage. Two different senses of efficiency in storage are: (1) the (opportunity) costs of resources used in the physical activity of storage (rental value of bin space, commodity deterioration, costs of loading and unloading the commodity), and (2) the optimal management of quantities held in storage so that the expected benefits of the stored grain are maximized given the costs of storage. This paper considers only the second sense and assumes that whatever quantity is stored, it is stored at least cost in the first sense. The issues to be analyzed involve efficient management of inventories in the sense of choosing the appropriate level of inventory at each point.

A common operations-research problem in firm-level inventory management is how much inventory to hold given random demand (e.g., how many gallons of milk to place in the grocery store display case on a July Sunday, or how many vans to place on the car dealer's lot?) At the industry level we ask similar questions, the main difference being that industrywide additions to inventories cause current market price effects that must be taken into account. At the multimarket level the issues widen to account for geographic price surfaces or price linkages among related commodities at a given time and place. Finally, at the macroeconomic level we consider the additional problems associated with interest rate, price level, and exchange rate problems.

The common element of efficient management at all levels is that it solves an optimization problem over time, taking into account current randomness in demand or supply and expectations of randomness contin-

BRUCE GARDNER is professor, Agricultural and Resource Economics Department, University of Maryland, College Park.

uing in the future. For agricultural commodities, we usually discuss problems of random supply rather than demand. In many specific problems it does not make an important difference analytically whether disturbances arise in supply or demand. At the firm level, for a competitive commodity seller or buyer, the problem can be reduced to one of optimal behavior given current market price and expectations of price in the future. At the market level, the problem can often be reduced to one of random excess demand or supply at a given current price level and market equilibrium in terms of current and expected market prices.

The firm- and industry-level problems have been explored quite thoroughly by economists, with much less emphasis on multimarket and macroeconomic issues. This paper briefly reviews commodity storage issues at the firm and industry level, and considers more speculatively some issues in efficiency in the multimarket context.

EFFICIENT COMPETITIVE STORAGE—SINGLE COMMODITY

There are two key results concerning efficiency in commodity storage. First, for given current and future supply and demand functions (with random disturbances having known probability density functions, given costs of storage and interest rates, and expected profit-maximizing behavior by firms), competitive industry equilibrium implies the existence of a well-defined demand function for commodity stocks. Second, the resulting inventory behavior is efficient in the sense that it maximizes the sum of current and expected future producer and consumer surpluses (see Newbery and Stiglitz 1981, Chap. 30, and references cited there).

DEMAND FOR STOCKS

The demand for stocks can be represented as a storage rule, showing the quantity of stocks held at the end of the current period for each realization of random variables at the beginning of the period. This is easiest to visualize for the special case in which the demand function is nonrandom and stationary, while supply is stochastic. The reason for holding stocks is that if current supply is larger than expected production in the next period, it may be profitable to hold stocks at the end of the current period. The bigger the supply, the more should be stockpiled. But if supply is smaller than expected production, it is unlikely to pay to carry stocks into the next period (because price will usually be lower next period). The resulting storage rule is of the form shown in Fig. 14.1, upper panel. The corresponding stock demand function is shown in the lower panel. The storage rule is derived such that whenever stocks are

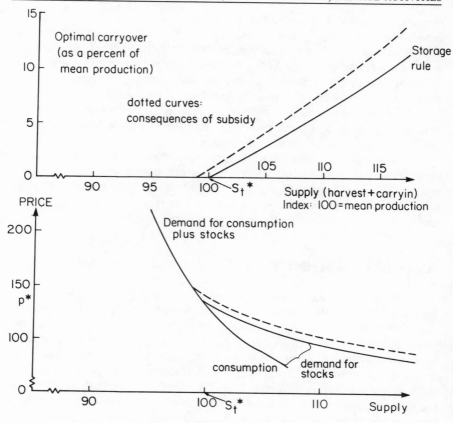

FIG. 14.1. Optimal stock rule and corresponding prices.

nonzero, expected price in the next period equals current price plus storage costs (including interest).

The supply of storage literature (e.g., Working 1949; Brennan 1958) incorporates the observed result that stocks are *never* zero through the concept of convenience yield. When stocks become small, near "pipeline" levels needed to keep mills operating, trains and ships in service, and animals eating in the transition period between harvests, the value of stocks per bushel can become quite large. This means that some stocks will be held even at the end of a crop year when a new bumper crop is coming in that everyone expects to depress the commodity price well below the year-end price. Accordingly, we specify equilibrium in storage as being attained when

$$E(P_{t+1}) - P_t = Z(I_t); \qquad I_t > 0 \tag{1}$$

where $E(P_t + _1)$ is expected price next year, P_t is current price, and $Z(I_t)$ is the net marginal cost of holding stocks, which can be negative if convenience yield (a negative cost) is high enough.

This specification is the basis for linking single-period commodity models to a multiperiod model in which current prices and quantities are mutually determined with expectations of future values of these variables. The details of this type of model will not be detailed here since they do not bear on the conceptual issue of efficiency. What the model does, for example in Gardner (1982), is to provide a framework in which all the variables in (1) are determined so that efficiency is identified with market equilibrium in the sense of (1) being satisfied.

EFFICIENCY IN STORAGE

Efficiency in storage in this model is achieved by equality of first-order conditions for expected profit maximization between periods, analogous to the condition that marginal cost equals price within a period in a static model. This leads to identifying competitive equilibrium in storage as specified in (1) with efficiency. This provides a simple criterion for optimal storage, although planning the optimal carryover in the absence of price signals involves a complicated stochastic dynamic programming problem. It is noteworthy that the main proposals for commodity price stabilization (buffer stocks defending fixed price bands or linear adjustment rules for floor and ceiling points) are inconsistent with this criterion and hence are not efficient storage regimes (Gardner 1979, Chap. 5). And since the storage regime, given the variability of supply and demand, determines price variability, efficiency in storage defines efficiency in price stabilization. Consequently, efficiency in price stabilization cannot be achieved by buffer stocks with fixed or linearly adjustable price bands.

To be policy relevant, the criterion must be social efficiency, not just private efficiency (i.e., we need to consider market failures). Reasons have been given why market failure might be more prevalent for an intertemporal than for a static situation. They include problems in forming and defining market expectations, risk, and time-dependent externalities.

Market Expectation. The model of competitive storage presumes that the concept of expectation has a meaning in a market context analogous to an individual's expectations. However, if any price (such as the price of a futures contract) were put forth as "the market's" expected price, we would surely find many individuals having expectation of a higher or lower price and even taking a speculative position on that expectation.

Many economists have attempted to model different aspects of market behavior when different agents have price expectations higher or lower than a futures price. In the present context, if different groups of agents have different expectations (e.g., commodity speculators are more bearish than farmers) the question arises of how we can specify the behavior of either as a function of the market's expected price. If we cannot, and different economic actors are responding to different price expectations, then the intertemporal marginal condition for a social optimum will not hold.

The market mechanism for thwarting this outcome is apparent if a futures market exists. The bullish can buy and bearish sell until they each have as large a position as their portfolio risk and capital constraints permit. At this point the futures market price reflects price expectations as surely as a spot market price reflects current price judgments. In the spot market, too, there are people who value the commodity at more than the market price and others who value the commodity at less than the market price. If the high valuers hold the supplies of the commodity, they will not sell. It is true that one quite possibly would be unable to explain their behavior in terms of market price. This creates problems in assuming that the market price is a reasonable aggregate valuation leading to surplus measures that involve a whole new set of problems. My point is not to deny the importance of any of these problems, but to assert that a futures price as an indicator of market price expectation is not greatly different from the cash price as an indicator of current market valuation.

One difference in the case of futures is the bias that many economists have hypothesized and some have found empirically. However, this difference between futures and expected spot prices is not fundamental. The bias means that there exists a nonzero basis between the market's price expectation and the futures price. But there is a similar basis in cash markets. Most people cannot, for example, sell cash corn at the Chicago cash price. Nonetheless, if the basis is constant, we can use the Chicago price as an explanatory variable for the marketing decisions of central Illinois farmers. In just the same way we can use the futures price to explain behavior that responds to expected spot price in the future. Indeed, I would venture that the bias-generated basis between the December Chicago futures price of corn and the market's expected December Chicago cash price of corn confronting farmers in May is smaller and more stable than the basis between the Chicago cash price and a central Illinois farm price. Fortunately, the relevant empirical work cannot be done because of the lack of data on the true "market's" expected December Chicago cash price.

Risk Aversion. It is commonly thought that risk aversion provides a reason for private competitive storage to be socially inefficient. It is easy to see how this result would arise formally in terms of (1). If equilibrium requires a risk premium in addition to expected price gains covering storage costs, then private stockholders will behave as if storage costs were higher than they really are. Thus, too few stocks, on average, will be held, and price instability will be greater than is optimal.

Buy why should holding stocks require a risk premium? Because the returns to storage are highly uncertain. (Just imagine yourself buying 10,000 bushels of soybeans to be held six months and then sold.) Still, people who hold soybean stocks are not just holding soybean stocks. They may be soybean processors who actually reduce their risk by holding stocks, farmers who reduce risk by holding stocks, or exporters or importers. And whoever they are, they may be hedged by means of forward sales.

Newbery and Stiglitz (1981) stress incomplete markets as a reason for market failure. After defining "constrained" Pareto efficiency as Pareto efficiency given the (incomplete) set of markets that exists—the most plausible missing markets being long-term futures and contingent claims (insurance and options) markets—they state that with risk-averse producers the market system will not even be constrained Pareto-efficient. The essential reason seems to be that farmers will not use the same factor ratios in all states of nature even though the ratios of value of marginal products and factor prices are the same. For example, farmers would tend to overuse pesticides.[1] This misallocation could ideally be corrected by appropriate taxes and subsidies (e.g., a tax on pesticide use). But as Newbery and Stiglitz say the tax would have to vary with each individual's economic situation and utility function. So hope for policy to correct the market imperfection is not high.

Intertemporal Externalities. Intertemporal externalities arise when people in the future are affected by current decisions, and their interests, like the interests of breathers of polluted air, are not taken into account in an unregulated market. With respect to storage of food grains, a notable set of such people are future victims of famines who will be impoverished when the famine occurs (because they earn their subsistence income from the crops whose failure causes the famine). Private markets will store for the contingency of future high demand, but people who will starve in poverty do not generate potential demand. This is really an income distribution issue rather than a matter of efficiency in the sense of maximizing real income. Yet aid to starving people is perhaps the least controversial case in which we would be willing to argue for the existence of a net social gain due to redistribution from people at average or better income levels to the lowest income group. If we accept this argument, then private storage is socially inefficient in this slightly broadened sense. However, this does not mean that the appropriate remedy is a public storage activity, a food reserve, or a subsidy to private storage. The externality could more straightforwardly be internalized by an ongoing commitment by government to provide food aid whenever people are starving. This would effectively monetize the needs of the potentially starving and generate the appropriate signals for socially efficient private storage.

A different source of intertemporal market failure is imperfect competition, particularly monopoly power in storage. Wright and Williams (1984) examine monopoly in storage. They show that a profit-maximizing monopoly storage industry always holds less than the stocks that would be held by a comparable industry of competitive stockholders. This would justify additional public storage, but a more direct policy would be a subsidy to storage or antitrust action in the storage industry. The problem with the monopoly power rationale for market failure in stockholding is empirical implausibility. Stockholding is much less concentrated than grain trading, processing, and transportation industries; much of it is done by farmers. A monopoly in storage would need to control the supply of bin space, but it is too cheaply available to make this feasible.

In short, the reasons commonly given why private storage is socially inefficient and should be supplemented or replaced by public storage are fairly weak. And this is before bringing in the main reason for skepticism about a public regime—that, like regulatory activities generally, it will be utilized to further the economic interests of those immediately involved rather than the bearers of externalities and that this may lead to even less socially efficient storage than private storage.

EMPIRICAL EVIDENCE

Beyond these conceptual issues is the empirical question of whether private storage in fact has characteristics of optimal storage. This is a real issue in that some have questioned whether farmers, for example, would actually sell stocks at appropriate high-price periods or would hold stocks too long and destabilize the markets. The desire to guard against this possibility is the rationale for "release" and "call" prices in the Farmer-Owned Reserve Program (FOR), preestablished prices at which farmers are encouraged to place FOR stocks on the market. Wright (1985) provides a helpful review and development of evidence on U.S. grain storage by the private sector. Using the fact that an optimal storage rule under plausible assumptions is approximately a linear function of supply over a large positive range of stocks (see upper panel, Fig. 14.1), Wright compares the slope and position of simulated optimal storage behavior with actual storage behavior. He finds that in a range of stocks in which optimality requires a slope of .81 (for every 100 tons of additional output, 81 tons go into carryover stocks), actual wheat storage has involved a slope of .84 (Wright 1985, 262).

Salathe (1985) criticizes the simulation of optimal storage rules on the grounds that it requires knowledge of parameters about which we in fact know little. These include the elasticity of demand for grain, the elasticity of supply, the variance of future demand and supply shocks, and future interest rates. Anyone's assumption about these matters must be questionable, so it is hard to be confident in a simulated optimal storage rule. Granting the validity of this criticism, this sort of evidence still seems worth taking seriously. Decisions based on judgments about very uncertain parameters are what private stockholders and governmental decision makers must be making. Wright (1985) has modeled behavior in this situation very much in the spirit of the rational expectations approach. Inconsistency with rational expectations when a policy regime changes is a problem with alternative approaches to explaining storage behavior that use simulation based on more traditional econometric models (as in Salathe et al. 1984).

The issues in this area of empirical work are far from resolved and we may hope for further advances in the approaches used by both Wright (1985) and Salathe (1985).

EFFICIENCY IN MULTIMARKET STORAGE

Optimal storage rules are efficient given the characteristics of supply and demand for a commodity in a single commodity setting. Bringing in related commodities will make a difference, if only because own-price supply and demand elasticities are affected by the existence of substitutes or complements. But will these complications be more than of second-order importance and thus negligible in empirical work? They can easily be empirically important as has been shown in several examples.

SPATIALLY RELATED MARKETS

Consider grain storage on a global scale. Most countries insulate their domestic markets from world price changes by means of tariffs, quotas, export subsidies, and the like. The United States has done less of this than most countries, but has imposed export restraints when world prices were high and export subsidies when world prices were low. In this context, each country could establish an optimal storage and price stabilization rule given its domestic price history and prospects. Thus, wheat importing countries would rationally plan for export embargoes under the contingency of worldwide crop shortfalls by acquiring their own stocks in times of abundance. What is inefficient about this? There is little if any inefficiency if (1) all countries have the same storage costs, and (2) random supply and demand shocks are perfectly synchronized across countries. Neglecting the first, the opportunity for improved efficiency arises when some countries have transitory excess supply of grain in the same years when other countries have transitory excess demand. For commodities produced in many countries (e.g., wheat) the gains from such transitory trade are likely to be even greater than the gains from trade based on static comparative advantage. The gains arise because reliance on trade to meet shortfalls is cheaper than stockpiling.

The size of the efficiency gain depends on the covariances of different countries' supply and demand shocks. Johnson and Sumner (1976) undertook an interesting empirical simulation of optimal storage, comparing regional insulation with global free trade in grains. It is an empirical simulation (as opposed to an arbitrary simulation to test out the performance of a model) in that the covariances of shocks, demand and supply elasticities, and other relevant facts are based on information available about the regions (many of them single countries).[2] They find that the mean optimal stock level is about eight times higher for the regions acting autonomously as for the world as a whole under free trade. In the randomly generated high-stock years, when supply is in the upper 5 percent of quantities that the yield probabilities generate, the aggregate optimal ending stocks of the regions acting autonomously is 162 million metric tons of grain. But with worldwide free trade it is 18 million tons. Thus, the efficiency gains achievable in storage could be quite considerable.

FUNCTIONALLY RELATED MARKETS

For similar reasons to those just discussed for spatially related markets, efficiency gains in storage of a commodity can be increased if one or more substitute commodities are available. Again, the gains depend on random supply-demand shocks being not perfectly synchronized across the commodities. Here, though, there are additional complicating parameters, the cross-elasticities of demand among the commodities. If they are zero, no gains are possible. If they approach infinity (perfect substitutes), the situation approaches the spatial problem (wherein commodities from different locations are perfect substitutes under free trade).[3] Simulations reported in Gardner (1979, 39–44), with cross elasticities half the (absolute) value of own-price elasticities for two crops with positively but not perfectly correlated yields, generate modest reductions in optimal stocks. For example, Table 14.1 shows a storage rule for corn and wheat under the assumptions just outlined. The entry in the row and column both labeled 10 indicates that when both wheat and corn supplies are 10 percent above mean production, amounts equal to 6 percent of mean production should be held in stocks for both crops. In a corresponding situation in which there is no substitute crop, 7 percent would be stock-piled. Taking another example, if corn supply is normal (0 column) and wheat is 30 percent above normal, 18 percent of mean wheat production should be held in stocks; but if corn were not a substitute, the optimal wheat stock would have been 22 percent of mean production.

An idea resembling the one just discussed is that of pooling the financing of buffer stocks used in international commodity agreements (ICAs). This was a key element in the Integrated Program for Commodities endorsed by the United Nations Conference on Trade and Development (UNCTAD) IV Conference of 1976 and discussed in many international forums since. A big problem for ICA buffer stocks has been the occurrence of sustained periods of low prices during which the funding necessary to remove commodities from the market to support the floor price runs out. The agreement then fails. Of 39 ICAs established since World War II, only two (for coffee and natural rubber) survive as arguably effective in stabilizing markets (Gordon-Ashworth 1984). Behrman and Tinakorn-Ramangkura (1978) simulated the financing necessary for ICAs for ten UNCTAD commodities (cocoa, coffee, tea, sugar, cotton, jute, rubber, sisal, copper, tin) to protect price bands 15 percent of trend price. They found that funding requirements were reduced by 30 percent when financing was pooled in a common fund. This is not enough to make formerly failing ICAs a success, notwithstanding the extraordinarily favorable assumptions about ICA buffer stock managers (notably that they know the true commodity price trends in advance). With sufficient negative correlation in yields across commodities, it is even possible that funding for all ten commodities jointly would be less than for any one of the ten individually, since some are selling commodities while others are buying. In this case the funding requirement would be reduced by more than 90 percent as compared to the 30 percent above.[4]

It is important to recognize that this funding issue, despite the similarity to the preceding corn-wheat discussion, has no implications for efficiency in storage. This is because no cross-elasticities of demand are involved. There is also no implication for the profitability of an ICA. If a buffer stock loses money, it is little consolation to have lost it on the basis of less than maximum financing for the overall system of ICAs. The average level of financing, the capital outlays per ton of commodity pur-

TABLE 14.1.   Simulated optimal inventory levels (ending stocks) crops

Excess supply of wheat	Excess supply[a] of corn				
	−10	0	10	20	30
−10	0, 0[b]	0, 0	0, 2	0, 8	0, 16
0	0, 0	0, 0	0, 6	0, 12	0, 18
10	2, 0	6, 0	6, 6	6, 12	6, 20
20	8, 0	12, 6	12, 6	12, 12	12, 20
30	16, 0	18, 0	20, 6	20, 12	20, 20

[a]Excess supply means carryin stocks plus production minus demand at mean price, minus mean production (which equals mean demand), as a percentage of mean production. Thus "10" could arise from supply 10 percent above mean production with normal demand or demand 10 percent below mean production with normal production and zero carry in stocks.

[b]The first entry is the optimal wheat carryout, the second is the corn carryout. The units are percentages of mean production.

chased and the gains or losses from given price changes, are the same whether buffer stocks are pooled or not.

SUMMARY

This paper has reviewed the concept of efficiency in storage as a matter of satisfying intertemporal marginal conditions for social optimization that are analogous to the standard marginal conditions in static economic models. Although special reasons exist for market failure to be a problem in storage, they are not well established enough empirically, nor are remedies well established enough to make market failures in storage policy relevant. Extension of the discussion to a multicommodity, spatial framework brings in some additional issues but does not alter the conceptual basis for defining efficiency in storage.

NOTES

1. This is not an example used by Newbery and Stiglitz (1981), and indeed I am not sure that this paragraph gets their quite diffuse argument right. They do not give real-world examples.
2. The separate entities are: Burma, India, Indonesia, Pakistan-Bangladesh, Philippines, Thailand, other Far East, Africa, Latin America, Near East, Europe, North America, Oceania, USSR.
3. For an interesting simulation of regional wheat trade in which wheats grown in different parts of the world are not perfect substitutes for one another, see Grennes et al. (1977).
4. Negative correlation across commodity prices is not to be expected because movements in all commodity prices seem so much dominated in recent years

by nominal changes in all commodities, attributable to global inflation, interest rate movements, or changes in currency values (typically the dollar) in which buffer stock rules are expressed. Buffer stocks, pooled or not, cannot deal with these macroeconomic events effectively.

REFERENCES

Behrman, J. R., and P. Tinakorn-Ramangkura. "Evaluating Integrated Schemes for Commodity Market Stabilization." *Econometric Modeling of World Commodity Markets,* ed. F. G. Adams and J. R. Behrman, pp. 147–85. Lexington, Mass.: Lexington Books, 1978.

Brennan, M. J. "The Supply of Storage." *Am. Econ. Rev.* 48(1958):50–72.

Gardner, B. L. *Optimal Stockpiling of Grain.* Lexington, Mass.: Lexington Books, 1979.

———. "Public Stocks of Grain and the Market for Grain Storage." *New Directions in Econometric Modeling and Forecasting in U.S. Agriculture,* ed. G. Rausser, pp. 443–70. New York: North Holland, 1982.

Gordon-Ashworth, F. *International Commodity Control.* London: Croom-Helm, 1984.

Grennes, T. J., P. R. Johnson, and M. Thursby. *The Economics of World Grain Trade.* New York: Praeger, 1977.

Johnson, D. G., and D. Sumner. "An Optimization Approach to Grain Reserves for Developing Countries." *Analyses of Reserves,* ed. S. Steele, pp. 56–76. Washington, D.C.: USDA ERS 634, 1976.

Newbery, D. M. G., and J. E. Stiglitz. *The Theory of Commodity Price Stabilization.* Cambridge, England: Oxford University Press, 1981.

Salathe, L. "Commentary." *U.S. Agricultural Policy,* ed. B. L. Gardner, pp. 277–82. Washington, D.C.: American Enterprise Institute, 1985.

Salathe, L., J. M. Price, and D. E. Banker. "An Analysis of the Farmer-Owned Reserve Program, 1977–82," *Am. J. Agric. Econ.* 66(1984):1–11.

Working, H. "The Theory of the Price of Storage." *Am. Econ. Rev.* 39(1949):1254–62.

Wright, B. D. "Commodity Market Stabilization in Farm Programs." *U.S. Agricultural Policy,* ed. B. L. Gardner, pp. 257–76. Washington, D.C.: American Enterprise Institute, 1985.

Wright, B. D., and J. C. Williams. "Anti-Hoarding Laws: A Stock Condemnation Reconsidered." *Am. J. Agric. Econ.* 66(1984):447–55.

A DISCUSSION

Jerry A. Sharples

BRUCE GARDNER reviews concepts of efficient management of stocks, the conditions for optimal storage, and arguments for why the private commodity-storage industry in the United States might be socially suboptimal and thus public intervention (i.e., government owned, controlled, or subsidized stocks) is justified. He implies that (1) theory can be used to refute many of the conventional reasons why private storage might be suboptimal, (2) empirical evidence of market failure is weak, and (3) direct and indirect costs of government intervention are high. He concludes that market failure in the U.S. commodity storage industry is not an adequate justification for public intervention.

I was reared on the same theory so it should not be surprising that I agree with Gardner's concepts. I also agree with his conclusions. What I wish to do is start where Gardner left off and discuss U.S. stockholding in an international context. I will also point to several research issues that I think we should be examining.

U.S. STOCKS OF GRAIN IN A GLOBAL CONTEXT

Over the last several months of 1985, Congress considered a wide variety of farm policy alternatives. Our colleagues prepared many evaluations of these alternatives. One of my reactions to these studies is that we do not have a very good understanding of the relationships among U.S. farm policy, the world commodity markets, and policy responses by other countries. I believe U.S. carryover stocks of grain play an important role in world markets and any significant change in how those stocks are managed will force other grain importing and exporting countries to make adjustments. It is in this context that I will discuss stock management, market efficiency, and research needs.

Over the last 25 years an interesting grain trade and stockholding interdependency has developed among the countries of the world. To

JERRY A. SHARPLES is agricultural economist, International Economic Division, Economic Research Service, USDA, Washington, D.C.

describe this interdependency I will do some generalizing, although I recognize that I am glossing over some expectations. Much of the research behind these comments is in Sharples and Goodloe (1984).

The United States and its farm policy played a central role in the development of this interdependency. Its price-support policies and grain stocks added substantial stability to global grain markets. In recent years, for example, the United States held 45–50 percent of the world's carryover stocks of wheat and 80–85 percent of the coarse grain carryover stock. (Carryover stocks refer to year-end stocks in excess of normal pipeline levels that are the insurance against a shortage the next year.) Since the United States had few grain trade barriers, those stocks were available to either the domestic or world market. In the past, those stocks increased with low world prices and decreased with high world prices, absorbing both domestic and external shocks to the market. Domestic grain policy, in its pursuit of domestic policy objectives, was a very important factor in determining the quantity of stocks held in the United States.

Another key country in this interdependency is the Soviet Union. The Soviet Union historically held large quantities of carryover grain stocks but in recent years those stocks have dwindled. There is evidence that the Soviet Union now looks to the world grain market to offset their own production variability rather than absorbing it domestically with belt tightening or with carryover stocks. This apparent change in policy would add more potential instability to the world market.

Other developed countries, including both grain exporters and importers, have held few carryover stocks. Importers adequately stabilized domestic consumption and offset production variability by adjusting their quantity traded, importing more when production was low and importing less when production was high. Most exporters shipped out all that they had in excess of domestic needs irrespective of world price levels. Domestic grain prices in most of these countries were state controlled so that no domestic adjustments were made to shortages or surpluses on the world market. There was little incentive for private stockholding and little public stockholding. Developed-country importers were wealthy enough to afford the luxury of a perfectly inelastic excess demand curve.

The less-developed countries (plus Eastern Europe) appeared to carry only a small amount of carryover stocks. The People's Republic of China may be in this category, but we have very little information about their carryover stocks. Domestic production variability in these countries was mostly absorbed by their consumers with only a little use of the world market to offset that variability. Internal grain prices usually were fixed to both producers and consumers so they tended not to make adjustments to shortages or surpluses abroad. Further, they could not afford to hold carryover stocks. In many of these countries the total annual storage cost would be at least half the value of the grain; thus their domestic policy would indicate that they had perfectly inelastic excess demand curves. But a shortage of foreign exchange may have forced some of these countries to be more world price sensitive (i.e., to have some slope to their excess demand curves).

What has evolved is a curious interdependency. Most countries hold few if any carryover stocks; they export much of their own production variability and protect themselves from fluctuations on the world market. The United States stabilizes the world price and holds much of the world's carryover stocks. This is a curious arrangement for two reasons. First, the stockholding pattern that has developed in recent years does not look all that inefficient from a global perspective. In the Sharples-Goodloe (1984) study we concluded that if we take all the trade barriers as given, global carryover stocks were only slightly above optimal during the early 1980s. Further, most carryover stocks have been very efficiently stored in the world's lowest cost storage facilities (mainly in the United States) and close to low-cost transportation routes to importing countries.

Second, it is curious in that this interdependency appears to depend entirely upon the United States' willingness to provide these stabilizing services to the world as an undesired byproduct of our domestic price support and stockholding policies. Was it these U.S. policies over the past 30 years that enabled many countries to rely on the world market rather than their own stocks to buffer them against poor harvests and shortages? I do not know, but my guess is that the answer is yes. It then follows that if the United States were to change its farm price support and stockholding policies, then other countries would change their domestic and trade policies. Stockholding would play a central role.

RESEARCH ISSUES

This view of the world grain markets leads to some interesting hypotheses and research topics.

Does the United States derive long-term social welfare gains from the stability it provides to the world grain market? For example, has that stability enabled developing countries to rely more on trade to meet their grain needs rather than striving for self-sufficiency? If so, the United States and all other grain exporters have gained. My hypothesis is that the gains are substantial for all exporting nations, but so are the costs to the U.S. taxpayers.

How would the distribution of global stocks change if the United States were to drop all government subsidies to stockholding? This policy alternative is implied by some of the policy options recently considered by Congress. Theory suggests that the private storage industry in the United States could hold privately optimal stocks, privately optimal in a global market context. What would be the implications for interyear price variation? Would other countries find it necessary to subsidize stockholding?

Some farm groups have suggested that the United States adopt a farm policy similar to that of the European Economic Community (EEC) where domestic prices are fixed. This policy option would remove incentives for private stockholding in the United States. Considerable world price variability would be expected. What kind of adjustment would this force upon the world grain market? The potential for increased world price variability should provide some incentive for private interyear stockholding somewhere in the world. Who would hold the carryover stocks?

We can be quite sure that the world will adjust to whatever farm policy (and stocks policy) the United States chooses. So as we evaluate farm policy options, that potential for change must be considered. Several of the above questions may be more appropriate for political scientists. Still, we need to do the best we can to understand how world trade and stability will change. The stakes are very high.

REFERENCES

Sharples, Jerry A., and Carol A. Goodloe. *Global Stocks of Grain: Implications for U.S. Policy.* Washington, D.C.: USDA ERS Staff Report AGES-840319, May 1984.

CHAPTER 15

Comments on Economic Efficiency, Public Programs, and Private Strategies

Richard G. Heifner

THESE COMMENTS reflect on the chapters by Bockstael, Gardner, Jesse, and Peck, which deal with a cross section of public decision problems in the marketing area. These authors differ markedly from each other in their approaches to the respective problems and in their use of the concept of efficiency. Jesse rejects the use of economic surplus for evaluating marketing orders because of measurement problems and because "social welfare encompasses far more than what can be derived from supply-demand diagrams." Efficiency is but one of nine elements that he suggests for evaluating marketing order performance. In contrast, Bockstael's review of grades and standards and Gardner's discussion of storage rest upon the concept of efficiency; they use economic surplus without apology. Peck, like other students of futures markets, denotes as efficient a market in which the price reflects all currently available information bearing upon supply and demand. She also uses bias and volatility in prices as measures of performance, but finds no need to use economic surplus or any other direct measure of welfare as such.

THE CONCEPT OF EFFICIENCY

These chapters and discussions show that the concept of efficiency plays an important role in our economic thinking and analysis. Econo-

RICHARD G. HEIFNER is a senior economist with the Economic Research Service, USDA, Washington, D.C.

mists use it extensively, but not always with the same meaning. Many avoid quantifying welfare explicitly. I shall use the term *efficient* to describe a market in which some measure of social welfare is maximized. An "efficiency condition" is a requirement that must be met, but is not sufficient to assure that the market is "efficient."

In contrast to the broader and more general approaches of Bockstael and Gardner, my remarks will relate to the application of efficiency and welfare concepts in assessing the need for and effects of specific public programs such as individual marketing orders. I suggest that market failures, reflecting monopoly, imperfect information, incomplete markets, or externalities are rather common, raising many needs for empirical analysis to determine if intervention is desirable.

A COMPARISON OF METHODS FOR EVALUATING PUBLIC PROGRAMS

I have grouped methods commonly used to evaluate public marketing programs into five categories: those based upon marginal efficiency, economic surplus, the money metric, multiple performance criteria, and price-quantity projections.

1. Marginal efficiency. Evaluating marginal conditions, especially equalities between marginal rates of substitution on the production side, in the search for gains that are possible without making anyone worse off. The possibility that gainers could compensate losers is not considered. I include in this category tests of the efficient market hypothesis as described by Peck.

2. Economic surplus. Use of the areas between supply and demand curves to measure welfare.

3. Money metric. A consumer welfare measure developed and advocated by McKenzie (1983) that amounts to quantifying Hicks's equivalent variation. Its main advantage over consumer surplus is that it takes changes in the marginal utility of money into account.

4. Multiple performance criteria. A scheme, such as proposed by Jesse, that involves determining the direction and perhaps the magnitude of the effects of a program on a number of variables that are believed to be important to decision makers or the public.

5. Price-quantity projections. Use of econometric models to project prices, quantities, and related economic variables under alternative program assumptions. This method is frequently used in analyzing the effects of major farm programs.

I will call methods 2 and 3 welfare methods since both involve explicit maximization of a social welfare function. The last two methods will be called multiple criteria methods.

Examples of alternative sets of criteria that have been used or suggested in evaluating marketing orders are presented in Table 15.1. The table shows that many possibilities exist. Some criteria are very difficult to quantify (e.g., orderly marketing). One should also note that measures of welfare for different groups (consumers or producers) can be used without maximizing total welfare.

CHARACTERISTICS OF ALTERNATIVE METHODS

The different methods for evaluating public programs are compared in Table 15.2 in which the rows represent characteristics or advantages of each:

• Relatively easy to apply. Marginal analysis is popular in part because it is relatively easy to perform. It allows one to look at one condition at a time.

• Handles lumpy changes. The need to measure welfare instead of merely examine marginal conditions arises when changes are lumpy (when fixed or overhead costs are high). Building a bridge is a good example. Decisions about grading programs, information programs, and regulatory restrictions tend to be of this nature. The costs can be about the same for a sizable program as for a small program. Sometimes welfare measures are useful for gauging the importance of a decision or problem even when incremental changes might be made. Examples include the work by Harberger (1954) and Parker and Connor (1979) on monopoly overcharges and the study by Hammond et al. (1979) on the welfare effects of prohibiting reconstituted milk.

• Ranks alternatives. In general, only the methods involving explicit welfare measurement actually rank alternatives. Marginal analysis may allow ranking of alternatives in some cases.

• Based upon observed preferences. The welfare methods make use of information about consumers' preferences contained in estimated demand relationships. Empirical information about consumers' preferences is not available for some types of performance criteria.

• Avoids interpersonal comparisons by the analyst. Any method for analyzing public decisions that rests on efficiency or welfare measures requires the analyst to make interpersonal comparisons of utility. When program performance is measured against multiple criteria, the task of

TABLE 15.1. Example criteria for evaluating marketing orders

	Multiple performance criteria			
Welfare criteria	1937 Act	USDA M.O. Review	Jesse-Brandow	Price-quantity projections
Total economic surplus	Orderly marketing	Efficiency	Profits	Price
	Parity prices	Income distribution	Stability	Output
Consumers' surplus	Protect consumers' interests	Indepen-dence	Equity	Producers' revenues
Producers' rents	Research	No. and size of firms	Coordin-ation	Consumers' food cost
	Stability		Safety	
			Efficiency	
			Progres-siveness	
			Selling costs	
			Extern-alities	

making interpersonal comparisons is transferred from the analyst to the decision maker.

• Accommodates varied objectives. The multiple criteria methods allow a wide range of objectives that can be tailored to each situation, whereas the welfare methods are limited to one specific objective.

• Avoids assuming that other sectors are efficient. The welfare methods lead to a social optimum only if sectors of the economy not included in the analysis are efficient. However, it is not clear that the multiple criteria methods actually avoid this problem.

THE CHOICE BETWEEN WELFARE METHODS
AND MULTIPLE CRITERIA METHODS

Jesse is surely correct in asserting that economic surplus is not broad enough to encompass the wide and varied concerns of society. Efforts to identify operational sets of performance criteria that more nearly capture

TABLE 15.2. Comparison of alternative methods for evaluating public programs

Characteristics	Methods				
	Marginal efficiency	Economic surplus	Money metric	Multiple performance criteria	Price-quantity projections
Relatively easy to apply	X				
Handles lumpy changes		X	X	X	X
Ranks alternatives		X	X		
Based upon observed preferences		X	X		
Avoids interpersonal comparisons by analyst	X			X	X
Accommodates varied objectives				X	X
Does not assume other sectors to be efficient	X			X	X

these broader interests and concerns are to be encouraged. Such efforts have considerable pedagogic value for decision makers and analysts, but their use in facilitating actual decisions presents several difficulties:

1. Reaching agreement among decision makers on what the list of objectives or criteria should contain.
2. Quantifying the elements on the list.
3. Weighting or combining the various measures together.

As an alternative I suggest that in some cases more effort might be spent in building the other social concerns into the demand and supply functions used to calculate economic surplus. Richard Just has suggested ways of doing this. Stability, for example, might be entered by taking the present value of rents estimated for a series of periods into the future. Or, if it is really risk or uncertainty that is important rather than instability per se, then ways might be found to measure rents in something akin to certainty equivalent income. Indeed, measurement of relationships involving uncertainty and imperfect information is the key to resolving many marketing program issues. In this respect the chapter by Antonovitz and Roe is very interesting.

Even with our best efforts we cannot capture all of the important variables in a social welfare function. Some will need to be handled in other ways. This suggests to me that we should look at the welfare methods and the multiple criteria methods not as alternatives, but as possible complements. Often, both approaches need to be applied.

THE CHOICE BETWEEN TESTING FOR EFFICIENCY AND MEASURING WELFARE

The step from applying marginal efficiency conditions to evaluating overall efficiency or welfare involves two major problems: (1) summing utility changes for the individual over some interval of change in price and quantity, and (2) aggregating over individuals. Willig (1976), McKenzie (1983), and others have shown that the first problem can be handled. That is, quite satisfactory individual welfare measures can be constructed from demand functions. Indeed, I believe that to neglect such measures in advising individuals or homogeneous groups about projects or programs can be unsound economics.

The second problem, how to aggregate welfare across individuals, remains basically unresolved, but this does not necessarily rule out the usefulness of welfare measurement. If a program is aimed at overcoming some market failure rather than simply redistributing income, for example, then it may be reasonable to add gains and losses across individuals, particularly if a scheme can be devised to compensate the losers. Moreover, welfare measurements for subgroups of society may be useful even if they are not to be aggregated.

THE CHOICE BETWEEN ECONOMIC SURPLUS AND THE MONEY METRIC

A key limitation of economic surplus as a measure of welfare is that it disregards changes in the marginal utility of income. Willig (1976) has shown that for relatively small changes in the price of a single commodity, the errors in measuring welfare with consumer surplus are tolerably small. More recently McKenzie (1983) has proposed methods for calculating a money metric that he argues provide the proper measure of consumer welfare.

Consumer surplus is generally conceded to be a valid welfare measure only for small changes in the price of one commodity. This seems to be satisfactory in many cases. For larger changes and more than one commodity the money metric approach as developed by McKenzie (1983) holds promise.

FURTHER SUGGESTIONS

Many of the differences among economists about the use of efficiency and welfare measures appear to rest upon differences in views about the objectives of society. Some analysts, like Harberger (1954), find the objectives implicit in the economic surplus approach quite useful for applied analysis of public decisions. Others, like Jesse, advocate criteria that imply a quite different set of societal objectives. Still others appear to despair of finding any satisfactory set of objectives at all.

We must be clear about the objectives if our analyses are to have meaning for public policy. This does not mean that we must agree with the objectives assumed or that only one set of objectives should be considered.

The measurement problems with economic surplus that Jesse mentions are very important. Our information about the demand functions for agricultural products leaves much to be desired. The situation on the supply side is generally worse and information about decision makers' risk-return trade-offs is extremely limited.

For reasons we all know, the problems of measuring supply and demand and risk aversion are not going to be soon overcome. Nevertheless, I think it behooves those of us interested in analyzing programs and policies to encourage and support continuing studies aimed at quantifying these parameters. Often there is not time to estimate the parameters as precisely as needed once a request for a program analysis is received. Thus, we need a stock of such estimates on the shelf to draw upon.

In conclusion, I suggest that the methods of applied welfare analysis can make an important contribution in evaluating public marketing programs. To avoid use of these methods deprives decision makers of important insights and information about preferences of the public that economic analysis can provide. Of course, these methods are easily misused. One danger is that they appear more precise than they are. This calls for extreme care so that both analysts and decision makers correctly interpret results. Welfare analysis should be viewed as only one source of information for public decision making. I suggest that both welfare analyses and multiple criteria methods are needed for many problems.

REFERENCES

Hammond, J. W., B. M. Buxton, and C. S. Thraen. *Potential Impacts of Reconstituted Milk on Regional Prices, Utilization, and Production.* Agric. Exp. Sta. Bull. 529, University of Minnesota, 1979.

Harberger, A. C. "Monopoly and Resource Allocation." *Am. Econ. Rev.* 44 (May 1954):77–87.

McKenzie, G. W. *Measuring Economic Welfare.* Cambridge, England: Cambridge University Press, 1983.

Parker, R. C., and J. M. Connor. "Estimates of Consumer Loss Due to Monopoly in the U.S. Food-Manufacturing Industries." *Am. J. Agric. Econ.* 61(1979):626–39.

Willig, R. D. "Consumer's Surplus Without Apology." *Am. Econ. Rev.* 66(1976):589–97.

PART IV

Summary and Research Directions

Economic Efficiency and Future Research

Richard L. Kilmer and Walter J. Armbruster

WHAT HAS BEEN LEARNED from the preceding chapters? The theory underlying efficiency analysis is subjected to criticism, largely because of the assumptions that must be satisfied for it to hold unequivocally. This is particularly damaging for welfare economics, which is normative, requiring the assumptions upon which it is based to be realistic for the analytical results to be applicable. Or, more realistically, the model results must be robust when the assumptions are violated. Recent research results have been damaging, particularly when the perfect information assumption is relaxed (Grossman and Stiglitz 1980) and/or constant risk aversion (Just, Chap. 2) is not attained. Thus, direct application of welfare economics as an empirical tool is reduced to those situations that satisfy the assumptions. Such situations are few in number.

This does not mean that welfare economics/economic efficiency is of no analytic value, however. We choose to separate the allocation of scarce resources from welfare economics and discuss their empirical and theoretical usefulness. First, we start with a basic discussion of the allocation of scarce resources.

ALLOCATION OF SCARCE RESOURCES

The analytical models of economists are used to analyze the allocation of scarce resources. The accepted decision rule for the buyer to use in determining how much to pay for a product is based on the marginal benefit derived from the last unit consumed. For a seller, the price charged should be the cost of the last unit produced. The buyer is irrational to pay more than the minimum price for which the seller is willing to supply the product. Thus, an exchange that is in equilibrium is one in which the marginal benefit from the last unit equals the marginal cost of the last unit.

When a consumer consumes more than one product and has a budget constraint, a budget allocation decision is required. In the final analysis, the marginal rate of substitution between goods equals the price ratio for each pair of goods. This rule must hold for every pair of goods, and requires that the ratio of marginal benefits must equal the price ratio of the two goods. If this rule is violated, the consumer is better off adjusting the quantities of each good consumed. This rule applies even as the number of consumers increases.

Thus, an economically efficient allocation of resources is one in which: (1) the value placed on goods by an individual (marginal rate of substitution) equals the cost of transforming one good into another (marginal rate of transformation); (2) the value to consumers of consuming input factors directly (marginal rate of substitution) equals the cost of transforming the inputs into goods (marginal rate of technical substitution); and, (3) the value placed by consumers on consumption of an input and output (marginal rate of substitution) must equal the cost of transforming an input into an output (marginal product).

The problem that economists have is determining which allocation is the preferred allocation. Economists can indicate what the consequences are of changing from one allocation to another. For example, when a new government policy is introduced, economists can say who will benefit and who will lose by measuring the change in income of the gainers and losers. Economists cannot say which allocation is better unless no one is hurt, because the economist has no objective means of making interpersonal comparisons. By the definition of gainers and losers, at least one person generally loses. Therefore, the economist can only provide those in policy positions with an analysis of the redistribution that will take place and the characteristics of those gaining and losing.

Given that the allocation of scarce resources will take place in the real world, economic theory provides an analytical framework from which the analyst can begin to analyze the potential reallocation. It is up to the professional to operationalize the theory on empirical problems and to explain what can and cannot be said using the theory. Thus, economists can analyze the allocation of scarce resources and can identify the magnitude of any income redistribution; however, they cannot indicate which allocation is best unless no one is made worse off by the reallocations and all assumptions of a first-best solution are met and/or the results are robust even with violated assumptions.

To step into the normative world and indicate which alternative allocations of scarce resources increases societies welfare the most requires operationalizing the theory of welfare economics as addressed in the next section.

WELFARE ECONOMICS

THE RELEVANCE OF ECONOMIC EFFICIENCY MEASURES

Rausser, Perloff, and Zusman (Chap. 1) suggest taking the route of dividing agricultural and food marketing efficiency problems into those problems that lend themselves to conventional welfare analysis and those that do not satisfy the assumptions of the conventional model. They then elaborate on each approach, highlighting its strengths and weaknesses and illustrating its usefulness for analysis.

The difficult problem with using either approach in empirical analysis is that the researcher must initially decide when the conventional model can be used and when it cannot. Even when the researcher is satisfied about which model to use, peers must be convinced. For those peers who accept the conventional welfare model in its theoretical form, the next task is to satisfy them that the assumptions of the conventional model are met empirically. That is a major task, particularly the question to what degree should the assumptions be satisfied? Should the satisfaction be 100 percent or 95 percent? The question in an empirical or theoretical analysis becomes one of how robust are the model results to a violation of the model assumptions. Many times the results are assumed robust without formal analysis only to find out later through formal analysis that the results were not robust for the assumption that had been violated.

This is unfortunate, particularly if decisions were based on erroneous model results. Hopefully, the violated assumptions only affect the magnitude of the results and not the direction of change. In the context of economic efficiency (welfare economics), what does the current state of knowledge say about the robustness of the conventional model and what research is needed to further test the robustness of the conventional model? A requirement for an economically efficient allocation of resources is perfect information on the part of producers and consumers. Grossman and Stiglitz (see Rausser et al., Chap. 1) show that prices cannot reflect perfect information unless the information is costless. Otherwise, costly information will be purchased only up to the point at which marginal benefit equals marginal cost. Thus, the property of efficiency cannot hold.

Rausser, Perloff, and Zusman also indicate that the achievability of a first-best solution to economic efficiency is virtually impossible. The first-best solution is not attainable when information is incomplete and/or asymmetrically distributed, states of nature are uncertain, or nonconvexities exist. Without first-best solutions, conventional efficiency measures cannot be used. They suggest two alternatives. First, define a new norm such as a political preference function. If that is not acceptable, then stay with the conventional economic efficiency measures but turn to the theory of second best. Then relative efficiency is evaluated by comparing the observed outcome to the second-best solution rather than to the first-best solution. Thus, we are concerned with constrained Pareto efficiency and the theorem of second best.

Rausser, Perloff, and Zusman further argue that economic efficiency and welfare concepts are inappropriate for use in markets in which prices and output levels are intertemporally determined. There is need for the development of general equilibrium measures of economic efficiency. More research is needed on the impact of contracts on economic efficiency. They also suggest that a general framework should be developed that would at least incorporate dynamics, uncertainty, limited and asymmetric information, and transaction costs.

Ladd (Chap. 1) is less optimistic than Rausser et al. about the usefulness of conventional welfare theory. He maintains that efficiency is defined with respect to specific criteria and given constraints and that we do not know societies' criteria. Ladd does favor Rausser's idea of using a political preference function to make equity evaluations among alternative allocations of resources.

MEASUREMENT IN A DYNAMIC, UNCERTAIN MULTIMARKET WORLD

In the last decade, significant advances have been made in welfare economics, which are basically concerned with relaxing many of the assumptions that keep welfare models from being directly applied to certain real world problems. Just recounts some of the advances made in handling a dynamic, uncertain multimarket world and indicates where additional work is needed. Just (Chap. 2) reports that conventional welfare measures cannot be used when the following assumptions are violated: (1) an economy has multiple markets in which some of the markets are distorted and others are not, (2) externalities exist in consumption and/or production, (3) markets are dynamic, (4) uncertainty exists in markets, and (5) information is limited and/or asymmetric.

Just states that conventional welfare measures do not allow researchers to separate the problems of economic efficiency and distributional (equity) issues. He also suggests that a two-stage decision process, known as the constitutional approach, be used. First, the formulation of rules should be based on impartial moral and social considerations. These preferences should form the basis for the interpersonal comparisons that are required in ranking alternative allocations of resources. Second, conventional welfare evaluations can be carried out with considerations given to improving the current welfare state.

Just believes that an uncertain world can be handled analytically when there exist constant absolute risk aversion, externalities, transaction costs, moral hazard, and adverse selection. However, difficulties arise when nonconstant risk aversion is encountered. This requires that the supply and/or demand functions be conditioned on the level of risk aversion, on the utility level, or on the level of wealth. Only the latter is currently possible and requires the solution of a differential equation. Nonconstant risk aversion cannot be handled under conventional welfare analysis.

Just goes on to argue that two of the most difficult analytic issues in a dynamic world are how to incorporate the social discount rate and investment. Investment will shift supply curves over time. When measuring producer surplus, the change in investment that shifts the supply curve over time must be subtracted.

Finally, Just notes that conventional, market-based welfare measurement is strictly applicable when: (1) all producers have constant risk aversion or face no risk; (2) all consumers have zero income elasticities for all goods that have prices that change; (3) a perfect capital market exists; and (4) market participants and preferences are fixed over time.

Pope (Chap. 2) generally supports Just's view of the usefulness of welfare economics. He feels that the assumption of constant absolute risk aversion is a valid assumption and that institutions and markets that affect risk must be included in welfare analysis. Pope does not view the constitutional approach as an improved substitute for conventional welfare analysis.

THE ROLE OF OTHER PERFORMANCE CRITERIA

Up to this point, economic efficiency has been the primary performance criteria used to evaluate markets. Milon (Chap. 3) indicates that criteria other than economic efficiency are also worth attention. For example, income distribution, quality, safety, and research to enhance productivity may all be desirable social goals. Pareto's utility has nothing to do with economic utility as we use the term today. It is a social concept that includes ethical, moral, religious, and political as well as economic elements. Pareto believed that we needed to understand noncommodity as well as commodity values to evaluate individual and social welfare. Modern welfare economics only considers the noncommodity values in its analytics. Milon emphasizes that socially desirable policies are selected for both magnitude and distribution of benefits and costs, whereas conventional welfare analysis only considers the magnitude.

Babb (Chap. 3) concurs with Milon on the need to incorporate noncommodity values into efficiency analysis. Babb recognizes that Milon discusses other performance criteria such as equity but does not incorporate still other performance criteria such as growth and quality. Babb indicates that the use of simulation analysis would allow the incorporation of multiple performance criteria more easily than do optimization models and further suggests the use of experimental economics to assess the impact of special interest groups on the allocation of scarce resources.

An Overview

Even though progress has been made in extending the theory of economic efficiency and welfare economics, additional work needs to be done and care needs to be used in determining what problems lend themselves to welfare analysis and what can and cannot be said from the analysis. Shaffer (Chap. 4) is concerned that judgments about rights and equity are imbedded in the concept of efficiency. However, the basis for judging regulations, laws, policies, and public programs does not exist in the theory of welfare economics based on the perfectly competitive norm. Shaffer finds cause for concern in applying the simpler efficiency concept of the ratio between outputs and inputs because someone may be harmed even though there is an increase in the ratio. Rights determine costs as well as define output; hence a judgment is required about which rights are better—a judgment economists are not qualified to deal with. Care must be taken to point out the limitations of economic analysis for developing inform public policy. Shaffer would abandon efficiency analysis to help develop a pragmatic political economics.

French (Chap. 5) notes that the adoption of the global view of efficiency focusing on aggregate social welfare adds greatly to the difficulty of making efficiency comparisons. But this approach has undoubtedly resulted in more useful analyses than the simpler comparison of end results to resources used. His suggested research on dynamic impacts of new production or marketing technologies may indeed help anticipate adverse impacts and suggest approaches to mitigate them, though the analysis is unlikely to be very simple. French supports the view that conventional welfare analysis has many shortcomings and limited use; however, strides that have been made in advancing the theoretical basis of welfare economics can be of value to policymakers as the consequences of alternative policies can now be more thoroughly analyzed.

The preceding chapters have been very critical of economic efficiency and welfare economics. Of what value is economics in explaining resource allocation? Should the models be abandoned? It is as easy for one person to accept economic theory as imperfect and of no value as it is for another person to accept it as perfect and an excellent analytical tool. Some middle road seems in order. All disciplines have theories that are less than perfect. Rather than reject a theory because it is imperfect, it seems wise to note its shortcomings and conduct research that either reduces them or evaluates their effects. Friedman (1984, 423) indicates that, "The greatest danger is to fall back on the foolish priority of either doing 'nothing' or doing 'anything.' Such a strategy is as sensible as conceding a chess game because you are unable to deduce the optimal strategy. Of course, it would be nice to know the best thing to do; failing that, do your reasoned best!" Thus, this book continues to pursue the concept of efficiency and explores new models that can be used to evaluate today's more complex marketing system.

CONCEPTS FOR EVALUATING ECONOMIC EFFICIENCY

ALTERNATIVE FORMS OF BUSINESS ENTERPRISE

Todays marketing systems are much more complex than the perfectly competitive, homogeneous product markets of the past. A merger can significantly influence the types of organizational forms operating in a market or marketing system. For example, if a conglomerate food processor buys into an industry composed chiefly of non-conglomerate firms, the performance of that industry is likely to be influenced. The types of organizational forms that firms may adopt become an endogenous variable and may have an impact on economic efficiency.

Cotterill (Chap. 6) reports that not much research exists on the economic efficiency of alternative forms of business enterprise. This, in part, is due to the lack of a theory to guide analysis. He develops a comprehensive theory of business enterprise. Cotterill states that the frontier production function approach cannot be used to measure the firm-level management efficiency deviations in areas such as marketing, distribution, investment planning, and coordination among several divisions. The research agenda to evaluate the impact of alternative business forms on economic efficiency includes the impact of (1) managerial capacity, (2) organizational structure, (3) degree of ownership by managers, and (4) the goals of managers and owners. Cotterill proposes a general framework for the strategic analysis of enterprise organizations and markets that merges organization theory with economic theory. General tenets of organization theory have emerged from empirical findings rather than deductive theory. Several general concepts provide management guidance in their effort to minimize the administrative costs of obtaining the desired objective. First, an optimal structure is needed that attains a balance between differentiation of management into departments and integration through establishment of effective communication channels. Second, loss must be controlled. Third, opportunism must be controlled. Fourth, management information systems must be efficient. Finally, the impact of bounded rationality must be controlled.

Given these basic concepts and criteria that provide insight into the design of an efficient organization, social scientists have developed four major schools of thought. They are (1) the classical administrative process school, (2) the human relations participative management school, (3) the cognitive process decision-making school, and (4) the bureaucratic school. Economists have developed the agency theory/contracts approach to corporate organization and the Coase/Williamson neo-institutional transaction cost theory of the firm.

Schrader (Chap. 6) concurs with Cotterill on the issue of the internal organization of the firm having an impact on efficiency. Schrader is a believer in X-efficiency, which deals with the inefficiency of the internal workings of a firm. He cites research that demonstrates that today's environment tolerates less inefficiency within fertilizer firms. Schrader feels that more research needs to be done on the ownership/management link and its effect on efficiency. Finally, Schrader finds the task of evaluating the efficiency of alternative business forms quite challenging and the data requirements formidable.

ALTERNATIVE EXCHANGE MECHANISMS

Just as organizational forms are endogeneous variables in todays marketing systems, so are the exchange mechanisms used by firms. Contract, spot market, cooperative bargaining, formula pricing, administered pricing, private treaty, vertical integration, franchises, tying arrangements, output royalties, sales revenue royalties and lump sum entry fees are alternatives for firm use. Exchange mechanisms influence economic efficiency.

Moving from alternative forms of business enterprise to the arena of markets and exchange arrangements, Kilmer (Chap. 7) argues that exchange mechanisms differ by (1) the amount of information conveyed, (2) transaction costs, (3) productive efficiency allowed the firm, (4) risk, and (5) market power. Agricultural economists have conducted considerable research on the impact on market performance from violating assumptions of the perfectively competitive model. The extent to which these assumptions are violated is influenced by the exchange mechanism used.

Kilmer found that exchange mechanisms do influence market performance. Further research is needed on relaxing the assumption of perfect information, making the model dynamic, analyzing market power, and having the exchange function performed by the firms themselves rather than an intermediary.

Tomek (Chap. 7) questions the notion of a supply schedule for exchange services, suggesting that little basis exists for determining the relative slopes and elasticities of the supply functions for the alternative exchange mechanisms. He also sees problems with applying the model. Furthermore, Tomek feels that transaction costs are very important to the understanding of why firms choose among alternative exchange mechanisms.

ECONOMIES OF SCOPE AND CONTESTABILITY THEORY

Increased understanding is needed about the internal operation of firms. Todays firms are multiple-output, multiple-input organizations that do not resemble the one-firm, one-plant, one-output entities of the past. Automatically policing the market and insuring economic efficiency through large numbers is a thing of the past in todays environment. Increased understanding of the influence on barriers to entry and economic efficiency obtainable through contestable markets is needed. MacDonald (Chap. 8) looks further at the marketing system and the structure of the market. He states that contestable market theory is essentially quantification of barriers to entry theory. The contribution of contestable market theory is the development of the multiple product theory of the firm. Empirical problems arise when applying current economic theory, even though the theory of monopoly and perfect competition are well developed and accepted. Much of the real world falls into categories between those for which models have been developed. Much work is needed to fill the gaps, and contestability theory is one major step. Contestability attempts to specify the conditions under which oligopolies can be expected to have a pricing result that approximates a competitive result in that it is allocatively efficient without relying on the assumption of large numbers. The competitive result is realized because of the threat of entry.

MacDonald is very complimentary of the contributions of Baumol in the area of multiple product theory. The concept of economies of scope is developed, but the sources of the scope economies need additional research. The reason for multiproduct firms to exist is currently considered to be both technological and related to transactions costs.

Taylor (Chap. 8) concurs with MacDonald that the source of economies of scope is not well understood. Furthermore, Taylor feels that the

definition used in describing economies of scope is so vague that it leads
to two definitions of what constitutes a contestable market. Thus, a technical definition of economies of scope is needed to assess its implications
and importance to contestable market theory.

OVERVIEW

Ward (Chap. 10) feels that questions of economic performance are
particularly important in the complex marketing and distribution system
of agriculture. He recognizes that the current efforts are providing a
useful framework that addresses efficiency in a broad context. However,
to operationalize much of the framework requires significant additional
work.

APPLYING EFFICIENCY ANALYSIS

MARKET INFORMATION

An important assumption of perfect competition that impacts economic efficiency is information. As concentration continues to increase
and barriers to entry in some markets grow more formidable, information
can be substituted to help accomplish an efficient allocation of resources.

Antonovitz and Roe (Chap. 9) examine the role of efficiency analysis and the value of market information. They are concerned, since the
competitive market model is not robust to slight alterations in the assumed perfect information. Though they favor *ex ante* measures of the
value of information, difficulties due to data problems lead them to *ex
post* evaluation based on numerous assumptions that make the estimated
values approximate. Antonovitz and Roe see the need to incorporate
imperfect information and its effects on market efficiency into neoclassical analyses. They hold out hope that such efforts could provide a sound
basis for public policy designed to influence generation and processing of
information. Henderson (Chap. 9) reports on some interesting laboratory
experiments suggesting that market information does not always result in
improved marketing efficiency, thus supporting the Antonovitz and Roe
findings in the cattle feeding industry.

MARKETING ORDERS

Over time, certain markets have been identified as not allocating
resources efficiently. The characteristics of these markets include (1) the
presence of externalities such as individual marketers acting in a manner

that negatively impacts the entire market, (2) individual firm decision making yielding suboptimal production of a good, and (3) differences in the market power of buyers and sellers that may cause undesirable price and output performance. One institution for market intervention that is used to improve market performance in some such cases is a market order.

Jesse (Chap. 11) argues strongly for using performance criteria in addition to economic efficiency to provide useful evaluation of market order performance. He is particularly concerned with the ability to accurately measure social welfare gains and losses, but even more concerned that program goals transcend common definitions of economic efficiency. Jesse proposes performance criteria based on elements that orders are expected to positively influence as well as elements that orders should not affect negatively. He sees this set of criteria as useful for assessing the efficiency as well as the broader impacts of orders. A widely recognized set of performance criteria could ease the enforcement burden and provide clear guidance to those concerned with using marketing orders. Kenney (Chap. 11) suggests that economists should not go beyond measuring the relative cost effectiveness of orders. This analysis could be incorporated with input from political and other social scientists into evaluation of the overall impacts of marketing orders relative to articulated societal goals.

GRADING AND MINIMUM QUALITY STANDARDS

Another facilitative aid to market operation are grades and standards. Products that can be graded on a basis valued by consumers will improve the economic efficiency of markets. Grades improve economic efficiency by increasing the information used by buyers and sellers in making an exchange.

Bockstael (Chap. 12) integrates the value of information and marketing orders as she focuses on the potential impacts of grading schemes on consumers. She argues that there is no obvious reason that a perfectly competitive industry with perfect information would not supply the optimal amount of grading. However, the difficulty of transmitting information about consumer preferences for quality vertically through the marketing system implies more complexity than in a perfectly competitive market. Minimum quality standards may serve a useful function to formalize rules that are common knowledge among marketing agents when quality is observable by all parties. But Nichols (Chap. 12) argues that the most important reason for grading is to provide trading information that has permitted more efficient resource use.

Bockstael does see the potential for minimum quality standards to improve welfare when quality is uncertain, but only on the condition that an optimal choice of the standards is made. Otherwise, they could lead to socially undesirable ends. She argues that if growers and handlers cooperate to set grades and standards, such as through market order committees, they will be set suboptimally and possibly screen collusive behavior. On the other hand, if set by unorganized, highly competitive growers, grades and standards may improve the flow of market information for consumers about unobservable quality characteristics. This information about quality, rather than quality per se is a public good. Bockstael identifies a number of researchable issues about grading and its impact on market participants and consumers.

FUTURES MARKETS

The intertemporal allocation of resources is as important as allocating resources in the current time period. Futures markets and commodity storage improve economic efficiency by infusing information into the market which allows consumers and producers to decide between current and future consumption and production.

Peck (Chap. 13) ties the information questions to the futures markets. She notes that while we all accept that futures markets facilitate intertemporal pricing of commodities and improve the information efficiency of commodity prices, the underlying empirical evidence is not very strong. In fact, information-specific market efficiency analyses have raised profound questions about whether optimal intertemporal allocation through futures markets may conflict with informational efficiency. Thompson (Chap. 13), building on Peck's analysis, identifies some additional research hypotheses and suggests the need to investigate under what circumstances informational inefficiencies in futures prices are, in fact, optimal from the welfare perspective for resource allocation.

COMMODITY STORAGE

Gardner (Chap. 14) reviews the concept of efficiency in storage, emphasizing that policy relevance requires social efficiency rather than merely private efficiency. He argues that while special reasons exist for market failure to be a problem in storage, empirical confirmation of such failures is lacking. Further, remedies to deal with market failures are not sufficiently documented to serve as a basis for sound policy decisions. Gardner posits that opportunity for improved efficiency does arise due to transitory excess supply and demand in various countries, something that can be balanced more cheaply through trade than through stockpiling. Sharples (Chap. 14) confirms this result when he observes that most carryover stocks have been very efficiently stored in the world's lowest cost storage facilities and close to low-cost transportation routes to importing countries.

An Overview

Heifner (Chap. 15) categorizes methods commonly used to evaluate public marketing programs as marginal efficiency, welfare methods, and multiple criteria methods. The most straightforward is the marginal efficiency analysis since no compensation is provided and gains sought are those that make no one worse off. Heifner favors using welfare methods and multiple criteria methods as complements rather than alternatives, since both approaches often have something to offer. While favoring attempts to operationalize sets of performance criteria that incorporate broader interests and concerns, he recognizes the difficulties in using them to facilitate actual decisions. He points out the importance of clearly specifying the objectives being analyzed and carefully interpreting the results, if analyses are to be meaningful for public policy decisions.

FUTURE RESEARCH

Despite heavy criticism of the theory underlying efficiency analysis in the early chapters, a number of adaptations and developments hold promise for even greater usefulness of efficiency analysis in policy decisions. Additional research is needed on the robustness of the first-best solution of welfare economics to the violation of assumptions. These include imperfect information, risk, transactions costs, alternative exchange mechanisms, externalities, nonconvexities, the income effect, and the intertemporal dimension. This will accomplish two things. First, professionals will gain additional insight into the subtleties of empirical welfare analysis through an increased understanding of theoretical models. Second, knowledge about the sensitivity of the welfare model to the violation of assumptions will help researchers determine which real-world markets can be analyzed with the first-best solution model. The book by Just et al. (1982) is an example of a work that increases our understanding of welfare economics.

When the first-best solution is not applicable in real-world analysis, second-best solutions are applicable. Second-best solutions are difficult to achieve. If one of the Paretian conditions is not attainable, all conditions are changed to attain an optimum that is second-best to the first-best but unattainable optimum (Lipsey and Lancaster 1956, 11). The first-best solution is analogous to an unconstrained optimum and the second-best solution is analogous to a constrained optimum. Two problems exist. First, the utility functions, production functions, and all constraints need to be known to determine the first-order conditions for an optimum. The data requirements are currently beyond our capabilities. Second, even if the first problem were nonexistent, adjusting all prices to the second-best level is impossible in our economy. Generalizable results to second-best solutions do not follow predictable paths. Research is needed to uncover ways of identifying and implementing second-best solutions.

First- and second-best solutions do not address the issue of equity. The constitutional approach identified by Rausser et al. (Chap. 1) and Just (Chap. 2) needs to be explored theoretically and empirically for its feasibility. Frequently, efficiency alone is not sufficient as an analytic base for policy analysis. Modifications to incorporate additional social goals into analytic models offer some promise. Multiple criteria approaches may have potential for further development for complementary use with efficiency approaches. The relationship of efficiency to the performance dimensions of equity, technological progress, growth, full employment, product choices, quality, workable competition, redistribution of income, safety, and environmental protection needs further exploration.

The current industrial environment is one of leveraged buyouts of a firm with the subsequent disaggregation and sale of the firm's parts. This suggests that the value of a firm's parts are greater than the value of the firm as a unit. It appears that such firms are inefficient. The current restructuring of firms should lead to a set of firms that are more efficient. The threat of buyout has caused firms to reorganize to thwart forced reorganization and disaggregation by new owners. Research is needed to more fully understand the forces causing the current restructuring and the economic efficiency of alternative forms of business organization.

This work is tied very closely to research into the economic efficiency of alternative forms of exchange mechanisms. Alternatives include the spot market, contracts, vertical integration, cooperatives, formula pricing, administered pricing, and private treaty. The percentage of farm output produced under production and marketing contracts has increased from 20.6 percent in 1960 to 24.8 percent in 1980. Vertical integration has increased from 4.8 percent in 1960 to 6.0 percent in 1980 (Marion 1986, 15). The vertical integration beyond the farm gate is expected to increase by 1996 except in the case of retailers who are projected to dis-integrate (Kilmer 1986). Additional research is needed on the forces causing the reorganization of the vertical system and leading to use of exchange mechanisms other than the spot market and the impact on economic efficiency.

Finally, the concept of economic efficiency is used most frequently when analyzing the effects on markets of information, marketing orders, quality, futures markets, and storage. The work to be accomplished on first- and second-best solutions and multiple performance criteria will further that analysis.

Numerous researchable hypotheses have been identified explicitly or implicitly by the authors. They range from the most abstract theoretical to the most concrete applied in their content. There is no doubt that much progress has been made in developing efficiency analysis as a useful tool for evaluating marketing policy and market performance. Research in the many areas identified herein should contribute significantly to the usefulness of economic efficiency in agricultural and food marketing.

REFERENCES

Friedman, Lee S. *Microeconomic Policy Analysis*. New York: McGraw-Hill, 1984.

Grossman, S. T., and J. E. Stiglitz. "The Impossibility of Informationally Efficient Markets." *Am. Econ. Rev.* 70(1980):393–408.

Just, Richard E., Darrell L. Hueth, and Andrew Schmitz. *Applied Welfare Economics and Public Policy*. Englewood Cliffs, N.J.: Prentice-Hall, 1982.

Kilmer, Richard L. "Vertical Integration in Agricultural and Food Marketing." *Am. J. Agric. Econ.* 68(1986):forthcoming.

Lipsey, R. G., and R. K. Lancaster. "The General Theory of Second Best." *Rev. Econ. Studies* 24(1956):11–32.

Marion, Bruce W. *The Organization and Performance of the U.S. Food System*. Lexington, Mass.: D. C. Heath and Company, 1986.